From The Streets of My Village

Eufemiano Moniz

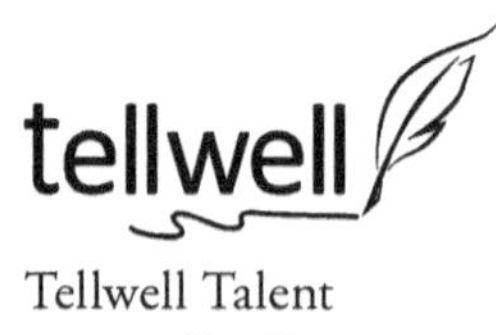

Tellwell Talent
www.tellwell.ca

ISBN
978-1-77941-781-7 (Paperback)

Table of Contents

**FROM THE STREETS OF MY VILLAGE
MEMORIES OF OUR ANCESTORS**

A 200 PLUS YEAR RETROSPECT OF
FOUR FAMILIES JOINED THROUGH MARRIAGE
MONIZ/MENEZES AND PEREIRA/MENEZES

THIS BOOK COMES WITH

1. Dedication with loving memories to the Ancestors of the husband-wife duo: Eufemiano (Emano) Moniz and Ethelwyn (Ethel) Pereira.
2. A show of deep gratitude to our parents Caetano and Marcelina Moniz and Francisco Xavier (F.X.) and Phoebe Pereira.
3. A grateful special mention of: Xamae (Grandmother Menezes), Albertina Menezes, Rosa Maria Sardinha, Jose Menezes and Riario Moniz, for their unique influences on my life.
4. A special vote of thanks to Marcelina Menezes and Marta Pereira for navigating me through the multitude of the family links and being a great source of stories about our families.
5. A sincere thank you to a number of cousins who, through their contributions, have embraced and enhanced the intended "family" aspect of this project.
6. A vote of appreciation to my daughter Larissa and cousin Antonio Costa for editing parts of this book.
7. A Thank You to Luis Gomes Pereira, the designer of the cover page photograph, for providing it to me. He designed it for the CLR Association. A Thank you to Lorraine and Dilip Nogueira for their input in the book-cover design.
8. Thank you to Nathan and Grace Moniz, with digitizing some of the photos included in this book.
9. Last but not the least, a Vote of Thanks to my wife Ethel, for her patience and tolerance of both my enthusiasm for this project and the inordinate time I have put into it.

Eufemiano (Emano) Moniz

INTRODUCTION

Learning about family connections and the history and stories that go along, has always been something close to my heart. I forget lots of things, and folks close to me will attest to it. But I will not forget the roots and the branches of my family connections, and how we are interconnected, whether they are families I am related to by blood or families adopted through marriage.

The principal objective of this book is to pull together genealogical information and stories related to four families, the ones I was born into, and the ones I married into when I married Ethelwyn: the **Moniz** family (aka Menkar) from Maina, Curtorim (my father's side) and the **Menezes** family (aka Godd) from Suclem, Curtorim (my mother's side). **Pereira** family from Margao - originally from Benaulim – on my father-in-law's side and finally the **Menezes** family from Raia, on my mother-in-law's side.

Looking back, I have come to the conclusion that I was probably born with a natural love, bordering into passion, to talk to my elders, with unique and ultimate objective of unearthing "stories" of our family's past or elaborating on their own lives, more than just family links. Now the extension of this passion is to pass on this knowledge about our families to members of our family spread across the globe.

When I would mention my project the first thing that came to people's mind was that I was creating our family tree(s), and not too long ago, that would have been a satisfactory achievement for me and others. Knowing the ancestral and current family links has always been of interest to me.

Of greater interest to me has been the personal stories associated with our ancestors.

Years ago, before the thought of writing this book crossed my mind, I had my first formal interview with my maternal grandfather, we called Xapae. It was in 1969 and I was 22. I made notes of this interview in Portuguese and I still have them in my possession.

Of the innumerable sit-down chats I have had over the years with various family members, two persons deserve special credit, for being great sources of information, which I know, I would not easily gather otherwise: my mother Marcelina for the Moniz and Menezes families (the latter, her own birth family) and Tia Marta for the Pereira side family. Marta was the youngest of my father-in-law F.X. Pereira's siblings. Follow-up research, has confirmed to me how sharp their memories were, and how blessed and lucky I have been having both these women feed me with so much important family information.

The title I have chosen for this book of family stories is "**The Streets of My Village**." I grew up in the village of Curtorim in a rural environment, and even 50 plus years after leaving Goa, almost every street and nook and cranny of the village where I grew up, are still vivid in my memory. For me it is an effortless recollection of every street, every house, every fruit tree by the side of the road. In our village of 13,000, all families knew each other and most took care of each other.

My family (the Moniz/Menezes) originated from three adjoining villages, Curtorim, Loutulim and Raia (CLR). The Pereiras have their ancestral links to the village of Benaulim even though the last four generations of Pereiras have been city folks. They did not fully lose their village roots, as many of their children lived village lives upon marriage.

The original idea of putting these stories down on paper came from repeated observations of how little our family members knew about their ancestors and how enthusiastic and eager they were to know more.

This book of our family stories is the result of my love of the social history of the broad community I lived in, with particular reference to our own families. I believe there are stories here and they need to be told for the posterity to know where our ancestors came from, what successes they attained and how they achieved their successes. When we learn about our ancestry and family's past, we know a part of ourselves.

There is a saying in Portuguese "Se nao quizer considerar o que hoje somos, trate ao menos de lembrar o que fomos". Rough translation goes as "If do not wish to deal with your present, try at least to remember what you were." Or maybe simply put "don't forget your roots".

My original sources of our family information are no longer living. More recently, I have tried to add to my gathered knowledge or to fill in the gaps, through chats with cousins and people of my generation and bit older. My chats or informal interviews, with our elders – grandparents, parents, uncles and aunts and other relatives - have been out of my curiosity. In hindsight I wish my interviews or conversations with these elders, were a little more structured and in greater depth. I realize now, that my ability to conduct oral history interviews was less than desired. How I wish now that I had access to the same ancestors and others gone before us, even for a brief time period, to dig deeper into their own personal experiences, memories and dreams for themselves and those who followed them.

As I mentioned earlier, writing a book on these conversations from our families' past was never my intention. It came about as a retirement project, and driven by an African proverb I read a few years ago, *"when an old man dies, a whole library burns down"*. With my accumulated knowledge about our families, I did not wish to be that library. I believe most of our family members would agree with me, if they thought about it.

I was surprised at some of the people's reactions, once they knew that some of this information may end up in my book. Most often it would be, "you are not writing this, are you?" or please do not include this amongst your stories. To me they are all interesting stories. It is also not my intention to use this book, to air our families' dirty laundry, if any. Truthfully, I am glad, there is not much in that category that may interest many, in particular in posterity.

First of all, it was not and is not my primary intention to publish this book for public consumption, but rather as a reference for the current and future generations of our family, spread worldwide. But as I've put pen to paper, I've come see this as a proud testament to our ancestors and current family. I believe a reader will be impressed with the cumulative achievements, including the public offices and scientific heights attained over the last one hundred years by the members of the family trees of the Menezes and the Moniz families and on my wife's side, the Pereira, Valeriano Barreto, Menezes and Miranda. Add to this, the contributions to the high public office of the Pinto Rosario and Majumdar families, who are part of our extended families through marriage. My hope is that someone in our family, in not-too-distant future, takes off from where I have left and proudly extends the history of our families. By the way, the above facts led me to have a chapter in this book, dedicated to the Eminent Meritorious Members in our families, who have primarily excelled themselves in public office and science.

As a convenient reference source for the reader, the first few chapters of this book lead the reader through the historical background of Goa and Goan identity. This is followed by an overview of the villages (lay of the land) and life in the villages of our ancestors, before I get into what I intended to write about in the first place: the stories of our families.

To me the lives and stories of our ancestors from our four families, are our history. And may I say, I am very proud of our family histories.

Remembering the past is itself part of life. I trust the memories of my elders from whom I have gathered most of the family stories. I would not be surprised that there are some gaps here and there.

I wonder how many of my ancestors would be happy to see me write about them, in particular on events they may not have considered important at that time. On the other hand, I wonder how many members of our families, from the current or future generations, will be interested in reading about this family narrative. I know they will. I hope they will.

Private lives become public through such a book of stories. It is not my intention to hurt anyone's feelings. I take very seriously my responsibility of writing a non-fiction narrative. My intention is to tell stories truthfully as I know them or as I believe them to be true, as they have been passed on to me.

In my lifetime I have seen such dramatic changes of the way we record and gather information. In the days of my grandparents and even my parents taking family photographs was rare. One would have to make special arrangements with a professional to take photographs, which were black and white. It was even more rare to own your own camera, that is, until some of us moved out of India and returned on visits, equipped with a camera, which by this time could take color photographs.

Gone are the days when we wrote letters to our dear ones. Gone are the days when, for example, we had to wait for a week or two to receive just a letter or card sent from Canada to arrive in India. By the time our parents received the letter the news was old. Our child's cold or fever was gone long before they received the letter with that news. Now the grandparents were worried about their grandchild and storming the heavens with their prayers, when these prayers could have been reserved for a more needful occasion.

With great advances in technology, the transmission of data is now instantaneous. We create and leave all kinds of information written or digital or audio and visual, which can easily be searched or archived.

I have already paid my tribute to my mother and Tia Marta for contributions towards elucidating me on family inter-linkages and pertinent personal stories. I would now like to acknowledge some people, whose work or contributions, have facilitated my work.

An important mention should be made of **Berardo** Pinto Pereira from Benaulim, my wife's first cousin, who, to my knowledge, was the first person to produce a written document whereby the Pereira descendants could find information about part of their ancestry.

Berardo came across a family tree document, prepared in Portugal for "de Quadros" family of Maria Aurora's mother's (Ludovina de Quadros) side of the family. Berardo picked up from there, adding substantial more information on the current Pereira generation. He then distributed copies of the document to many interested members of the Pereira family. There was lots of excitement, knowing such a document existed and for a few years it became a reference document for our family links.

Berardo's document was one of my initial sources of information, which I used to confirm with Tia Marta, who was a living, fully dependable thesaurus of family information. Berardo's document preceded Geni.com.

Most of the genealogical data is now easily and freely available from the website **Geni.com**. The data on Geni.com in Goa is derived from the historical archives maintained in Goa, and thus, in my opinion, very dependable. What is needed is for this data to be added or downloaded to Geni.com, after necessary checks. Even with pockets of information missing (more is being added by different members), I find it to be a treasure of information, for our family connections, although the information does have to be confirmed on a case-by-case basis. To get an idea of the utility of this website, let us look at the latest Geni.com statistics (February 2023) relating to the families, who are the story subjects of this book.

Pereira Family: (**F.X. Pereira**, my father-in-law), Family Tree 4,313, Blood relatives 10,000, Ancestors 92, Descendants 20; **Phoebe** (Menezes) Pereira (my mother-in-law), Family Tree 4,250, Blood relatives 265, Ancestors 12, Descendants 20. The last number does not make sense to me.

Moniz Family: (**Caetano Moniz**, my dad), Family Tree 4,043, Blood relatives 292, Ancestors 10, Descendants 48; **Marcelina Menezes** e Moniz, (my mother), Family Tree 4,151, Blood relatives 3,3303, Ancestors 60, Descendants 48. You get the idea.

In order to supplement and enhance my own knowledge of our families' stories, I approached many of our cousins for their written input about their own nuclear families, into this book. I am happy to report a few responded positively and I am so thankful to them.

Fr. Albert Menezes made a written submission on the Roque and Ofelia Menezes family, besides giving me an insight into the Pereira Margao household of which he has sweet memories, when he and his siblings paid a visit to their grandma Maria Aurora and other members of the family; **Oscar Souza** has written about the Souza family life in Dongrim and then their move to Panaji for the sake of children's education; **Fr. Joe Moniz** and **Avito Moniz**, each gives us an added insight into my uncle Riario's family. Tio Riario has had the most positive influence on my character, when it comes to the pride I feel for the Moniz family; I wish to remember Avito in a special way, for his timely contribution to this book, before he succumbed to pancreatic cancer in late 2023; **Lira Moniz D'Mello**, was kind enough to make a contribution, honoring her mum and dad Belmira and Alcinho Moniz, for which I am doubly thankful, as Alcinho happens to be my godfather. I have adopted for this book the family tree **Fr. Luis Menezes** completed on his mother Ofelia's (Pereira family) and his father Roque Menezes families, saving me a significant effort and time.

This book was originally set to cover the lives and time period of my parents' generation and their antecedents. To write about my generation and the ones after, would be such a mammoth task. Not only have the families in discussion grown by leaps and bounds, but they have also spread around the world.

I came up with an alternative plan. In this book I have tried to trace the path of our ancestors' migration ending in Goa. Over the last 50 plus years, many family members have migrated out to parts of India and the world our grandparents probably never heard about. I added a chapter with input from the current generation family members about their own experiences in their new adopted countries. To me this is like closing the family migratory circle, for now.

I thank the family members, who agreed to share their experiences in their new countries and these submissions have been collated without redaction into the chapter titled "Our family Emigration from Goa and India": Heriberto Moniz (Canada), Egidio Moniz (Brasil), Tony Moniz and Valerie Viegas (USA), Oscar Souza (Portugal) and myself (Canada).

What is a culture without discussing the native cuisine? Goans have been known to be good cooks whether professionally or within their own home. The Monizes do justice to this fact. It seems to be in our blood. I have collected recipes which take me back to the "village cuisine", I grew up with. I did this with input principally from the Moniz family members. Credit is given to the contributor for each recipe. However, I believe my sister Blanche Moniz Viegas and my cousin Chrisann Misquitta Barnetto deserve special mention for their extra help with the recipes.

CHAPTER 1

A Brief History of Goa

The Goa of today, with its different districts, came into being only in 1764, when the Portuguese attached the last of the New Conquests. Prior to that, over centuries, it consisted of parts carved out and mostly occupied by Hindu dynasties and for short periods by Muslim kingdoms and their armies to the south and north.

I have purposely made an effort to keep the information relating to the History of Goa and such matters simple and relevant to understanding the historical background of our own families.

I am aware that a reader interested in a more detailed treatment, can dig deeper starting with the references listed herein.

Archeological explorations in parts of Goa, have demonstrated that, going back 20,000 to 30,000 BC, the region was home to a population of hunters and gatherers, before the advent of agriculture.

For centuries the name Goa (variously referred to, in ancient literature as Gove, Gomanta, Govapuri, Govarashtra) referred principally to the Port of Goa and its environs, on the Mandovi River.

The succession of dynasties that controlled Goa are the Scytho-parthians (2nd -4th century AD), the Abhiras, Batpura, and the Bhojas (4th - 6th century AD), the Chalukyas (from 6th - 8th century AD) and the

Rashtrakutas of Malkhed (8th to 10th Century AD). This was followed by the Kadambas (1006-1356 AD).

Other than during the Kadamba dynasty, which was a local dynasty, the invading armies would occupy a portion of the territory, now known as Goa. The conquering king would then withdraw the bulk of the army placing a family member or a chieftain in charge. In return for paying the king an annual fee, the occupied territory was promised protection from the king against internal rebellions and foreign army attacks.

The port of Goa, being proverbially rich, due to its trade connections, attracted more than its share of quick attacks and plundering from neighboring kingdoms or their rogue army commanders.

Goa has a prominent place in the history of India. The geographical location of Goa made it a strategic and safe port of call for ancient traders that plied their trade along the coastal trading posts stretching from the East Coast of Africa, along the Arabian Peninsula and down the west coast of India and over time stretching all the way to China. Prior to 1400, China was a major maritime power and India was a major trading nation. These two nations were technologically far more advanced and wealthier than the European nations that through the sea route around Cape of Good Hope, now part of South Africa, came to "discover" India.

Goa is endowed with a large natural harbor, Marmagoa, at the mouth of River Zuari, emptying itself into the Indian Ocean. This harbor could not only accommodate a big number of ships at a time, but also acted as a safe place to take refuge during monsoons when the heavy rains and rough seas made sailing in the high seas treacherous. Located twenty five kilometers up the river is Rachol, which served as a fortification for various occupiers of the land, including the Portuguese, against invaders from the sea; ten kilometers further interior is Chandor (Chandrapur), capital city of the Bhoja and Kadamba kingdoms (the latter 1006 AD-1356 AD). These two villages are located to the south of the river adjoining to and sandwiching Curtorim.

Little further north is another natural harbor Panaji, at the mouth of River Mandovi. This harbor though not as large or deep as the Marmagoa harbor still afforded sufficient protection from the monsoon and rough seas and was the preferred port of call of the ancient sea faring ships. The old capital of (North) Goa was located 15 kilometers up the river and it was this city that the Portuguese first conquered in 1510 to start their four and half centuries of the Portuguese stay in Goa.

Vasco da Gama is credited with the "discovery of sea route to India" in 1498, when his ships sailed into Calicut in Kerala. Twelve years later Afonso de Albuquerque sailed to India with an armada of 23 ships, looking for conquests and chose to conquer the rich port of Goa.

It took Afonso de Albuquerque two tries, one in March (easy victory) and the second (brutal warfare) in October 1510, to conquer the Port of Goa (Tiswadi) from Adil Shah, the Sultan of Bijapur. There were significant losses in personnel on both sides. The darker side of second victory is that the Portuguese resorted to plundering and massacre. Women who were spared were forced to marry Portuguese soldiers and convert to Christianity.

Bardez and Salsete belonged to Sultan of Bijapur and were under the jurisdiction of the Governor of Belgaum, whose troops were posted across the river Mandovi. When there was a rift between the Sultan and the Governor of Belgaum, the Portuguese offered to help both factions. Both agreed and in 1553, the Portuguese quickly annexed Bardez and Salsete, but reneged on their offer of help. This completed the Old Conquests, made up of Tiswadi, Bardez and Salsete.

The port of Goa was a bustling city of trade and riches and it was bringing Goa and Portugal vast profits. This was the time when it acquired the name Goa Dourada (Golden Goa).

Goa's harbors were important places of call. Exports were gold, silver and brass, spices, vegetable oil, silk and cotton fabrics, perfumed oils and many other items to the Arabian and Persian countries for their consumption and for onward land trade to the Mediterranean countries. The same ships brought in various tradable goods and horses from those countries; the latter were destined for the rulers of Goa and also for the cavalry of the Vijayanagar Empire located in the Deccan plateau to the east and south of Goa.

CHAPTER 2

Goan Identity

A Macro Historical background of
Post-Portuguese conquest of Goa

Discussion on the Goan identity would not be complete, without touching on the fact that Goa as it is constituted today, is conveniently broken down as "Velhas Conquistas" or the old conquests, or old acquisitions and "Novas Conquistas" or the new conquests. The cultural and religious characters of these two areas are starkly distinct.

The old conquests territories, which came under the Portuguese tutelage within the first fifty years (by 1560), include Salsete, Tiswadi and Bardez. A period of respite from wars and attacks from neighbouring powers ensued. For about two centuries, these regions which came under Portuguese possession early on, were subjected to Christian evangelization by different waves of priests of religious orders (Franciscans, Jesuits, Dominicans and the Augustinians); Their zeal was relentless, often fanatical, coercive and sometimes brutal (including inquisition). Hindu temples were destroyed and in their location catholic churches were built. Often material for construction came from the destroyed structures. The result is that these territories have relatively higher proportion of Christian population.

After a couple of centuries of peace, Goa was attacked by the Marathas in 1739, in retaliation for the help the Portuguese gave to a rebel Maratha general in Bassein. The Marathas took possession of most of the territories,

5

except the forts, held by the Portuguese. A peace treaty followed, with Portugal ceding Fort of Bassein and Salsette area north of Mumbai, to the Marathas.

The acquisition of the New Conquest territories came in two phases: first in 1764, the southern Goa areas comprising of Ponda, Sanguem, Quepem and Canacona from the Raja of Sonda in return for protection against attacks from Haider Ali from Mysore to the south. Haider Ali himself had to retreat as he was being attacked by armies from his neighboring powers.

By now the Portuguese were making treaties with neighboring feudal lords, principally for their own protection. The remaining Novas Conquistas of Bicholim, Satari and Pernem, in North of Goa were acquired from Sawant of Wadi, in return for protection from Raja of Kholapur who was attacking Sawant's territories.

By the time the current dimensions or make-up of Goa came into being, the Portuguese power and the religious zeal were both on the wane. The forced conversions and destruction of the Hindu temples had stopped. To this date the population of the New Conquests is predominantly Hindu.

Goa post-liberation or political integration with India

After numerous approaches by the Indian Government (Jawaharlal Nehru) to Portugal about giving up their rule over Goa, India decided to "liberate" Goa from the Portuguese. The military operation (December 19, 1961) was swift and with very little bloodshed. Portugal neither expected India's action nor had the wherewithal to fight back the Indian military. The only military presence of significance was a frigate named ironically Afonso de Albuquerque in the Marmagoa harbour.

The air strikes were pointed and limited, commandeered by a son of the land: India's Air Vice-Marshal Eric Pinto Rosario. Legend is that without higher political approval, on the appointed day he piloted the leading attack aircraft / bomber, as he wished to minimize the damage inflicted by aerial bob attack. It turned out that there was minimal resistance from the Portuguese military.

Eric Pinto Rosario, happens to come from the well-known Goan family Pinto Rosario from Porvorim and brother to Vice-Admiral Fausto Pinto Rosario. Fausto's son Geoffrey Pinto is married to Maria Aurora (Pereira) Pinto who is the sister of my wife Ethelwyn (Pereira) Moniz.

Goans were now Indian citizens. The Catholics, in particular the Catholic elite, so used of thinking of themselves different and closer to Portugal than India, had a tougher time to adapt to the new reality, than the Hindus, who always felt alienated by the Portuguese, because of their deference and favouritism to the Catholics.

Rapid economic changes came about; educational opportunities were plentiful and easily accessible to many more than the Portuguese days. The Portuguese had established in Goa the first Medical School in whole of Asia. On the other hand any further studies in Portuguese, beyond the bachelor equivalent, such as law and engineering, were only available by going to Portugal, which was not easily accessible to many.

My personal experience through years of observation, has taught me that education is the most potent instrument of societal change. That has happened to our family (more on this later) and it was so apparent in the 'new" Goa.

Within a year of Goa becoming part of India there were three Colleges, Chowgule College in Margao, Dempo College in Panaji and St. Xavier's College in Mapuca in the north. The first two colleges were opened by mining industrialists of the same name and St. Francis Xavier was a Jesuit run College.

These colleges were all affiliated to the University of Mumbai and initially offered education leading to Bachelor Degree in both the Arts and Science streams. The curriculum and final exams were identical to those followed by all the colleges affiliated to the U. of Mumbai and spread throughout Mumbai region. This full integration with the U. of Mumbai, allowed the Goan students to compete for higher learning Colleges in Mumbai such as Engineering and Medical schools. Goa now has its own University and more affiliated colleges.

When my turn came, I joined the Chowgule College in 1964. I was there for two years, when I moved to Mumbai to pursue Engineering, as an Engineering College was not yet in place in Goa. The original Chowgule College premises for classes were temporary structures in the form of the old Portuguese military barracks. It was not uncommon for the classrooms to be flooded with the monsoon rain water, and we would have to climb up on the benches. I must say the teaching staff was of high caliber. Chowgule College has since been housed in modern buildings built 2 kilometers to the east.

With these changes in access to education, coupled with greater mobility and employment opportunities for many in the Middle Eastern countries, more people have climbed the wealth ladder. The nuveau riche want to enjoy the same privileges enjoyed for so long by the elite, resulting in high inflation as too much money is chasing too few goods. New societal classes are challenging the old classes. The age-old dominance of the upper castes, especially Brahmins and Xhatriyas, among both Hindus and Catholics is being challenged.

The Goan culture as is defined today, started with the conquest by Afonso de Alburque in 1510, of Port of Goa. As colonizers the Portuguese differed from the British in two essential aspects.

To the Portuguese, christianization (enlarging the frontiers of the Christian or catholic faith) was as important as the commercial trade, in contrast to the British, whose motives were purely commercial. Two, unlike the British who were class conscious, the Portuguese intermingled freely with the natives. The 450 years that the Portuguese stayed in India, have borne a culture wonderfully unique to Goa, and which persists to a great extent, till today.

The Goan identity has been built upon the belief that Goans are different from the rest of Indians. Whether you are Christian or Hindu or born and brought up in Goa or you are part of the Goan diaspora previously settled in other parts of India or Pakistan or East Africa and more recently in North America, Europe, Australia or any other corner of the world, you are a Goan first and then citizen of the adopted country.

To this date it is still predominant for a Goan (particularly a Christian Goan) to think that "Goa is part of India, but Goa is bigger than India". As for me, if anyone should ask about my heritage, my initial response is "I am from India, from a place called Goa".

It is not uncommon to meet "Goans", who have never been to Goa. Their grandparents or parents were economic migrants to shores far away either to one time British colonies in East Africa or one of the Portuguese colonies. They do not speak Konkani, the language of Goa, because, in part they were brought up believing Konkani was culturally inferior to English or Portuguese, the language of the colonizers. This is so, even though their grandparents or parents spoke Konkani in the house, because their formal education was limited when they migrated. Konkani was considered the language of servants. To be fair, "the Portuguese policy of suppressing the local language and enforcing the Portuguese language on Goans, never underwent a great change during the four and half centuries of their rule" (R.S. Newman).

"By insisting on Goa being Catholic and Portuguese, the colonial rulers forced the Hindus even further towards glorifying the past and adapting to the regional culture of the state of Maharastra to the north. The same process prevented the Catholic elite from recognizing its own Indian-ness and encouraged cultural dependence on Europe, the perceived centre of learning and civilization".

Still they are all proud of their "Goanness".

Some Goans take this sense of "Goanness" to extremes even in this day and age. In 2010 or thereabouts, I was at the Canadian Passport Office to renew my passport. When the lady officer at the counter saw that I was from Goa, India, she said to me "Oh you are from Goa?". Glad that she recognized Goa, I retorted "What do you know about Goa"?

She says to me: "do I know about Goa? Last week there was an individual born in Goa, who would not accept Goa being part of India. To him Goa is still part of Portugal or as we used call India Portuguesa." She had to call for help from her supervisor, to put some sense of reality into this individual that Goa is part of India, for Canadian passport issuance. It Is my belief that this desire of being different from other Indians is stronger and more prevalent among Christian Goans. I would believe that amongst the Hindus this feeling is lot less visceral.

I believe that two factors have led to the belief amongst Goans of a separate identity: centuries of the Portuguese rule, combined with the unremitting drive to Christianize the locals with or without coercion, along with the geographical and political isolation of Goa from rest of India.

I did my engineering studies in Mumbai 1966-1970. These were still early years of Goa becoming politically part of Republic of India. My classmates told me on various occasions that the Goans are different from the rest of Indian population. It was kind of, there were the Goans and the rest of Indians. That surprised me. Surely I knew I was culturally different from my Hindu and Muslim classmates, but I did not see myself as "different" or having a separate identity.

Jawaharlal Nehru, the architect of modern India and its First Prime Minister, had this to say in a speech he delivered in Goa on May 22, 1963. "I have felt for a long time that Goa had a distinctive personality, and it would be a pity if anything were done to take away that personality. It may be that gradually, time and other factors will bring about changes, but it is not for the government to enforce changes that will affect Goa's personality…" Pointing to Goa's future he said, "It would be wrong to divert your energy to anything but the task of building up Goa, building up India and thus bequeath a great heritage". (Rahul Tripathi, Times of India, Nov. 14, 2018)

For four and half centuries of the Portuguese rule, much of Goa was virtually an island of peace, amidst turmoil in India, and was unaffected by the feudal wars, British colonization through force and divide and rule approaches, Indian rebellions against the British rule, the Second World War and the non-violent movements, which led to India's independence in1947. Even in the World War II, Portugal (and thus Goa) managed to stay neutral and out of the theatre of war.

"To all Goans, Hindus and Christians alike, Goa as it was demarcated by the Portuguese, is synonymous with a homeland. It is the very center of the world and those who do not belong to its soil are outsiders. It is as simple as that: purely a matter of birth (or ancestry)" (Malgonkar).

Malgonkar tells a story of the boatman who transported him (1980) across the river Sal to the Kavlesi beach in south Goa. When asked if he knew the couple he had just transported, his non-chalant response was "Enh! They are Indians!" The "Indians" were from Karwar, barely ten kilometers from Goa's southern border or to be more precise less than 30 kilometers south of where they were.

Thankfully the boatman did not say they were "Ghattis", i.e. a fairly common pejorative term of the day for "outsiders from India" but literally meaning people from across the Ghats, the imposing border mountains that form the eastern border of Goa.

The Portuguese did little for the economic advancement in Goa. The dearth of economic opportunities resulted in Goans migrating to other cities of India, in particular Mumbai, for higher education and in search of job opportunities, or to Pakistan or British East African colonies and to a lesser extent to Portugal, usually for higher studies. For the most part the Goan diaspora (principally Catholic Goans) greatly benefitted from their foreign forays. Remittances from this diaspora to their families in Goa made up a substantial contribution to the Goan economy.

There was this huge diaspora of Goans, many of them single men, longing for their Goa and the life as they knew in Goa. These single men would travel back to Goa to find brides. Marrying a "Goan Africaner" or for that matter a "foreign based" Goan was a catch and a way to ensure a better economic future for the bride, and by extension for the bride's family.

My observation is that historically more of Bardez and Tiswadi (North Goa) people would migrate out of Goa. It is my understanding that this may be principally due to the fact that Salsete had more fertile lands for rice and coconut plantation and agriculture produced satisfactory incomes.

It can also be a domino effect: once you have a family member or friend who has migrated and willing to help, more people follow.

It is worth noting, that many of the Goan diaspora residing in the east African countries, maintained their strong ties to their motherland by sending their children for high school studies to Goa. A couple of noteworthy boarding schools run by clergy are Arpora and Guirim, in Bardez.

By late 1960s it was time for the Goan diaspora in East Africa to move again, as the political and economic changes in that continent were negatively affecting Goans. The colonies were gaining political freedom and the locals were becoming masters of their own affairs. There was less of a role for the foreigners, even though by now many in the Goan diaspora consisted of second and third generation, born and brought up in those countries.

Many of the older, retired folks decided to move back to their beloved Goa, and to their ancestral homes, which they had continued to support and maintain all these years. Others, in particular the younger and married ones with young children, moved to welcoming countries such as Canada, Australia, U.K., and the USA.

Canada has attracted many Goans. More recently the Middle East has been the intermediary work stop for Goan immigration to Canada. Toronto is the big magnet, followed by Calgary, Vancouver and Edmonton. Each city has its G.O.A. (Goan Overseas Association) and I had the privilege of being a founding member of the Calgary G.O.A in 1973. It is estimated that Greater Toronto Region alone (including Mississauga, where I have been residing since 1986) has approximately 25,000 to 30,000 of Goan diaspora. G.O.A. associations and a handful of village associations - in Toronto the prominent villages being Aldona, Saligao, Calangute and the CLR-Curtorim Loutolim and Raia, as well as Salsete - have been active through holding picnics and annual social gathering, in catering to the cultural and social needs of the Goan diaspora. Over the half century of their existence and activity, the greatest challenge is to attract the younger generations and keep them connected and interested in their roots.

Many medical doctors educated in Goa, Mumbai and elsewhere have migrated to USA, UK, Canada and Australia. USA has been favoured due to higher demand, greater financial and work opportunities and ease of requalification as compared to other countries. There is a relative over-representation of Indian ex-patriate (including Goan) doctors and other medical service providers in the USA healthcare industry. Add to this the children with Indian parentage, but born in the USA who are in the health system and other professions. It is more probable than not, that an American person has had an "Indian" doctor attending to them. In my opinion, based on my experience when I lived in the USA (1971-1972), Americans hold "Indians" in high regard and respect for their educational and professional achievements.

To me the final confirmation of the Goan identity happened in 1987. First Konkani was entered in Schedule of official languages in the Indian Parliament and was made the official language of Goa, which at that time was still a Union Territory of India. Four months later on May 31, 1987 Goa attained statehood, becoming the 25th state in the Republic of India. Thus the Goan Identity moved from the virtual concept to the political confirmation.

It was not a straight path for this recognition of the Goan Identity. The first party in power after the liberation, MGP (Maharashtra Gomantak Party), did not recognize the existence of Goan culture and unique identity. It echoed the Portuguese claim that Konkani was a non-language. MGP's raison-d'etre was to merge Goa into Maharastra.

Fortunately, the Government of India held an Opinion Poll on 16 January 1967, for voters to choose between merger with Maharashtra or continuing as Union Territory. The result was in favour of continuing as Union Territory by 54 percent. It was not a huge margin, but it was enough to move on.

In December 2021, Goa celebrated its 60-year anniversary of becoming politically part of India. On this occasion, I read a few articles from political analysts and journalists, aggrieving the gradual loss of the "Goan identity" or Goanness, which Goans and outsiders, have come to expect and which has been used to market tourism to Goa.

This effect is most experienced by the catholic population, who make up today less than 25 percent of the population, down from 40 percent in 1960s. This is a combination of migration into Goa, the wealthiest per capita state in India, of people from other parts of India and migration of Goans (principally catholic and young men) leaving Goa looking for employment opportunities and better future, and heading out to European Union countries, principally the UK. The migration of Goans includes not only individuals with professional degrees, but also individuals who know well that only unskilled or blue-collar work is what they can expect in these foreign lands.

The migration to European Union is facilitated through acquisition of Portuguese passport, which is a thriving business on its own. For a fee, the agents that facilitate the Portuguese Passport acquisition, know how to get you a Portuguese passport, whether you have Goan roots or not.

References

1. "The Struggle for Goan Identity", Robert S Newman, The Transforming of Goa, Norman Dantas, Editor, 1999.

2. Inside Goa, Manohar Malgaonkar, 1982, The Govt of Goa, Daman and Diu

3. Amchi Khobor, Our News, Inside Goa, Philomena Lawrence and Gilbert Lawrence, 2003

I came across recently a reference (not used herein): Goan Identity by Sushila Sawant Mendes:

https://www.heraldgoa.in/Edit/By-invitation/GOA%E2%80%99S-PA O-BHAJI-A-MELTING-POT-OF-CULTURES/208147

Chapter 3

Migration of the Gowda Saraswat Brahmins

The Indigenous people of Goa (Kunbis) were gradually conquered by Aryans who advanced into the south around 1000 and 700 BCE. Prominent amongst these were two groups of Gowda Saraswat Brahmins (GSB) who migrated to Konkan and Goa.

The GSB group itself is so called because these folks lived on the banks of (mythological?) river Saraswati, which has since either dried up or is buried due to eartquakes or other geological events. Having lived in the north, they were labeled Gowd, meaning those belonging to the northern sect of Brahmins.

The GSBs are credited with developing the northern languages, from which Sanskrit (the root of Hindi and other northern Indian, non-Dravidian languages) and Konkani, the language of Goans, have derived.

Couple of groups of GSB are also thought to have migrated to Bihar and Bengal. Closeness to their languages to Konkani, is given as proof of GSB contribution to their development.

Legend has it that ninety-six GSB families came to Goa. Of these sixty-six settled in the area called Sasti (in Sanskrit Sasast means "66") and thirty families settles in Tiswadi (Tis for "30"). Sasti is today's Salsete (Sashti in Konkani). Tiswadi is the region of Old Goa (including Panaji) and Ilhas (islands).

In later years many GSBs, in view of lack of work opportunities in Goa, migrated along the coastal regions north till Thane in today's Maharastra and south to what is today Karnataka and Kerala.

As a group, GSBs prosper today both in and out of Goa. They perform their priestly duties, but unlike other Brahmins in India, they eat fish, probably influenced by living by the sea and on coastal regions over centuries.

In 2006 the CLR Mando Group (Curtorim Loutulim and Raia), of which I have been the Group leader since 1999, was invited to perform in Hamilton, Ontario, at the Konkani Samelan of North American Konkani Association (NAKA), whose objectives are the "promotion of Konkani language, Konkani community social and cultural activities and to preserve the Konkani language and traditions". The members call themselves Konkanis and claim lineage to the Gowda (or Goud) Saraswat Brahmins (GSB).

It was on this occasion that I was introduced to the GSBs for whom Goa is their ancestral land or have had historical links to Goa. Since then I have tried to learn more about the GSBs, in particular the earliest known historical reference to this group of people and their migration route to Goa.

What follows is my best effort to succinctly summarize the migration path and settlements of the GSB. The bulk of the information herein is drawn from Ref. 1 (see below). Other references given at end of this chapter are sources of historical information on Goa, summarized in this book.

The lineage I can trace through the Comunidade (Community) records and other related research, lead me to conclude that our families are descendants of the GSB and converted by the Portuguese from Hindus. The origin of the Comunidades and their role in the community is discussed later in this chapter.

Ancient tradition places Saraswat Brahmins with the Sarasvata tribe on the banks of the Rig Vedic Sarasvati River, whose exact geographic location is not certain. It is now believed by some scholars, Saraswat Brahmins are Aryan migrants from Central Asia who came to Afghanistan's Kandahar region circa 3000-4000 BCE.

Coincidentally Sumer, located in Mesopotamia, is the first known complex civilization, developing the first city-states in the 4th millennium BCE. It was in these cities that the earliest known form of writing, cuneiform script, appeared around 3000 BCE. Early formal agriculture was also taking root. (Google)

In the first millennium BCE, around the early age of wheeled cart, Sanskrit literature places Saraswat Brahmins on the banks of the now extinct river Saraswati of Punjab, probably travelling through the Bolan pass. A substantial Saraswat community remains there to this day.

Some scholars have suggested that the Rig Veda- one of the four sacred texts of Hinduism known as the Vedas-. was composed on the banks of a river in Haraxvaiti province in southern Afghanistan (Persian: Harahvati; Sanskrit: Sarasvati; possibly the Helmand or Arghandab, though their conclusion is considered controversial. The origin of the name "Rig" is unclear. It is noteworthy that the Kandahar region is adjacent to a large (now mostly desert) domain known locally as Rigestan (stan = place).

The mythological river Saraswati (named after the Goddess Saraswati), flowed in Northern India in the present Punjab and Rajasthan region, from the Himalayas to the Indian Ocean near Dwaraka in Gujarat. The river has long since dried out because it flowed from the receding glaciers of the great ice age 10,000 years ago.

The Saraswats, who were a priestly Hindu caste, settled to an agrarian life, supplemented by cattle grazing. Education was of great importance to the Saraswats and so they taught their young the Sanskrit language and enlightened themselves from the Rig Veda. Although they spoke Sanskrit in public, they innovated a simplified version of Sanskrit called Brahmani which they spoke only at home. This language was the grass-root for the present day Konkani language.

When a severe famine, which lasted for about 12 years, hit the region and the crops were not enough to feed everyone, the survival of the Saraswats was at stake. When they could find no apparent solution to their vexing problem, and at the advice of their pragmatic Guru, they started to feed on fish from the Saraswati river for survival. Thus they became the only fish-eating Brahmins ever known.

Because of continuing famine, the Saraswats migrated in three directions - mostly following the river routes and migrated to the South-West (Sind), North (Kashmir), and South East (Bihar).

The Saraswats who moved South East, followed the Ganges and reached Trihotrapura or modern Tirhut in upper Bihar. This was in 400-350 BC.

With a strong ability to adapt, the Saraswats easily mingled with the locals, but did not try to compete with them in agriculture, the major occupation in that area. Instead, they relied on their superior educational background to secure administrative positions during the reign of the Maurya and Pala dynasties. After the Pala kings, the kingdom was plundered repeatedly by hordes of Muslim invaders and local kings from central India.

Because of repeated attacks by various invaders, life in Tirhut became quite unbearable for the Saraswats, and so, around 1000 AD, almost 1500 years after they left the Saraswat desh (home), the Saraswats decided to move again. This time, however, they moved out mainly in two groups.

One group moved east and settled in Bangla (now Bengal) where in the course of time they assimilated the Bengali culture. The striking similarities between some aspects of Bengali and Konkani languages and cultures probably bear witness to this historic link.

Goa and Migration of the Saraswats

The first migration (700 BC) to Goa by Saraswats was directly from the Saraswat river banks via Kutch (Saurashtra) and southwards mostly through sea routes probably fleeing constant Arab Muslim attacks in the region. These Saraswats in Goa immersed themselves into farming, fishing and trade. The Saraswat Brahmins worked in partnership with the local indigenous people, the Kunbis, who exist still today.

There is not much information about the origin of this "tribe" of Kunbis. Scholars call the earliest settlers, the Proto-Australoid tribe known as the *Konkas,* from whom is derived the name of the region Konkan, which covers Goa and regions to its north and south; it is thought this tribe of people came prior to 2000 BCE from places to the south and east of India (Australia and Melanesia, potentially via Maldives islands). Their intermingling with the Dravidians from the Indus valley Civilization and the Kannadigas from south of Goa, today's Karnataka, produced a tribe called Kunbis. Today the Kunbis are classified as Scheduled Cast in Goa. To me another denomination would be Indigenous people.

The second wave of Saraswat immigrants via the sea route, followed (300-400 BC); they were representatives of other clans and they settled at Keloshi (Quelossim) and Kushasthal (Cortalim) and were named after those villages as Keloshikars and Kushasthalikars. These Saraswats primarily sought professional careers in the fields of teaching, writing, and accounting.

As the southern Brahmins had domiciled in the south for a long time, the Saraswats who had newly migrated to the South were described by the local brahmins as Gowda (Goud) Brahmins (meaning northern).

The third significant migration (circa 1000 AD) of the Saraswats was part of the groups moving south from Trihotra, Bihar. They travelled south to the Godavari River, and then proceeded along the south bank towards the source of Godavari near Nasik, and then moved into Go-rashtra which is

Goa. From here some clans proceeded to Uttar Kannada district (south of Goa).

Goa was chosen mainly for its fertile soil and sea ports with flourishing overseas trade. Another reason for their migration into Konkan is the marital relationships between the Kadamba king Jayakeshi (1050-1080 AD) of Goa and a Saraswat king from Trihotra.

Some historians believe that the king of Trihut sent ninety six families from ten clans to the new land to propagate religion and philosophy at the request of the Kadamba King. Sixty six settled in Salsete (Sasti 66 in Sanskrit) and thirty families settled in Tiswadi (tis for 30)

The families of Loutulim, Raia and Curtorim claim a common membership in the GSB community, but Curtorim Brahmins may derive from a distinct migration event from Trihotra (Ref. 2). This makes sense as Kadamba king's capital was in Chandor, bordering Curtorim.

Once settled down, they continued in their traditional professions of agriculture, administration and education. Those Saraswats who were lucky, got royal patronage and positions in governance in due course of time. But the opportunities in the administration and education professions were limited in Goa at that time.

Many Saraswats (mainly traders) sailed south from Goa, along the Konkan coast all the way to Cochin and Travancore, and disembarked at several ports to start a fresh new life in these places. Some moved north along the coast up to Thane (part of modern Mumbai). The successes of these pioneering Saraswat traders encouraged many other Saraswats to whole-heartedly adopt trading as a main-stream profession.

Various dynasties that controlled Goa from 2nd to 10th century were for the most part Hindus. The Kadambas, who ruled Goa from 930 AD to 1356 AD, were unique, because they were a local dynasty that slowly came to dominate the scene by forging alliances with their neighbors and overlords, the Chalukyas. They made Chandrapur (today known as

Chandor, neighboring Curtorim) their capital (937 AD to 1310 AD). The period of the Kadambas is considered to be the first golden age of Goa.

The Kadambas subsequently moved their capital to Govapuri on the banks of the Mandovi river, the site of today's Old Goa (Goa Velha), because foreign sailing ships were having difficulty navigating up the river due to the silting at the mouth of river Zuari. The death of the last Chalukya king in 1198 weakened their alliance and this exposed Goa to the vulnerability of Muslim invasions that took place repeatedly after that.

After enjoying peace and prosperity for 400 years, Goa came under repeated attacks by various Muslim kingdoms. The history of Saraswats again took a turn for the worse due to continued military attacks on Goa.

The Muslims destroyed many temples and forced the Hindus to get converted to Islam. To avoid these insults and religious persecution, several Saraswat families moved to the neighbourhood Kingdom of Sonde (east of Goa), more to Kanara (south) and a few to even far off south to Kochi on Malabar Coast.

Those Saraswats involved in farming and trading were less willing to abandon their farms and businesses. They stayed back in Goa and slowly rebuilt their lives as farmers and traders.

It is appropriate at this juncture to introduce how the institution of Comunidade came into existence and its role in identifying the gaumkaris (also written as gaunkar). The agricultural land was jointly owned by the group of oligarchic villagers, the gaumkaris (now commonly known as gaumkars); they had right to auction/lease the land; this rent was used for development and maintenance of the village, and the remainder was distributed amongst the *Gaumkaris yearly (known as "zonn"- think of it as a dividend from land ownership)*. The agricultural land consisted of definite boundaries of land from village to village with its topographic detail, its management and social, religious and cultural interaction. Gaumkaris thus were in existence long before the arrival of the Portuguese colonialists and constitution of the state of Goa itself. Today the name "gaumkar" means the original descendant of that particular village.

Even before any king ruled the territory, a kind of democracy in the form of Gaumkari existed in Goa. This form of village-administration was called as *Gaumponn*, and despite the periodic change of sovereigns, the Gaumponn always remained; hence the attachment and fidelity of the Goans to their village has always surpassed their loyalty to their rulers (most of whom were extraterritorial). This system for governance became further systematised and fortified, and it has continued to exist ever since. Even today 223 comunidades are still functioning in Goa, though not in the true sense.

The Gaumponn, with its rights, was and still is passed down through the male lineage only. All the male persons of the gaumkaris need to have their birth registered at the Comunidade and become eligible, at age 18, to receive the zonn amount for the year, as and when declared. For example even though I have been a non-resident for the last 47 years, I am eligible to receive this zonn from the Comunidade of Raia, which is collected by the person with my power of attorney.

Even more interesting is the fact that my son, Francis, who was born in Canada and always resident of Canada, is also a gaumkari of Raia with all its rights once I register him at the Comunidade, with the baptismal certificate as proof of his lineage.

The Portuguese linked the Comunidade rights of the gaumkars to religious events. In Goa, at the village religious (Christian) events, it is usual to have processions. The men dress up in colourful garments, the colours indicating which "confraria" (brotherhood or fraternity) they belong to, whether gaumkars or non-gaumkars of the village proper. Some of these people will hold Cruxifixes, holy images and such, in the procession. Until more recently Gaumkars of another village were not allowed to participate in their own confraria garbs, in the procession outside their own village.

It is not difficult, to study your ancestry, if you are a gaumkar. The Comunidade has all the records. I understand that due to high humidity and poor upkeep, some of these records, may be in poor state of usefulness.

From the Comunidade records (ref 3), **1575** is the year of conversion to Christianity of the first of the Moniz family in our line of Gaumkars. The name taken was Antonio Moniz, son of **Goinda Poi**, the Poi or Pai being known founder families (others being Camotim and Naik) in the Raia and Loutulim comunidades. The conversions to Christianity (forced or voluntary) of the Hindu Gaumkars in these two villages, took place starting in 1560 and 1630.

To satisfy my own curiosity about my ancestry I had my DNA analysed in 2010 by Ancestry. They had a sale price of C$69 for the test. A sample of my saliva was shipped to Ireland, where they analysed it and came back with their findings. *The personal details provided were: name, age and sex, besides my mailing address (Canada).* They did not have any further information on me, including my place of birth or reason behind my Portuguese name.

The findings: I was 90 percent North Indian, 6 percent East Asian and 4 percent Melanasian. There was a note to me that they had encountered similar DNA in some individuals with last name Prabhu, Desai and Pai. There was no mention of geographical location of these individuals. Yes, these are GSB from Goa. Curiosity led me back to the Ancestry site in November 2023. As it says on the website, the DNA has not changed but science has. The new ethnicity estimate from my DNA based on over 70,000 test samples: 63 percent Northern India, 35 percent Southern India, with a note "your community with a connection to this ethnicity region: Goa and Western Deccan; 2 percent Central Asia, mainly Afghanistan.

More recently I came to know about the DNA test results (myheritage. com) of my cousin who lives in Portugal. She is the daughter of my uncle (mother's brother); her mother is of Portuguese and Indigineous Timorense mix heritage. Her DNA results had many similarities to mine, even though the percentages of our ancestral origins were different. I am believer of these DNA results.

References

Khabbar, a Quarterly newsletter of NAKA, History of Saraswat Migrations, Volume XXX1V, 2011-2012 http://ekhabbar.com/2011/Khabbar%20 XXXIV-2.pdf

Genetic and Cultural Reconstruction of the Migration of an Ancient Lineage, a Research Article, BioMed Research International, Volume 2015 by Desmond D. Mascarenhas, Anupuma Raina, Christopher E. Aston, and Dharambir K. Sanghera

https://www.hindawi.com/journals/bmri/2015/651415/

Os Primordios, Chapter One

Inside Goa, Manohar Malgonkar, 1982

Amchi Khobor Philomena Lawrence and Gilbert Lawrence, A Historical, Religious, Social, Cultural and Economic Review of Goa

Wikepedia, https://en.wikipedia.org/wiki/Goa

C H A P T E R 4

The Golden Goa

Goa is relatively a small state in India, 400 km south of Mumbai, approximately 3,700 km2 area, with a 100 km of the Arabian Sea sandy beaches to the west and Ghat mountains to the West. It has a coastline of 160km and 80 km at its widest point.

From the west to the east, Goa's topography can be roughly divided into three. In the western coastal sandy region the land is basically flat, with abundant coconut trees. The middle part of plains and rolling hills, consists of rice fields with fruit trees interspersed all over the place. The easternmost third of the state, rising up to the Western Ghats is predominantly hilly, forested and with abundant cashew trees as the cash crop.

Goa has seven major rivers, the Mandovi (north) and Zuari (south), being the most important, both in size and as transportation arteries for barges carrying iron ore and manganese, mined in the hinterland. It should be noted that our three villages of Curtorim, Raia and Loutulim lie on the south bank of river Zuari.

Goa's tropical climate can be described as warm (September to March), hot (April to June) and hot and humid during the monsoon (rainy) season (June to August / September). During the winter months, night and early morning temperatures are cool and you can experience the morning dew. For us Canadians these temperatures are really pleasant. As an example when our older daughter Celine was close to 3 in age, she would roam around the house care free dressed in light clothes. My folks would

25

warn us that she would catch a cold, if we did not protect her more. It never happened.

There is greenery in Goa year around. The trees in Goa are always green. They drop old leaves, as they rejuvenate themselves, normally before the monsoon season. In the rural areas, the dry leaves and dry wood were collected and used for cooking and heating the water for showering. Cooking with gas has now replaced the old way of cooking over wood fire in most of semi urban households.

The rice fields and other open fields, including children's playing fields turn dry and brown or reddish during summer. The reddish colour derives from the lateritic soil.

When the monsoon rains come, the paddy or rice fields become a carpet of greenery. The rice plant is green, before the rice is ripe and ready for harvesting, when the crop turns brown.

In the post-Portuguese era, Goa has become a magnet for tourists. It is visited by large numbers of international and domestic tourists each year for its white sand beaches, nightlife, places of worship and world heritage architecture. Goa is a biodiversity hotspot. It has rich flora and fauna, owing to its location on the Western Ghats range.

There are two views of Goa. One is the way the tourists, whether Indian or foreigners, look upon Goa. The other, is the way native Goans or the Goan diaspora see Goa along with the real and romantic feelings about Goa. After mining, tourism is a huge contributor to the local economy.

Goa is a traveler's paradise with its pristine beaches, verdant cocooned hills, exotic locales and more. A traveller is spoilt for choice with boutique hotels, budget getaways, party hot-spots to serene wanderings.

For the tourists, Goa is a tropical holiday paradise with beautiful, broad beaches with white sand, warm waters of the Arabian Sea (Indian Ocean), a tolerant and welcoming population, party hot spots and liberal drinking laws. The latter, even to this day, is a major attraction for Indians from outside Goa, for whom liquor is not readily available, due both the societal and religious norms, and local liquor control regulations. For example, if you do not plan well ahead of time, travel by air or train and hotel accommodation is close to impossible during Christmas and New Year holiday season.

What is a vacation without indulging in local cuisine, abundant with fresh seafood, local produce and rich use of coconut!

I read it in the Financial Post Magazine, February1, 1984, on a write-up on Goa: "When Indians of any religion sing, they sing for religion. Goans sing and dance for the senses".

The native Catholic Goan and the Goan diaspora revels in celebrations: whether they are the multitude of village church feasts, or weddings or any occasion to celebrate, such as birthdays. Food and drink are the center piece of celebration, with music, song and dance, to go with it.

I remember that when soon after the 1961 liberation, the prime Minister of India, Jawaharlal Nehru, paid his first visit to Goa, he alluded that Goans were well known as cooks and musicians. Many among the Goan elite took exception to this categorization. I am sure Nehru meant it in a good way and not intended in a pejorative way. I personally feel proud of the Goan cooks and musicians, who have historically contributed so much to the Goan culture, both at the village level and in hotels in major cities across India.

Goa, with her 160 km long coastline is blessed with some of the best and most attractive beaches in the world. I can vouch for them. From my own travels and TV viewing, I have the tendency of comparing the world beaches to the beaches I have known in Goa. And for the most part, Goa's beaches surpass them all in their beauty and vastness in terms of width and length.

In the olden days the most popular were the Calangute beach in the north (Bardez) and Colva beach in the south. The northern beaches are not as broad, or as continuous (length). In my youth (1960s) I used to hear that

Calangute beach was the happening place for fun and merriment in Goa. The recently returning diaspora from East Africa, of which there was lot more in Bardez than Salcete, added to gaiety, with many groups of girls and boys reveling with guitar music and singing.

In the post-Portuguese era, the hippie folks were the first foreigners to discover Goa (starting in 1965) as the place for fun and relaxation. Goa was every hippie's dream of tropical paradise, the real thing. Kathmandu, Nepal, was their previous hangout. Anjuna beach became a destination and a centre of activity of its own.

The Goans, who are naturally very welcoming and tolerant, extended those courtesies to the hippies. Once the novelty wore off, Goans became less tolerant of the hippie crowd's perceived excessive liberty with their life styles, including nudity and drug usage. The latter was being spread among the local youth. As a result, mutually acceptable ground rules were established.

When the Portuguese conquered Goa in 1510, the port of Goa on the Mandovi, was already a well-established maritime and trading centre and a prosperous and bustling community. So enchanted were the Portuguese with their new conquest, they called it "Goa Dourada" or Golden Goa. This description has been longingly and often used to this date. Another of the famous historical sayings as applied to this city is "Quem viu Goa, nao precisa de ver Lisboa", (who has seen Goa, does not need to see Lisbon).

Manohar Sardessai, a highly acclaimed intellectual and poet, composed many poems, one of which is sung with pride by many Goans. Part of it goes "Sobit amchem Goem, Sundor amchem Goem" (basically Beautiful Goa) and is widely and proudly accepted by the Goans. Mr. Sardessai, a humble and unassuming gentleman, was a professor of French language at Chowgule College, during my days at the same institution in 1964-66.

This port of Goa on the Mandovi River, became the original capital city of the Portuguese possessions in India. With passing of time it came to be known as "Velha Goa" or Old Goa. It attracted not only traders but also

Catholic missionaries from the different orders starting with the Jesuits, followed by the Franciscans, Dominicans, Augustinians, and others.

As the Portuguese power was waning there were plans to move the capital from Old Goa. However these plans were hastened due to a bubonic plague in 1738, that decimated the local population. The new capital Pangim (now Panaji) was founded in 1843.

Each religious order thought it necessary to build their own church or convent, with the result that within a perimeter of less than 2 km, there are six large churches and a convent for the nuns. Goa was the headquarters and departing point for the missionaries travelling to regions stretching from East Africa all the way to Japan in the West. Velha Goa came to be known then as the Rome of the Orient.

In recognition of the services rendered in the propagation of the catholic faith, the Pope bestowed on the Bishop of Goa the title of Patriarch, of which there have been only five in the catholic hierarchy, others being Rome, Lisbon, Jerusalem and Constantinople in Turkey, all with a special place in the catholic church. The Pope also bestowed on the Goans a unique privilege of being exempted from consuming meat on Fridays during the lent season. It was called Bula. The faithful had to make a small monetary payment for the paper (Bula) which gave you that privilege..

The Archeological Department of the Government of India has taken all these old religious buildings in Old Goa, under its management due to their historical and touristic value. Maintenance costs for the churches or monuments require a deep pocketed entity.

For Goans and many Indians including Hindus, the most important church in Old Goa, is the Basilica de Bom Jesus, where lies, in a mausoleum, the body of St. Francis Xavier, patron saint of the Indies. He arrived in Goa in 1542, but did most of his missionary work in Kerala, Sri Lanka and the Far East (Malacca and Japan). He intended to visit China on his return trip to the Far East, only to die just off the coast of China.

His allegedly incorrupt body, after being first interred on the Sancia island and then reinterred in Mallaca, has been moved around three or four times without any visible damage. The damage has been dealt by mutilations of the body on the request for body parts prior to the canonization, from the Pope, the Jesuits and even a toe bitten off by a worshipper overcome by devotion to the saint. What you see now is a body with skin over the bones.

Every village in Goa has a church, and normally they are big structures. Many of these churches in the Old Conquest territories have been built where once Hindu temples stood.

Even though close to three quarters of the population of Goa is principally Hindu, big Hindu temples are relatively few, in particular in the Old Conquest territories. This is the result of destruction of the Hindu temples, first by the Muslim invading armies and then by the Portuguese, whose religious zeal was ruthless in the early years. For example in Curtorim, those in the population (hindus) who did not wish to be converted to christianity, took their idols moved across the river Zuari, to Shiroda of the Ponda taluka. They were welcome there by the current ruler, who happened to be Muslim. To this date, Curtorim which is now predominantly Christian, has many churches but only a small Hindu roadside temple.

The Portuguese also brought in Inquisition and established coercive measures to Christianize their subjects around 1560. The Inquisition was in force in Goa for close to 250 years, from late 16th century to early 19th century. My understanding is that Inquisition's initial objectives were more to control the behavior of recently converted Christians rather than forcible conversion to Christianity of the still non-converted, as it is widely believed.

CHAPTER 5

Our Villages: An Overview

In 1999, six couples, including Ethel and I, came up with the idea of creating an Association in Toronto, Ontario, Canada, of the three neighbouring villages of Curtorim, Loutulim and Raia, and named it The CLR Association.

What follows is the research and write-ups on our annual social function handouts. I had done the original write-ups on Curtorim and Raia. Venusto Deniz had done the same for Loutulim.

Venusto is responsible for the bulk of the material you read in this chapter, on these three villages: pulling it together and adding material where necessary. I have added material to Venusto's write-up, in order to complement my narrative.

Through the CLR Association, we hoped to treasure our rich and diverse heritage and ensure that it continues to live in the hearts and minds of those that follow. It is quite amazing that some 9,000 plus miles away hundreds of families with their roots in these villages like to associate and socialize with such enthusiasm.

In addition to the social activities, such as the picnic, and the Sao Joao Feast celebration, the Social is the principal annual event held annually on the last weekend of September and attended by 300 plus "villagers" and their friends. The guests are treated to a cultural taste of Goa, including annual performance by eponymous CLR Mando Group of the Mando singing and dance; Kunnbi dance, Dekhni and other items such as Portuguese dance, corredinho, would also be performed. Once a typical Goan (Christian) wedding reception was enacted, a performance which is fondly remembered to this date, with lots of requests for its re-enactment.

Over the years, at our CLR Social the Mando dancing has been performed by adults and the other types of dancing performed by the youth and children of the villages.

At the 2019 Social event, the 20th Anniversary of the founding of the CLR Association, the CLR Mando group members decided to do something different than the normal performance. The troupe members both sang and performed dancing of the Mando, Kunnbi Dance and the Dekhni to live music. The youngsters danced the corredinho, to pre-recorded music. Due to Covid-19 pandemic, the annual CLR Social was not been held for three years, till September 2023.

There are indeed some "binding agents" that keep these villages together and some "catalysts" that trigger the enthusiasm. For starters all three villages are located on the southern/western bank of the river Zuari as it snakes its way into the Arabian Sea, which is a few kilometers downstream. For centuries, several dynasties that ruled this area found the location to be of strategic importance because it is conveniently accessible and yet tucked away from the rough sea during monsoon as well as maritime invaders.

Until the Portuguese invasion in the 16th century, most residents were Hindus of common origin namely the Saraswats from northern India. Already at that time most residents of the three villages traditionally participated in and celebrated common Hindu feasts being descendants of similar origins. When the Portuguese conquered south Goa they continued to use Rachol (a sub-village of Raia) as their fortress and military base.

A few years later the Portuguese invited the Jesuits to commence the major aggressive process of christianisation of South Goa. The Portuguese rulers initially housed the Jesuits in Rachol and the process of christianisation started in Raia and then spread to the neighbouring villages, namely Curtorim and Loutulim. The forced conversion to Christianity and the resentment towards the Portuguese drove these three already blended communities even closer together.

During the four centuries of the Portuguese rule, their focus was on education in the Christian faith. During the Portuguese rule, the majority of the marital unions in these villages took place between the residents of these three villages. As a result, most residents had family connections in all three villages.

Finally, some 40 years ago, emigrants from these villages who lived in Bombay (now Mumbai) were aware of the existence of three village associations Curtorim, Loutulim and Raia. And there was one obvious observation. Pretty much the same people patronized all three associations. So when the founders of the CLR got together in Ontario, Canada, they wisely saw no point in having separate associations.

The following are the historical and cultural profiles of each of the villages.

Curtorim

Curtorim, being the biggest of the villages (in area and population) referenced here, is getting an extensive treatment in my writing. It happens that being born and raised in Curtorim I know more about life in this village than in the other two villages. Readers of this book can assume that life and events in the other villages were not too dissimilar.

I was fortunate to get my hands on a copy of The Commemorative Supplement of the newspaper Diario de Goa, dated February 1, 1956, and dedicated to the village of Curtorim, with articles written by respected sons of the village. To me, this issue of the journal has been a good source of information and deduction of historical and cultural aspects and of village life in general, along with confirming my own observations and information passed on by our family elders. I wish to thank Rafael Viegas, from Curtorim, for sharing with me a copy of this supplement and his deep knowledge of the people and events of the village, past and more recent.

Curtorim (Curtore or Kurhtori) is a straddling village bounded on its northern side by the Zuari river, to the east by Chandor, to the south by Sao Jose de Areal, and Fatorda/Margao to the west and Raia to the Northwest. It is set in a fertile valley, vivid green during monsoon season, earning the name of Granary of Salsete Taluka (Saxtti Bhatacho Koddo, or "Celeiro" de Salcete, in Portuguese).

The name Curtorim was assigned to this village by the Portuguese. The ancestors of Curtorim were Saraswat Hindus, usually surnamed Pai, Prabhu, Desai and Kamat, the latter being the majority. In the 16th century, the Portuguese and the Jesuits changed the religious and cultural landscape of the village.

Curtorim's main interest since its evangelization in the 16th century centers on the Church of St. Alex (Santo Aleixo), one of the oldest churches in Goa. It was built in 1597 (rebuilt in 1647) on the site of the former ancient Hindu temple dedicated to the deity Ravalnath (a form of Lord Shiva), the remains of which are visible even today.

The builders of the Church of St. Alex certainly had an eye for location and, refusing to accept the obvious, built the church with its back to the center of the village, allowing the front of the church and its square to face across the serene waters of a palm-fringed lake and wooded slopes, an enviable setting.

Despite the fast changing of the population make-up in Goa, Curtorim continues to be a predominantly Catholic population. The Church of St Alex is the central feature of the village.

Over the years, Curtorim has earned an outstanding reputation for heroics in the armed forces and in the field of music. The village boasts of having perhaps the greatest number of its sons decorated for bravery in India's conflicts with her neighbours than any other village in Goa. It abounds with retired military officers and former freedom fighters. The latest name of prominence is General S. Rodrigues who retired as the Chief of Indian Armed Forces.

Another distinguished son of Corjem, Curtorim, Padma Bhushan Dr. Jose Pereira stood tall in his achievements that benefited not just Goa but India, and the world in general. At the time of his death, in January of 2015, Goan Press described Dr. Pereira as" Goa's intellectual giant", "Goa's Michael Angelo or Da Vinci", a theologian, an Indologist, a singular Indian of his generation, an artist, a painter (see his beautiful frescoes on the ceilings of sacristy at the Chapel of St. Joaquim in Margao), a teacher (Fordham University, USA), an author/writer, historian, a linguist and a staunch collector and publisher of Goan folk music.

Dr. Pereira left a rich legacy with 24 books and 145 articles covering the fields of arts, architecture and religion, and languages. His research and publications of the Konkani language were a contributing factor to Konkani being acknowledged by the Sahitya Academy of India, as a full-fledged language in India. As a tireless researcher of our Goan folklore, Dr. Pereira authored 3 books and co-authored six more with Prof. Michael Martins from Orlim and my cousin Antonio Da Costa also from Curtorim. Antonio and Jose Pereira are themselves first cousins. While the Goa Government shamefully did not value the immense contribution of this great son of Goa, the Indian Central Government conferred upon him the highest honor of <u>Padma Bhushan</u> for his distinguished service of high order in the fields of Education and Literature.

A number of world-class performers of contemporary Goan music and, believe it or not, western classical music have their origins in this village. There was a period between late 19th century and early 20th century, the peak period for Mando compositions, when the most prolific mando composers to date, Arnaldo de Menezes, Giselino Rebelo, Sebasteao Costa Fernandes, Ligorio Costa, Aleixo Antonio Costa, Aleixo Azavedo Diniz, Erminia da Veiga Estibeiro, and Francisco Sardinha, called Curtorim their home. In the post-Portuguese era, Curtorkars have continued this tradition, with one or other group bagging top prizes at the Annual Mando Festival, organized by the Goa Cultural and Social Centre. Many sons and daughters of Curtorim grew up learning western classical music and then went on to make their mark in many of the world's most elite centers for music.

Curtorim Brahmins were known as Kashti Bamon. Being true "xetkars" (farmers), it was not uncommon to see many of them going to the fields in their beloved kashti.

Kashti, is a kind of male G-string, or loin cloth, commonly worn by the worker class. Interestingly the hippies (men) liked it, and thought it cool, and many enjoyed wearing it on the beach.

I remember till in late 1950s, seeing my grandfather wearing a kashti when he would go to the fields / farm. It was on prodding from his children, by now well-educated and holding high public positions, that my grandfather stopped wearing the kashti.

Loutulim

Loutulim, also pronounced as Loutulim, is situated on the left bank of the river Zuari and is flanked on the north, west and south by luxuriant hills and the villages of Quelossim, Verna and Raia respectively. The river, the hills and the rice fields in-between, contribute to the diverse beauty and complement the rich and diverse heritage of the village. The name Loutulim was derived from the words "Lov" a luxurious growth of wild grasses and "Tollem" meaning lake or pond.

Legend has it that the Goud Saraswats founded the settlement of Loutulim when they came to Goa from northern India. The saraswats were learned in Vedic lore and this group concentrated on studying subjects like astronomy, metaphysics, medicine and allied subjects and disseminating knowledge. As a result Loutulim became an important seat of Hinduism with several temples and an "agrahar" or university where Vedic studies and other subjects were taught and the people of Loutulim embraced a culture focussed on religion and education.

In 1567, the Portuguese dealt a severe blow to the village of Loutulim. In their continuing efforts to "Christianize" south Goa, the Captain of Fort Rachol ordered the burning and destruction of all the temples in Loutulim including the main temple of Shree Ramnathi. Many Hindu gaunkars left with their idols for safer grounds across the river.

Most of those who chose to stay embraced Christianity. Following the destruction of the temples and simultaneous evangelization and conversion, the missionaries consolidated their religious successes by building churches and chapels to promote Christian worship and schools to boost religious teaching and development of future priests.

The church in Loutulim was built in 1581, under the Patronage of St. Bartholomeu and later renamed Saviour of the World Church. Adjoining the church, there is a Portaria (lobby), which traditionally was the meeting place of the villagers after Sunday mass. Here they would talk, discuss, and party. One can take it as a habit rooted in the ancient past and continues to this day. Very close to the Portaria is the sundial standing on a circular pedestal, which provides sitting accommodation. Here the village elders would spend the evening, exchanging views and opinions on various topics of interest. It was for them a well spent evening.

Today, the village of Loutolim consists of five wards namely Vanxem, Devotte, Orgao, Carvota and Rassaim. The Saviour of the World church still stands magnificent (recently refurbished) and is the main church in the village, while each of the wards has chapels affiliated to the church. Hindus and Catholics coexist in peace and harmony respecting and sharing both their cultures, which were originally one.

Through all its history and turmoil, Loutulim has retained its focus on religion and education and has been known for these two attributes for centuries. It is not surprising that for hundreds of years Loutulim has nurtured an unusually high number of priests and learned professionals who have served and made their mark in every continent.

Loutulim is well known for the finest examples of Goan architecture observed in the houses and mansions providing a natural Goan feel to visitors. Among tourists. Loutulim is known for "Big Foot" also known as "Ancestral Goa", an open air museum that recreates the Goan rural life as it was a hundred years ago.

Loutulim was a major contributor of Mando composers. Torquato de Figueiredo, as a member of the Mando Trilogy, (Arnaldo de Menezes and

Giselino Rebelo being the other two), deserves special mention. Other prominent composers of mando in Loutulim are Paulo Milagres Silva, and Eduardo Menezes.

A son of Loutulim, Mario de Miranda, the world-famous cartoonist, was awarded Padma Vibhusan by the Government of India. Mario has left his indelible mark with his drawings of typical Goan scenes.

Raia

Raia is nestled between Curtorim to the east, Loutulim to the West, the River Zuari to the north, with Nuvem, Fatorda and Margao making up its southern boundaries. The lower-level eastern plains along the river bank are ideal for rich paddy fields suitable for two yearly rice crops: one from the monsoon rains and one from the irrigation from monsoon rain waters collected in reservoirs, locally known as "tollem"

The name Raia has its origin from Agni-Mukha-Roy, the first Kadamba ruler, who came from present day Mysore, to settle in Salcete. Upon the fall of the Kadamba Dynasty, the place came to be known simply as Raya and later Raia.

Raia was of strategic economic and military importance to South Goa, with the river to the north and the Rachol harbour. Trade flourished with distant Arab ports, as early as in the 7th century. Over centuries, Rachol, a sub-village of Raia was significant for its strategic location on the river Zuari and in the hinterland of South Goa. For many years Rachol was the capital of South Goa. It acted as a big obstacle to many invaders and because of its importance successive rulers continued fortifying Rachol. At its peak, the fort had as many as 100 cannons and provisions to withstand an invasion for up to three years. There is little evidence left of this fort, save a gateway and some walls.

The Portuguese used the Rachol fort as its strategic military base and later permitted the Jesuit missionaries to use Rachol as its operating base for the Christianisation of South Goa. Raia happens to be the first village in Salcete to be evangelized (circa 1558), and the first Church in south Goa was built in Rachol (Our Lady of Snows) in 1565 over a Hindu temple site. The church was made of mainly mud/clay and attached to the fortress. This church was demolished many years later.

The present-day church of Our Lady of Snows was built in Raia on the original site of the temple of Goddess Kamakshi or Shantadurga after the Portuguese destroyed the temple. The church was completed in 1699 after 30 years of construction work.

Today this church is the focal point of the village and is famous across Goa for the "Konnsanchem Fest" (Feast of the Harvest). Although this feast takes place in most villages in Goa to celebrate the rice harvest, the feast in Raia is celebrated with great pomp including the elaborate traditional rituals with the sheaves (konnsam) of rice harvest. It is attended by people of all faiths and a large number of devotees from all over Goa.

Since I have given credit to mando composers of the other two villages, it is noteworthy to honor Frederico de Melo from Raia, who penned the song, "Sorgu nittoll go nirmollu" which is identified as the first Mando composition.

CHAPTER 6

Village Lives of Our Families:
A Brief Introduction

I may be repeating here information I have already spoken about, as I try to capture the essence of life of our ancestors and my own, in the villages of Curtorim Loutulim and Raia, when I migrated to Canada in 1971, at the age 24. In the last 50 years of my absence from Goa, I find there has been a rapid and unbelievable change in lifestyle. For me this feeling is accentuated because I am not there to experience the ongoing, gradual transition from a purely rural life to today's semi-urban and semi-rural life.

I see that the village youth of today live a semi-rural and semi-urban life and have little idea of the mainly rural community life of their parents, let alone of their grandparents. I am therefore attempting to describe the village life going back, say 100 years. Prior to that, life was even more rural, less mechanized and as a consequence slower paced.

The changes have been brought on by a combination of increased globalization, including labor demand, travel mobility and greater overall wealth level on account of higher formal education which allows people to pursue better employment opportunities, in Goa and outside Goa. Two noteworthy overseas employment opportunities for Goans would be in the Middle Eastern region countries (principally Kuwait, United Arab Emirates and Oman and to a lesser extent Saudi Arabia, Qatar and Iraq) and work as seafarers, in particular as stewards on the cruise ships.

I expect this chapter will have a bias of information towards the village of Curtorim. This is due to the fact that I grew up in Curtorim, and my first-hand knowledge before I migrated, and information obtained by me both by word of mouth and a useful source of information, via a special Supplement of Diario de Goa, 1956, are significantly Curtorim-centric.

It is my firm belief that life in these three villages, and the achievements of their sons and daughters, run parallel paths. Curtorim, being the larger (approximately 15 sq. km) of the three villages, has probably contributed greater number of illustrious people, who left their mark for the posterity. From my observation, it is sad that the achievements and contributions from these illustrious sons of the village, have not received a due and lasting recognition.

The intended objective of this book is first and foremost to put in writing the cultural and societal history and living habits of our ancestors and their contemporaries, who grew up in these villages. Thus a reader, who is currently living in Goa, may have difficulty relating the current village life to day-to-day life of our ancestors, or even my age generation merely 50 years ago. Woven in the narrative in this chapter and following chapters, will be the stories of my own family members and those of the extended family through marriage.

The accelerated pace of the technological and industrial advance of the past fifty years, has affected the life in the villages, and it cannot be compared to the relative changes people experienced in these villages in previous fifty or hundred years. All societies across the world, have been affected by these changes and the pace of change has been greater or lesser in different regions of the world.

For example I spent a few days in August 2018, visiting a dear friend, retired priest, Fr. Albert Castelino, in St. Louis, Missouri, USA. He is a resident of the Redemptorist Priests Retirement cum Nursing home in Ligouri, St. Louis. Since writing this book was top of my mind at the time, I took the opportunity to have conversations with Fr. Albert and several other resident priests, about their own experiences growing up, in Pune, India, for Fr. Albert and across the USA for a handful of resident priests.

What struck me, is that the life experiences recounted by these elderly priests of their ancestors and their own during their growing up years, are to my knowledge, no different than those of our ancestors in the rural environment, and the more recent changes experienced by our parents and their generation.

A few years ago, I came across a relatively new composition of Mando and Dulpods, its subject matter being the village of Curtorim, and aptly named Curtorim. This poetic composition resonated with me, as a son of the village.

This particular Mando and Dulpods refer rather sarcastically, to societal changes which may be normal to the new generation but which reflect the changes in the cultural fabric of the village of recent past. I believe the composition was the work of my uncle Lourencinho Menezes, a person from the older generation, and it left me with "saudades", or longing for the "good old days".

Here are the lyrics for the Mando and my attempt at translation, keeping it as literal as possible. My CLR Mando group in Toronto, sang this Mando in 2003, at the Annual CLR Social in Toronto. CLR stands for Curtorim Loutulim and Raia.

Curtorim -mando

Xasttintulea ghanvam modem
Kuddtorecho ghanv ek dennem
Ravonk zainam Kuddtore vinnem
Kuddtoreant Kuddtorkar zatat unnem
Among the villages of Salsete (District)
Curtorim is a gift
I can't live without Curtorim
Even though the number of Curtorim original folks is on decline!

CH. Ghirest itias aslo Nove pillgen to samballcho
It is up to the new generation to maintain the rich heritage

Kuddtorkaru rovun xetam
Kutumbachim bhorlim pottam
Ghanv ghor soddun dhaduxi atam
Disgras! lagleat vikunk xetam bhatam
Through cultivation of the rice fields
Curtorkars filled families' stomachs
They are happy after leaving their homes and village
It's a disgrace, that they are selling their properties.

Dulpods

"Reference is made to "tigur and pittoll", fish types grown in the 5 water retention ponds (tollem), but which local thieves or miscreants, fish out or rob the rightful owners, a day or two before the designated official fish catch date (tolle marunk).

The dulpods continue with a dig at the youth who have too much money at their disposal and are not interested in tending to the properties / farms, but instead enjoy themselves going to the theaters / films and dances.

The new generation pays little attention to formal education and shows lack in good manners.

It ends with a reference to elder parents being shunted to "albergue", a home for the needy and destitute, with the son not being allowed by his wife to visit his elderly parents."

The reader will find a little more description of what Mando is and its place within the Goan Christian culture further down in this chapter.

The People of the Village

Even though people did not explicitly talk about communal living, you felt and lived a communal approach to doing things in the village. In general, everyone in the village felt responsible for each other's wellbeing. In particular parents could rest assured that their children would follow the societal norms. You do anything to the contrary and the news would filter back home in no time, often before you arrive home, and the children may have to face parental discipline. I guess that this is where the saying "it takes a village to raise a child" came about.

A classical example of the community helping each other was the agriculture, where neighbours helped each other, both at the time of cultivating the fields and at harvest time. Even the domestic animals, in particular the pigs and the poultry were free to roam in the adjacent neighbours' properties. There were no stone walls or barbed wire fences separating individual properties. The custom to demarcate the property boundaries was to bury a building stone in the ground at each end of the property and it was respected by related parties.

The society in these villages could be broadly divided into two classes: the landlords (bhattkars) and the labor class. Aside from a few rich families, with excessive properties within their residential village and elsewhere, most land holdings were of modest size and normally adjacent to your home. Families produced enough for the family's food needs, and some excess produce, which would be used for barter or converted into cash necessary to pay for all other necessities.

Before 1900 and even in the first quarter of the twentieth century, walking was the main mode of moving around and one-way walking distances of 2 to 4 km were routine. Bullock carts were the principal means of transporting bulky or heavy material, such as building material or the harvested paddy and such.

I am told that on rare occasions, when he had to go into town (Margao) for any work at the municipality or a government office, my maternal grandfather used to walk the 6 km distance, with a short stopover at his mother's family home, the Cruz family in Borda, which is a walking distance of fifteen minutes to the center of the city. There he would help himself to "canjee" or "pez" (local rice porridge) and then proceed onward.

Then the bicycles showed up. In my youth days (1950s and 1960s), in households that could afford it, there would be one bicycle per household, which would be shared by all the male members of the family. The same was the situation in our household, and we would have to plan with our dad for the use of the bicycle, for any trips to the city or neighboring villages.

The bicycle has long been replaced by motorized bikes or scooters. The new fast pace of the society is reflected in an individual household commonly having more than one scooter.

Even in the early nineteen seventies there probably were less than a handful of families, in the village, owning their own private vehicle. And they would have a driver to drive the family around. Today ownership of a private car is a common occurrence, and you drive yourself around.

Local mini-buses, called "carreira" had started to run between the village and Margao in 1950s. Two images of the carreira travel are that most of the time, the mini-bus would be packed like sardines, by the time it arrived from one end of the village to our place (Maina) with about 6 km still to go to town (Margao).

Things have not changed all that much, after all these intervening years. The transportation vehicles are still cramped, due to a combination of more frequent travel by people, increased population, government inefficiency or corruption of not allowing more of these mini-buses to ply the route.

The main employment for the labor class was in the form of manual labor in rice field cultivation, other works in the farm properties and other village civil works, such as building and maintaining roads and ancillary works. The labor class owned their own abodes, but for the most part their land holding was limited to the property where their residence stood and a few meters surrounding their home. The houses were all built of stone and mud construction with tiled roof. Contrary to what is common in rural parts or slums in India, or in some remote regions in Goa, no huts with tin roof or thatched roof existed in our villages. There was no abject poverty among the village folks, wherein people would go hungry. The community took responsibility to look after the few needy people, who, for health reasons could not be part of the labor force and fend for themselves.

With the dawn of the twentieth century and with gradual increase in mobility and limited work opportunities being available in Goa, many men from the village would take up temporary work outside Goa to supplement their income from working in the village. An attractive and lucrative option was to work as a "shippy" (seafarer or tarvotti), either on ocean plying passenger or merchant ships. This marine employment exposed these folks to new and more developed worlds and enhanced the living standards of their families in Goa, which in turn gave an early boost to education opportunities to their children.

Schooling / Formal Education

The generations of our ancestors up to our grandparents limited themselves to formal education in Portuguese, at the Primary School level (escola primaria, completing segundo grau, corresponding to English Grade 4), say up to the ages of 10-12. Exceptions would be boys joining the Seminary and embracing the priesthood, as we see them in our own families. Very few girls would be privileged to complete the full primary school course. On the Moniz side of the family, my dad's siblings did not pursue further studies beyond the primary school level. Dad did a further couple of years of schooling at the Seminary.

After all these years I had forgotten that even my generation of school kids attended the primary school in bare feet, until a colleague originally from Rajasthan, India, brought it to my attention as she was recounting her own childhood school experiences. The same applied to playing football. I got my first football boots, already well used, and handed down from my brother Heriberto, when I was in my third year of Seminary. I also remember that in the following year, having the boots led to my selection to Seminary's football team.

Schooling in Goa was in Portuguese, as Konkani language studies were discouraged and not officially available. Most Hindus chose however to do the primary school studies in Marathi, a language with same roots as Konkani. Hindu population was relatively small in the villages of our ancestors. During my Seminary studies, I had a course of Konkani language. The first half of the course involved learning the Marathi or Devnagari script, as the correct pronunciation of the Konkani language is best achieved through that script. Amongst Christians, any literature such as church booklets or newspapers in Konkani were and still are in Roman script.

Before mid-twentieth century, it was also rare for kids from the worker class families to even complete the primary school grades (primeiro grau and segundo grau) which kids from the landowner class (usually the brahamin class) would complete by ages 10 to12. A limited number of students, principally from the urban areas, would continue into the Portuguese studies, Liceu (or lyceum) studies. This was equivalent of going to High School and a couple of years of college. Those who completed the maximum of 7 years course (Setimo Ano) could then proceed to studies in Medical (in Goa) or Engineering or Law (in Portugal) or did a special teacher's course called "Normal". A few students would proceed with their higher studies outside Goa, normally Belgaum (e.g my uncle Constancio Menezes did his Agriculture degree there), or Pune or Mumbai.

The start of the school year in early June coincided with the arrival of the monsoon, with all classes and exams completed by early March. The school break happened during months of March, April and May. These are also the months of rising temperatures (day temperatures rising to 32C plus) until the arrival of monsoon rains, which on one hand had a cooling effect, but on the other hand increased the levels of humidity.

The school break time was also the time for folks to **go to the beach**. The closest beach to Curtorim is the Colva beach, approximately 10 km away. Families that could afford it, would rent a place near the beach for a month or so (usually part of a residence) and family members would take turns of a few days each. They called it "mudança" literally change. Before the arrival of the automobile, travel to the beach would be on a bullock cart with people and provisions all loaded in the bullock cart. By early 1950s, at the height of the beach going season, a bus or two (carreira) with passenger capacity of 30 to 40 passenger would take the village people to Colva late afternoon with return trip around 8 pm.

I remember that as a kid of 6-7 years, accompanying my mum's unmarried cousin Tia Esperança once at one of these trips to the Colva beach. We and other holidayers would make two trips to the beach every day: one early morning before the hot sun came up and one in the evening around the sunset.

The routine consisted of getting your feet wet in waters at the beach and then congregating with other ladies under the shade of a coconut tree, for the gossip of the day. I had to sit nearby and be seen but not heard! As I remember there was one constant topic of conversation, and that was "what did you have for lunch or dinner", and my aunt would often respond that we had chicken (just to show off), when we actually had sardines (tal'le) picked up fresh at the beach as the fishermen pulled in their nets to the shore. And the fishermen did not mind us picking up those few sardines, and not paying for the catch. I guess that was life then. By the way, I still remember that Tia Esperança's cooking with sardines or anything else, was delicious.

Starting in the second quarter of the twentieth century due to increased mobility, and financial resources, the pursuit of higher education became feasible to more young people. Then after Goa was integrated politically into India in 1961, there was a big-time acceleration of access, desirability and affordability of further education not only towards completion of high school level of studies but also at college and university levels to all classes of the Goan society.

By now you are probably getting the picture that before early twentieth century, birth of a male child was more welcome than that of a female. This was on account of two factors: one is that boys/men would lend physical labour in the fields and the other is that there would be an outflow of wealth in terms of dowry, when giving a girl in marriage.

There is a saying "Bai zalear don fogetteo, Bab zalear tin fogetteo" meaning "if a girl is born light 2 packs of fire crackers, and if a boy is born, light 3 packs of fire crackers". Even though I did not experience it or hear about it in our families, I know of some older folks in not too distant past, actually giving preferential treatment to the boys against the girls, and in their minds, there was nothing wrong with it. The rationalization was that the boy carried the family name forward. As an example such differential treatment could be as simple as the grandmother or an aunt setting aside the best piece of chicken meat for the boy.

In rural areas of Goa, it was a norm for babies to be delivered at home with the help of midwifes. All of my siblings were born at home in Curtorim. There was a custom that the delivery of the firstborn would be at maternal home, with the mother and the baby returning after a week to a month after childbirth.

It was also customary that on January 1, the mother would send a basketful of a variety of home-made sweets and fruit (bananas and tangerine) to the married daughter's house. This was called "janer" and was sent only to daughters and not the sons, who were part of the joint family anyway. With my aunt Tia Albertina in charge, we knew that both the quality and quantity of goodies in that "janer" basket, were something to look forward to.

It was customary to name the first grandson and granddaughter after their grandparents. Usually the passing down of the name skipped a generation. For example, my dad was named after his grandfather Caetano, my elder brother Loyola, was named after our grandfather and I have been named after one of my granduncles, Eufemiano.

Prior to 1964, there was no electricity supply in the villages in Goa and no television anywhere in India for a few years after that. After Goa was integrated politically with India, bringing electricity to villages became a priority. Curtorim was selected to be the first Goan village to be electrified in 1964. It helped that the new Chief Engineer of Electricity of Goa, had his ancestral roots from Curtorim.

The first radio in our house was a Grundig box radio purchased in 1965, and powered by an external battery, like the one used for cars. Not too many other households had a radio at this stage.

There was a limited number of hours per week of music of our taste and our choice, on Radio Goa and Radio Ceylon (now Sri Lanka), and we tried not to miss these time spots of radio music transmission. On radio Goa, it was the listeners' request program of one or two hours, once or twice a week. On radio Ceylon, it was a program called Binaca Hit Parade, broadcasting the current top 10-12 songs on the chart (US or UK?).

In my childhood days, say till approximately age 10-11, kids from the neighboring 7 to 8 houses, would get together and play various outdoor games, which depended on the season. Also the game activity was limited to non-school days. We did not have or play any indoor games, such as cards, any board games (e.g. Monopoly, Connect-Four, Boggle, Memory, etc) to keep us occupied.

The most popular games that I remember playing with other kids are listed below.

Seven Tiles. We would have two teams each taking their turn alternatively. The game starts with piling seven pieces of tiles. Part 1: one of the attacking team members attempts to hit/break the pile with a ball from a certain distance marker. If one of the defending team members catches the ball you are out. Part 2: Then one or more players would try to rebuild the pile, without being hit by the other team members, with the ball. If the ball hits you below the knees, it does not count. Therefore the attacking team members can kick the ball far away from the defending team members. We would use a tennis ball covered in a sock. This way the ball would last longer, as well as it would hurt less if you get hit with it by the defender.

Gilli Dandda (Barra): players try to strike a small stick called a gilli (with both ends made pointy) with a longer stick called a dandda/danddo; the objective is to hit the gilli the furthest possible.

Cashew Nut/Seed (with shell on): you line up 6-8 seeds vertically on the ground and draw a square of a certain size in front of the line of cashew seeds. Then from a fixed distance, the players with a cashew seed in hand, alternately take turns to hit the lined-up cashew seeds. The objective is to hit any seed from the line-up and, get it out of the marked square in front. The player takes all the cashew seeds to the right of the one he successfully hit out. We would play this game around the time fresh cashew seeds would be available, say March-April, which coincidentally were school summer vacation months.

Marbles: similar to the Cashew Nut game. Another version of marble game is digging a shallow cup (hole) in the ground, and again mark an area around the hole. Players take turns in getting a marble into the cup. The person who successfully gets the marble into the cup, takes all the marbles within the marked-out area. This game was played more during the monsoon season.

Once we entered the youth stage, the boys with sport inclination, would move on to football (soccer). In my youth days (principally post-ortuguese days), high school and college attendance by girls, increased tremendously. They were also taking part in sports like throw ball and athletics. Thus my own sisters not only graduated from college or University degrees, but also participated in college sports team of throw ball.

Just as a point of reference, my grandfather (mother's dad), who by the standards of the day had a good level of education, believed that educating girls beyond the minimum level, was a waste of time; I understand that one sweet day, he went down to the convent where my mother was a boarder doing her Grade 3, and brought her home. By the way, this thinking, regarding education, was not shared by his wife, my grandmother; interestingly her ability to sign was her limit of formal education.

In our family my brother Heriberto and I played football (soccer) at relatively high level, having played for the Curtorim team, and for our College teams both in Goa and Mumbai. Remember, we never had the fortune of having a coach to hone up our natural football abilities.

Somewhere along the way Goans have come to be known as "susegaad," a term derived from Portuguese word "sossegado" which stands for peaceful, calm, restful or care-free. And most Goans enjoy this epithet and use it as a distinguishing badge of honor. The way of looking at Goans as 'susegaad", was compounded by the fact that, in olden days all the offices (in particular the government offices) used to close for siesta from one to three in the afternoon. This was something unheard of, in the rest of India.

The office hours in Goa went from 8 am to 1 pm and 3 pm to 6 or 7 pm. I believe this office hour timing was an outgrowth of, and transfer to urban office times, from the rural or agricultural work force hours. The labour force in the fields would start early but take a long break, to avoid the high noon sun and heat. The Portuguese, who, back home, were used to "siesta" break, went along with the long noon break or the siesta.

The local native language spoken by the common folk Goans is **Konkani**, which is the prevalent language, with regional variations, of the people living along the Konkan coast, extending from Ratnagiri in the north and Mangalore to the south.

The Konkani language spoken in south Goa is lot more influenced with the Portuguese words than the Konkani spoken in central and northern Goa, and there is a tendency to truncate the words. This is the result of Goan territory, south of the river Zuari, having been occupied and Christianized (1560) for more than 200 years before annexation of the central and northern parts of Goa.

I will illustrate this with a simple example for the English phrase "what are you saying" would be: "Tum kit sangot re" in Salsete or south Goa. The northern and the more correct version would be 'Tum kitem sangtai re".

In other words the language spoken by the non-southerners and the hindu population is closer to the purer Konkani language. Interestingly it is the southern Konkani style which is considered to be more lyrical and is adopted in the composition of most of Konkani song lyrics.

It is my own experience that when a person (adult) takes up learning a new language, a list of bad words or curse words is the first thing they seem to want to learn. A few examples of words or expressions derived from the Portuguese language and which have become part of common, daily usage in the Konkani language to this date, and whose origin is not known to most people: Malcriad (stands for "badly behaved" and derived from Portuguese word "mal criado", literal meaning: rude), "Vasimbor" (to convey "get lost" and derived from Portuguese phrase "vai se embora"), "best" (when somebody wishes to call you an "animal" and derived from Portuguese word "besta"), "merd" (stands for "person of low character" and derived from Portuguese word "merda"), "Fujadaput" (stands for "son of a bxxxx" and derived from Portuguese word "filho da puta").

In Goa the tiny, hot chilli is commonly known as "putkepar" (outside world calls it most commonly peri peri, or even Thai hot chiili, and it is chilli type, originating from East Africa and which was spread throughout the world by the Portuguese). Legend has it that when a Portuguese white man tasted it and found it unbearable he exclaimed "puta que pariu" which is equivalent of "son of a bxxx", and the local person, thought, "what a beautiful name"!

The Portuguese worked very hard to discourage formal education in Konkani, and for Government Office employment, they favored those who had Portuguese education. Thus there has been an elitism ingrained into the Goan mind, that the languages of the colonial masters, first the Portuguese language and now the English language, are superior to their native Konkani language. I have observed that this attitude is more prevalent among the Chistian folk, who because of their religion, still relate more to the western culture than the Indian culture.

The **Church** played a central or an important role in the lives of the Christian folk in the village and in Goa. The church was also located centrally, with farthest house being at maximum of 20-30 minutes walking distance. This is similar to the European model, where the church edifice and the "plaza" or "town square" are the city center of today.

Unlike the attitude and relatively independent thinking by the catholic population in the western world, the practice of faith, even today, is strongly ingrained in the community. This deep faith is manifested through overwhelming church attendance, multitude of feasts at the local chapel or the feasts of patron saints and other major religious feasts at the central parish or church. Each of these feasts is preceded by novenas, held in the evenings.

On the feast day the main mass or the high mass, is a big celebration including a procession on the church grounds. The feasts are also an occasion for local markets (feira) where folks buy various sweets on their way home, after the church celebration. It has become a custom and folks have come to expect for these goodies to be on sale at such occasions near church grounds (laddoo, kaddio boddio, chonne and such). The market would also be an occasion to buy household items, such as cooking utensils. The most important aspect of the village feast was the opportunity and custom of a get together of grandparents, uncles and aunts, first cousins and other close family members, the highlight being the expected sumptuous festive lunch, with all the trimmings.

As for most Christians, the principal church events in the life of our villagers are the baptism, the first holy communion, the wedding and the funeral. In villages with predominantly catholic population, the church bell played an important role.

The church bell announced the morning mass, a few minutes before the start of the mass. There is also a daily church bell tolling for Angelus, at 7 pm (at dusk), at which time most people would pause to say the angelus prayer.

In our house, the daily rosary recitation started at eight in the evening and all family members had to be home before then. The time between the end of the rosary and serving of dinner was for the kids to wash their feet and such, if they had not done so before then. Since there was no electricity or TV in my youth days people went to bed following dinner. Reading the daily newspaper or reading a book were not a normal practice.

For the young people in higher study grades, studying in the late hours when the adults were already in bed, was with the light of a small kerosene lamp (divo). Everybody was used to wake up early in the morning, most of them around six. To this day the first Sunday mass is at seven in the morning, with the last mass being at ten.

The Bishop of Goa, had the title of Patriarch (one of the 5 in the Catholic world), in recognition by the Holy See, for the role played by Goa in propagation of the Catholic faith in Asia, in the sixteen and seventeenth centuries. The Vatican had also bestowed on the Goan Catholics, a special dispensation, allowing them to consume meat on Fridays, during the lent season, when the rest of the catholic world could not. There was a catch. The family had to pay a small charge and receive a piece of paper, called "bula". I find this European thinking applied to Goa, a little funny, because Goans are normally fish eaters, with irregular consumption of meat, and that too, predominantly by the well off and usually not on Fridays.

A special tolling of the church bell, of one beat followed by two beats, was to announce death of a villager. The body of the dead person was kept in the house to allow for visitation from people of the village. From time to time there would be wailing for the dead, some of it genuine and some from some semi-professional wailers, I understand. The funeral would take place the following day, with cortege of villagers accompanying the hearse, leaving the house directly to the church. A jazz style music band accompanying the cortege was not uncommon, where the family could afford it. The burial would follow the mass and the prayers for the departed. On the third anniversary year of the burial, the grave would be excavated for reuse for another interment. The remains (usually the skull and some other bones) would usually be added to a big well of such bones from the predeceased. More recently, families who can afford the costs involved, have the bones cleaned and put in an urn in the wall of the cemetery.

Going back to 200 to 250 years, most families, including ours, had three to six children, the latter being more of a norm, in the nineteenth century and the first half of the twentieth century.

Families lived in a **joint-family system**, where the elders were highly respected, whether they earned their respect or not. Within our families and in most village households and for that matter in the Goan culture, women managed the household, including the finances and children's education and all family affairs. The men were the bread winners or "hunters-gatherers" of the past. Outside the home the men acted as spokespersons and bragged about family successes, giving an impression that it was they who were in charge.

"A joint family or undivided *family* is an extended *family* arrangement prevalent throughout the Indian subcontinent, particularly in India, consisting of many generations living in the same household, all bound by the common relationship". (Wikepedia)

It is in this system of joint-families, and my observations confirm it, that the notorious, controlling mothers-in-law, got their bad reputation. Within our own families, to my knowledge the mother-in-law ruled the roost, but fortunately I did not see or hear of that mother-in-law from hell.

It was usual that the eldest boy would marry, whilst the remainder of the boys would remain single, and contribute to the joint family "pot". It was truly a combined family affair. With a few exceptions, family members lived in harmony and supported each other. For that matter, and I can attest, supporting each other, neighbour helping the neighbour, was how the whole community thrived as an agricultural clan. It was a communal type of life to a great extent even in early nineteen seventies, when left India for Canada.

When I talk to people in my age group (70s-80s), who were born and grew up in rural areas or farms in Canada, they tell me that neighbour helping neighbour was also the norm in their "good old days".

Among the Brahmin families, it was fairly common and often expected that the oldest or second oldest of the boys would join the priesthood. This was a remnant of their ancestry before their conversion to Christianity. The Brahmins are the caste from which Hindu priests are drawn, and are responsible for teaching and maintaining sacred knowledge.

Becoming a priest was probably the cheapest higher education available at the time. I believe the cost involved, was provision of a certain quota of rice. Having a priest also brought prestige to the family. In the village, the households were often known as the house of so and so priest.

The villages of Curtorim and Loutulim and Raia produced more than their fair share of Goan priests, who exercised their priestly duties in Goa, other parts of India and various Portuguese territories in Africa and Asia. I am positive that proximity to the principal Goa Seminary, in Rachol (part of Raia), a respected go-to institution for post-elementary schooling, was a major factor in producing a large number of priests from these villages.

The joint-family system was already on its way out, in favour of the modern nuclear family system, starting with my own uncles on both sides of the family, and on the Pereira side too. To be specific it would be at the dawn of the second half of twentieth century. The change to the nuclear family came about as the children, armed with higher education, moved out of the village to urban centres in search of professional opportunities in Goa, India or overseas. They were also marrying women with higher education, principally in the teaching profession. With combined incomes they had the means to rent or buy their own place to live.

Marriage and Weddings

Within the joint family, the custom was to 'arrange" marriage for the girls anywhere between ages of 20 and 25. Normally the boys got married between ages of 30 and 40. There was an unwritten expectation that the boy would wait till all his sisters were given in marriage. I heard of this custom, when I was getting married at age 28, by then already four years in Canada; I was told that some members of our extended family, pointed to this custom, and in their opinion, what was the hurry, when I had two unmarried sisters.

For families and in particular mothers, getting their daughters married, would be an emotional and all-consuming affair. Families truly believed that in marriage, it is not just the boy and the girl marrying each other, but also that the two families joined together.

Marriage by proposal (or arranged) was the predominant way to marriage. There were matchmaking ladies (raibari) in the villages or in the cities, who were well versed in this art of connecting families and young girls and boys. To these matchmakers, the most important deciding factor was knowing the families, and much less the boy and the girl who were being matched. Courtship time would be a luxury and was most often not a factor to be considered.

Not marrying within your own social class (caste) was a rare event, and even less common marrying across religious lines. After the Portuguese exit from Goa in 1961, and establishment of a number of Colleges in Goa, higher education became available to wider segments of the society, than before 1961. This in turn led to much greater social contact among the youth, from the two predominant religions (Christian and Hindu), as well as from social classes. Intermarriages across religious lines and social classes were not an exception any longer.

My sister-in-law Benildes's mother, Simpliciana Coutinho, from Divar, recounted to me her own story leading to her own arranged marriage. Simpliciana (or Sumplu-man) was one the most pleasant and endearing women I have come across. She was a calm and wise woman, and has left a lasting impression on me.

A prospective husband, hailing from the same village was at the time working in the oil fields in Iraq. It was quite common in those days for such ex-pats to come back home on vacation of one to three months, every two years. There was a need to send her photograph to the prospective husband. Remember that in a village the families knew each other, and had enough background information about the prospective bride. To take that photograph, but to avoid alerting neighbours' curiosity, her folks took her to the nearest town (Panjim) walking through rice fields. Then the first time he actually laid his eyes on her, was from a distance at the church.

Due to limited time before he would have to go back to Iraq, there was urgency in getting the marriage done. He was 13 years older than she was. Remember, in those days, it was not just the man and the woman getting married. It was, in a way, a union between the two families. Not only did the wedding take place in a hurry, but they also managed to arrange to have a marriage between the groom's sister and the bride's uncle on the same day.

The groom was off to Iraq, for his "well paying" job, just a few days after the wedding and his next trip back was after two years. Such a story was not uncommon in those days, in particular amongst the North Goa population, where lot more men left Goa to the British and Portuguese colonies, than would be the case in the south. The job opportunities and pay scales in these far away places were immeasurably better than in Goa, or even in rest of India.

From mid-twentieth century, the rigidity of this system of marriage by proposal amongst our folks has experienced much loosening and currently I would not be surprised if amongst the college educated, fifty percent or more of the couples come together on their own, through social interaction, either during school days or work or some other social environment.

Normally a dowry was given to the girl, at the time of the marriage, with the marrying girl, signing off any further share of the family property. The monetary value of the dowry, depended on bride's family's means, expectations or demands from the prospective husband's family. Many families paid attention to wanting their daughter (or son) to marry "higher" from the point of family social status and wealth.

The dowry system was originally intended to help the girl settle down within her new family, as well as giving her a share of the family wealth (usually not accounting for the land ownership, which was precious as agricultural land but would not fetch the high property prices of today).

As it happens with such customs, this dowry system often became an impediment for marriageable girls to get a husband. There were many instances, the dowry became a tool of oppression after the marriage by the in-laws, looking for greater share of girl's family wealth, often where there was none. It was not unusual for families to go into debt, to give the bride a dowry, to help the bride, her husband and his family financially.

Forgotten was the fact that the husband and his family were gaining a young lady to bring children into the family, be a worker/manager in the house as well as being the future caretaker of the household. In the days of joint family system, the husband's mother, or grandmother would still rule the roost, as long as she could. The young bride's turn at being the matriarch of the family would come with time.

Amongst some populations in the world, the dowry system prevalent in India, is reversed, and it is the husband's family that pays the bride's family, at the time of marriage.

More often than not, the dowry asset became part of the joint family wealth. With my grandmother's advice, the cash component of Marcelina's (my mother) dowry was used to buy a parcel of land five to 10 minutes from our home, and thus the new property asset did not co-mingle with the joint family property assets.

There is a folklore saying that families in Goa came into wealth in the olden days in three ways: Casar, Herdar or Merdar. "Casar"- to marry, and receive dowry; "Herdar"- to inherit, from parents or an aunt or uncle who may be childless; and "Merdar"- literally to be a shit disturber, or through cheating or illegal means. In olden days, in many Brahmin families, (who in their Hindu past were a class of priests), it was not unusual for the family to benefit from the earnings or savings from a priest, normally upon retirement.

Before we move on, it is worth mentioning two important aspects of marriage and property inheritance, governed by the Civil code set up by the Portuguese and applicable to all Goans, of all faiths. Goa is the only State in India to have the Civil Code governing their inhabitants, even to this day.

Before the religious wedding ceremony, the couple had to register their marriage in the Municipality. From the government (official) point of view this was more important than signing the book and be registered in church (or a temple or mosque). For example, in my own situation, Ethel and I had our civil marriage registered in Margao, and it was on the basis of this document, that her Immigration to Canada was processed and approved. We had our church wedding, in Calgary, upon Ethel's arrival to Canada.

Upon death of your parents, the Portuguese Civil Code assigned equal property rights to all their children, sons and daughters. This is the reason why a daughter upon receiving a dowry, signed off or renounced her share of paternal property rights.

Christian Wedding

Marriage ceremony in the church, the wedding vows, the woman's wedding dress and suit for the men, dress code for the wedding party and guests, and wedding reception, were and continue to be typical of a western catholic church wedding. Most of the village clan, which includes your own family and relations and relatives of your relatives would be invited, including young children. Probably 200 to 300 wedding guests would be expected. Normally there were two receptions. The first one, following the church ceremony, would be at groom's place and after a couple of days a reciprocal one (tornaboda or "aponnem") at the bride's place.

Wedding receptions were held during the day and plenty of ball-room dancing to a local live band was a must. The venue would be either inside the house if a big enough hall was available for all the guests, or outdoors in a pandal (large open-sided temporary pavilion). There was a routine to wedding reception menu: a plate of appetizers, with about three or four different items, was served to start the function followed at set time intervals with soup (caldo) served usually in a tea cup; this would be followed by serving the main plate consisting of pulav (Goan pilaf rice), Goan "stew", and a slice of sandwich bread. This would be followed with a fruit salad for desert and a piece of wedding cake to end the day. There never was a buffet at the wedding receptions. Beer, Scotch Whisky, red wine (either dry red wine or "tinto" or sweet wine, Port wine style) and soft drinks (including Orsata) were drinks of choice.

Wedding receptions of today, which are mostly evening affairs, have become such extravagant affairs with 500 – 1000 – 1500 guest count being easily the norm. The costs are usually equally shared by the groom's and bride's families.

The number of dishes and the amount of food served does not seem to have limits. It is always a huge buffet layout, with such variety of dishes served (Goan, Indian and Chinese). I do not know when this opulence started and the way I see it, it has a long way to run its course. Even though snacks are served at the early stage of the reception, the buffet dinner is served at late hours. It has become a routine for the guests to avail themselves of the buffet food, and then head home. It is not unusual for many of the wedding guests to arrive late for the reception, knowing well that the buffet is served quite late in the night. COVID-19 pandemic (2020-2022) led to severe limitations on the number of wedding guests. The big wedding receptions have returned.

One custom that continues to this date is serving a piece of "wedding" cake (fruit cake) as a parting gift. I remember my parents bringing home for us, one or two pieces of this wedding cake and we really enjoyed the cake. I have followed this habit, and brought such treats from my office parties for our kids. Unfortunately our kids did not appreciate my gesture or care for the fruit cake or even some other delicious cookies.

An interesting custom prior to the wedding day deserves a mention. A week before the big day, the known "poor" people (bikari) of the village, say within one or two kilometres radius, were invited for a meal (bikranchem jevonn - meal for the poor). As I recollect it, it was a sumptuous meal, including a piglet. Prior to the meal, the routine would be a few prayers for the good health of, and blessings on the couple and their families.

This leads me to another fact about the village life and how folks looked after each other including their "neediest". There was no abject poverty amongst the people in the village, when it came down to daily necessities of life, including food. There was however an unwritten communal social security system. During the Portuguese rule, begging in public places was against the law in Goa. The community looked after the downtrodden of the society. Goa is the only state in India which still has that law against begging in public places, although it is not evenly enforced.

I will illustrate this with two examples. In my days of growing up in the village, there were two "needy" men who would go around from house to house once a week asking for alms, be it in the form of rice, coconut, condiments and the sort.

Two of these eventually preferred being fed a wholesome luncheon meal. The routine was for the individual to drop by in the morning and inform my mother he would come back for lunch that day. One would show up on Tuesday and the other on Thursday. My mother never had a second thought about feeding these individuals. And I am sure there were other households which would do their part.

If you look deep into it, it is an unorganized but effective social security system, which the community adopted for the welfare of their needy.

Performance of Mando

There was a period of approximately 100 years, from mid nineteenth to mid twentieth centuries, when the wedding reception function among the well-off families (normally the Brahmin class) would end with the singing and dancing of the Mando. It was the golden era of the greatest mando composers, and most of them were the sons of these three villages.

Often a new Mando would be composed for the occasion; otherwise another composition would be sung, followed by a set of Dulpods. By the time of my youth, crowning of the wedding reception with a set of Mando and Dulpods, was more of an exception than the norm. Within our family there were occasions such as weddings or "ladinh" where an uncle (Remedios Soares, Raia) or family member (Licurguinho from Loutolim), pull out the Goan drum Gumott, and would lead and others would join. The session would go on for a while, starting with the Mando followed by Dulpods with different people coming in with a different dulpod each time.

Here is a paragraph taken from a write-up by Felix Almeida for the CLR Mando Group, when we performed at the opening session in 2006 of the Konkani Samelan of North American Konkani Association (NAKA).

"The **Mando**, is a characteristically Christian Goan form of song, traditionally accompanied by dance, and an outgrowth of the music brought to Goa by the Italian missionaries. Sung in a harmony of blended voices, classically the Mando consists of three verses; each followed by a refrain, in 6-4 time; a slow, stately tempo. Often profoundly melancholic, the theme of the Mando usually revolves around rich sentiments of love, a yearning for union, and lamentation over the tragedy of lost love. **Dulpods** (or dulpoddam) are couplets, most of which predate the Mando in antiquity and serve as a repertoire of the history of the Konknnis. They are rendered in typical Konknni melody and rhythm. In the Gaud Saraswat custom, following the Mando, a collection of Dulpoddam is delivered in accelerating tempo, rising in crescendo to a climactic finale."

I spent two years at age 8-9 at ti Rosa Maria Sardinha (mum's first cousin) as a boarder and did my last two years of the Elementary or Primary school from her house. Ti Rosa Maria was extraordinarily kind to me, even though she was known to be a tough lady, having to deal with nine of her own sons. I have very fond memories of ti Rosa Maria and one of them is her habit of picking up on our conversation, and sing parts of a mando or a dulpod. Three of ti Rosa Maria's children Constancio, Francis and Inacinho inherited her love of the Mando. Inacinho has been honored a number of times as the best Gumott player ate the annual Mando Festival in Goa.

I also remember well at the Seminary, my cousin Antonio Costa, who was a few years ahead of me, putting on Mando and Dulpods show. These exposures to the Mando music enhanced in me a hidden love for this genre of music.

In Canada my opportunity to sing in a Mando group came in 1996, i.e. 35 years after my arrival in Canada. I like to say that amongst the blind, the one with one eye is the king. For three years I was a member of the

Mando group in Toronto, led by Dr. Lucina (Cordeiro) Pinto (grandchild of Loutulim), until in 1999, a village association (Curtorim Loutulim and Raia – CLR) was founded by six families, including ourselves.

On this occasion we also formed the CLR Mando Group with members from these villages. I took on the leadership role, and we have been together as a group all these years, only interrupted by the Covid-19 pandemic. I am thankful that in the early years I had help and guidance from my cousins Inacinho Sardinha, and brothers Rosarinho da Costa and Antonio da Costa; the latter is co-author of the best selection and treatise of the Mando and Dulpods (The Song of Goa, by Jose Pereira, Michael Martins and Antonio da Costa) and additional books on Dulpods and religious songs.

Goan (Christian) Music and Song

Goan Christian population, adopted the Portuguese musical and dance traditions the way they were in that country. Portuguese music itself evolved through influences of other European countries, in particular Italian music. Even before they arrived to the Indian subcontinent, the Portuguese had been exposed to and had adopted elements of Moorish and African (through the slave trade) music and dance. Fado, the national song of Portugal, came about through coming together of the European modinha and African lumdum.

The catholic missionaries transported the musical forms prevalent at the time in Portugal, to Goa and the Goans quickly acquired expertise in western music, starting with church music. Many parochial music schools were established, through which a large number of proficient musicians were trained and excelled themselves. Many musicians made a good living in Goa and plying their trade in the rest of India and throughout the British colonies. (ref: Song of Goa, by Jose Pereira, Michael Martins and Antonio Costa)

At the local level, at every wedding, small or big, it was normal to have a music band play and the majority of guests dance during the function. Every village would also have an annual large ball (we called it 'dance") attended by young and old. The latter would normally attend only the early part of the function, which normally would start at 10 pm and go through to 6 am. In my youth and early adult stage, a few of us would rent a vehicle and attend such balls in nearby villages and in particular in the city, Margao. In those days, dancing was our main entertainment and probably an opportune time and place for girls and boys to mingle in a relaxed environment.

There were two other occasions to showcase the musical talent (song and music), and that was through plays or the European equivalent of operettas. One was a stage production, locally called "tiatr" (theater) produced by and acted by professional actors. These plays would usually be held in the evening, on the occasion of the village feast and thus move from place to place, to villages or towns. I have called these actors professionals, which for the most part they were, although some were holding a day job. These were individuals with unbelievable natural talent, as there were no trade schools for this profession. Many of these actors are still fondly remembered, long after they have passed on. Now-a-days village people go the nearest town to watch the "tiatr" where it is performed in a cinema type hall.

The other type of play was locally called "khell" (or play). These were local productions, at the Carnival season. Whenever I hear a mariachi band (Mexican) it reminds me of music accompanying these khells or plays. The repertoire of this small group of actors would be one or two plays, and the actors would go walking from place to place and perform at select locations. The locations would be homes of well-off people, who would reward the group with a reasonable money donation. Other locations would be open places where the attendants would hopefully also make some contributions to the participants of the play.

Another typical Goan feast is the Festa de São João to celebrate the nativity of St. John the Baptist (June 24). This again is a celebration adapted from Europe (big in France) and in Brazil. In Goa, the date falls at the height of the monsoon season. The revelers with colorful head crowns go to water locations such as wells in open fields (which by this stage are near full of water to the surface) or locations near the local river. The custom is for some of these folks to jump into the pond or the well and make merry, and shout Viva São João. I remember some of these revelers coming to our house and my parents would then gift them with some cash or a late season jackfruit if we had any at the time.

Seasons of the Year

Being a tropical country, the Spring, Summer, Fall and Winter are not distinctly observed seasons in Goa. Rather one can say there are two distinct seasons: Monsoon season which is basically the summer in Goa, and extends from end of May to end of September or mid-October. The other season, I like to call it, non-monsoon season period, which includes winter, spring and part of summer.

Goa is not different, when it comes to the changes in the climate patterns, being experienced currently all over the world. The start of the monsoon season and the amount of rainfall are not as predictable as in olden days.

The **monsoon** season brings heavy rainfall to Goa. It rains almost every day, with intermittent periods of rain and sun during the day.

The indigenous people of this region must have been agricultural geniuses the way they carved the rolling hills and managed the river flood plains for paddy rice cultivation. They built an amazing drainage infrastructure directing monsoon rain waters to retention ponds, locally known as lakes (tollem). Water from these ponds is distributed under gravity to the lower lying, vast stretches of agricultural land (addi) for a second crop of rice, after the first crop grown during the monsoon season. Excess water is released to the river.

After the water is drained out of these retention ponds (tollem) to irrigate the rice crop, part of the exposed lake bed is utilized to grow crops such as onions, chillis, brinjals and other vegetables.

The drainage system was very efficient, with flooding in the rural areas almost unheard of. More recently, the uncontrolled and unplanned building construction has altered the drainage system and I understand that this has affected the old drainage efficiency leading to flooding in some rural parts of Goa. I believe that the CLR villages have been spared from monsoon flooding thus far, because of the low hilly topography draining towards the flat areas and the nearby river.

Agriculture, Flora and Fauna

To Goans, Goa is part of India, but Goa is bigger than India. Extending this thought process Curtorim is part of Goa, but to Curtorkars, Curtorim is bigger than Goa. You can extend this thought process to Loutulim or Raia or Benaulim, all villages of our family ancestors- Moniz, Menezes, Pereira and Valeriano Barreto. There is something about Goans and their ingrained love of their village of birth or the village of their ancestors.

The CLR villages and in particular Curtorim have been blessed with a rich and fertile land which has been carved into upper level and lower-level rice fields, with abundant water resources and shallow water table, in particular in the lower level fields, normally bounded by the river and the water retention ponds (tollem). Other than the fact that Loutulim and Raia are relatively more hilly and thus more forested than Curtorim, the lay of the agricultural land is similar in nature.

With the arrival of the Saraswats, more advanced agricultural techniques, and greater variety of production were introduced.

The ponds or lakes (tollem) also became a source of sweet water fish farming, very much appreciated by the locals. One fish that comes to mind is "pittol", the fish of choice, for the lucky ones or those with greater financial means, which besides being appreciated as fresh fish was also be the fish of choice to be dried and pickled as "para" for consumption during the monsoon season. There were other fish varieties, including "tigur" (jack fish), "khall" and the big meaty one "ghuri" usually 2 feet (60 cm) in length. Harvesting of the fish from the lakes is done in the months of April and May, that is before the arrival of the monsoon rains.

In these villages in general, cashew plantations covered most of the hills. Teak trees, whose timber was highly sought for higher end furniture, would often be present in many locations at the foothills. The lower reaches of the hills and the river plain land is rice growing agricultural land, with three distinct zones of cultivation.

Every household lives in their family owned house. The bigger houses had walls built with quarried laterite stone whilst the smaller homes were of stone and mud construction. The roofs were tiled with what are known as Spanish tiles or locally also known as Mangalorean tiles. By the law of the land, even the tenants (mundkar) living on your property, have full ownership of their houses and a road leading to their house.

The tenants on the land are free to seek employment of their choice, including choosing to be employed by the property owner. The tenant is expected to keep an eye on the property (principally fruit trees including coconut trees) but in return receives a share (10 percent) of the produce.

Whether you were a landlord with significant land holdings or you belonged to working class, with limited land ownership, who made their living doing manual work on land or elsewhere, everybody had the basics of living and abject poverty was absent.

It is widely accepted that the fertile land, relatively large property holdings, self-sufficiency and good living, and limited formal education levels, resulted in limited migration of the village folks in south Goa, to other Portuguese colonies (principally Mozambique) or parts of India (principally Mumbai) or other British colonies of the day - Karachi in pre-partition days and Eastern Africa (Kenya, Uganda and Zanzibar). The out-migration of Christian Goans, in search of economic opportunities, was far greater from North Goa districts of Bardez and Tiswadi. As the old colonies were getting their political freedoms, many of these folks have now migrated to Canada, Australia and the UK. For example just in Toronto there are over 25,000 people, mainly Christians, who trace their heritage to Goa and Mangalore.

In the 1950s the transport system connecting the villages to the cities, had relatively improved to the extent that more young people from the villages were attending secondary and post-secondary studies (Lyceum) in Panjim and Margao.

After 1961, when the Portuguese era ended, many English language high schools were set up in villages and cities and Colleges (all affiliated to University of Bombay) in the major cities. Suddenly higher education was available to the masses. The increased mobility, was paramount in changing the character of the villages from pure agrarian to the current state, when not even twenty five percent of rice fields is cultivated.

The new reality is that it is already difficult to find a local (villager or Goan) trade person, such as a carpenter or a mason or a fruit plucker, and for those few left, the demand for their services is overwhelming.

My general observation of the layout of the streets and houses lining up these streets with a definite setback, tells me our ancestors knew a thing or two about village planning.

The households that I know well in Goa, The Moniz, and Menezes on my side and the Pereira family on Ethel's side all had large homes, close to 30-40m from front to back. I have not seen Phoebe's family ancestral home as her parents had moved from Raia to Mumbai more than 100 years ago (first quarter of 1900s) and the family did not maintain any rights to the ancestral home. Each of these homes was originally built approximately in late 1700s to early 1800s. Then late in the nineteenth century and early twentieth century (1890s to 1930s) the growing size of the joint families led to additions to the original construction, almost doubling the original size in each case.

Till the first half of the 20th century, the Moniz and Menezes families were self-sustaining farmers, the main crop being rice paddy.

Very few villagers owned properties large enough for commercial use. Rather, until early twentieth century, property ownership was limited to the parcel of land, ranging from 100m to 300m x 20m of arable agricultural land adjoining their home, either in front or back. Over time, individual family landholdings increased through marriage (for example, dowry or inheritance from a married childless aunt). As the family wealth increased, opportune purchases were made of properties put up for sale by other families.

The limited size of land holding forced people to make maximum utilization of available land. On this land, besides cultivating the rice crop, they planted at the edge of the property, utility fruit trees, the most common being coconut trees, mango trees, jackfruit trees and tamarind trees. In a close knit community, exchange of produce was quite common.

Coconut tree plantation in Goa was predominant in the sandy soil villages along whole sea coast of Goa (Benaulim is one those villages). In the interior villages like Curtorim Loutulim and Raia, there were plenty of coconut trees but mostly confined to areas near the banks of the river and other water bodies.

The coconut fruit and the tamarind fruit are important elements of the Goan cooking, which at its foundation is a sweet and sour style of cooking. The sweetness is achieved via the coconut milk, and sourness with the use of tamarind (or ambtann) or coconut vinegar. Kokum (bhindi solam) and dried green mango slices (amchur) are two other spices or elements used to create sourness in the Goan cooking.

Rice Fields

The upper zone rice fields, known as "morodas", originated from sculpting of the lower slopes of the hills draining towards the river Zuari. The fields are therefore more of lateritic nature. Chemical fertilizers were not used or available before India's annexing of Goa in 1961. There were a few ways adopted to enhance the quality of the soil and improve its productivity.

It was common to spread every three years, a silty clay dredged from the river bottom. Landowners, with larger properties, often owned their own buffalos for work in the fields, and providing milk for the family and sales to the neighbors. Some of the (cow) dung –xhenn- was made into cow dung cakes to be used as fuel for cooking. Most of the cow dung however was collected in a pit during the year, and allowed to organically break down under the tropical sun. This accumulated material was spread over the fields before the arrival of the monsoon, again adding to the productivity of the tilled land. The morodas were cultivated once a year during the monsoon season, the growing season being early June to mid to late September.

In the days of abundant fish catch, usually small size sardines or mackerel, the fisher folk would dry the excess fish under the sun on the beach sands. Well off farmers would buy this dried up fish as another source of natural fertilizer, to be spread out on the fields, before the growing season.

Looking back, all agricultural and fruit crops were organic farming, even though nobody called it so. Now-a-days chemical fertilizers are lot more convenient and probably cheaper to utilize, than adopting the old organic farming methods.

The middle zone of the cultivated land, also known as "addis", is more of a plain or flat land in nature, of silty/clayey soil. It is my educated guess, it was created by the river Zuari overflowing its banks over pre-historic times. This zone has two cultivations, one being rice during the monsoon season. The second crop could be either rice or vegetables: rice crop was viable, where the fields could be irrigated with monsoon rain water harnessed in ponds (tollem) and released in a controlled manner and draining under gravity to the growing fields. Where direct access to pond water was not available, crops of vegetables are grown with water drawn from field wells, where the water table was just a meter or two below surface. The principal crop is chillis, with sweet potatoes, onions, brinjal being the other vegetables of choice. Watermelons are grown in more sandy areas.

The third zone is "Khazan" land reclaimed from the river bank; this land is also known as mangrove. This land is defended throughout its length from the river waters with a "bhund" or a rudimentary clay embankment structure with gated openings to manage the flow of waters to and from the river. Again there is only one rice crop grown in this zone.

After the onset of the monsoon season, the entire villages of Curtorim Loutulim and Raia, which were mainly agricultural land, were a sea of green rice fields, from June till harvest time in September, when rice stalk turned brown.

It is interesting to note that the rice type cultivated in each zone was of a different type. During the Portuguese era, there was very limited scientific research in the improvement of the yield of the rice crop. It was left to the ingenuity of individual farmer and the willingness of the farmer to share his higher yield seed with his neighbor.

I am told that my grandfather (mother's dad), who was a dedicated farmer, through and through, won the first prize a couple of times for the best crop yield in Goa. I understand that my grandfather would also grow on a limited basis, a special breed of rice, which was reserved for use at special occasions at home, such as weddings, baptisms or church feasts.

Today's farmers can now avail easily of much higher yield seeds (yield of three to four times more than the old seed) as well as a greater variety. The irony is that much less of the arable land is cultivated today as compared to even 50 years ago, when I emigrated to Canada. This decline had its beginning in the (1900) fifties and sixties, when working in the mines and related industries was more profitable for the labour class than working in tilling the land. Accessibility to college and University education, and the new opportunities that higher education created, has completely changed the agricultural character of Curtorim and all across Goa.

Monsoon season and the monsoon rains normally arrive in the second half of May. Preparations for the arrival of this liquid gold, would have been going on for at least a month or two and would include having enough parboiled rice to last till October by which time the new rice crop would be harvested.

During the monsoon season the sea waters are rough and the fishing season takes a break. In absence of fresh fish to go with daily fish and curry, the alternatives of dry salted fish, pickled dried fish ("para"-most commonly mackerel) and pickled tender mango fruit (cheppni tor), needed to be provisioned too. The provisions were required not only for our own family use, but also for the labour force, who were fed two meals per day, one mid-morning (cangee) and one mid-day (lunch). The feast of the Holy Spirit in Margao, held in May, and the accompanying three-day market (feira), was the time to make any last minute purchases of provisions for the monsoon season for folks from all the village around the city.

Once there had been enough of rain showers to flood the rice fields and soften the ground, the tilling and seeding of the rice fields took place. The tilling was solely done with a buffalo drawn and hand-held plough.

The rice paddy variety grown in Goa was grown in flooded fields, which were subdivided into small land parcels with small dikes (mer) all around. These small dykes allowed water flooding, with any excess water being allowed to drain away with a shallow opening at one location.

The plough was the most agricultural implement since the beginning of history, used to turn and break up soil, to bury stubs from the previous crop, and to help control weeds. The only plough that I know being used consisted of an iron blade fixed on a wooden implement and drawn by single buffalo or ox, and a worker guiding the animal; these implements could break up the topsoil which was softened due to the monsoon rain.

After ploughing, levelling the ground was achieved with a flat wooden plank implement, which looked like a giant comb, again drawn by buffalo, the labourer standing on top of it for weight. The field was now ready to receive the pre-germinated seeds.

In our house the process of germination was my father's job. Through natural selection, the best seed was used for germination and sowing. The best seed was selected and stored separately for this purpose, at the time of previous harvest. As I remember it, two or three large baskets (ojem) filled up with rice seed were stacked in a corner of our shower bath area. My dad watered these baskets two or three times a day, the water draining from the bottom.

I believe it took close to a week for germination to occur. The germinated seed was then loosened up by hand. The seedlings were then spread by hand. Obviously there is a technique to do it, but more than one plant would sprout too close together.

A month or so after the fields were sown, there was a process of thinning the rice plants by manually uprooting the saplings, and replanting them at a desired spacing. This process also involved getting rid of any weeds growing with the rice sapling.

Customarily the transplanting task was a job for a "specialized" labour force: in our case it was hindu women who were brought in for this particular operation of uprooting and replanting the saplings. The ladies came from outside the village (from across the river or "peltoddi") and they were housed and given food provisions for the period of their stay to complete the task. After completing their work at our rice fields, this group of workers would move on to properties of nearby families.

Once the fields were cultivated there was nowhere for the buffalo to graze during the day. If the animals were left free, they would graze on the young rice plants. It was a routine then to make arrangements to send the buffalos across the river (peltoddi) to locations where the seasonal rice plants were not cultivated and thus the buffalo herd had more freedom of movement and enough land to graze on.

The herd of animals and the men accompanying them, would cross or swim the river waters at a time of low tide and at a location (Xenabog, Corgem), where the width of the river was relatively narrow. The animals would do the return journey when it was harvest time.

The rice plant when ready, was harvested with a sickle, which is an agricultural implement consisting of a curved metal blade with a short handle. Normally this task was carried out by women workers. When the rice plant was cut, a stubble of 2 cm to 4 cm was left behind. The grain stalks were then transported for threshing.

In our house the threshing or separating the grain from the stalk was carried out with buffalos and a few workers. Imagine a central tree trunk size pole to which a rope would be tied and then three to five buffalos with bamboo basket muzzle on, would be attached in a line to this rope. These buffalos would walk round and round, on the harvested rice crop plants, thus separating the grain from the chaff. The workers would loosen up or lift the stalk from time to time, with a pole that had a hook at the end. This process achieved two things: it allowed the separated grain to move down and move fresh stalk with grain still on it to move up. The rice grain is known as paddy.

Folks with small size rice plantations, and or their own buffalos, would resort to hand threshing the paddy stalk, a more laborious task.

The chaff was then moved away and piled up as dry grass fodder during the year for the buffalos. The grain was sun dried, making sure that it was protected against the late season rains if any.

It was not uncommon for houses of families, like ours, with significant size rice crop, to have big halls where the paddy rice was spread out, to further air dry the crop. Our hall for this purpose was probably 20 m long. This hall was a multi-use place. For example it would be the place where workers fabricated the multi-use bamboo mats, or coconut leave mats used to protect the front balcony from the monsoon rain. This hall was also the place to spread the mango crop, covered with hay, and jackfruits waiting for them to ripen.

The next steps after the satisfactory drying of the paddy would be: storing enough for family's yearly provisions in a bamboo mat round shaped silo; the surplus to our needs would be sold, usually to regular local families.

Two more steps are needed, before the paddy rice is ready for consumption. The first is parboiling, which the Wikepedia describes as: "Parboiled rice (also called converted rice and easy-cook rice) is rice that has been partially boiled in the husk. The three basic steps of parboiling are soaking, steaming and drying. These steps make the rice easier to process by hand, while also boosting its nutritional profile, changing its texture, and making it more resistant to weevils. About 50% of the world's paddy production is parboiled."

In our house we had two big copper containers, for this specific use of boiling the paddy and the process was carried out outside with wood fire at the back of the house.

The next task was drying of the boiled or steamed paddy and then taking this parboiled paddy rice to a husking mill located about 5 minutes walking distance from our house. The grain was for human consumption and the paddy husk was utilized as feed for the pigs and the buffalo.

In the rural environment of the villages, domestic animals such as a dog and a cat were common presence in the households. In the urban areas these animals are often raised as pets, but in the villages they had an utilitarian purpose. Being a tropical place and deep-rooted community trust, it would be rare for the front door of the house to be closed. A presence of the dog on the front porch acted against strangers walking right in. A cat was there in every home and its main raison d'etre was to keep the mice away.

Local Fruits and Vegetables

The fruit trees would start flowering in December and different fruits would mature at varying times between March and June. Most of the fruit was plucked before the monsoon rains as it would be difficult to access the fruit or it led to spoilage of the fruit on the tree. As I remember it, the first fruit to mature was normally the cashew fruit (caju) and the laggards would be a certain variety of jackfruit and an occasional mango variety.

My observation is that the fruit trees in Goa, are of the hardy type and have a long life. I understand the mango trees have a life span of over 100 years. Other than the cashew trees (height 3-4 m), the fruit trees in Goa are tall (20-30 m) and with a large canopy. In more recent times, the Goa Agricultural department has introduced and supplied shorter varieties of all types of fruit tree plants.

Almost every tree around the place was a utilitarian tree. Some produced fruit that was consumed as a dessert or snack - mango, jackfruit, little apples (bhoram), jamum (zamblam). The fruits of the other trees were used in our cooking –coconut, tamarind, kokum, drum stick. The coconut and tamarind have the greatest use and together form the sweet and sour elements of the Goan cooking.

Cashew tree plantation was widespread on the rolling hills of our villages. The cashew tree produces cashew apple or cashew fruit with a single nut/ kernel attached on the outside. In India, cashew apple is extensively used only in Goa to prepare cashew liquor called caju feni. The cashew crop season usually runs between March and May.

Feni is synonymous with Goa and somehow the sentimental drink with Goan diaspora. There are two types of Feni produced in Goa. The Cashew (caju) feni, is the more desired variety by the Goan connoisseur and it is distilled from Cashew apple, during months of March to May, the maturing season of cashew fruit.

The coconut feni is derived through distillation of the 'toddy", which is the sap collected from the cut flower of palm tree. An earthen container is fastened to the flower stump to collect the sap. A tapper climbs the tree to collect the sap twice daily. The white liquid that initially collects tends to be very sweet and non-alcoholic before it is fermented and turned into vinegar or distilled to obtain the feni.

The traditional method to process the cashew apple, consisted of crushing the fruit in a basalt cistern under feet (not unlike crushing of grapes) and collecting the juice in an adjoining cistern leading to a big earthen pot (kolso). The crushed fruit is then piled and tied in a mound, a heavy weight placed on the top, collecting the last bit of juice, called "Niro", which is a very appetising drink and I carry sweet memories of it, to this day.

The Rodrigues family were the landlord of the closest local cashew plantation with "Curru" Santan a tenant and feni producer on site. The Rodrigues family worked and lived in the Middle East and had requested my dad to be their eyes for this property.

A side benefit of this arrangement was that we had a regular supply of cashews and niro. Dad knew when these would be available, and as a young man, I would take a short cut through the rice fields and get there in less than ten minutes, to get a few cashews or pick up a bottle of niro.

My Loutulim grandmother's family (Monteiro Soares) had a hillside property, Bindalle, in Loutulim, with plenty of cashew trees. Ti Licurguinho, their adopted son, managed the property and produced, a high-quality Feni.

Once when I was visiting there, along with my cousin Zezito Menezes, Ti Licurguinho sent us home with a small vessel full of niro, which the two us were still consuming, as we were lying on our sleeping mats and retiring for the night.

The first distillate of the cashew juice is known as Urraca. It is light (20-25 percent alcohol content), and consumed usually undiluted or without being mixed with any type of sodas.

Further distillation (part urraca and part juice) produces 30-40 percent strong liquor Feni. Locals will tell you that Feni has a long shelf life, urraca less so. Therefore urraca is usually produced and consumed locally. Feni is available bottled commercially, and some of it is exported overseas, where there is huge demand, from the Goan diaspora in places such as Toronto, London and other world cities with high concentration of first generation immigrant Goans. To my knowledge the demand for feni, far exceeds the supply originating from Goa.

Coconut. I would say that in Goa, the coconut is the king of all fruits, as the Goan cuisine revolves around this fruit. Products derived from coconut kernel or the white meat of the coconut are innumerable: grated coconut is used directly in preparation of vegetables and sweets or it is ground to produce the coconut milk, which is so predominant in preparation of curries.

The coconut milk is not only used in preparing curries, but also an important and ubiquitous ingredient in most of the Goan sweet delicacies, including the famous Goan Bebinca, a seven layered rich pudding, and whose main ingredients are coconut milk, egg yolks and sugar.

The dried coconut kernel also called copra is cold pressed to obtain coconut oil, which in Goa used to be the most used oil for cooking. After Goa's integration into India in 1961, other oil varieties, such as peanut oil and sunflower oil have become widely available and have been popularly embraced due to their lower prices than the coconut oil price. The coconut cake after the oil extraction was used as feed for buffalos, principally the milking buffalo.

A coconut tree is one of the most useful trees in the world: besides the numerous uses of the coconut water and the kernel or meat, everything in the coconut fruit is put to great use. The outer shell (kotti), holding the kernel, is used as medium of fire for old style clothing iron and the outer husk provides coir fiber, with its own multitude of commercial uses. Locally the coconut makes an excellent fire burning medium in place of firewood for cooking. The green coconut leaves would be woven as mats with multiple utilitarian uses, and the trunk is used as a building material. Anything of the tree which is not put to some specific use, becomes a very good and combustible source of fire for cooking. Now-a-days use of firewood for cooking is much more limited as gas stove and electric range have replaced much of the old style cooking.

Mango fruit is very dear to the heart and the palate of Goans. In the Hindu religion, the coconut and the mango are the fruits the devotees offer to their deities. These fruits reflect health, wealth and beauty (mango).

The Portuguese introduced the mango (mangifera indica) from India to other tropical parts of the world, principally South America and Africa. In return the Portuguese introduced the chilli to India, originating from Brazil. The Jesuit priests and monks had a major role not only in the trans-oceanic transfer of flora, but it turns out they had a significant role in creating new improved varieties of fruits, in particular mango, coconut and chilli.

Mangos of India are famous in the world for its sweetness, richness and unique flavour. India is the largest producer of mangos in the world and it's an important agricultural, cultural and religious fruit of the country.

Goans are proud of their home varieties of mangos and at a practical level, they can be broadly divided into two categories: one type of mango is the one that you normally slice to eat, and these mangos are larger than the second category (called "gonttam" for the sweeter ones and "pochram" for the less sweet ones), which are smaller and people just suck on them.

The smaller variety of mango fruit, principally the "pochram", but also the "gonttam", lent themselves to three important uses, for the Goan cuisine: the young, non-mature fruit, where the inside seed was still soft, was used to prepare pickles - Chepnim Thor (water pickle, without the red masala), mescut (the tender mango fruit is slitted and stuffed with a unique red masala). An important use of the mango fruit, before ripening stage, is when it is sliced, salted and dried to prepare what are locally called "ambea solam" or "amchur" in rest of India and which like the tamarind is used in the Goan and Indian cooking to bring sourness to the dish.

There are many taste and size varieties of mangos in Goa, some more common (malcorado, muserat) and other more rare (Hilario, Ferdinando). Amongst them the most appreciated is the king of Goan mangos, the "malcorado" (meaning badly colored in Portuguese), both for its taste and smoothness or absence of fibre in the flesh. The name malcorado, has now been adulterated and known locally as "mankurad". I remember that when I had referred to the British Encyclopedia in 1970s, I read it there that the malcorado mango from Goa, was considered one of the best in the world.

A mango variety that tries to compete with the goodness of the malcorado, is the Alphonso mango, which originated in Goa, but the variety was exported to north of Goa (Ratnagiri) and other parts of India. Its name is now more widely known as "apus",

From my childhood memory, three other mango varieties, that I remember being most appreciated were Fernandinho, Colaço varieties (to eat) and the fleshy muserat, the latter being the desirable variety of mango for preparing the greatly loved Goan mango jam "mangada". The flesh of the muserat mango is first mashed and the pulp sieved through a cloth, to remove the fibrous material. The juice with some sugar added, is slowly boiled with continuous stirring, until the desired consistency is achieved. When less sugar was added the jam would be a spreadable type, whilst higher amount of sugar would produce a more solid mangada, which in the days of lack of refrigeration, was a way to make it have a longer life. A piece of this mangada was often given to us in place of a snack at tea time.

For example, in North America the two most common market varieties are "Ataulfo" with minimal fibre and the "Hayden" variety, which is more meaty but with relatively more fibre. After close to fifty years out of Goa, we have become quite accustomed to the taste of these two varieties, and very much enjoy them. The mango season in North America, for these mangos originating from Mexico, runs from June to August. One can get mangos originating from South America during a few months of the year, but are lot more expensive.

Recounting of my childhood memories related to fun derived from fruit trees would not be complete, without a mention of how a strong breeze blowing through, would prompt pre-youth age kids including me to action. In my case that was the signal for us to run from the back door expecting to pick up some tree ripened delicious mangos falling from a certain tree two houses from ours. To this day it is not uncommon for a certain type of breeze here in Canada to bring back memories of those childhood days in Goa.

By the way, if you take into account the mango crop at our own house and that at grandma's house, ten minutes away, we had plenty of mangos to eat. But to me, they were not the same as those from our neighbor's tree, both in type of mango and sweetness and color. Add to it the excitement of racing to fetch the ripe mangos falling off the tree, upon a good burst of wind. Fortunately there were not many kids my age to compete for these fallen mangos. If left uncollected, the pigs would eventually feast on them.

The account of the tropical summer fruits in Goa is not complete without a discussion of the **jackfruit**, which happens to be the largest tree fruit in the world. Just like the mango trees, there are jackfruit trees spread all over the place either in non-arable land or on the edge of the rice fields.

The maturity period for the jackfruit varies among different types. Even though at my mother's house they had a very early maturing jackfruit tree –I remember eating jackfruit once at Christmas time – most of the jackfruit would ripen relatively later than most mango varieties, and some after the monsoon rains past the month of June.

In Goa the jackfruit varieties matured to an average size of 5 to 8 kg (10-16 lb). In comparison, more recently we have been getting in Toronto jackfruits imported from Thailand and Mexico, the size of these jackfruits ranging from 8-15 kg, (16-35 lbs),

When pruned, the inner part (core) secretes a sticky, milky liquid. A little coating of the hands and the knife with cooking oil, will tackle this stickiness problem. The jackfruit has a strong pleasant aroma; the pulp of the opened fruit resembles the odor of pineapple and banana. This odor is something one has to get used to and can be a bit too strong for some folks' smell tolerance; for those who have grown up in Goa, it seems this tolerance to jackfruit smell, came naturally. The eatable flesh consists of many little individual fruits (ghore), each with an edible seed inside (bhikna). When the seeds are dried thoroughly they can be preserved for use over time as snacks or added to dishes, such as Goan sausage preparation.

There are basically two varieties of jackfruit: the soft fruit variety and the stiffer fruit variety. The soft fruit variety (ponos) can be consumed straight or it is often utilized in combination with rice in preparation of snacks (bakhri) or drying them up, with or without addition of sugar, for later consumption as sweets (sattam). The stiffer flesh variety (borkoi) is the desirable type for eating the jackfruit flesh straight as snack.

The scaly or pimple shaped outer cover and the internal parts of the jackfruit not used for human consumption, were fed to the cattle, who would be more than happy to have it. Thus nothing of the jackfruit was wasted.

We ate jackfruit in the season, as a snack, and we had not heard it was nutritious too. Nobody in the village had heard of utilizing a green jackfruit as it is currently used in the West, as a great vegan alternative to animal meat and it is replacing chicken, turkey, beef and other meats in dishes like curries and in pizzas, burgers. Back in Goa, jackfruit is still a sweet snack.

In the yard, you would find other fruit trees. The most common were banana, papaya, guava or "per" (Green/yellow outside and pink inside, guava is a fruit you will commonly find in Goa and we always had it in our backyard), custard apple (also called sugar apple, dark brown in colour and marked with depressions giving it a quilted appearance, a favorite of my wife), chikoo (known as sapota outside India). We had them all in our front or back yards.

Monsoon season was the time for families to grow their own **vegetables** in their yards, the most common being okra (lady fingers), karela (bitter melon), pumpkin and long beans (vir-vir). The pumpkin vine would be directed to climb to the roof of the house or shed, where large pumpkins would grow nicely, exposed to rain and sun.

As young lads, walking down the street, during the summer fruit growing season, it was a temptation and a challenge to throw stones aimed at that ripe mango or tamarind or other such small fruit. I had my own special tree here and there, and to this date, I do remember these trees and their locations. Some of these trees of my youth days do not exist anymore at the old locations. Most of the time we got away with "naughty" kid behavior, but occasionally we would be shouted at or chased away by the owner of the tree. When a fruit tree was too close to a home, an errand stone would lead to some damage to the roof tiles and the owners would have to fix the damage before the monsoon rains. For the most part stoning a tree for fruit big or small, ripe or not, was more a kid's play than a want or need for the fruit itself.

There were other fruit trees, which if by the road side, would be free for all. Included in this category I recollect being the jamum (zamblam) and little applets "bhoram". The ripe fruit would fall to the ground, and we were happy to pick it up, just wipe off any dirt, and into the mouth it went. We never got sick eating fruit off the ground.

Being a tropical place, and blessed with abundant rainfall, Goa has its share of a broad variety of **flowers** to brighten the garden. These plants are hardy and perennial in nature, the most common being Hibiscus plant, bougainvillea and roses. A common, colorful plant one sees everywhere in peoples' gardens is one or more varieties of croton.

In addition to the flowers, which give beauty to the garden, there are two flower categories, the marigold and the "abolim" which are in high demand, as they are the most popular flowers in the preparation of garlands. Local women, in particular amongst the Hindu population, like to tie their hair in a bun at the rear of the head and adorn it with a flower garland. Even greater demand for the flower garlands is for the purpose of making offering to God at the church, temple or your home altar and at the multitude of roadside crosses or Hindu places of worship, erected to honor a dear deceased person or in gratitude for some divine favor.

Goan Diet

In Goa the village food diet revolved around rice, fish, red chili and coconut (the latter two for curries, along with onion and other spices).

Waking up around six o'clock in the morning was more of a norm than exception. The daily eating routine was the early morning tea, with or without some accompaniment, such as fresh daily bread or home-made chappatis (rotti) and then three meals: rice gruel or canjee or "pez", basically rice with broth and accompanied by some kind of pickle, midway between breakfast and lunch; lunch at approximately one o'clock consisting of rice, curry and fish; dinner at approximately eight o'clock, again consisting of rice, curry and fish. The frequency of consumption of vegetables and meat depended on seasonal availability and or family's affordability. Between four and five in the afternoon, tea would customarily be available, along with some home-made sweet or snack (merenda).

Early morning, and almost on a timely basis, freshly baked (wood fired) bread (Goencho pao) of different but limited variety, was delivered to your doorstep by an individual (padeiro in Portuguese or "poder" in the local language) on a bicycle with a good size basket resting on the back of the bike. Prior to the bicycle era, the "poder" made the rounds on foot. For most households it was a fixed quantity of bread, which thus dictated the quantity the said delivery man had to cater. Besides the pao, two other items were supplied by the "poder": Bakri or poyee and Kanknam (bangle shaped baked dough).

Our ancestors, as was the case with the general Christian population, ate pork, chicken and beef. The frequency of meat eating depended on the days of the week, that these meats would be available and your means. Remember that in absence of refrigeration, all meat was of an animal slaughtered only a few hours prior to the sale. Also on special days, such as weddings, feasts or other special occasions, chicken and pork, often home grown, would be on the menu.

The staple food for the Goans, whether well-off or with limited means was rice, curry and fish (xitt koddi). The main differentiating factor in a fish curry was the presence or absence or the amount of the coconut juice. There are curries, such as "ambot tik", where no coconut juice is added. Families self-sufficient in coconut production for their own needs or those with means to purchase the coconuts, would add the coconut juice in the daily fish curry, which resulted in a richer and more balanced sweet and sour taste. True and typical Goan cooking consists of different ways of achieving the classic sweet and sour balance.

The fish was a fresh catch of the day from the Indian Ocean (10 to 15 km distance) and brought to the village by one or more individuals in a basket tied at the back of a bicycle. I remember to this date having had a run-in with one of the bicycle riding fishmongers. I was 8 and heading to school, but in a playful mode, crisscrossing back and forth from one side of the street to the other. In those days the vehicle traffic, including bicycles was minimal. My playfulness was stopped in my tracks, by the fishmonger bicycle, which actually hit me and ran over me. Either the fishmonger had no bell on his bicycle or I did not hear one. A woman who was walking close by, came to my assistance, dusted me up, and seeing there was no outward damage, sent me back home.

The type of ocean fish catch changed seasonally, the most common and affordable being the sardines and the mackerel. These fish types lent themselves to greater versatility in kitchen preparation, as well as for salting and drying, for use during the monsoon season. The other common sea catches were shrimp, clams (tisreo), king fish and shark fish.

During the monsoon season, when the fresh fish from the sea was not available, dry fish was consumed instead, as side accompaniment with rice and curry (principally mackerel, sardines, sole and Bombay duck). It was quite common to prepare pickled dry fish (para) to provide change and variety from the straight dry fish. In our house, the most common "para" fish would be mackerel and "pittol", sweet water fish from the lake.

In our own house we enjoyed abundance of fresh fish from the ponds off the river (muus) and lakes (rain water catch reservoirs – "tollem"), that our dad would lease through the Comunidade properties.

Most villages in Goa, were built on the coastline or the banks of rivers. River Zuari, the largest river in Goa runs on the north boundary of Curtorim, Loutulim and Raia. Along the river there are many man-made ponds (muus), with heir inlets to the river. These ponds were owned and maintained by the Comunidade, or the village community body, and were used for farming different types of fish. My dad would lease a couple of these properties, and then sub-lease them to others. His profit was limited to receiving a share of the fish catch. Thus our household had this added supply of fresh river fish many times during the year.

A great number of hotels have now sprouted all along Goa's sea coast to cater to tourism. The demand from the hotels, has taken away the availability and affordability of daily sea catch from the common people, whether in the villages or the cities. On the other hand, poultry, pork meat and beef, are now commercially more readily available than before. With increased ownership of a refrigerator in the households, a gradual change to the society's diet can be observed, compared to the diet even 50 years back.

I read once that the Portuguese people could prepare and eat bacalhau, or salted cod fish in 365 ways per year. Similarly Christian Goans, given the choice, know to prepare **pork meat** in as many ways, and with different spices and varying levels of spiciness. It is generally known and accepted that the native population of south Goa prefer spicier food than the folks in North Goa. The best known pork dishes from Goa are Vindalho (anglicized as vindaloo) and sorpotel. Both of these Goan delicacies are an outgrowth of Portuguese cooking, but with a definite Goan spice touch. The original Vindalho is a pork meat dish. This dish style preparation has been popularized by Indian restaurants world over as chicken "vindaloo".

The Goan pork sausage (**choris** in Konkani or chouriço or linguiça in Portuguese) is a hallmark Goan delicacy. Every Goan knows about Vindaloo, sorpotel, Goan Choris and the Feni, the Goan rum made from Cashew fruit juice or the coconut toddy.

A pork dish I am particularly fond of, is "presunto", which is a salted pork and spicy dry preparation, one of the few non-curry Goan dishes. Presunto, which translates in English as ham and in Italian as prosciutto, may have a few common elements in preparation with its foreign cousins, but very little in common when it comes to its taste, due to the spices used in its preparation.

Serving of **chicken** meat (in olden days, free range and always home grown) was normally reserved for special occasions. Chicken was commonly prepared as a coconut curry. A non-curry dish where chicken is used and is a favorite of mine is what is known a "mixed stew" (I call it Goan wedding stew) where chicken meat is one the triumvirate of meats used, others being pork and duck or beef. This was a marquee dish served at weddings, and besides the meats, it included pasta, peas and carrots. The dish would be served with a triangular shaped half bread slice.

Beef was the least consumed of the meats. During my growing up days, beef was available only on Thursdays, and probably was bought by families with better financial means. I believe Goan cuisine has relatively less variety of beef dishes. Other than your regular curry dish with beef, the ones that come to mind are "biff assado" or beef roast and beef croquettes

Consumption of **vegetables** in the olden days was seasonal. Monsoon rains facilitated growing vegetables, the most common being, okra, long beans (vir-vir), cucumber and karela. Many a folk also grew pumpkin with vine climbing to the roof of the house and the pumpkin fruit thus exposed to sun. In our house okra, karela and pumpkin were regularly grown vegetables in the monsoon season. As I remember the karela plant would germinate from the seeds fallen on the ground in the previous growing season, the seeds not being eaten by animals due to their bitter taste. The pumpkin vine would be directed to the top of the cattle shed. Local small-time growers would go house to house to sell their monsoon season vegetables.

Prior to 1980, **cooking** (frying, grilling and boiling) was carried out on open fire flame which is the oldest and most primitive method of cooking. We are talking of the kitchen in the house. Open flame cooking is almost non-existent now. Wood was the main source for fire, but dry tree leaves, coconut palm leaves, coconut fruit husk, or dried cow dung patties, were the other good sources. Since almost every tree on the farm was a fruit bearing tree, there were no trees to be cut down for firewood. Instead firewood would be derived from dead tree branches or from trees cut down because of their age or disease.

Cooking on open fire flame causes lot of smoke. Hence the kitchen was always located at the back of the house. The smoke from the cooking fire was not all wasted. It was natural and customary to smoke the home-made sausages by placing these on a bamboo rod suspended approximately 2 metres above the flame. The need to allow air circulation, and the tropical warm weather, led to the design of the tiled roof and the wall interface not to be sealed, as it is in colder climates or even in urban highrise buildings in India.

Most of the cooking was in earthen utensils ("kun'nem" for curries and "bullkulo" for rice). Copper utensils were usually used for frying as was warming of the milk or baking. It is said that cooking in such earthen utensils, in combination of the open flame and the smoke gave the dishes a special flavour, which supposedly you cannot recreate with the modern metal utensils.

Piped **water** in the villages is a more recent phenomenon and it arrived in the village in 1970s and 1980s. Prior to that and even after availability of piped water, well water was the water of choice. Normally most larger homes had a well attached to the house structure. A copper metal vessel (bhindul) or an earthen vessel (kolso) would be lowered with a rope and pulley arrangement to draw the water, which was always cool and fresh. Some folks could not afford to have their own water well. In this situation four or five surrounding families would share the water from the community well in the open field.

The water table in most parts of Goa is relatively high. During the rainy season the water level in the well would rise almost to the ground surface. It was not uncommon for a chicken that came roaming into the house and as it flew out of the window in the process of being shooed out, would end into the water well. A basket tied at one end of the rope would be lowered and the chicken coaxed to get in. Failing that, a person (and I did it a few times) would go down the well on a ladder tied to another rope, and grab the chicken up. These are the memories of my younger days!

CHAPTER 7

Our Families and their Village Origins: An Introduction

This chapter is my attempt to be the prologue to the next four chapters, dealing individually with each of the four families, I am part of: two families I was born into, and two families I embraced through marriage.

Right at the outset, I wish to remind the reader that the life in the villages described here, relates to lives lived by our ancestors and on my side that includes as recent as my dad and my grandparents on both my mother and my father's side. I am talking here till late twentieth century. Also some of the contents of this chapter may be repeated in the chapters that follow, as I write about each of the four families involved.

When I say our four families (Ethel's and mine), I refer to the families of our mothers and fathers, going back approximately 150 to 200 years. From information available to me, I would suggest that Ethel's and my great grandfathers, all four of them, were born circa 1870s.

On the Pereira/Menezes side of the family, the earliest that I have been able to trace back the family members, is 1675, the birth date of Manuel Antonio de Quadros from Loutolim. Maria Aurora Valeriano Barreto (DOB 1877), the modern-day Pereira family matriarch, is the fifth-generation descendant of the Quadros family.

On the Moniz/Menezes side, with the help of Geni.com, I was able to go back to 1758 which is the approximate date of birth of my great-great-grandfather Antonio Francisco de Menezes on my mother's side.

I have arrived at a general conclusion that our ancestors from both sets of families, Pereira/Menezes and Moniz/Menezes and branches thereof have enjoyed longevity. Other than diabetes, which affects a large section of Indian population, occurrence of other common health problems, such heart disease and cancer, has been minimal. The latest deaths in our families were: Ethel's aunt Marta Pereira, 2015, age 95; Fr. Luis Menezes at age 85 in December 2019. On my side my mother Marcelina Menezes at age 93, in April 2014 and my uncle Constancio Menezes at 87, in December 2019.

How often do we hear the expression "it's a small world after all". This expression is so true when it relates to inhabitants of the three South Goa villages of Curtorim, Loutulim and Raia (CLR) where our families have their origins. I extend this to the village of Benaulim, when it relates to the Pereira family. The cumulative population of the four villages around mid-1900, was no more than 40,000, Curtorim being the bigger place geographically and by population; Curtorim was also probably little more prosperous, having been blessed with more fertile land and with moniker of granary (rice) of south Goa. This is the "small world" we are talking about.

The life and stories of the four families covered in this book relate to a period starting 1860s to year 2020. Specifically, we are talking about the time period covering the lives of our grandparents and our parents. Prior to 1860, it is accepted wisdom that all the families lived an agrarian life. Information on one or two generations prior to 1860s, is limited to names, with scant data on their lifestyles.

The Pereiras and the Menezes (Phoebe) families had a head start in the urbanization race, followed closely by the Menezes (my mother) and the Monizes a generation behind.

Within the 1860-2020 period of time, our families have grown in size by leaps and bounds. We take it for granted that we have many first cousins.

But when one takes the count, what you see is amazing. For example Ethelwyn and her siblings have 24 first cousins. My siblings (6) and I have 41 first cousins.

To get a broader bird's eye view, I referred to the Geni.com website which is a good, but not a complete source of family tree data. A search for Ethelwyn, indicates that her family tree is currently made up of 4,873 members, she has 102 ancestors, and 10,000 blood relatives. My own research tells me that the Pereira family branch in Benaulim, prior to and from the time Ethelwyn's great grandfather moved from Benaulim to Margao, has unfortunately been severed from the Margao Pereira family tree.

A similar search on Geni.com for Eufemiano, indicates that his family tree is made up of 4,836 members, he has 64 ancestors, and 3,143 blood relatives. Again, a few branches of the Menezes side of the family have not yet been catalogued on Geni.com. If and when the missing data is added, the number of family members should rise significantly.

Before the onset of the twentieth century, walking was the main or sole means of getting around the rural areas, which the three CLR villages were at the time. Even in my youth days (1960s) and before we had a bike in the house, we walked to school, and our relatives' homes. For example, my paternal grandmother's house (Loutulim) and one of my married aunt's house (Raia) were close to two hour leisurely walk. For the villagers, in the rare occasion of needing to travel longer distances, a hired river paddle boat would be the vehicle of choice. The social network, including marriages and relationships, was built normally within walking distance of approximately one hour to a maximum of two hour. Over time, family relationships are spread throughout the three villages, and surprisingly with the village of Benaulim, mainly driven by the desire of marrying within the same social group (caste).

The caste system followed by Christian Goans, is inherited from their Hindu ancestry, with the division of India's Hindu society into rigid social groups, with roots in India's ancient history and persisting to the present time.

The caste system in India goes back to times long before colonialism, or arrival of the Portuguese to Goa. The caste system basically reflected the social hierarchy. The wealthy, royals and priests were at the top, whilst those with manual labour jobs were at the bottom. The caste system is deeply ingrained in the Indian society, immaterial of what religion you belong to. However the economic significance of the caste system in India has been declining, even though so slowly, as a result of urbanisation and affirmative action programs - (parts of the last two paragraphs taken from Wikepedia).

In Goa it is very common to call somebody "prim", for cousin or primo in Portuguese" or "soiro" for a relation. The interesting part is that, due to inter clan marriages over many years (centuries) and limited mobility, in these villages there are lots and lots of inter-relationships. Other than first or second cousins, most people accept the relationship without bothering to know the lineage.

If it was not for the Catholic Church's prohibition of marriage between cousins (first and second cousins) the gene pool would have become even smaller than it is today. For first cousins to marry, one needed special dispensation from the church. I read recently that because of the inter-clan (within same caste) marriages, the DNA within the Saraswat community has not changed significantly over a few centuries of their migration to Goa.

As a kid, I would often ask my mother to clarify the various family relationships. Both my interest and curiosity on our many family inter-linkages, grew with time and I would broach this subject with all the family members with interest and knowledge on such things.

I have spoken about the family inter-linkages spread through the four villages of our ancestors: Curtorim, Loutulim, Raia and Benaulim. Let me give the reader a perspective through relevant examples, of how these interlinkages through marriage happened within our own families.

MONIZ FAMILY. My father's family, Moniz, are gauncars of Raia, (primeiro or first vangor) even though we have been residents of Maina,

Curtorim for generations. Gauncar is considered a descendant of the original class of land owners. I do not have any information on when my ancestors made the move to Curtorim from Raia. My educated guess is, it was in late 1600s or early 1700s, after conversion to Christianity of our Hindu ancestors.

My dad is Caetano Moniz. His father Loiola Moniz, was married twice, the first marriage being to Rearinha Pereira from Raia, who died soon after giving birth to her first child, Riario. Approximately 5 years later, Loiola Moniz's second marriage was to Cecilia Monteiro from Loutulim, approximately an hour and half walk.

MENEZES FAMILY. My mother, Maria Florinda (Marcelina) came from the Menezes family from Suclem, Curtorim. The Menezes were gauncars of Curtorim (again primeiro vangor). My mum's dad Caetaninho de Menezes married Maria Fernades from Maina, Curtorim, but whose mother's ancestors (Figueiredo) originated from Loutulim, but later moved to Maina, Curtorim. My great-grandmother comes from Cruz family in Borda (near Margao) approximately one hour plus walk from their house.

PEREIRA FAMILY. Francisco Xavier Pereira (FX) is Ethel's dad and his family, the Pereiras, hail originally from Benaulim. FX's grandfather and his wife moved to Margao, in early 1800s. FX's dad Epifanio married Maria Aurora Valeriano Barreto from Raia.

The Pereiras are gauncars of Benaulim. Pati – short name for padre tio in Portuguese, Msgr. Aniceto Pereira, Epifanio's brother- had arranged through a third party to research the Pereira family tree when they were residents of Benaulim, going back to 1700s. This was summarized on a couple of loose pieces of paper and I was fortunate to peruse the info through Tia Marta, FX's youngest sister. From this research, I noticed that prior to 1830, a number of generations of Pereiras had their brides originating from Curtorim and Raia.

For the purpose of the narrative in this book, I consider Aniceto Pereira and his wife Josefina da Cunha (her family already resident of Margao) as the more recent patriarch and matriarch of the Pereira clan as we know them today. They moved out from Acsona, Benaulim and purchased a plot and built their original house in Tembim part of Margao township circa 1870. The location is right opposite to Hospicio, the old Hospital complex until the end of the Portuguese era. The main Margao Catholic cemetery is diagonally opposite to our old house. The family lived at this location till 2005 when it was replaced by a new, six storey building structure, of mixed use, commercial, office and residential. The construction was completed and occupancy given in 2011. The new building is named Pereira Plaza.

To my knowledge, Aniceto Pereira had three brothers: Sebastiao Vicente Pereira and Fr. Francisco Xavier Pereira, the latter joining Aniceto's family upon his return from missionary work in Calicut, Kerala. Sebastiao Vicente had two children, a boy (Joao Batista?) and a girl (Divina?). For reasons not known to me, the family links between Aniceto's family and Sebastiao Vicente's family have not been maintained. One of the three brothers, disappeared without leaving any trace. Fr. Francisco Xavier's will made provision for this lost brother, in case he made a reappearance.

Aniceto and Josefina's son, Epifanio married Maria Aurora Valeriano Barreto from Raia. Her mother, Ludovina Quadros, was from Loutulim. Epifanio and Maria Aurora had seven children of their own, including Francisco Xavier (F.X.) Pereira, Ethel's dad. Epifanio had two siblings: Mgr. Aniceto Pereira who took the virtual mantle of family Patriarch and Etelvina Pereira. The former, upon his retirement moved back from Mumbai to the Pereira Margao house. The latter was deaf and mute and never married.

MENEZES FAMILY. Ethel's mother, Blenure Phoebe also happens to come from a Menezes family, but from Raia. Her dad Antonio Vicente de Menezes from Raia married Filomena Fernandes from Curtorim.

If you cared to or have been able to keep your attention to the contents in the few preceding paragraphs, you will have noticed that over the last 200 years, the marriage unions in our families have been like import-export or barter trade business between these villages.

These inter-village linkages were brought closer to home or from my perspective full circle, with the marriage of Ofelia Pereira, the eldest of Epifanio and Maria Aurora Pereira's children, to Roque Menezes (originally from Loutulim). Just follow me here.

Roque's niece Elena Quadros from Fatorda (Margao) married my dad's older brother Riario Moniz, in early 1940s. Thus, Eufemiano's first cousins and Ethel's first cousins have a second cousin relationship.

Roque's another niece Anita (commonly known as Aurita) Pereira from Chandor (village adjoining Curtorim) married Sebastião Vicente Pereira and upon his death, she married his step-brother Daniel Menezes, both from Macazana (another village adjoining Curtorim). These men's grandmother, Idalina Menezes and my grandfather Caetaninho Menezes are siblings. In other words, Aurita's husbands and Eufemiano are second cousins.

Such a small world indeed!

As I was mentally getting ready to immerse myself into writing about our families, it was a coincidence that we in North America were celebrating on November 11, the annual Remembrance Day. This is a special day, when in the western world, people "remember" and thank their veterans of war, principally those who made the ultimate sacrifice with their lives, on the battle theatre in the World War One and World War Two, and then other wars or conflicts such the Korean War, Vietnam War, and Conflicts in Bosnia, Iraq and Afghanistan.

The eleventh hour of the eleventh day of the eleventh month is considered Canada's most meaningful moment to remember. It is a gesture of respect for those who lost their lives in the war. It is also a gesture of respect for those who came before us.

Remembering involves something one has seen or experienced. I like using the word "reflecting" on the sacrifices of both the Canadian soldiers who died in wars and the Canadian veterans. This reflection extends to our family ancestors, even though Goa being a Portuguese territory, and

Portugal having stayed neutral during the World War II, and also neutral for most of W. War I, our direct family members living in Goa, were not exposed to either World War I or World War II.

Hearing the news broadcast on November 11, was both somber and emotional for me. In the frame of mind I was in, my thoughts veered towards our own ancestors, and the sacrifices they made to bring our families to where we are today.

Let me echo some of the sentiments expressed by the political, military and religious leaders on this day and apply this to our own families "Let us continue to make our families worthy of their dedication and sacrifice, and live a life in which respect, harmony, inclusion, responsibility and kindness fill the air".

When I dig into the past, I find that in each of our four families there was somebody with a vision, often a woman, who led or guided the family with short term sacrifices, for what we see now, great futures for the family members spread across the globe.

Let us face it. Did they know or have a guarantee what success their actions would produce? Could they have dreamt or envisioned the world their descendants are living in? No, but they had their own visions, and for this we have to be thankful to our ancestral visionaries and the people who supported them. It is with this spirit of gratitude and pride that I wish to write about our ancestors.

There is a lot of wisdom that is handed down through the generations. I find lot of wisdom in the saying that "if you don't not know where you've (and by extension your family) come from, you don't know where you are going" Maya Angelou.

When you hear the elders say "in our days we used to do this and that or how different things were then, compared to now", they are trying to tell you their stories. And what did we do most of the times? We rolled our eyes, saying to ourselves, "here he/she goes again".

When people hear, elders say "in our days", often something negative triggers in our heads and the listener's immediate reaction is "that is the past, this is a new generation; the story teller has no idea of today's reality".

My take on this, has always been that we should learn from the experiences of our ancestors and profit from them. I guess it helped that I was born with or inculcated with a DNA of feeling a sincere love and pride for our families and in particular those who, through actions and advice, were sharing their vision for uplifting our families and those who were showing us the way forward with their own educational achievements.

I hope that by now the reader, whether living in Goa, or anywhere in the world, has a good idea of the geography and the glorious history of our beloved Goa in general and our ancestral villages of Curtorim, Raia, Loutulim and Benaulim.

What I am covering in the chapters that follow, are stories, facts and events spanning from early nineteenth century, which is approximately from the early days of our grandparents. The stories about our families are meant to be a narrative of the facts and events as gathered by me through numerous chats with our elders. I am thankful to Fr. Albert Menezes and Oscar Souza for their contributions, which helped me fill in some gaps in the Pereira side of the family.

I hope this book's contents will be a celebration of the people who had a vision, faced the challenges and either they grabbed opportunities themselves or guided their children towards those opportunities.

More recently, further research into publicly available digital information, has helped me to confirm what I learnt from the family narratives as well as to enhance my knowledge of our families' past.

During my childhood, my youth and early adulthood, the great influencers and guiding lights for me were my mother Maria Florinda (Marcelina), her mother (my grandmother, Xamae) Maria (Fernandes) Menezes, my mum's first cousin Rosa Maria (Menezes) Sardinha, and my uncle Riario Moniz (dad's older brother). Their own formal education levels did not allow them to guide us to career choices, but each one surely had a vision that, in their respective households, their children were going to be the first generation to pursue post high school studies. In India this is known as College education. The colleges are affiliated to Universities, leading to a University degree. For example, I did two years of pre-engineering studies at Chowgule College (1964-66), followed by four years of Engineering at the Victoria Jubilee Technical Institute (VJTI) in Matunga, Mumbai, 1966-1970. Both Chowgule Colle and VJTI were affiliated to University of Mumbai.

Later on in life, when I grasped the dynamics of our families, I learnt that my grandmother, a petite woman, a gentle woman and a woman wise beyond description, was the superwoman, whose advice and guidance was sought by her children and all her extended family. And they were all better off for it. The amazing thing about my grandmother is that she had no formal school education. Signing her name is all she could write. But she had a penchant for higher education for her children, grandchildren and extended family. Remember that, other than priests, there had never been professional public office holders in our families.

On the Pereira family side, Pati (Msgr. Aniceto Pereira), even with limited financial resources due to his priestly profession, took the role of being the influencer for and supporter of higher education for his nephews and nieces and supporting his nieces when the time came to getting them married. Till his death, he was highly respected and looked up to, by his nieces and nephews.

The individual family chapters that follow cover family stories through late nineteenth century and early twentieth century. In this period, with rare exception, it is the women in our families who excelled when it came to the vision for the future, the wisdom and smarts, and pushing their children towards education opportunities, which were just opening up and were now available for families like ours.

In the eighteenth century and early nineteenth century, higher education for various professional occupations, other than priestly profession, including doctors, lawyers and sometimes even priests, was principally limited to wealthier families.

In that particular time period, when I talk about well-off families, you can break them down into so-so rich, rich and super rich. Even in this group of families, some of them went into debt to send their sons for higher studies, in Goa, Portugal, England or other parts of India. Unfortunately the girls were not lucky to be included.

The male folks in our families, were for the most part, non-risk takers, even though they were hard working farmers or office workers, focused on their trade and task at hand of providing for the family. I attribute this non-risk-taking attitude, partly to self-sufficiency from farming and may be partly to the non-entrepreneurial ethos of the Portuguese, transmitted to the Goan Christians. I come to the latter conclusion from the fact that the business and trading in Goa, was carried out predominantly by Goan Hindu families, even after such a long rule by the Portuguese.

For example in 1960s and early seventies, most of the village shops and businesses in Curtorim, other than the bars or taverns were owned and managed by Hindu families, even though the population was predominantly Catholic. The Hindu religion frowns upon consuming liquor, and therefore access to and sale of liquor is very much controlled to this date in rest of India.

The first seeds for my collection of family stories were sown in April of 1969. I was 22 and just completed my third year of engineering in Mumbai. I could not join my class on their trip to North India (Chandigarh in Punjab, being the focus, as a famously planned and newly built city by French Architect Mr. Corbusier).

I had to undergo appendectomy, and was spending a few post-surgery days of rest at Suclem, my maternal grandparents' place. My grandfather, Caetaninho Menezes, whom we called "Xapae", was also convalescing from a fall.

He had a fall in the paddy field, shooing off kids, who were stoning his tamarind trees. He was 90 then. It was a very common hobby amongst kids 8-13 years of age, to throw stones to pick a ripe mango on a tree or other fruit trees such as tamarind tree or jamun (zamblam) tree. I had my share of fun doing that. Xapae had fractured his hip bone, and, after surgery, was house bound.

"Our son asked me news of the whole world today" is the literal translation from Konkani, of what Xapae told all sitting at the dinner table, with a satisfied and happy tone in his voice. That happened to be my first of formal and informal interviews with a number of our ancestors. Curiously I kept hand written notes from that particular chat with Xapae. I am positive Xapae had not had this opportunity, for a long time, of reliving memories of his earlier days.

Even with my penchant for knowing relationships and gathering stories about our families, writing a book about our family ancestry and stories about families spanning 150 to 200 years had never crossed my mind. However, I realized that I was becoming the "go to" person for my siblings and our cousins, regarding our family ancestry and relationships. I was glad to share my knowledge of these family relationships along with some little stories linked to these relationships.

For me, the most informative and valuable sources of family relationships have been my mother and tia Marta. The cumulative effect of the prodding and digging for information on the family relationships and life stories, is that I found myself with a treasure of family relationships and stories. When I found myself being the "the go to person" for my cousins, I decided that I would make an effort in putting down to paper this information and this book is the result of it. Interestingly my project has generated significant positive interest from the descendants of the members of the four families.

In the Greater Toronto region, which includes the city of Toronto and adjoining municipalities or cities, our circle of friends includes many who trace their ancestry to the CLR villages and have near or extended family relationships. In view of this, a good friend, Mario Coutinho, who traces his family roots to Aldona, North Goa, has said to me more than once, "it looks like in south Goa, every other person is related to each other"

Long before reference sources like Geni.com became readily accessible, I was digging for the linkages of our wide and extended families, and I have been successful in retaining these bits of information in various diaries and my mental library. Data from Geni.com has been helpful to confirm parts of our family trees. I have also found out, that data of whole branches of our trees have yet to be entered.

Not too long ago I came across the following saying, "when an old man dies, a whole library burns down". And I did not want to be that old man or that library. I was nearing 70, and was seriously planning to retire from work. And this project became a convenient task I could undertake, and I knew I could do it with love and pleasure.

When it comes to all the chats I have had with the elders in our families, my only regret is that I did not push further, dig little deeper, when I had the opportunity. Looking back, I write that off partly to my inexperience in the interview process and partly to my enthusiastic satisfaction, on listening to these folks recounting the past.

The bulk of the stories in the chapters specifically dedicated to each family derive from word of mouth gathered by me by sitting down with our elders and making enquiries. I do not believe that any of these stories can be classified as gossip. The stories that I write about our families, date back starting from mid-1800s to mid-1900s.

As I was preparing to write these stories about our families, I kept asking myself what was so important or different about our own families. All families have their own stories to tell, but do they pass them to the next generation? Even stories, which to us seem trivial now, may hold different significance for the future generations.

Since I have undertaken to write about our families, I have been taking every opportunity I get, to talk to people in their seventies and eighties,

Goans and non-Goans, who grew up in other parts of India, and even people who grew up in North America, and whose parents or grandparents were immigrants from Europe.

I noticed a few common threads amongst all these people I interviewed and the backgrounds of our families. If you look back 100 to 150 years, those who grew up in the rural areas, made their living from agriculture and those in the urban or semi-urban environment made their living being trades people or in administration. There were a few whose parents or grandparents were small business owners.

For a perspective of the early period covering our family history in this book, it is noteworthy that the US Congress passed the 13th amendment officially abolishing slavery in the United States on December 18, 1865. The vast majority of plantation slaves labored in the fields, while a select few worked at domestic and vocational duties in and around the owners' houses.

In Goa there was a labour class, but not indentured servants or slaves ever. They were free to work for whom and where they wished to provide their services.

Formal higher education is the main ingredient that has made the difference and has raised the living standard of the families. It did not matter whether the families grew up in rural areas or urban areas. There is no doubt that the urban dwellers had easier access to educational institutes, not only because these institutes were located in cities but also on account of greater mobility or ease of travel within and between the urban centers.

With urbanization, greater education opportunities, and increased mobility, the generations of our uncles' and aunts' age had started to move away from agrarian environment to professions such as medicine, administration and teaching. Once in the urban living situation, they also moved out of the joint family living to nuclear family living of husband and wife and the couple's own children. This slow outward movement from village life became more of an exodus starting with my generation in late 1960s and in 1970s.

Through higher education, our families were on a sure path to higher level of achievement both professionally and financially. I am talking about our family members of our parents' age, including our uncles. The treatise in this book relates to this generation and a generation prior to that.

Writing about the succeeding generations – my generation, and following generations, say post-1945 - would not only greatly increase the scope of this book, but also the effort involved.

The next generation of our family members (now in their late sixties to eighties) have had the fortune and opportunity to pursue college and University education. For the first time the girls from rural environment were enjoying the same education rights and opportunities.

We have enough Ph.D. graduates within our families, that it led my mother, to remark, why do we have so many Ph.D.s and not more medical doctors. Medical doctors, in particular within your own family, were always held in high esteem. My mother could not grasp the high value of doctoral research involved in getting the Ph.D. degree.

In the Moniz / Menezes families my siblings and first cousins have all completed University degrees and to the great pride of our respective parents, grandparents and families, there are professionals of every kind: priests, scientists, doctors, engineers, lawyers, public administrators, politicians, teachers, artists, musicians. On the Pereira side I see a similar pattern of educational and professional achievements and prowess.

I have also elected to honor some select family members (including extended families) who in the twentieth century have excelled themselves in science and the public service.

You will find these in the chapter *Eminent and Meritorious Family Members*:

Mgr. Aniceto Pereira,
Cpt Aniceto Pereira, ISP
C.J.V. Miranda,
Grevy Menezes,

F.X. Menezes,
Constancio Menezes,
Dr. Jose Menezes,
Enio Pimenta MLA,
Francisco Sardinha MP,
Commodore (ret) Gilbert Menezes,
Wing Commander K.K. Majumder
Dr Jose Luis Pinto do Rosario and his three sons
Air Marshall Erlric Pinto,
Rear Admiral Fausto Pinto and
Cpt. Norman Pinto do Rosario.

The last five are extended family members through marriage.

C H A P T E R 8

The MONIZ or MENKAR Family

The Moniz family derived their current family name in 1575, when our first Christian ancestor, was baptized in Raia from a Hindu family Pai (or Poi as the Portuguese would record the name). The name given was Antonio Moniz and he was son of Govinda Pai. Prior to 1575 there were two individuals from families Pai (not the same Pai as above) and Camotim, baptized in 1560, and they were the first Goan Christians baptized by the Portuguese not only in Raia but also whole of Goa.

Is it difficult to trace the ancestry? As Gauncar (original land owner) of the Raia Comunidade, belonging to the Primeiro (First) vangor, it is not too difficult a task and doable but it is laborious to trace it back, from the records maintained by the Comunidade. The male descendants of Gauncars registered with the Comunidade, continue to receive the "Jono" when it is declared yearly or every alternate year. The "Jono" is like a dividend, or bonus or an annuity paid to the original land owners going back hundreds of years. My brothers and I or our appointed representatives still collect our jono. This reminds us of our "patrimonio" (heritage). All the male descendants of Loiola Moniz are equally eligible for the "jono".

Interestingly, as the Comunidade rules stand now, our male children, immaterial of their country of birth, citizenship or residence can still be registered with the Comunidade, with a proof of birth certificate. And I have done it for my son Francis, for whom, at this moment, this whole thing of gauncar and jono, means nothing.

The Comunidades of Goa are among a rare kind of collective establishments in India with ownership and management of powerful land resource. The circumstances prevailing in Goa in the centuries prior to the Portuguese conquest favoured the survival of the Gauncarias, later known as Comunidades. The literal meaning of Gauncar, is son (original) of the land.

There are 223 State recognised private Gaunkari (Comunidade) villages of Goa which are not constituted nor established by any State/Central Government or ruler at any point in time. Governance of these Comunidade villages is carried out in accordance with their very own private laws compiled as Code of Comunidades.

The information on our ancestors from Raia, fell into my lap through a document in Portuguese language, procured by Pe. Santana Faleiro, my wife's cousin and also my prefect in the Seminary days. The document "Os Primordios" (The Beginnings) covers history of Raia and adjoining village of Rachol from IV Century. I am honestly very thankful to Pe. Faleiro.

My guesstimate is our ancestors moved sometime between 1600s and early 1700s to **Maina**, the westernmost part, and making up approximately one third of the Curtorim village. On the north and west, Maina borders Raia. They moved here from Curra location in Raia. The road to Curra, off the main road from Margao to Panji is relatively short and ends at the edge of the forest.

Coming from the main road, when you arrive at the first high point, if you look down to your right, you can still see some remnants of old houses in the middle of the rice fields. That's where, I understand, our ancestors resided before they moved to Maina, Curtorim. Coincidentally the last house on this road, is where my dad's sister Aurelia (Moniz) Soares resided after her marriage to Remedios Soares.

There are still some families with surname Moniz around this location. As far as I know they are not related to us. This is typical of clusters of unrelated families in various villages in Goa with the same last name. The Portuguese priest who baptized them, more often than not gave them the same last Portuguese surname, which was either his own or that of the military officer in charge of the area or some other person in authority, he wished to "honor".

The farthest in time that I have readily available information is on my great-grandparents Caetano Francisco Matias Moniz (1850?-1887?) and Otilia Lavinia Herminia Vas e Moniz (1857-1921, age 64). I extracted this particular information from the website Geni.com. My only problem with the Geni.com data, is whether she was Otilia or Atilia, the latter name given to my dad's sister, and who was no doubt named after her grandmother. Thus I feel tempted to call them both Atilia. But I will not.

Caetano supposedly had a brother priest, Pe. Alcinho. I was not able to readily get any information about him. I tend to believe it, as one of my dad's brother was called Alcinho, even though his given name was Alex.

Caetano and Otilia had the following children: Inacio de **Loiola** Joaquim Xavier do Rosario Miguel Moniz (circa 1878-1937, age 59), Zeferino **Eufemiano** Moniz (1881-1947, age 66), **Joaozinho** Moniz (circa 1884-circa 1913?) and Caetana **Amelina** Moniz Luis (1887-1960, age 73).

As was common at the time, the children did not receive formal education, beyond the primary school level (in Portuguese), which is Primeiro Grau (first degree) and Segundo Grau (second degree), which I would believe they would have completed by 10-12 years of age. By the time our turn arrived (1950s) we completed the Segundo Grau at age 10 and moved on to higher education.

Joaozinho's memory has basically been erased and hardly anybody knows about him or talked about him. More on Joaozinho a little further down.

The family was struggling to keep their heads above water, with the main source of food and income being the strip of land for rice cultivation, at the back of the house. The only fruit bearing trees on this strip of land were a couple tamarind trees. There were two mango trees in the front yard: one "musserate" whose fruit is used for making mango jam or mangada and one "malcurad", the prince of Goa mangos. For some reason I don't know, the malcurad tree would flower in alternate years only. In our front and back yards, there were other trees or plants, bearing edible tropical fruit, and these included banana plants, custard apple, lime, chikoos, guava (pera) and others. Some of these were planted by my mother.

Food self-sufficiency was attained by raising pigs and chicken. They were allowed to roam freely, and even though there were no physical boundaries or fences, the animals knew their virtual boundaries, with irregular encroachments of the neighboring properties. Remember droppings from the roaming animals were welcome as natural fertilizer for the rice fields.

Otilia confessed that she often would go walking to Curtorim (about 20-minute walk), with the excuse of attending the mass; the true purpose was that after the mass she could drop in at her sister Paciencia's place, who was married into the Borges family. The Borges family were relatively well-off, and they used to run a store and a paddy husking mill (ghuirin). Atilia would be happy to receive any scraps from the store, including the crushed chili at the bottom of the whole chili container at the store, and you could not sell it to the paying customers.

Addendum: A Brief on Vas Family
Branch Link to Moniz Family

A small digression here before, I pick up again the thread of the Moniz family history. This is my effort to connect a myriad of our cousins descendants from the Otilia Vas and Moniz side of the family. Even in Canada, we have plenty of them. The information that follows in this addendum, is composed from my own diligence and from referral to Geni. com. The latter was invaluable. The information is not complete, but what is given is factual.

Nicolau Conceicao **Vas** and Rosa Aurora da Costa and Vaz, from Curtorim, had four daughters: Paciencia, Otilia, Bernardina, and Quiteria. Just to reinforce the point, note that Loiola and his aunts' children, listed below, are first cousins and their grandchildren are therefore my third cousins.

Paciencia Vas married Joaquim Borges and they had the following children: Antonio Francisco, Afonsinho (1885-1961) (Aleixo, Elvira Sardinha of Ungirim, Celina Figueiredo, Lina and 2-3 others), Carmelina B Teles of Suclem (Carlotinha de Menezes, Sarto, Roncon, Clifton), Argentina Faleiro of Manora, Raia (Joaquim, Tomas, Ulorica, Estelito), Marquinha Colaco of Loutulim (Msgr. Manoel, Serolina, Pascoal, Alexandrino and Antonio), and Fr. Jose Maria Borges.

Estelito, known as Paul to some, and his wife Teresa have been long-time close friends, since we moved to Toronto. We see each other regularly. They used to be also part of our CLR Mando Group, until they moved to Peterborough, approximately 2 hours driving distance from us to be close to their son Warren. The other child Maria lives in the United States..

My family and I have had long term relationships with Carlotinha's children in Canada: *Aurea* married to Ricardo Miranda of Orgao, Loutulim (Desiree, Niobe, Wilburn and Blain), *Carl* married Barbara (Sujan and Sanjay) and *Agnelo* married Agnes (3 children). Ricardo's great-grandmother comes from The Valeriano Barreto's house. She was Joao Martinho's sister. Joao Martinho was Ethel's grandmother, Maria Aurora's father.

Desiree and husband Venusto Deniz, have been long-term friends and for the last eight years plus, regular bridge card game partners, along with two other couples. Venusto, who had prior experience in playing bridge, has prepared notes and taught the group the latest version of the game after himself taking the initiative and trouble of educating himself in the finer points of the game.

Serolina's four kids were in Toronto, until one, Freddy passed away a few years ago. We keep in touch with one of them Trevor, who is married to Melba Pimenta, daughter of Enio Pimenta. Melba is one of three lead singers, in my CLR Mando Group. Besides having a good voice, Melba is quite adept at various Goan cultural dances.

Celina (Afonsinho's daughter) and Joao Figueiredo have three children Efigenia (Efie), Daniel and Orlando. Efie, a close friend of ours, lives in

Toronto with her husband Derrick and their three children. She is a bubbly and socially active lady and has been active within the Goan cultural activities here for many years, including taking part in and training young and old, to dance the Mando, Corredinho and Dekhni at CLR Association functions and others.

Quiteria Piedade's marriage to Caetano Francisco Barneto from Orgao in Loutolim produced the following children: Joao Aleixo, Inacio Sebastiao (six children, including Anacleto) and Joao Pedro. Anacleto had three children of his own, including Fernanda da Fatima (Barneto) Montes, who with her husband moved to Calgary, Canada. Fernanda passed away in 2022.

I had an encounter with Fernanda a few years ago, when she informed me that my uncle Riario had told her the Moniz and Barneto families were related. Lina (Afonsinho's daughter) had also informed me that one grand aunt Vas was married into a Barneto family, but she could not remember her name. I connected the two pieces of information to complete this family branch.

Divina Providencia **Bernardina's** marriage to Constancio do Rozario de Menezes produced the following children: Quiteria, Claudina, Antonio Vicente, Pe. Miguelinho, Pe. Rozarinho, Carlota, Adelaide do Carmo Moniz and Jose Nicolau.

Claudina married Cosme Barreto and were our next-door neighbors in Maina. Claudina was of great moral support and mentor to my mother in her early married years. They had one daughter, Cacilda, who married Bernardo Diniz and went to have the following children: Maria Emilia, Santana (who was head of Goa Post Office and set up many Curtorkars in the post-office employment), Cosme and Alvito.

Jose Nicolau with his wife lived in Mahim, Mumbai They had the following children; Marina D, Flavia Dias, Eva and Dr. Constancio (Conny), a dentist practicing in Mahim; he was also my dentist, when I was studying in Mumbai He did not charge me for his services. Thank you Connie.

I remember well, when Jose Nicolau and his wife (by then elderly couple) were down in Goa, and come to visit his sister Claudina, our next-door neighbor, they would walk holding hands. This was unusual to village folks in Goa like my family members and I remember my elders' reaction as being kind of scandalized.

Adelaide married Rozario Francisco Moniz (no relation to our Moniz Branch) and had the following Children: Maria Aleluia, Pe. Sebastiao, Inacinho, Maria Adelina Salema (Goncoi).

Maria Aleluia married Joaquim Santana Rebelo and had 6-7 children, one of whom Lourdes married Adv. Antonio Menezes, my neighbor in Maina, and whose mother Liliana was my grandfather's grandniece and my second cousin from Macazana. Interestingly Antonio and Lurdes' older daughter, Dr. Anushka, married Dr. Oswald Mascarenhas, son of Dr. Clelia (Souza) Mascarenhas, daughter of Clarissa (Pereira) Souza, the latter Ethel's dad's sister. As you can see world is so small, at least in South Goa.

Pe. Sebastiao was instrumental in setting up the St. Xavier's School in Curtorim, in a building previously owned by a wealthy family, the Navarro family, but which was falling into disrepair, at that time.

End of the Vas Family Branch Addendum

Even in the face of such a tight financial situation, Caetano and Otilia Moniz decided that there was an opportunity to raise the family's financial standing, by sending Joazinho to East Africa (probably Portuguese colony Mozambique), with the expectation that he would send part of his earnings to help the family, as many families did in those days, particularly in North Goa.

They took a loan to enable them to pay the trip expenses, including the travel fare by boat. To their great dismay, they never heard back from or about Joazinho, until three or four years later, when they received the news that he had died. It would have been customary to have the village church bells tolled, to announce the death. However, Otilia, by now so heart broken, refused to do it.

There is a happy ending to Otilia's quest to raise the family standards. Her son Eufemiano, started a business of candle making from the family home, circa 1910. This business improved their cash flow and the family was in a position to add to their original sole piece of land behind their house, a number of productive properties, spread around Curtorim and one in nearby Sao Jose de Areal. The latter was leased to a number of local tenants (indigenous people); a few years after Goa's integration with India in 1961, and change in ownership laws (land for the tiller) we basically could not exercise the legal ownership of the property and the various tenants are now the virtual owners of their own parcels of that property.

The family nickname of **Menkar**, is derived from the trade of candle making, mentioned above. It literally means "waxman". Customers for the candles came from Maina and parts of Curtorim and Raia and in these villages everybody knew who the Menkar family was. Thus, when as kids we would get into any minor mischief, and people would ask us who our parents were, the name Menkar would easily identify us and often get us out of trouble.

Besides being hard working and entrepreneurial in nature, Eufemiano kept a good control on the household financial affairs. Candles were made of two or three sizes, depending on their utilization, such as funerals, Church feasts and such. The charges to the customer were based on weight of wax used. The customer paid for the full weight of the candles taken. Upon return of the used candles, the customer would be reimbursed for the unused weight of the candle.

As you would expect, the candle making was entirely a manual process. It started by melting big slabs of impure wax in oversized copper pots. The molten wax would then be emptied in a big tank of water. This would result in separation of impurities which would settle to the bottom and true wax, which would float to the surface. This wax was much lighter in color than the original slab form.

The next stage of candle making involved melting the purified wax, and the used, returned candles. The molten wax was poured over the candle wick or thread hanging from huge wheel suspended from the roof. The process consisted of pouring the wax over the wick, move to the next wick, by slowly rotating the wheel, and repeating the process until the desired shape or thickness of the candle was achieved.

As I remember this task was undertaken by a loyal employee also named Caetano ("hortantulo" Caetano), until the latter, due to his age, could not keep up with regular rounds of making the candles. All other tasks involved in the candle making business were handled by Eufemiano and later taken over by my dad.

The final step would be to dunk the freshly made candles in cold water, cut the bottom end off and then roll the candles for proper round shape. The candles were then ready for the customers. As you can see it was all manual labour.

After Eufemiano's death in 1947, my dad, Caetano Moniz, took over the running of the business. He was deeply involved in the manufacturing process. My mother was more often the one involved with the sale to the customer: weighing the candles, handling the cash, and preparing the receipts if needed.

The business was still going strong during my youth, but it was then discontinued, due to a combination of factors: lack of adequately trained person for the task, market forces and principally because there was too much traffic from the front door to the room at the rear of the house, where the trade was taking place. This situation was tolerable when you lived in a joint family with enough people to keep an eye on customers. With the end of joint family, and children moving away to school, my mother was finding this customer traffic unacceptable.

Loiola, my grandfather, occupied himself tending to the family's limited farm land holding. With increased cash flow from the candle making business, which Eufemiano had started, new properties were added to family's land holdings and that kept him busier than before.

Loiola's first wife Ana Maria Rearinha Pereira (circa 1890-1910), from Raia, had passed away soon after the birth in 1910, of their first child, a son whom they named Caetano Francisco de Conceicao **Riario** Moniz (1910-1979). Riario was wet nursed by a Barbosa lady in Raia.

I understand from Fr. Joe Moniz (Riario's son) that Riario was brought up by Riarinha's sister Ezeldinha (Maria Ezilda Marcelina Quiteria) Pereira e Gracias up to age 4-5 in Raia. Sometime after Loiola remarried, Riario was brought home to Maina, as now his new wife Cecilia Monteiro, would be able to take care of him.

Riarinha had two brothers, Joao Francisco Fermino Pereira (Constancio, Aida Ida, Maria Acelia Barreto, Francis) and Jose Maria de Jesus Valeriano Pereira (Acilia, Silvano and Maria Besmita).

Ezilda married Joaquim Inacio Gracias circa 1918. For convenience sake and information for those interested (Riario's side family), I give herein names of Ezeldinha's children: Carma Gracias e Gomes (Analia Gomes e Quadros, Lynette, Nelson and Oscar), Jose Rozario Gracias (Yvonne and Shirley), Sister Lira Gracias, Fr Fermino Gracias (Carmelite?), Fr. Urbano Gracias, and Fr. Tomas Gracias.

Loiola remarried after 4 years to **Cecilia** Claudina Expectacao Monteiro (circa 1890-1963, age 73) from Loutulim.

Loiola and Cecilia had five children: **Caetano** Acacio de Santa Rita Moniz (1914-1978, age 64), Joanita **Atilia** Moniz da Costa (1919-2007, age 88), Maria **Aurelia** Moniz Soares (1921-2005, age 84), Aleixo (Alex or **Alcinho**) Coceicao Moniz (1924-2008, age 83); and **Joao** (John) Moniz (1930-2001, age 71).

As years passed on, Loiola took up to drinking excessively and this led to his premature death in 1937 at relatively young age of 59-60. I was told by one of my aunts, that towards the end, he lived into alternate periods of 15 days or so of drunken stupor and sobriety. At his death, my dad, Caetano, was 23 years old, and Eufemiano was there to guide him in taking over the management of the family properties. Caetano married my mother

Marcelina 6 years later, and then had guidance from Xapae (my mother's dad), a farmer who excelled in his trade, to move his farming abilities a notch higher.

At the time of Eufemiano's death in 1947 (year of my birth and whose name I inherited), the Monizes were enjoying a good period of financial cash flow, due to a combination of higher prices for the paddy rice (as a result of WW II), revenue from the candle business started by Eufemiano and from sale of other produce such as coconuts, mangoes and such, in excess to family's needs.

In the days when formal banking was non-existent, all business was done on cash basis or at smaller scale on barter basis. After the death of Eufemiano, my grandmother Cecilia (avó) became the effective head of the family but she had a poor sense of money management or vision for savings for future needs. By the thinking of the day, Cecilia was now the "ghorkan" or the head of the house and for a while she took this role seriously but not very smartly. The simple and basic rule of attaining financial independence is saving and saving early.

In our house, all the monies from the candle business and sale of paddy rice were deposited in the left hand drawer, of the armoire on which the Oratorio (prayer room altar) was sitting. The right hand drawer was reserved for dad's monies from the small contracts, he got through the Comunidade or the Municipality, such as fixing a culvert or a secondary road here and there.

Here is the rub. All adult household family members, including my dad's younger siblings had free access to the monies in the left hand drawer, without having to answer to anybody. Even the younger married daughter would come "visiting" and help herself to some funds, because, in her words, she had a right to it, "as long as my mother is alive."

This lack of financial management carried on for the next 10 years plus, whilst our own family was growing. My mother, under the coaching of her own mother, was focused on savings for the education of her children, now numbering seven. A couple of examples will illustrate both my mother's focus on building up her "own" savings on one hand and the casual attitude to household cash flow management.

My mother, wishing to respect the "customary" handling of the cash flow in the house, had decided that she would not dip into the monies in that left hand drawer, or the right drawer, unless my dad or his mother handed it to her. That never happened as savings ethic was not a strong point either with my dad or his mother. Marcelina and an elderly cousin neighbour (two houses from ours), Claudina de Menezes Barreto, came up with the following scheme: my mother would send a few baskets of paddy rice on the boys' heads to the neighbour's (her) house, for Claudina to sell it and hand over the money directly to my mother, bypassing the customary cash drawers.

There was a time when the right hand drawer was the repository of big bundles of bank notes (bills), when dad would get paid by the government agency on completion of his civil construction project. Those were the days when cash was the king or the only method of payment, for most of ordinary transactions; these included employment wages and purchase or sale of most of the goods. Heriberto, probably 18 years old then and aware of this lack of control in cash management, on his own initiative, came up with the idea, that he would pick a few notes on a regular basis, from dad's bundle and hand the money to mother.

When I got wind of what was going on, I started doing the same. One day I noticed that the top note on the bundle had a cross made by pen on it. I had an inkling that dad may be getting suspicious of decreasing size of the bundle. I lifted that note and I picked the notes below. I forgot to warn Heriberto about it, and I guess he lifted a few notes including the one with the cross.

Thus dad's doubts, about the bank note bundle diminishing in thickness came to fruition and he asked my mother if she had been helping herself to the money. Mother told him to ask Heriberto, who when asked why, told him, that when he had asked dad for some money, he had refused to give him. As expected and typical of our dad, Heriberto suffered no consequences for his actions. My role did not come into play. We stopped this "import-export" business of bank notes from dad's money to mother, after that.

Then came the event that broke the proverbial camel's back. As was the seasonal custom or routine, my mother with help of hired hands, had gone through the whole process of parboiling the paddy rice, get it de-husked at the local mill and get the rice provision ready for the impending monsoon. One day after that, the young, married, bold aunt comes to our house, accompanied by a worker, and helps herself to whatever her family's needs were.

That was the final straw for Marcelina. With advice and encouragement from some of her trusted elders, she picked up enough courage to take control of the situation and put a lock to the room we called "dispensa" or provisions room. This applied to the candle business receipts too, even though by this time the candle making business was past its peak.

Marcelina had the silent support from her husband, but wresting away the control from grandmother Cecilia, the accepted "head of the household", created a few waves, to put it mildly, within the extended family members. However, this "taking control" of the household cash flow couldn't come earlier, as the three older children were attending College and others were following in our footsteps.

Amelina the youngest of the Loiola's siblings was a petite but a tough lady. Amelina had to be tough, as she had lost her father when she was merely 3 months old. She married in Batora, Curtorim, to Jose Vicente Luis. Jose Vicente was a seafarer and thus absent for long periods of time. Husband's absence from home did not stop Amelina from undertaking major addition to their existing home, which was completed circa 1924. Unusual for the Brahamin ladies of the time, she would not hesitate doing laborer's menial job, including climbing up the ladder and the sort. Amelina and Jose Vicente did not have children of their own.

Sometime after the birth of Loiola and Cecilia's first child (my dad) in 1915, apparently Amelina witnessed Cecilia disciplining Riario, then probably 5 or 6 years old, with a "doulo" (coconut shell spoon with wooden handle) and that was the trigger or opportunity for Amelina to convince her brother to let her adopt Riario. The rationalization was that Loiola and Cecilia would have more children together in the future. She also promised that Riario would inherit all her property and Loiola and his new wife would not have to worry about Riario and sharing their property with Riario.

Riario's adoption by Amelina was agreed. There was no formal document of adoption. In a few years time, the astute Amelina came back asking the Monizes for Riario's share of the property, as she noticed that the Monizes were doing well because of the candle making business started by Eufemiano. The request for Riario's share of the family property, caught them by surprise, but they met Amelina's demands by gifting a property they bought for this purpose in Batora, from a "Kulli Mari" (Crab Maria). Part of the property settlement also included a gift of a "grilhão" –a thick gold chain – from his uncle Eufemiano.

My memories of ti Amelina are not sweet ones. By the time I was in my youth, any time I would go to ti Amelina's house to visit my cousins, she would terrorize me with her uncalled for, stern comments, or let's say her attitude towards me, would make me very uncomfortable. She was like that with my siblings, my cousins and even my dad. I believe my dad was afraid of her too, but he got along through avoiding her and tolerating her temper tantrums. When I would complain about it at home, my folks would just ignore it. Years later, I learnt that she had a drinking problem and this added to her tough lady demeanor.

Riario was always respected as the elder brother by my dad and his siblings, even though they did not grow up in the same house. He did not in any way try wearing his elder statesman hat, when it came down to any of sibling's family affairs. On the contrary he acted as the older brother, and peace maker, if the occasion demanded.

Riario was extraordinarily proud of his family roots, and nursed a vision for his own children and his nephews and nieces rooted in greater education for them than he and his siblings did not have. He is one of those rare uncles who, in those days, took the time to impart on you their values for your own uplifting and that of the family. We are now in new times, when such advice would often not be appreciated. I have ti Riario as a great influencer of my character, in particular the pride in and love of, first of the families I was born in and next of the families adopted through marriage.

The first short one-on-one with ti Riario was at age 17, after my High School exam results were out, in 1964. The final year of high school, also called matriculation, is a public board exam for whole of Goa, and I had done well placing myself fourth in Goa.

My brother Heriberto also attained good results at the same exam and same year. The Portuguese rule in Goa, had ended in December 1961. As a result of us moving from the Portuguese studies curriculum to the English medium, the two of us had ended up being together in the final year of high school. Both of us brothers were also playing for the Curtorim Village Football team and ti Riario and our cousins, on vacation from Mumbai, would come to watch the games.

One day he takes me aside and says to me: "I have watched you, and you are a good boy. I know you are a good student and you participate in sports. This is all good. I don't have much in terms of advice to give you. But I have one advice for you: Stay away from drinking, because it is in our family."

I had no idea to whom he was referring, when he said "it is in our family". But his advice was good enough for me, and I was receptive to it. I made a resolution then and there, that I would limit myself to one alcoholic drink per day or function, no matter how long the duration.

I am proud to say now at age 77, I have stuck to my resolution. And in a way I have ti Riario to thank for this. My self-discipline on consuming alcohol, did not always earn me camaraderie, such as joining my office colleagues for a game of golf or a ball game. For my colleagues the game was an excuse for after-game drinking late into the night. For me the reverse was true.

The next one-on-one with ti Riario was in Mumbai two years later in 1966, after I started my studies at VJTI Engineering College (University of Mumbai). I was nineteen now. As usual he started by telling me how proud he was of my scholastic achievements and how I was making the whole family proud.

Then he told me something that not only profoundly touched me at that moment but it also deepened my sense of never-ending pride of the Moniz family tree with all its branches.

He told me that, as kid (probably 5), he witnessed, his father Loiola (my grandfather) being slapped by a Dr. Jacinto Silva. Typical of those days, this person, a prominent and respected doctor in our part of the village, felt his status allowed him to do what he did to my grandfather. It does not matter what the reason for the slap was. That incident must have left a permanent negative impression on him. Ti Riario told me "we must never allow such a thing to happen to our family again and the only way we are going prevent that and bring ourselves up, is through education". How true it is. That was then, when opportunities for higher education, were not readily available, and it holds true now, when opportunities are plenty. I am glad the current generation of the young in our families has grabbed these opportunities.

Riario is often remembered for being a disciplinarian with his kids and focused on their studies. From what I have shared with you, you can now see why: the childhood incident of seeing his own father ill-treated, lack of higher education opportunities he experienced, and early deep conviction and vision that education was the only path for his family to rise up.

Riario was a very simple and down to earth person. His mind and his heart could not feel any ill will or envy when it related to family members. However, Riario's enthusiasm towards his family and relatives, could sometimes overflow into the territory of the absurd. For example, there was this instance he was heaping praise on a family member's cooking abilities, when some of us knew well, that this person was not a good cook at all. Ti Riario had never tasted this person's cooking. Today, I can imagine Ti

Riario tasting his granddaughters' (Carol's kids) cooking, who, there is no doubt, excel in the kitchen. He would pee in his pants every time.

Riario married Maria Helena Quadros, (1919-2016, age 97) whose mother Maria Amelia Menezes Quadros is Ti Roque Menezes' sister. When the elders were arranging the match, Helena's mother died. An uncle settled the match, but unfortunately, he died soon after of stomach cancer (ref. Jose Pereira et al, Song of Goa, Crown of Mandos, July 2010). Roque Menezes then got involved with the marriage arrangements.

A short educational diversion in inter -family relationships is appropriate here: Ti Roque and his wife Ti Ofelia's children (Ofelia being Ethel's aunt or dad's sister) are Helena's first cousins from Roque's side. Helena's and Riario's children who are my first cousins, are also first cousins, once removed to the Menezes children. Riario's and Helena's children carry the double Luis Moniz last name, the former in honor of the married family name of Amelina Moniz Luis, Riario's aunt and adopted mother.

On the occasion of their wedding, Torcato Figueiredo, a great mando composer during that era, composed a mando *"Suria Uzvadd Fankarolo" (The light has blazed with the sun)*. Torcato, who was composing a different mando, was coaxed and assisted by Roque Menezes, in making modifications, and come up with the above mando, for his niece's wedding. Riario and Helena's children and grandchildren (including those born in the United States) continue to honor them by singing this mando, at family gatherings in Goa or North America.

The mando has been included in the book Song of Goa, the most authoritative mando collection book that I know, page 213. The book has been authored by Jose Pereira, Michael Martins and Antonio da Costa, the last one being my grandfather's (Xapae) grandnephew.

After marriage, Helena stayed in Goa with Amelina, whilst Riario returned to work in Mumbai The intention was for Amelina to have company and as kids were born they would initially grow up in Goa and then at the right time move to Mumbai It was also an economic decision. Riario would come visiting the family in Goa on his annual vacations.

I understand Amelina drove Helena half way to sainthood as Amelina was not an easy person to live with. The kids did their primary schooling in Portuguese before time came to uproot them and take them one by one to Bombay, starting with the eldest, Carol. Towards her final years, Amelina's comfort in Goa was a Fr. Sebastiao Moniz, whose grandmother and Amelina's mother were sisters. I understand my dad's occasional visits, were not very welcome.

Riario and Helena had the following children, all of them with last name Luis Moniz: Jose Vicente or Fr. Joe, Carolina Sara (married Linus Misquitta), Joaquim Sebastiao (married Maria Lopes Pereira), Egidio Aristedes (married Lourdes Lobo), Avito (married Grace Welch), Antonio (married Melanie Lobo) and Jeanette (married Ronald Dalgado)

The story about Riario and Helena, in my mind is not complete without a few words about one of my dearest cousins, and that is Carol. She is four years older than I, and in our growing up years, my siblings and I always looked up to her. She is and has always been the kind of girl, you want to take home to meet your mother: smart, affectionate, caring, a good singer and very family oriented, just like her father. And to boot, she is deeply religious and keeps us in her prayers.

Riario and Helena were like two peas in a pod. Ti Helena earned the "golden" aunt title in par with my Ti Albertina, my mother's sister. When we were studying in Bombay, we would visit Riario and Helena from time to time, at their place in Mazagon, Mumbai, unannounced. Within a few minutes we were dragged into their tiny kitchen, where Helena would serve us some delicious snack or dish, out of the family meal. I can never forget that.

After coming to Canada, Helena came to know that "doce" (made of gram dhal) was a favourite sweet of mine. And at each trip to India, she would make sure she made that favourite sweet for me, not just to eat a piece of it, but the whole thing.

At our last visit with Helena at my cousin Joaquim's place (their ancestral home), she pestering Joaquim to bring some chocolates to give us. It sounds funny, as we are used to take chocolates and plenty of them from Canada, for our family.

Riario (and my dad too) reveled in the (educational) achievements of his children and nephews and nieces, and I can only imagine his limitless joy at their successes. He died relatively young, in 1979, at age 67 of pancreatic cancer. When Helena died in 2016, she had clicked a good age of 97 having been adored by children and nephews and nieces alike.

Now here are the write-ups from Fr. Joe Moniz, and Avito Moniz, Riario and Helena's children in their own words. Fr. Joe (Babush) is the first of seven children and Avito, the fifth in line.

Riario and Helena Moniz by Fr. Joe Moniz

Was my Dad, an educator or motivator or both? Perhaps he was both. Though he had no formal education, he was a motivator for sure. Besides raising seven kids and providing them with a future, he extended himself to a larger family.

Being the oldest, I was the beneficiary of a Seminary education, which at that time was the best education opportunity available to boys. The rest of the kids got the environment, the support and the guidance for good careers and futures.

Dad was a master at social networking and he had friends at right places: they were priests, doctors and members in the community, who became part of our family and an amazing influence on our education and our future.

What money couldn't buy, and there was not much of that, social networking opened doors and gave us incredible opportunities for an unimaginable future.

In Mumbai, the Jesuits were our neighbors pastors and educators. The Jesuits took us for breakfast at the rectory. Members of the Jesuit community let us use study rooms for serious studying, when there was no room at our modest residence. The Jesuits gave cheese and grains recently arrived from charitable organizations in America and a sure relief for my family.

Raising seven kids on their own, the Jesuits were friends of our family, accepted the boys in their schools and with their experience, talents and generosity, guided them through the teenage years, up into their college education.

Even though I was a Diocesan priest, ordained for the Archdiocese of Goa, one of the Jesuits from the Mumbai province helped me get into the Jesuit University, the Loyola University in Los Angeles. And this miraculous admission had something to do with dad's connections with the Jesuit community. The Bombay and Spanish Jesuits stand tall in the MONIZ horizon.

Even though dad had a large family, if you could consider seven kids large, even for a good catholic family, his vision was much bigger. Dad believed in education and considered it as important as food and drink, and was a promoter of catholic education for all kids, boys and girls alike.

My parents kept a nephew and a niece, as boarders and offered them shelter and food in their very congested quarters. For mum and dad there was always room for one or two more and they shared our quarters for four years, benefitting from a better education than they would have gotten in Goa.

The mention of a cousin needs special attention. She was one of many kids of my aunt, who had limited resources to educate the family. My cousin wanted to be a nurse. She didn't have to knock at our door. Dad prevailed on the family and volunteered to help her in this effort. She remembers the date she got to Bombay, July 9, 1972.

With the help of my father and my siblings, who managed to get the admission paperwork together, and with the influence of a doctor friend, who owned a hospital, she got accepted in the Nair Hospital, that same year, on September 4. Staying at a hostel nearby and making the Moniz home her headquarters, she managed to get a degree as a General Nurse and mid-wife, after four and half years of education and dedicated service. After working at different hospitals, today she works as a Hospice nurse serving many patients, with varied medical needs, in the privacy of their homes.

By God's providence, September 4, 1972, the date my cousin got admitted in the school of nursing, was also the date when my brother Avito flew to New York, U.S.A., to begin a new chapter in his personal, academic and professional life. It was more than a new chapter, a new book, a new beginning.

My dad would have been very proud of us, his sons and daughters, but also those he adopted as his own. Dad didn't live long enough to see his wonderful creations, as he died at young age of 67. He didn't talk to us about his dreams and visions, and we were too young and too much into our own experiments, to pay attention to someone else.

But friend, this is just half of the story. The other half is much more interesting and worthy of imitation. I welcome you to the world of maids in the Moniz family. You will be very confused if you look at them as maids. They were not. They were a class of individuals, doing servile jobs at the beginning, but dreaming of fortunes not unlike ours. Why not a priest, a doctor, a scientist, a nurse, a chef or a tailor?

We had twenty maids, from ages 10 to fifties, all of these girls, except for one male, they served us for close to forty years from my birth to dad's passing away. The first batch were from Curtorim, as they were our tenants / mundkars, and they helped mum with taking care of the house of my grandmother and the first six kids who were born in Goa.

The rest were younger from different parts of Goa. The recent vintage were a group from Uttar Pradesh. They served in our home, but also learnt to read, write, sew, cook and prepare delicious meals and even practice their own faith, whether they were Christians or not.

One of them became a nurse and raised two daughters, a doctor and a scientist. Two of them went to Hong Kong and raised their economic status; one them has a son, who is a priest. All of them found a better future for themselves and for the kids they raised.

For mum and dad, the family was a village wider than the confines of their own.

This note is dedicated to Riario and Helena Moniz, my parents, to Carol and Jeanette, my sisters, to Joachim, Egidio, Avito and Antonio, my brothers and their amazing families.

Dad sowed the seeds that are bearing fruit for his children and the children of the world"

Write up from Avito Luis Moniz (Rajendra Prasad), (1952-2023)

Author's Note: Avito is the fifth child of Helena and Riario Moniz. He was a resident in Manhattan Beach, California, USA. Sadly Avito succumbed to pancreatic cancer in September 2023. He was one of a kind within the Moniz family, a good edition of Riario's legacy, and will be deeply missed for a long time. Avito wrote what follows two years prior to his passing.

A son's remembrance of an exemplary father

In the 7th grade at St. Mary's High School, in Mumbai, India, I sat on the family bed, memorizing my favorite poem. My dad sat next to me, helping me line by line, verse after verse, until I had it fully memorized. "IF" was Rudyard Kipling's gift to his son, overflowing with wisdom, love and life lessons. It continues to be a reminder of my father's gift to me, almost 60 years later, as lines keep rushing back, unsolicited at times…. a reminder in hard and difficult times to stay the course.

If you can keep your head when all about you
Are losing theirs and blaming it on you,
If you can trust yourself when all men doubt you,
But make allowance for their doubting too;
If you can wait and not be tired by waiting,
Or being lied about, don't deal in lies,

Or being hated, don't give way to hating,
And yet don't look too good, nor talk too wise

As a grown man living in the US for the past 48 years, looking back at my life, what story shall I tell you? How about a story about Riario as a father with a vision for his family?

If you can dream—and not make dreams your master;
If you can think—and not make thoughts your aim…"

Riario was a strict disciplinarian and set high standards for all his 7 children. He taught us to believe that we could achieve anything, ANYTHING! Growing up in a poor apartment building in Mumbai he would often say "maggots don't stay in the dung" and "a lotus rises out of the muck". Having barely achieved a Secondary School Certificate himself, he had a vision to enroll all the children in Catholic schools and used that as a foundation to advance them in diverse fields such as agriculture, chemistry, microbiology, finance, culinary arts and religious studies. The oldest child, Fr. Joe came to Manhattan Beach California in 1966 as a young 25-year-old priest and served the church in Los Angeles for over 52 years…and he continues to serve now, as a retired priest. Dad's guidance and Joe brought 3 of us to the US and 1 son to Brazil; 2 remained in India.

Or would you like a story about one of Dad's best gifts to us? Public speaking!

If you can talk with crowds and keep your virtue…

Dad was a master communicator with a silver tongue and charm. He could convince anyone! When mum and dad moved us from Goa to Mumbai, I was a shy 7 year old boy, who spoke only Konkani and not a word of English. My older brother Egidio was going to second grade, and Dad did not want to have two little ones in different grades. During a short meeting, Dad charmed and convinced the Irish principal to let me skip first grade, so he could mentor and tutor both us boys at the same time. I have my dad's unique baritone and style and have been asked in Goa… "are baba, Devan kosoli jib dil re tuka"? (So, what gift of gab, has God gifted you).

As a Food Scientist and Microbiologist, I have travelled all over the world to teach and lecture on seafood aquaculture, processing and food safety. The love of public speaking has made this a personal joy! Over 45 years, the gift of proclaiming God's word has been shared with a church community in Manhattan Beach, CA as a lector. Dad's passion has been my blessing too.

Or shall I tell an inspiring story?

If you can meet with triumph and disaster
And treat those two impostors just the same…

I am awed by how hard my dad worked at Scindia Steamship Corporation in the payroll department for over 35 years. He walked to and from work for decades. At age 38, walking to work at 2 am, he was run over by a drunk truck driver, and that resulted in an amputation of his right leg above the knee. We never heard him complain. He wore an artificial limb for the rest of his life, but at parties, he was the first one on the dance floor. He re-learned to ride a bike, and hopped from spot to spot happily doing his work around the house.

Dad had a joyful heart and a positive attitude. The glass was always half full. Together, Dad and Mum raised our family in a tiny 2 room flat and welcomed relatives, strangers and visitors with an open-door policy. Abundance did not mean possessions or financial wealth. Rather, it was a rich family life, attending daily mass, praying the family rosary, helping raise a niece or nephew, godliness, and spreading love, kindness, and faith to the community.

And how about one last story of sacrifice, hard work, and the love of being a parent.

If you can fill the unforgiving minute
With sixty seconds' worth of distance run,
Yours is the Earth and everything that's in it,
And—which is more—you'll be a Man, my son

My parents encouraged me to emigrate to the US, because prospects were slim for a Catholic in 1970s-India. Ultimately, five of the children left home and travelled around the world for a better future. Living in the US has not been all easy. Not having family nearby was initially a source of loneliness, sadness, missing birthdays, weddings and funerals, including my father's. Saving to educate children in the best of US private schools and buying a home were some of our initial challenges, but with time, we developed friendships and built relationships. America is home now.

Four years after completing my Master's degree, I fell in love with a young American girl, Grace, whom I met at church, and we have been happily married for 41 years. We have four beautiful children. Education, faith, and community were the pillars of their upbringing, just like my own. All four children left home to study in far away cities, and I felt what my father must have experienced as his own children left the nest: sorrow in letting them go, immense pride in their accomplishments, and gratitude for the adults they have become and the impact I know they will have on the world.

Riario taught us to seize every opportunity, squeeze joy out of every moment, and live life to its fullest. His legacy lives on, as we his children and grandchildren continue to strive for the seeds of greatness, he saw in us and everyone he met. He was the best Man, the best Father, we could have asked for.

End of Riario and Helena's Story

Inacio de **Loiola** Joaquim Xavier do Rosario Miguel Moniz (circa 1878-1937, age 59) got married in 1913 to **Cecilia** Claudina Expectacao Monteiro Soares (circa 1887-1966) from Organv, Loutulim.

They had five children: **Caetano** Acacio de Santa Rita Moniz (1914-1978), Joanita **Atilia** da Costa e Moniz (1919-2007), Aleixo (**Alcinho** or Alex) Conceicao Moniz (1924-2008, age 85) Maria **Aurelia** Moniz e Soares (1921-?) and Antonio **Joao** (John) Moniz (1930-?)

Caetano and Marcelina's Story

Caetano married Maria Florinda (**Marcelina**) Menezes (1921-2014, age 93) in 1941. They had seven children: Loiola (May 1943-, married Especiosa Benildes Coutinho), worked at Air-condition technician at Voltas in Mumbai; Heriberto (Nov. 1944-, married Maria Lurdes Barreto), worked as Marine Engineer and then Stationary Engineer at Imperial Oil (Exxon) Refinery; Eufemiano (Jan. 1947- married Ethelwyn Xavier Pereira), worked as Professional Engineer throughout Canada and last 25 years of work as self-employed Financial Planner; Violeta M. Fernandes (Fe. 1950 – married Albino Fernandes) and managed husband's family owned music store, Pedro Fernandes Music Shop in Panji and Margao, Goa; Blanche M. Viegas (Aug. 1953- married Placido Viegas) and lived a teacher's life and as the pillar and go-to-person in the Moniz/Menezes/Viegas families; Flaviano (Nov. 1957-Feb. 2015, married Amelia Misquita) and worked as kitchen chef, practicing the trade he trained for in Mumbai; and Serena M. Diniz (Oct. 1960- married Belrosario Diniz), registered nurse, worked for a short time in Mumbai, many years in Muscat, Oman for the Police Force Hospital and since early 2000 at Mississauga General Hospital.

The seven children gave Caetano and Marcelina 19 grandchildren, who have produced 20 great-grandchildren to date; the majority of the grandchildren have completed University studies and they and their spouses are holding professional positions to make the family proud. The great-grandchildren are spread worldwide: in Australia (Violet's Nadia's 6 children, in Goa (Loiola's Michelle's 2 children in Maina Curtorim, Violet's Pierre's 2 children in Porvorim, Flaviano's Agnetha's one child in Panji), in Dubai (Blanche's Muriel's 2 children), in Canada (Loiola's Rochelle's two children in Vancouver, Heriberto's Ralph's one child in Edmonton, Eufemiano's Celine's one child in Burlington, and Serena's Synuae's one child and Byanca's two children in the Greater Toronto Area).

My siblings and I called our parents, Caetano and Marcelina, pae and mae, which in the Portuguese language stand for father and mother respectively.

Caetano was probably the last of the typical land owner-farmers in Curtorim of mid-twentieth century. He knew the trade, he supervised the workers in the rice fields and did some menial chores himself. The two principal tasks he took charge of, were milking the buffalo in the mornings and taking full charge of the seed germination for plantation of the paddy rice. He was also fully involved in part of the manual work in the candle making for close to 20 years until mid-1960s.

There was a time period Caetano would also take on minor civil construction contracts, such as building culverts and side road repairs. I think these contracts were profitable, but he was not a good money manager on two aspects. I remember my mother reminding him repeatedly, after he received his payments from the government agency, to pay back the loans he had taken from his cousins to pay the workers on the construction project, on an ongoing and timely basis.

I remember his workers at these civil construction contracts talking about the "engineer" in very glowing terms. That and in my mind, the prospect of taking over dad's line of work, is how I set my mind towards pursuing a civil engineering career, to much disappointment for my maternal grandmother, whose wishes were for me to pursue medicine.

Dad had access to a good cash flow, from the candle business and his big weakness was that he was a poor money saver and he could not say no, to people wanting to borrow money from him here and there, with no record keeping of IOUs. I believe that, more often than not, he had no expectation of getting paid back.

My dad and his buddies used to play game of rummy (cards) on a fairly regular basis. They played for small stakes and I heard often, he was "lucky" and good at the game. I remember him coming home with coins jingling in his pockets, and we as little kids used to run to meet him, as we had learnt we would receive a fistful of coins for each of us.

I understand they used to play rummy even at social gatherings (in a separate room) on the occasion of village feasts and such. My brother Loiola recounted to me one such occasion, when he, with his diploma from

Escola Tecnica (Technical College) in hand, was about to leave for Bombay looking for job opportunities. Dad got up from the table and handed him a bundle of INR 2,000, saying that he probably could use it better than him having it and spending it. Back then INR 2,000 was a significant sum of money, and something Loiola could only dream about.

I found that gesture, not Caetano's typical attitude with us grown up kids. The way I remember him is that if I asked him for money, say to buy cloth for a pair of pants (ready made clothing was not promptly available in those times), it would not be easy to get it and he would even say on an occasion, "do you think, money grows on trees?". On the other hand if we asked him to buy it for us, he would promptly do it, and it would be of a good quality too.

Caetano had luck on his side too. He had a lottery winning of INR 20,000 in early 1960s, (a big amount in those days) and another smaller amount at a later date, of which he made a meagre savings deposit at the post office of INR 500 on my sister Violeta's name, and that too, after lot of prodding from my mother.

In our house we had a regular and abundant supply of fresh fish. That is because dad would lease from the Comunidade a number of fish producing riverside properties ("poi" or "mus"), located in close proximity to us and sub-lease them to others. His pay-back was getting a share or supply of fresh fish caught on these properties, for our family. He also had a share of the fish catch at the Curtorim and Maina Lakes.

You see, if one wishes to receive your due share both in quantity and quality of the fish catch, one has to be there in person. The timing of these fish catches depends on the tide, and dad would be there at the designated time, be it during the day or late in the evening.

When he would come home with a sack full of river fresh, and he would empty the bag on the kitchen floor, some of the fish was still flopping about. Normally there would be enough of it for our family and thus the immediate query by us kids would be "aren't we sending some to grandma's (mum's) house, which was 10 minutes quick walk away.

Caetano was an easy going and happy man. He was liked by all in the village and in particular he could relate to the common man or the labour class. I understand he used to be in popular demand to raise the toast at many of their weddings.

His popularity with a broad segment of village population, led him to stand for the post of Sarpanch. He was, without a doubt, not a corrupt man and to my knowledge never took advantage of his position for his monetary benefit. I hear that corruption is rampant at the panchayat level now.

"A sarpanch is a decision-maker, elected by the village-level constitutional body of local self-government called the Gram Sabha (village government) in India. The sarpanch, together with other elected panchayat members (referred to as commissioners or a panch), constitute the gram panchayat. The sarpanch is the focal point of contact between government officers and the village community and retains power for five years." Wikepedia.

For many years, Caetano had been a caretaker of a number of properties for absentee landlords, living out of Goa. After Goa became part of India in December 1961, there was a change of laws related to property rental or care taking. The new laws basically allowed the care taker or the one cultivating the land, to continue holding on to the property, (without the need to return it back to the rightful owner, as long as you made the old, agreed annual payment. I believe it was known as "land for the tiller".

To the astonishment of these rightful owners, dad returned each of the property back to them, without demanding anything in return. At the time, so many absentee landlords were suddenly placed in an unexpected situation, where the rightful owners had to pay big sums of money to the lessee or the tiller, to get their properties back. In so many instances the court cases to rectify such matters, went on for years.

I understand that one of these absentee landlords was offering my dad a good deal pricewise for buying one big land property "Uddo" next to the Maina lake. This property was not only a farmland, but also had all kinds of produce trees and it could have been developed into multi use or multi-residential location. Dad did not have the investment sense to grab the opportunity. The owner sold the property to another individual who developed the place as a residential sub-division, and surely made good profits out of it.

I am so proud of dad for his correct behavior, as a private person or as holder of a public office as village head or sarpanch. He has not left us a legacy of underhandedness or cheating. As they say, we can live with a clean conscience. An heir to one of these properties, who is living in Canada, keeps reminding me of the honorable behavior of my father. Under the table payments and corruption are the scourge of life in Goa and rest of India.

Caetano's honorable behavior did not help, when it came to our own property. The Moniz family (dad and his brothers) had inherited a sizeable paddy field property in Sao Jose de Areal, less than 5 km away, which was sublet to a number of indigenous people (gauddi) who had been cultivating the fields for a number of years. They would dutifully come and pay their annual rent to my mother once a year.

However, with change of laws to "land for the tiller" we needed to do our part to salvage our property, for example by paying off the tillers, as other landlords did. Caetano did not take interest in this matter and this whole property is now lost to the tillers, even though the ownership on paper remains on Moniz family name.

Caetano never neglected his responsibilities for the day-to-day management of the family property affairs, in special with respect to the cultivation of paddy fields (whether our own or the ones he was looking after for others) and all related aspects. However, he lacked the saving ethos and vision and business drive, which would have made a huge difference in our financial self-sufficiency.

Thankfully his wife Marcelina, on the other hand, had those qualities. Just like her mother in the house of the Menezes (Godd), and with her guidance, Marcelina became the visionary, the financial manager and in the end the backbone of our family.

The dowry money she received, was immediately used in the purchase of a property, located about 5 minutes from our home. Marcelina was very money savvy and frugal. Tight cash was no barrier in the acquisition of couple properties, one a plot in Aquem, Margao, and another bordering the property bought with the dowry money.

As much as the children learn from their parents, there is always one parent who plays the dominant role. Our mother had that role, and she built our characters not only by example but by actions.

She was the disciplinarian, and as little kids we experienced our share of the proverbial stick. I remember a phase when the three older ones, the boys, would tease each other by the nicknames, we had given each other, and then the little fights ensued. And mum would have to intervene, the cane being the instrument of punishment. One day out of desperation, I heard her say, "I don't even know why you were born." I felt so hurt, and do you know what? These niggling brotherly fights stopped after that.

To our mother no work was beneath us. Each one of the children had tasks assigned to us, such as watering a specific plot of flowers in the garden. A Hindu lady would come to pick these flowers on a regular basis and pay for them by the size of the lots. These flowers known as "abolim" are used to make garlands as offerings to God, or by some women folk on their hair. My mother kept this money aside and she was herself surprised by the impressive sum of money that had accumulated over time.

Our mother would send us to the fields, not only to serve as supervisory eyes, but also to be an additional person at work, such as filling up the baskets, with composted buffalo dung, and lift them on the heads of the women workers, to be spread it as fertilizer on the fields, prior to monsoon.

All the kids contributed their share to the kitchen related work. For example, the older kids were tasked to take their turn for a week at a time, in making chappatis or rotis (rolling them out and frying them) in the morning for breakfast for every household member. The dough would be made and kept ready overnight by the house maid. For us kids, cleaning and preparing fresh fish for the kitchen was routine. We did the frying of the fish of which there was routinely plenty.

I did not prepare any dishes (with masala, etc.) in the kitchen, but I remember mum advising me to learn to cook if I wished to continue to enjoy our home cuisine. In her words "when you get married, your wife will cook the way she has learnt from her mother." In this day and age, when cooking is not just a woman's job, my mother's words may not seem to project a foresight, but sixty years back, it was a true vision.

Once I had to carry on my head a large basket of paddy to the husking mill, a distance of 5 to 10 minutes walking. Kids of families of our ilk would never, and I repeat never, would have to do such a chore. This is the only time I felt mortified inside for doing a type of work, usually carried out by the labor class.

To our mother, bringing up her children doing any and all tasks, entailed not only building their characters, but also in the process saving money she would have to pay one additional hired hand.

In the "good old days" families lent a helping hand to each other and broader community in general. Our mother made good use of the family members who were willing to help, with the four older kids. Loiola and Heriberto spent a school year at Loutulim grandmother's house. I spent a year with my uncle priest Fr. Rosario Menezes (Patiu), when he was chaplain in Sarzora, Chinchinim. Violeta also spent a year with Patiu, who by that time was posted in Utorda, Majorda.

Following my stay at Patiu's, I was back home for a year. Then I was exported to stay with my mother's cousin Rosa Maria Sardinha, in Curtorim, where I boarded for two school years (ages 9 and 10) completing the final two years of primary school primeiro grau and segundo grau (Portuguese studies)

In the Sardinha house they had an unmarried uncle (professor) Roque Sardinha, who used to give afternoon tuitions on the second floor of the Borges house behind the Church. Most parents who could afford the fees, would send their kids for tuition at Prof. Roque, not only for his teaching abilities but also for his tough discipline.

Tia Rosa Maria, is one of my favourite women in our family. Unlike other ladies in our families who wore dresses, she always dressed up in tollop bazu, the outfit worn by most ladies prior to 1950s. She was a no non-sense lady, and she had to be, with eight boys of her own. My memories of her are of a sweet aunt. Years after, or at least six years prior to my departure to Canada, I used to love to pay her a visit now and then, never missing to drop by on the Christmas day. I felt a special connection with ti Rosa Maria, and looking back, at our conversations, I believe we had a soft corner for each other.

When we were growing up, money was very tight in our house because there was a costly new expense in terms of having to pay for the college education of seven children. On more than one occasion, to pay the college fees due, our mother would take a short term loan from one her brothers, which would be paid back with the proceeds of paddy rice and other agricultural products.

When Heriberto and I were studying engineering in Mumbai, mae arranged with our elder brother Loiola, to pay part of our expenses. Mae and Loyola kept accounts of Loiola's payments, which she then paid him in full when he was buying his first apartment in Chembur, Mumbai, after marriage to Especiosa Benildes Coutinho in 1970. This was my mother's way of helping Loiola through forced savings; but she was also able to plan her cash flow better than would otherwise be.

You could say frugality was Marcelina's middle name. But through that thriftiness, she exhibited huge softness of heart supporting charitable causes and lending a helping hand to people in need in our community. For example, she was a donor to an Orphanage in Mapuca, as long as I remember, and which I started supporting through her once I came to Canada. To this day I don't know the name of the orphanage.

When we were in our final year of High School (Matriculation), she invited one of our classmates to move in to our home, during the last couple of months of exam preparation, as she felt his widowed mother could not provide nutritional food and proper study environment. She helped in a similar way a couple of my cousins too.

She helped a number of village wives, whose husbands were away on work, such as seafarers, to tide over, until their husbands returned. They would then pay her back any accumulated dues, from purchase of rice and other produce or even borrowed funds.

Even though their personalities were quite different, in the end my parents recognized each other's strengths, and worked successfully to the ultimate goal, which for parents in our community is solely to give their best to their kids.

Pae died in 1978 as a result of a motorbike accident, where he was a passenger. For a person still full of life, and only 64, it was without a doubt a premature death, which nobody expected. I often think about how much dad would have loved to visit us in Canada, and I can only imagine the glowing stories he would have taken back to Goa and would share with people down there. Unfortunately, it was a bit too early in my life in Canada, to bring dad to visit us here.

Upon his death, the people of Maina erected a commemorative monument in my dad's honor. Caetano deserved it and would have been mightily delighted. After forty plus years the monument still exists, and in reality some beautification has been carried out recently.

Doing my readings on easily available information, Curtorim and Maina have produced many illustrious men, such as doctors, administrators and lawyers who have excelled in their trade in Goa or in India or Portuguese territories. A number of them have made significant contributions, monetary or in kind, for the betterment of the village. It is unfortunate that there is nothing there to remind the future generations of their contributions.

When Caetano died, the four older children were already married and out of the house. Loiola was in Mumbai, Heriberto and Eufemiano in Canada, and Violeta in Panji. Marcelina had to still take responsibility of the three younger ones, Blanche, Flaviano and Serena, aged 25 to 18. Suddenly she had to manage cultivation of the rice fields and related matters. It was tough for her but she rose up to the task.

Marcelina made two trips to Canada, and I believe only after the second trip, did she reluctantly come around to thinking her two sons were better off in Canada, the second one in 1993. Serena had not migrated to Canada yet.

You see her wish or dream for us (and for herself) was that we would have been working in the Middle East, as so many from the village did, and we would return to the village with that earnings wealth, build a modern style home and have a nice car in which she could ride. In the end she would have the company of at least one son, and also enjoy the "good life", such as being driven around, and no doubt in her mind, this would raise her standing in the community.

When I was leaving for Canada pae was excited for me, as I am told, he was with mother's youngest brother Jose. Mother's thought process was different. She was afraid that I would find a bride in Canada, and practically she would lose a son, whose bonds to his original family would only weaken after that.

Marcelina had a good long life, the last seventeen years spent in the company of and care from Blanche. She was taken in with open arms by her husband Placido Viegas and their children Olancio and Muriel.

About a year after dad's death when all the boys were in Goa we decided to undertake property partition in a friendly way. Heriberto and I opted for a property in Margao (two adjoining house plots) and the remainder of the properties and the house for Loiola and Flaviano. In return of mae giving up her property rights, it was agreed that s would receive regular support allowance from the sons. Especially after she moved in with Blanche, the elder three sons exceeded their financial responsibilities to her. After many years of thrift, all for the sake of her children, toward the latter part of her life, mae did not have to worry about money. She was free to enjoy the little luxuries in life, she so deserved.

Marcelina died at age 93, after having being in coma for approximately 6 months as a result of a stroke. We the siblings have been fortunate to have Blanche to be her companion and care giver in those last seventeen years.

We all have our own ways of remembering our parents or those dear to us. I am not talking about the big influences they have had on our lives, but those little things that from time to time remind us of them. I asked myself how do I reminisce my mother and father. And here is what I came up with.

They say outside food tastes better than home food. When as kids we were at grandma's place or some other family's place, I guess our appetites were getting the better of us, and I remember mae saying, we behaved as if we had never seen food. To this date that attitude to food, away from home has not changed much. It reminds me of a Konkani saying "Deklem moddem, ailem roddnem". The literal meaning is "you see the dead body, and tears come to your eyes." The saying is used to indicate that "when you see the food, you feel like eating" or in other words you have no control over eating.

In Canada all non-evergreen trees lose their leaves before the onset of winter. Each time I am raking the dry leaves for garden waste collection in the fall, I remember doing it with mother a couple of times. This collection of dry leaves (potro) was used as fuel to heat the water in a big copper pot (bhaan). Then you have your bath from a bucket where some of this heated water was mixed with freshly drawn water from the adjoining well.

In the last 10 years of mother's life, I visited her more frequently than I used to prior to that. And each time it was the same thing from my mother: "You look old to me. Why do you keep that grey beard? Doesn't it bother your wife?" And my response was also the same: her little boy is now over 60 and I wish to age gracefully"

When it comes to dad there are two of his sayings which have stayed with me. One was "nobody has died by not eating one meal, people have died eating one meal." This I heard enough times when we kids had fallen asleep, during rosary, which always started at eight at night. After the rosary, dinner was served and the old folks were trying to wake us up and we were more interested in sleeping than eating. I have adopted the same approach with our kids, whether at home or when visiting with friends. My wife has applied this approach to our kids, when we visit with friends and family.

An observation from my dad, about me, even though he put it in a bit crude way, has been so correct and it was that "he will even eat shit if you tell him it is good for his health."

Dad also introduced me to the art of catching frogs, which was a special experience and was in a way a kind of coming of age for the boys in those days. Frog meat was a delicacy in our family, and unlike many other people, we consumed all parts of the frog other than the head, the innards and the skin.

I was 15, and on the second day of heavy rains at the start of monsoon, the frogs had just come out of hibernation and croaking mightily looking for a mate, and ripe for being caught. Dad woke me up and told me we were going to catch frogs. We went down on the strip of rice fields at the back of our house, with a big flashlight and a sac or maybe a pillow cover. You see at this stage, a flash light thrown on frogs' eyes, freezes them in place, and all you do is go grab the frog and place it the sac. It is like they say, deer in the headlights. In a matter of another day or two, the flash light does no longer have the same effect on the frogs and it would be lot harder to catch them.

With the overhunting of frogs for commercial consumption and the introduction of chemical fertilizers in the Goan rice fields, the frog population has significantly decreased over time. The government has now banned catching of frogs for human consumption.

What probably has had the deepest influence on me, of my dad's actions is the joy, and pride he experienced each time his children excelled in their exams, starting from Segundo Grau (I did it at age 10) and then High School and finally in Engineering. I suppose he must have given me a virtual pat on the back but I do not remember any special father-son chat on this matter. But I surely knew of his bragging and celebration, and that was my inspiration, as moved on in life, not to let him down.

End od Caetano and Marcelina's Story

Joanita **Atilia** Moniz da Costa (1919-2007, age 88) was an aunt whom I got to know when I was 16, even though she was married and living approximately 45 minutes walking distance from our home. She married young at 17, to Roque da Costa and they had six children together: Alzira (unmarried), Sr. Laura (nun), Fr. Caetano, Carlos da Costa (married Alzira Rodrigues), Belivia da Costa Miranda (married to Arlindo de Miranda) and Mario da Costa (married to Maria Rita).

The three older cousins used to come visiting their grandmother and the rest of the family at regular intervals, at least once a year. My siblings and I did not visit my aunt's family. It is odd that I never heard a conversation on where our aunt resided or why we were not going to visit her. My first visit was in 1963, when our parish priest, who was also the school principal, sent me to fetch a bell, which was part of the little chapel adjoining their house, as Ti Roque's brother was a priest (Pe. Vicente) and he resided in the house.

I was so happy to (finally) meet my aunt, and our joy of this meeting was mutual. I liked to think of Ti Atilia as "saibinichi bhoin" (Our Lady's sister), as she was such a nice person and appeared always calm and at peace. On Christmas day, I made it a point to pay her a visit, in addition to my grandmother and ti Rosa Maria.

Sometime around 1942-43, a village neighbor Dr. Paulo Jose da Veiga, instituted a legal case against Ti Roque, related to some matter that took place within the confines of the Comunidade building. Ti Roque used to have the lease rights from the Comunidade for the open market vendors (Tintto) in Curtorim.

Caetano was listed as one of the witnesses by Dr. da Veiga, as he was supposedly seen sitting at the back of the hall. I assume that Caetano was afraid of Dr. Paulo Jose da Veiga (a powerful personality at the time and that too living in our vicinity) and probably (in consultation with his elders) did not fathom the consequences of appearing in the court as a witness against his own brother-in-law.

After the court case ti Roque came straight to our house to complain about the matter with his mother-in-law, Cecilia, who unfortunately was diplomatic enough: less sympathetic to his complaints and more supportive of her son's actions. In view of this Ti Roque told Cecilia, that this side of the family was henceforth dead to him. Ti Atilia was thus forbidden to visit her mother after that.

We knew Roque to be our uncle, and we would greet him, whenever we met, and he would politely return our greeting. Thankfully neither family, brought the children into this family rift, and it was never talked about in our house. As time passed by, the cousins got along quite well. I used to visit Pe. Caetano in Long Island, N.Y. regularly when we would go down to New York City visiting Ethel's sister. He also came up on vacations to Edmonton and Mississauga and stayed with Heriberto's family and with my family and we had memorable times together. At his last visit with us in 2010, Pe. Caetano was showing early signs of forgetfulness, but we had a good time watching a lot of the World Cup matches together. Caetano was a very good soccer player in his late teens and early adult years. He would play for the village team, with his cassock on, as the Seminary would not allow him to play dressed up in uniform of the team.

In 1964 at the time of celebration of the first mass by Fr. Joe Moniz (Ti Riairo's son) and Fr. Caetano's mass the following year, Ti Riario through his mediation brought Roque and Caetano to speaking terms, which I believe did not last long. But at least Atilia was able to come visiting her mother a few times before her death.

Maria **Aurelia** Moniz Soares (1921-2005, age 84), **Tia** to us, was 25 when she married Remedios Soares. Their house in Curra, was the last house on that road, as beyond that was pure forest. Ti Remedios had a brother who lived in Santemol, Raia, quite far from this location. It would be only a guess on my part, to think that the ti Remedios moved up there just before or after getting married.

They had seven children together: Aida S Cabral, Augusto, Antoneta (Neta), Alcina, Miguel (Miguelinho), Maria das Neves S Noronha and Olavo. Relative to her siblings' families, Aurelia's family had greater financial hurdles to put all the children through education. My mother and Ti Riario and his daughter Carol have done their part in helping the family. In the end the children and the grandchildren have lifted up the family through education and marriage.

Here is an interesting story I like to tell, when one compares the way we grew up in the "good old days" to what the modern generation has. On more than one occasion my brother Heriberto and I were sent to Raia to spend a few vacation days at Tia's house. It was a long walk of approximately 1 hour plus. At our leisurely pace and with all the interruptions along the way – picking a cashew fruit, or stoning a mango tree to get a ripe mango up there- this walk probably was a 2 hour journey. It was a joyful walk and there was never a reason to complain.

With no telephone at either end and the societal trust accepted as a given thing, I believe my parents never worried about the safety of their children. After a stay of a week or so at Tia's place, we came home trudging all the way back, and in the end everybody was happy. Compare this, to today's helicopter parents' behavior.

By the way, in our house, we made do with one bicycle, which was our dad's bicycle. Even in our youth days, the three boys (the older children) would have to plan with dad, to get its use for some special trip to the city or a football game. I don't remember when the second bike finally arrived at our house. Today there is more than one motorized bike or scooter in every household in the village and ownership of a car is more common than not. Bicycles are ridden by older folks, who can still ride them, or by foreigners, either ex-pats or out of state.

Aleixo (Alex or **Alcinho**) Conceição Moniz (1924-2008, age 83) is my godfather. He always had a quiet demeanor, but left a lasting impression in me as being fond of his nephews and family.

I remember that when he came down from Bombay, he would bring one or two baskets of fruit, such as oranges, apples and grapes, which during the Portuguese era, either were not readily available or we could not afford. When I was doing my pre-engineering college studies, it was compulsory to join either the Army or Naval cadets (NCC or national cadet Corps). When after my second year of college, I shared with him that I was dabbling with the idea of joining the Indian Navy, Ti Alcinho told me summarily that with my scholastic abilities, that career was not for me. Since he was himself working in the merchant navy, I took his advice and thus one door was closed.

Alcinho had an unfortunate accident when he was little kid. Supposedly work was going on in the house of making bamboo mats. One day during rosary, his older sister Aurelia, playfully threw a bamboo strip at him, which hit him in one eye, which could not be saved. He lived with this handicap for the rest of his life, and I am sure, it hampered his work opportunities.

Alcinho married Belmira Misquita from Loutulim. The wedding took place in Mumbai. My dad, who was attending the wedding, took me along, as I was his godchild. I was 6 or 7 years old, and I have no recollection of the journey to Mumbai or even the wedding ceremony. But I surely have memories of visiting the Victoria Gardens zoo, the Mumbai Aquarium and I was very fascinated with the street cars or trams, where I couldn't believe my eyes, people would get up or get down the moving vehicle. It also turns out it is the only wedding of my uncles or aunts on dad's side that I attended.

Alcinho and Belmira had four children: Lira M D'Melo (married to Cornel D'Melo), Ralph Moniz (married Rohita), Cecilia M da Silva (married Stephen da Silva) and Kevin Moniz (unmarried).

Lira is a cousin, close to my heart. Now-a-days in conversations among folks of my generation, a wish that is constantly heard, is the hope that our kids will keep in touch with their cousins. Lira has kept in touch on a regular basis, through the years, with all the family members in Goa and elsewhere. I also admire her personality. I make a special mention of Lira (and Carol earlier), because, as I have said elsewhere, I consider some folks amongst us, are more equal than others.

I have a special gratitude to Ti Belmira, who volunteered to advance me a loan for the price of the airline ticket for my first trip to Canada. After initial delays at the Canadian Embassy, my visa papers were expedited, as the school year in Canada had already started.

On my way back from the Canadian Embassy in New-Delhi, with visa papers in hand, I did not even have time to ask my folks in Goa, on how we would round up the funds for the ticket. Ti Belmira figured out I needed money help and she offered it to me. In fact, with this loan facility, I was able to finalize travel matters in Mumbai (through a Mr. Lobo, at Air France), before I went down to Goa for a day, to say goodbye to family and pack up my travel bags.

Alcinho and Belmira moved to Goa, to spend their retirement years in Maina Curtorim. They built a nice bungalow and lived there till a few years after Alcinho's death in 2008. In the interim Belmira put in lot of effort in trying to get back our family property in Sao Jose de Areal. But the task was too much for one person and she bemoaned lack of support from the other Monizes.

Here is a contribution from **Lira (Moniz) d'Mello on Alcinho and Belmira**

My Indelible Memories

Youth is a time of formation, a time when memories are crystallized of people and events, and these slowly but surely form our core. I see myself as blessed to have had amazing parents, a good home environment, life which extended beyond immediate family to include my aunts and uncles and cousins and friends who became family.

Though we were born in Mazagon in Mumbai, my vivid memories take me back to the villages of Curtorim and Loutulim and Raia where we spent our summer holidays. To me, that's where my roots are, as memories come rushing to my mind's eye. Maina in Curtorim, my Dad's home village was a buzzing place of energy and local politics which you could listen in to and get caught up in. Dad's childhood home was just opposite the school and now Church of St. Rita. I remember it always buzzing with conversation and people dropping in as they passed by.

My Dad, Alex, was the fifth of six children and he was the quieter one of his siblings. His childhood was at a more laidback time when things kind of just flowed from one day to another and were not so competitive as they are now; where the village school was not the organized setup it is today. So a lot depended on the support system at home, conversations around a dinner table and on the "bolkanv" (balcony) and if you could lay your hands on books that would have been the teacher. Dad had a playing accident as a child because of which he lost the function of one eye. It affected him but he was not one to complain.

He came to Mumbai as an adult, so in that sense my parents, like so many others from the surrounding areas, were migrants to Mumbai – a city where one could earn a living. Dad started working as an engineer on board ships – a large part of his work life was on ships that did the Mumbai-Goa run. He met my mother, Belmira, through Tio-Joao who was the youngest of the Moniz family and a very popular guy. Dad, the quieter brother, married Mum in Feb 1953 and I was born a year later. My Mum, Belmira Misquita, came from the village of Vanxem in Loutulim.

My mother and father were so complementary to each other in every way. Dad was handsome, a good listener, a good observer and generous to a fault. He drew people to him as they felt relaxed and comfortable in his presence. However, his work took him away from home for days at a stretch, which made Mum the parent who was always around us and cared for our every need. Mum was delicate of constitution, with the most impeccable, creamy skin and she excelled at everything she did. If we, Ralph, Cecy and Kevin and I love music, she inculcated that in us, her detailing of her day via her jottings in her diaries (which is something I am still amazed by), her sewing pretty things for her family – we were always well turned out – thanks to Mum. She was an excellent learner and passed on her love of learning. After her marriage, Mum moved from Goa to Mumbai where they set up home in Nesbit Road, right across St. Anne's Church. Mum did her Teacher training and taught in Rosary School for more than 25 years. They saw to it that we went to the best possible schools in the vicinity.

Mum and Dad together made sure we always had a holiday …. And Goa was the go-to place. I look back on those holidays and those memories always enrich me as we would spend time in many homes – grandparents' homes, aunts, uncles – each visit enriched us as we had close encounters with wonderful family members. I remember long conversations with my aunts, long walks every evening to the "musher" (river bank), trips to the Colva beach over the weekend and umpteen visits to most fascinating people in the village. Those were days of the freshest ever fish, sausages made at home from home reared pigs, mango picking and pickling and jamming from trees on the property. The learning we had through those interactions is crystal clear even today, and brings a prayer to the lips.

I could name and go on naming the people individually but rather this is a time for me, on behalf of my siblings, to salute my parents who listened, who taught us to dream to reach out and love life. Dad, (Tio-Alcinho) and Mum (Tia-Belmira) were exceptional people. They lived by Faith always and always reached out to their own and to their friends and neighbours. Those were times where people were the greatest wealth, and we can proudly say that in that respect, we were very wealthy.

Joao (John) Moniz (1930-2001, age 71) is the youngest of my dad's siblings, and also the only one who was still calling our home his too, till I was ten years old.

He left for Aden in 1953, through assistance from Mr. Joao Francisco Rodrigues, who was the Consul General for Portugal at that place. My dad was a caretaker or the eyes, for the Rodrigues property, which was mainly a cashew farm property, and where we would go to get cashew fruit in the season and from where we got the delicious "niro".

The main juice was extracted by the ancient method of crushing the cashew fruit with bare feet. This juice was then distilled to make the famous Goan cashew Feni and the lighter distillate the Urrak. The fruit remnants after the crushing, were then tied in big mound and the last of the juice collected, called "niro", was the delicious drink, very much in demand.

Joao worked at Cable and Wireless, a British company, and it was the only company he worked for, first in Aden and then in Bahrain. He and his wife Maria **Filomena** Costa (1933-2011, age 81) returned to Goa for good in mid 1960s.

I understand Joao and Filomena were a "couple" from primary school grades (7-10 age), something unheard of, in those days. They got married in late 1950 or early 1960 and Filomena joined him in Aden, where she would give private tuitions to school kids.

They had three boys: Dean (married to Ioona Conceicao), Shailesh (unmarried) and Seville (married to Tina Pereira).

Joao left a lasting negative impression on me as a little lad of 8 or 9. At that time, Joao was the only Moniz family person who was "overseas". He was returning for the first time from Aden, and my expectation was that my uncle would bring me some chocolates, or some other gift. That did not happen. Nada.

To add insult to injury, I would be sent every day or on alternate day to bring him a bottle of Urrak, a less potent cousin of Feni, the famous Goan liquor made of cashew. Each time, after paying for the bottle, there was small change (coins) left, and I was hoping that one day he would let me have it, so that I could go down to the main road and buy some "bhajias", or what we now call pakoras. That did not happen either. No other visiting uncle or aunt, whether coming from nearby or from Mumbai, came empty handed to our house, as far as the kids were concerned.

My disappointment as a kid deprived of his little expectations, has been so intense, that it has influenced in a positive or reverse way, my attitude towards my own nephews and nieces, in doing for them everything and more of what I was hoping to receive from Ti Joao, as a little lad.

I must confess that it has given me lots of pleasure taking gifts of all kinds from Canada, for my siblings and their children in India and deep down, I am sure some of the enthusiasm in showering my nephews and nieces, has been derived from my interaction with Ti Joao. I must thank here my wife Ethel who has been my willing supporter and shopper for the gift giving.

As years went by and we were coming back to Goa on regular visits from Canada, we would take some cheese and other such gifts for Joao and Filomena. As the tables had turned and recognizing that he had failed to do his part for his nephew, Joao was once somewhat apologetic with me, saying that he had been remiss in his duties with his nephews, and in his words "that's not the way we were brought up." I knew what he was alluding to and I did not delve in the matter.

C H A P T E R 9

The MENEZES (GODD) Family

The earliest record that I was able to access is four generations of the Menezes family ancestors going back to Antonio Francisco de Menezes (1758?-?) and his wife Ana Maria de Menezes.

Their son was Aleixo Manoel de Menezes (1793?-) married to Theodesia de Menezes. Their son Antonio Francisco de Menezes married Ana Florinda de Menezes.

Their son Manoel Xavier Rosario de Menezes (1831?-) married Maria Severina Conceição da Cruz, from Borda, Margao. These are my great-grandparents who had eight children of their own: Francisco Xavier, Fr. Joao Piedade Milagres, Fr. Carminho, Idalina (married Joao Francisco Menezes in Macazana), Maria Quiteria (married Romualdo Francisco da Costa in Xhennoibagh, Curtorim), Felicidade (married Sebastiao Veiga of Maina, Curtorim), Lourencinho and Caetaninho.

The stories in this chapter relate principally to **Caetaninho's** family, i.e my mother's father. Caetaninho married Maria Teresa Fernandes and they had eight children of their own, including my mother, who was the eldest. My principal objective is to cover the two generations: my grandparents and their children. The next generation, the grandchildren of my grandparents, is not the subject of this work. I have made an honest effort to pull together material on my uncles and aunt.

155

Ideally, I would have loved to have covered the families of my grandfather's married siblings. Any attempt to do a reasonable job on these families would be laborious and would sidetrack me from the principal focus as mentioned above. A look at the numbers will give the reader an idea of the magnitude of this task:

Caetaninho: Children 8, Grandchildren 19
His 4 Siblings Total: Children 22, Grandchildren 79

The above-mentioned numbers are all from the Menezes or Godd side of the family alone and spread out across the same village, Curtorim. No wonder that in my youth it looked like every second or third person in the village was our cousin. From his mother Conceição da Cruz's side, Caetaninho had four first cousins, (Cruz and Pereira from Solva, Raia); these first cousins had fifteen children of their own - da Cruz, Pimenta Pereira and do Rozario families. These fifteen members became my mother's second cousins.

How much planning went into the planting of the sapling from which Caetaninho's family tree grew? Caetaninho was in the Seminary studying towards priesthood and getting married was not on his mind. Then his brother Lourencinho, a young adult being groomed to be the caretaker of family properties, passed away suddenly. His name was only once mentioned to me by my mother, during all my probing into the family history. My educated guess is that his cause of death is the Spanish flu which had taken many lives in the village around that time.

The family made the decision to pull Caetaninho out of the seminary for him to play the role for which Lourencinho was being groomed. Caetaninho was not happy with his new role in the family, and he was found a few times crying at the base of the tamarind tree, in front of their house, and saying he wished to go back to the Seminary. As time went by, the elders in the family had other plans too for Caetaninho.

His eldest married brother, Francisco Xavier had seven daughters (the youngest being Rosa Maria, I've spoken of already), and the two older brothers were priests. His three sisters had been given in marriage.

Caetaninho was happy with his life of a farmer and part-time musician. By now he was in his early forties and unmarried.

Just imagine this circa 1920. You are the youngest boy in a family of eight children. You are in your early forties and unmarried. Your eldest brother is married and has seven daughters, and the other two brothers are priests. One brother just older to him died as an adult. Your three sisters have been given in marriage. You are happy with your life of farming and part-time musician.

Then a major change was to take place in Caetaninho's life and this is how it has been narrated to me. It was a normal day at work looking after the workers in the rice fields. Your father comes down and tells you, "son we have decided to marry you". The "You" is my grandfather or Xapae to us, who is shocked; he tells his father that he is happy with his single status and is not interested in marriage.

The father tells Xapae that they have already found a bride for him. He has to marry her as his elder brother Francisco Xavier has only daughters and no male heir in the family. What is he to do? He agrees to the family's wishes and marries my grandmother or Xamae (Maria Teresa), a girl some 20 years younger. That was in 1921.

Their first born arrived a year later. The child was a daughter, and that is my mother. There was not too much joy yet in the Menezes household. They would have to wait a year for the much-longed arrival of a boy, Rosario. Xapae and Xamae ended up having eight children of their own, two girls and six boys.

My mother's family Menezes, are converts from **Hindu Desai** clan from Curtorim. My estimate is that the conversion took place in late 1500 or early 1600. When I was growing up in Curtorim, only a handful of Hindu families were left, principally goldsmiths and grocery shop and tea-shop owners. These families lived into three or four small clusters.

All the Hindu families who resisted (forced) conversion by the Portuguese just took their idols or gods and settled across the north bank of the river, where the Muslim ruler at the time was welcoming the fleeing Hindu families.

Interestingly between 1960 and 1970, Curtorim was being serviced by medical General Practitioner, Dr. Camotim, who was not native to Curtorim. Medical needs of the population in adjoining sub-village of Maina were met by Dr. Eloi Figueiredo, who would travel from Loutulim. Later Dr. Fernando Menezes from nearby Santemol, Raia, would take his place.

There is not much information, that is known about the family, prior to my grandfather's generation. Typical of the small-time landlords of the day, the family was paddy rice crop farmers (xetkar). They had modest land holdings where they grew sufficient crop for their family's daily needs and usually some additional quantity which they would sell or exchange to purchase other necessities of life. They were thus the middle class of the day.

The family has had a nickname of "Godd", which stands for juggery. Everybody in the village knew the family as "Godd". Through a hand-me-down story about its origin, I was told that the family owned at one time a small grocery store, and the owner (my great grandfather or great-great grandfather perhaps) would give a piece of juggery to any kid that came to his shop. In those days, a piece of juggery, was as good as a chocolate piece or a bonbon today. They called him "Godda Tiu", or literally "juggery uncle"

Like most households they had coconut palm trees and other fruit trees, such as tamarind, mango, and jackfruit spread through their property. These fruit trees produced enough for the family needs.

When the marriage proposal for my grandmother was accepted, there was the matter of negotiation of dowry. My grandmother's only sibling, the spinster older sister, Leopoldina, whom we called Mauxi, helped to close the deal, by forfeiting her rights to their property. This way, another significant size property was added to the Menezes land holdings. By the way, part of the deal was that Mauxi would move in, with the Menezes family.

The onset World War II resulted in highly reduced imports of rice to Goa. This led to significant rise in price of paddy rice, and the rice growing farmers like our families in Curtorim (the granary of Salcete (Saxticho koddo) were the beneficiaries. Some additional properties were acquired with the extra farm income which provided the necessary financial means towards children's higher education.

At this stage in time, the size of their residence was modest and it reflected their means. With added income and also financial help from the retiring brother priest Pe. Milagres, addition to the existing house almost doubled its size. My grandfather was the principal hand-on person, behind the new construction and he did an excellent job of it.

With the help of word-of-mouth information and supplemented with info from Geni.com, I was able to trace back the family tree to my grandfather's great-grandfather Antonio Francisco de Menezes, (DOB circa 1758). My grandfather's DOB is 1880.

My grandfather, Caetaninho Menezes, (Xapae to his grandchildren) was one of seven siblings, four brothers and three sisters (Appendix). Of the four brothers two became priests, Pe. Milagres and Pe Carminho. The elder brother Francisco Xavier was married and had seven daughters. The family needed a son or a boy, to carry on the family name and the family wealth. That prompted the family to marry my grandfather, who went on to produce eight children of his own.

The three sisters, were geographically spread out within a perimeter of 6 km, when they were given in marriage: Idalina Menezes (Macazana), Maria Quiteria da Costa (Xenabhag in Corjem) and Maria Felicidade Veiga.

Two of Xapae's brothers became priests. Pe. Carminho, I am told was academically the smarter one. His first and only posting was as the Treasurer of the Rachol Seminary. Sadly, he died very young. He tried to separate a fight between two kitchen cooks fighting with knives and in the process received a major knife wound in the leg, which festered and led to his death.

Pe. Milagres, was originally posted in North Goa or Ratnagiri region. The latter part of his career he spent at the Rachol Seminary. It was when he moved back home upon retirement, that addition to the old existing home in Suclem led to the current home, as I have always known it. He died in 1948.

I am proud to say that next two generations (including the current one) of my grandfather's family have excelled in the field of music. I am not surprised about this musical gift in the family, as besides farming, my grandfather's other profession was music. He was part of a local music band and he told me that he often travelled by canoe to places as far as Quepem, to play for weddings and other occasions. He told me that to keep themselves awake, they would munch on pickled tender mango (Cheppni tor). He also gave violin lessons, charging two annas per session.

In Goa, in the Christian villages, it is a common occurrence to have small roadside monuments (locally known as crosses) lining up the roadways. These are erected by folks as a sign of thanksgiving for some favor from God or to placate a dead soul.

It is a custom to have an annual celebration at these religious monuments with singing of litany (ladinh for Portuguese Ladainha) and say rosary or some prayers. I am told that, even after my grandfather had lost his touch with the violin, people would still coax him, (probably more out of respect), to play the violin to accompany the singing of litany and to an educated ear, it would not be the best of violin playing sounds. My memory as a child of these "ladinh" events, was the fun part of it when snacks in the form of homemade sweets and small chunks of coconut meat, were distributed at the end of the ladinh.

Many homes had a custom of having an annual litany to celebrate a special occasion or anniversary to which a few of the neighbors, relations and recognized litany singers would be invited. Another established custom was for the image of our Lady to move from house to house, within a limited number of nearby homes.

Speaking of the violin, my grandfather decided one sweet day to get rid of his violin, as all the children were pursuing higher studies and none of them was living at home or had taken up to playing music. He sold it to their tailor (known as Hadda Francis, or Francis with a beard). In those days the tailor would come to your house to sew men's or women's clothes. There was a rumour, later on, that that the said violin may have been a Stradivarious or at least a violin of high quality.

The irony is that Francis the tailor did not know to play the violin, but he would talk about this precious violin which he had figured was a precious thing. The tailor lived not too far from my house and, other than in the monsoon season, people kept their windows wide open for aeration. I remember hearing him many evenings, practicing to play the violin and the saxophone, and it was rough on us to listen to his playing the music.

Francis, the tailor was one of three established tailors in the village. He was considered to be a good tailor, but was known to be undependable to finish off what he started. At the end of working day, when asked about whether we should expect him to return the next day, his retort would be "see I am leaving my scissors here, and you can surely expect me tomorrow". Guess what! There was no sign of Francis for a few days. He was giving the same tall tale to a few other families, and leaving scissors at each of these houses, and leaving everyone's job unfinished. Maybe it was his way of trying to please everybody or his way of cornering business for himself. And in those times of laid-back living, most people would tolerate this behavior of his.

Xapae was kind of a gentle giant: about 6 foot in height, which is relatively tall within the community, and lean and in good shape physically. Even in his early nineties, before he had a fall in the fields you could see him always walking tall with no walking stick. Upon greeting him, when I was passing him by on the bicycle and he was walking home, he would call out to me to stop, and would share a bonbon or two.

One day in my youth I happened to walk by, when an elderly gentleman Constancio Veiga, with a walking stick, called my Xapae "titiu", which is reserved to address your real uncle. When I got home and asked my mother why Constancio Veiga was calling Xapae titiu. I was shocked to learn Xapae was really his uncle, but looking at the two, you would think the reverse to be true.

Xapae was a hardworking man but also a smart farmer. I understand that he received awards for high paddy rice yield, but he never bragged or talked about it. I never saw him raise his voice within the family or with the workers in his property. He was a father figure not only within his direct and extended family, but he exercised the same role equally well with the tenants (munkars) in his properties, and in turn won respect from everyone around him. In many an occasion, learning that his tenant would get out of societal norm, such as over-drinking liquor, he took on the role of having a calm, supportive, fatherly talk with the offending party, and I am told in most instances he was successful at it, because he had earned their respect.

A good reflection of a person at peace, Xapae could take a nap anytime anywhere. I mean at home or at the base of a tree, enjoying the shade on hot sunny day. I probably inherited this extreme gift from him. He used to say that he could nap any time, as he had a clean conscience and he was always at peace with himself.

I am told that once when in his 70s or 80s he was at church attending mass, he started dosing. A grown-up guy (known to be mentally handicapped) sitting nearby in the pew, landed a knock on his head (kutt) to wake him up. I don't know what was Xapae's reaction, but I am sure he was not amused.

Through his dedication and hard work in farming and managing of the properties, Xapae was a good provider to the family. Unlike his wife, he was rooted in antiquated thinking, and it was his wife who, behind the scene, was pulling him into the new age.

My mother, his eldest child, was a boarder in a convent in Margao and about to complete Grade 3. In those days girls were boarded at a convent, to give little bit of formal education and teach them other domestic trades such as knitting and sowing. He went there and pulled her out of school, because in his thinking, she had had enough of formal education and "girls don't need to study too much".

It kind of surprises me, about Xapae's thought process. He had, by the standards of the day, a good basic education from the Seminary school (geographically and conveniently a "go to" school for boys of families who could afford to send them there). On the contrary, my grandmother had no formal education, and signing her name was the only thing she was able to write.

Maria (Fernandes) Menezes, (Xamae to her grandchildren), who had the vision, determination and drive to guide her sons to higher education in Goa and outside Goa. Xapae's input was not there as he did not see any value in his boys pursuing higher education. My mother told me that she heard Xapae often complaining, and saying to his wife "Look at this woman; I don't understand why she is spending all this money and what is she trying to achieve with all this education for the boys." But thankfully he did not stop her from her journey of higher education for her sons, who embraced her dreams for them. I believe my mother, who did not benefit from her mother's penchant for her sons' higher education, made it her mission to facilitate higher education for all her children (4 boys and 3 girls). College /University education for girls was still relatively new at the time.

Xapae was a hardworking man with no vices such as smoking or drinking. He was a man with a very good heart and love of the family, a good man and a decent man. He was highly respected by everybody but he did not get himself involved in other people's affairs, fairly easy thing to get into in the day, when people looked up to you.

I have been told that that when Xapae died, Dr. Camilo Severino Rodrigues, an influential man in the village and the first village Sarpanch (head of the village) came to pay him his last respects. His words were "It is not my style to visit a home when somebody dies. But he deserves it, as there are no more people like him left in this world."

Xapae's major shortcoming was that he did not have the vision or could not bring himself to accept the reality that higher education was what would change this family from a middle class, to what turned out to be, at one point, one of the most educated and accomplished families in Goa. Here I am referring to the combined accomplishments of his children, grandchildren, and his nephews. I am told that Xapae had no interest in keeping tabs on where his sons were or their educational and professional achievements.

For example, I never heard Xapae take interest in our educational or sports activities, when my brothers, sisters and I, being the eldest of his grandchildren, were all pursuing college or university studies and achieving good to excellent grades. The fact that all seven children from the household were pursuing college /university education was in itself a new trend.

Xamae on the other hand was showing so much pride and encouragement towards us. Xamae made it a point to know and remember all that was happening with us. For that matter we heard from some uncles more than once, that Mana's children in their youth were the pride and joy for both on the Menezes and Moniz side. My mother being the eldest of her siblings was called "mana" by all her brothers and sister.

When my brothers and sisters were heading to college, Xamae very much wished one of us to become a medical doctor. I am only guessing that she probably wanted to have a doctor in the family not only to attend to family, but also because, in those days, a doctor in family meant great prestige.

On more than one occasion Xamae tried guiding me towards medicine. But my brother Heriberto and I became engineers. To this date I feel that she would be a little more contented, if I had become a doctor. Well Xamae had to wait a little longer as two of my uncle Constancio's sons, Edgar and Noel and uncle Jose's daughter Natasja became doctors, and that must have pleased her a lot.

My mother's youngest brother Jose, had innately high interest in and knowledge of the farm animals and fruit trees and everything related to the farm. Before he left for Portugal to do his Veterinary Medicine, he had a conversation with Xamae, wherein he offered to stay back, to help Xapae in managing the farms, as Xapae was worrying that none of his sons was there to take over the management of the properties.

Xamae, placed her hand on his head, and told him "No, you proceed for your higher studies. Education gives you knowledge. It is enough that I have suffered for lack of education and the resulting ignorance." That is Xamae's vision of education for her children.

Xapae and Xamae's 8 children gave them 20 grandchildren and 40 great grandchildren. Through Xapae's 4 married siblings there were 20 nephews and 72 grandnephews. Bringing this down to the personal level and make it more relatable, this means I am one of 20 first cousins and amazingly one of 92 second cousins, on the side of Xapae and his siblings alone.

In this era of virtual reality, if we could have a Menezes family reunion today, I can only imagine my grandparents feeling an overwhelming pride and sense of fulfillment seeing all this highly educated progeny. They would include scientists, politicians, priests, holders of high public office, medical doctors, engineers, musicians, teachers, accountants, IT professionals, entrepreneurs. Most importantly I feel they have turned out to be good and decent people, contributing for the betterment of the societies in which they live. To me it is also heartening that for the most part the descendants have not forgotten the old family bonds and still keep in touch.

Xamae was a petite lady, endowed with indescribable qualities. I am amazed with Xamae, a woman, whose ability to write was limited to signing her name, and who still had the wisdom to guide her sons towards their educational dreams, and great achievements in public and scientific fields. Xamae was the support and guiding light to my mother in all aspects of life, ranging from her married life challenges, to financial management and to the education of her children. Her nieces, some of whom had been given in marriage at a very young age leaned on Xamae, their aunt, as their advisor and as the shoulder to cry on.

Xamae was 20 year junior in age to Xapae, and early on in the marriage she had to adjust living in a joint-family household, with much older brother-in-laws. She had a natural temperament for it. Xamae also adapted to changing times and I noticed that quite often she was ahead of my own adaptation to changing thinking, even long after I was in Canada. The only way to describe it, is amazing. She was versed in political correctness, long before the rest of the world adopted it. Without ever giving a hint of interference, she would have a one-on-one chat about her own family and marriage with her daughters-in-law, not intimidated by their much higher formal education. Supposedly her advice was down to earth and laced with common sense.

One of my early confirmations of Xamae's modern and practical thinking happened in 1970. It was the week that her husband, Xapae, had died and she asked me whether I was going for the dance, that weekend. She had known about the dance event and that I had planned to go for it, as the band leader was her nephew (Floriano Sardinha) and he was bringing his band from Mumbai for the occasion. Besides playing soccer, attending a dance was the most important entertainment for us, in the days of non-existence of TV.

I was shocked because the local custom was that one would not go for a dance for at least three months after the passing of a close family member such as your grandfather, and from all the people, I was not expecting Xamae, his wife, to ask me the question. My response was "what are you saying Xamae; are you out of your mind? Xapae just passed away last week; what will people say?"

Xamae's immediate response was: "I know how much you love going to a dance and on top of it Floriano is playing. I know how much you loved your grandfather. I will handle what people may say. You go for the dance." I went home and told my mother about it, and since she did not say anything to the contrary, I went for the dance and enjoyed myself.

Compare this incident to what happened when my dad's mum (avó) passed away just a few years earlier. I was 17 years old. We were instructed to put even the radio away. In those days, the latest in English and Portuguese music was broadcast only on select days and for one hour or two. For us, the young people, it was the only amusement. The radio was put away in a trunk. When the time came for that select time slot, I tried surreptitiously to listen to the radio music, with my head in the trunk. And I got caught in the action by an aunt of mine. I received a good tongue lashing for my action, and it does not need further description.

On the matter of Xapae's funeral there is another important story to tell. It was and still is the custom for the wake or visitation of the dead body to be in your own home; the funeral consists of the body being led in procession (sometimes to the accompaniment of a local music band) directly to the church for the religious services prior to moving to the cemetery.

As time was nearing for the body to leave the house, probably under the influence of seeing my mum and uncles and aunt in tears, I experienced a huge burst of tears and crying. It was so overwhelming that I cried through the journey to the church (say 15 minutes), during church ceremony and burial. I just could not stop crying. I have not had such an experience either prior to this or after. I loved my Xapae but was it so deeply?

Xamae, I guess, observed what was going on with me and kept it to herself. That is, until my uncle, Jose Menezes, who was already in Canada, came down for the first time after thirteen years out of Goa in 1970 soon after Xapae's death. I had been close to this uncle writing him letters regularly from age nine. I had applied to various Universities in Canada to pursue further studies and I had got admission in a few of them. However my uncle was trying to sponsor me for landed immigrant status, now called permanent resident (PR) status.

So Xamae tells my uncle "you have to take him to Canada. Do you know how much he loved your father and how much he cried at his funeral?" I am glad all those tears were not in vain! Fortunately for me, my uncle was already convinced on helping me migrate to Canada, in particular for his gratitude for being the regular family link all those years, when even his siblings were not as regular in writing to him. I must mention that my uncle on his way to Goa, travelled through Hong-Kong and felt he should reward me in a special way with a gold watch (Enicar), which I passed on to my sister Violet, when I was departing to Canada in September 1971.

I must narrate an amusing incident of either political correctness or just what Xamae was. One day my sister Blanche and her husband Placido, who already had two children aged 10 and 8, decided to play a little joke on Xamae. So Placido walks in front to announce to Xamae that Blanche is pregnant again. Xamae with a straight face congratulates them and says she is so happy for them. Once they were gone, she turns to my aunt and says "why do they want more children now?" I remember Xamae for having this kind of sense of humor!

My mother Maria Florinda, was 21 when she married my dad in 1942. Florinda was her great-grandmother's name, but soon after she received the name, family members started commenting that it was more of a "lower" class name. My mother happened to have a (second) cousin of similar age, Marcelina Cruz in Borda, Margao. Thus, **Marcelina** it was, and that's how the whole world knew my mother, even though they never changed her real name.

Being the eldest, her siblings called her Mana, which translates as sister in Portuguese, but in reality in Goa, the term was reserved for the older sister. For a boy it would be mano. When my mother was getting married her youngest brother Jose was only two and half years old and my mother was a second mother to him. I understand that on the day of the wedding, he was hanging on to her, begging her not to go away.

The first son and second in line of siblings, is **Fr. Rosario** (DOB 1922). He became a priest, and was known for his piety and rectitude. It was his habit to make regular visits to all his parishioners, which endeared him to his flock. Every church he was posted to, he would exhort his parishioners to be on time for the Sunday mass, as he would have the front door of the church closed when the mass started. It is quite common in Goa to see enough people standing outside the main door whilst attending the Sunday mass. Jokingly these are known as "standout catholics".

In the family, everybody, including my mother, looked up to Patiu (from Portuguese padre tio, uncle priest) with respect and for his guidance. In fact my mother kept me with him for one year, when he was posted as Chaplain in Sarzora, Chinchinim, and I benefitted surely from his strict discipline. I was 7-8 years old then.

As time passed on, my siblings were slowly getting discontented with Patiu for his self centered behavior and open favouritism towards his brother Carminho and his family. The latter may in part have to do with the fact that uncle Carminho was cajoled by Patiu to move back home from Mumbai, where he was comfortably employed at a Bank, with a promise that he would inherit more of the property than his brothers.

Today (2024) Patiu is 101 old and is a resident of the South Goa Clergy home. Lots of his old parishioners still trek to this place for confession. Other than failing eye sight and some parts of mental abilities, he appears to be in good health.

Carmo Menezes (known to everyone as Carminho), is the third child in the family. He was working at a Bank in Mumbai, until he was coaxed to come back to Curtorim to help Xapae, who was getting on in years and they needed to have one of the sons take over the day-to-day management of the family's properties. Unlike his brothers he had not pursued college level studies, but had secured a good job at the bank. In Mumbai, his older cousin Esperança, a tough lady, was minding the household chores for him and Esperança's nephew Rosarinho Sardinha (he worked at the Mumbai Central post office) and later on, his brother Floriano Sardinha (who would go on to become a great musician and band leader). These were the sons of Esperança's sister Rosa Maria.

I understand that Carminho's brother Pe. Rosario (Patiu), took the initiative to convince him to leave his job in Mumbai and come down to Goa, sweetening the pot with a promise that Patiu would bequeath to him his and his sister Albertina's shares of the family properties.

The move turned out well for Carminho and his family. For a short while, before the end of Portuguese era, he was the regedor of the village (something like justice of peace). He also became an entrepreneur as property developer. He died at age 87 in 2013, a year before my mother as a result of a car accident and ensuing complications, including diabetes.

Carminho was known to have a love for good food, in particular for fresh fish, and he was known to go into town, specifically to get it. I also remember him always having something to criticize about meals not prepared by his wife. He appreciated us visiting him, in particular once he became house bound. But he did not know to show that appreciation in words.

Carminho's wife Carolina, has a special place in my heart. Every time we would go to say good-bye to Xamae and others at my grandparents' house, before we traveled to Mumbai for our Engineering studies, she always made it a point to gift us some pocket money. This gesture of giving some pocket money was very rare in those days. In the days when extra money or pocket money was hard to come by, this gesture was really appreciated and has not been forgotten by me to this day.

Albertina Menezes is the fourth of my mother's siblings. She was a spinster and took upon herself the role of being the home manager for Xamae and uncle Lourencinho who was a teacher by profession but a bachelor staying at home. Besides being the care giver to her mother, Xamae, she was always ready to help with caring for nephews and nieces and even grandnephews and grandnieces.

Ti Albertina doted on her nephews and the young ones of extended family; in return they loved her to no end. Within the family she was the most generous one, whether feeding us as soon as we arrived there or with gifts of money or jewelry. I like to say she ran an "import-export" business when it came down to cash flow in her own hands, even though she did not have a definite source of income herself.

From the support payments from her brothers, including Lourencinho, to meet the household expenses (Xamae, Lourencinho and herself), she budgeted out of this cash flow both for the household expenses and her never ending needs for gifts to nephews and others. In later years, as the needs multiplied, I came to know through my mother, that besides the physical gifts we would take for her from Canada, she would dearly love to receive some cash gifts, not for her own expenses, but to enable her to make gifts to her nephews and nieces.

Ti Albertina had such a generous heart and "large" hand, that before her final days arrived, she had already distributed all her jewelry and things of value. It turned out that she gifted a gold cross, to a nephew visiting from abroad; it turns out, that gold cross was kept with her for "safekeeping" by Patiu. Patiu was not amused and in fact livid with her, once he found out about it, after the fact.

Ti Albertina did not have a match, when it came to cooking, whether it was daily cooking or cooking for special occasions. With respect to my siblings, she has had a big role in my sisters, in particular Blanche, excelling in our typical village cooking and thus kind of passing down those unwritten recipes to us. Our mother's cooking abilities did not match ti Albertina's and we soon learnt not to come home and sing praises of our aunt's cooking.

Ti Albertina had a problem with eye vision. The eye doctor suggested to the family that reading books may strain her eye sight, which resulted in her not receiving much formal education. Fairly early on in life, the operation on the one eye was not successful. Thus, she lived many years with good vision just from one eye. With age, the vision from the second eye kept deteriorating to the point that less than two years before her death, she lost vision completely.

This was a real shock to her and she did not know how to handle it. I understand she would be simply terrified to move around or even take a seat when guided to it. Ti Albertina had a close relationship with Blanche, and they had an understanding she would move in with Blanche if and when she might be incapacitated. In addition, my mother would also be company to her. On this basis, Ti Albertina moved in with my sister.

Unfortunately, the family, i.e. Patiu, felt that she belonged in her own parental house. This was to address the gossipers in the community saying "look she had to move in with her niece, as her own family is not willing to attend to her".

Even though there was full time attendant to look after her, ti Albertina was lonely, without a family member to give her company, suffered unnecessarily towards the end and did not live much longer. Many within the family believe their most beloved sister and aunt deserved a better end. She passed away at age 78, approximately six months before her brother Francisco Xavier, just a year younger to her, and who, upon retirement, used to come down to Goa to enjoy her company and her cooking.

(Dr.) Francisco Xavier de Menezes is my uncle, whom I had the least time to get to know. He left Goa by ship for Portugal in 1951, when he was 22 years old and I was only 4. And when I got the opportunity to know him, I must say, I was taken up by his personality, which was quite distinct from all other uncles of mine. On our (Ethel and I) first visit to Portugal, we stayed ti FranXavier and tia Angela and at that time I spent some time individually with tiFranXavier. He was a consummate story teller and had lots of interesting stories from his days in Timor, Angola and Portugal.

I had plans to sit down with him and listen to more of his interesting stories when he had tentatively accepted our invitation to come to Canada in May 2006, to attend my daughter Celine's wedding. It was not meant to be, as he cancelled his trip for medical reasons and he passed away in October of the same year of heart failure, when he was on a leisurely bike ride with his son-in-law. He had lived with type-2 diabetes from relatively young age. He took care of it, but also knew to be a "bon vivant".

The story I heard of his early formal education in Goa, is that he had joined the Medical School in Goa, but left the medical studies as one professor who disliked him, made his life difficult. He did matriculation and completed a Diploma in Accounting from Delhi University. All this time his heart was on going to Portugal. But Xamae resisted, for various reasons, including financial.

The opportunity came about, when a neighbor in Curtorim, who was on vacation from Mozambique (then a Portuguese colony) and was holding a

his cap, but no doubt for the Menezes family. His first posting after joining the Department was in Diu, followed by Pilerne and Margao or South Goa.

During his years in-charge of South Goa, he facilitated family, friends and Curtorim villagers to avail of coconut tree saplings and mango plant graft cultivars.

Constancio was the first in the family, to pursue his studies in India, when Goa was still governed by Portugal. He received his degree in Agriculture from Belgaum University. I understand that on his trips back to Goa, he would bring along some cow tongues, highly appreciated at home, but probably not of much sale value in Belgaum.

Constancio has the distinction of being the first family member to own a car in Goa within our Menezes or Moniz families. It was a white Volkswagen Beetle (Bug) bought in 1961, from a departing Portuguese military officer.

I paid him a visit in February 2019. At this time he was spending most of his time on bed, but came out to see me, with the help of his care-giver. He recognized me promptly and was happy to see me. His memory was not all there, but each instant I would mention the name of my sister Blanche, he would say "Blanche is a very good person". He passed on in December of that year at age 87.

Lourenço Menezes (1937-), also known fondly as "professor", was Elementary School teacher. To this end he completed a Portuguese teacher's course "Normal" and prior to that he also completed the matriculation. The latter came in handy with the change of teaching medium from Portuguese to English, after Goa was no longer Portugal's territory and became part of India.

My early memory of him was that, around age 6, I was sent to him for help with my studies. I am not sure whether I needed it or not, but my mother probably wanted to keep me busy with more of studies and less play time. He did not seem to have much patience teaching me, and I was subjected to his discipline of knocks on my head with his knuckles (kutt). By the way this kind of disciplining was not frowned upon, in those days.

Anyways, one day, I guess, I had enough of it, and complained about it to Ti Carminho, who, I can picture even today, was busy getting feed ready for the buffalos. He gave him a good tongue lashing and Lourencinho dropped his discipline of knuckle knocks. Looking back in time, I am surprised he even had to discipline me on my study shortcomings. I remember being always a good student from the Primary school days through to my Engineering studies, and my grades are a proof of it.

Most of his postings as a school teacher were within reasonable distances, and he could get there and back daily on bicycle. His presence in the Suclem household and his financial help to Xamae and Albertina were mutually supportive.

I believe Lourencinho's intellectual capabilities were much greater than required for his teaching job. According to me he would have had great success in a research type of a job, where attention to detail is a desired commodity.

In the days of communication by letter writing, Lourencinho would occasionally write to us in the name of Xamae and Albertina, in response to my letters, giving lots of family news. I can say he was proud of successes he could see in his older nephews and nieces. Even though Xamae's thinking was very current and broad minded, Lourencinho would on occasions try to use Xamae to impart on us his conservative ideas.

One such instance was, when he learnt that I was a regular blood donor in Canada, he did not believe I was cut out for it. It befell on Xamae to advise me that I should discontinue my blood donation, as, according to them, I was too weak to do it. I respectfully nodded, but I am glad I continued with my regular blood donations (50+ donations).

Other than Albertina, I believe Lourencinho has done more than his share for a few of his nephews and nieces in Goa, in terms of both moral and financial help. In the old joint family type situations, bachelor uncles made such sacrifices not only out of duty, but also in expectation that in their old age they will in turn be looked after by the younger generation.

Jose Menezes (1939-) is the youngest of my mother's siblings and as referred to it earlier, with whom I developed over time the greatest bond. Our age difference is seven years, but in early stages of growing up, that age difference looked larger than today. Being in Canada we have continued to be good friends, sharing family bonds and soccer stories.

Before my uncle left Goa for Portugal my memories of him range from him carrying his rooster for cock fights with neighboring friends' roosters, his friend Juju Lourenco coming over, giving me a ride on his bicycle, and him coming over to our house on Sunday to take me to church, and may be back to his house too, at Xapae's instructions. At one of these occasions, when he started combing my hair, he found that I had a wound on the top my head, which had not been attended to, and I remembered that he was scolding my mother that they were not looking after me properly.

The head wound was probably a result of a stone from some kid landing on my head, as we were throwing stones on trees to pick a ripened fruit such as mango, tamarind or applets (bhoram). I had not told my mother about it for fear of being punished. The general rule in our household was not to bring home the little fights or problems between neighborhood friends. To my mother it was never other kids' faults, and the blame stopped at my feet.

Ti Jose's great love was animals, in particular their herd of buffalos and his roosters. When he would return home after couple of weeks or a month away at school (Lyceum), he would go straight to the backyard, visiting his animals even before he entered the house. To satisfy his love of animals he decided to pursue Veterinary medicine and left Goa for Portugal in 1958. Xamae would have wished he had gone for human medical studies, and therefore she was keen on one of my siblings pursue that route.

At this stage, my grandfather was more concerned about one of his sons joining him to help manage the family properties, including the rice fields and two-yearly crops in some of them and less about their higher education. Jose being the youngest of the sons was ready to sacrifice his desire to pursue the veterinary medicine, and confided in his mother about his intention. His mother's retort was "it is enough that I have suffered because of lack of education; you pursue your education dreams."

In Portugal, he was not happy with the level of instruction at the University of Lisbon, and after one year there he got himself admitted in the University of Perugia, Italy, for the same line of studies. Upon graduation, instead of working in the veterinary field, he decided to apply his medical knowledge to research at Institute Pasteur, in Paris, France. Money was tight even with some financial support coming from his brother Francisco Xavier. Early on in Paris, before he received his scholarship funds from Institute Pasteur, arrangement was made via guarantee in Goa, to have some funds conveyed to Jose via an order of nuns in Goa who had a presence in Paris. I understand Jose paid back all the funds to both his brother and the nuns.

Even through the times when he was not that comfortable financially, Jose never forgot to send annually, around Christmas time, some gift money for his nephews and nieces. This unique gesture made a deep and lasting impression in me. I followed his example once I migrated to Canada, towards my siblings and their children, mainly the latter. In 1971, even when I was struggling as a student, and would mentally convert every dollar spent into rupees, my first remittance home was $25 ($150 in today's dollars), this sum increasing as time went on. Ethel and I continued with this annual gesture of sending money, to our nephews and nieces, until they joined the work force themselves.

After two years at the Institute Pasteur, Jose migrated to Canada and did his Ph.D. in Microbiology at the University of Ottawa. That was in 1971, a year after he got married to Guilhermina Gouveia and the same year I arrived in Canada to do my Master of Engineering at Carleton University, Ottawa. I came to Canada as landed immigrant or permanent resident, thanks to the sponsorship from Jose.

I arrived in Ottawa approximately three weeks late for the school year and I struggled in my studies in the first term. The first shock to my system, and I remember it so well, was experiencing a sinking feeling like I had never felt before. Three days after my arrival to Ottawa Jose and Guilhermina, departed for Sweden, where Jose was going to do his post-doctoral research.

I had a scholarship from Carleton University, covering fees and boarding and lodging. Jose was wise enough to know that I would need some funds for various supplementary expenses. Before he departed for Sweden, he gave me $2,000 towards that end. When I started working and wanted to pay him back, he was suggesting that it was not necessary for me to pay him back. If I so desired, I could similarly help somebody else in our family. In spite of his magnanimous gesture, I insisted I should pay him back.

Jose returned to Canada, after two years and took up a research-cum teaching position at University of Montreal, initially with the title of Scholar of Government of Canada. Through this denomination he was receiving funding from the federal government agency, allowing him to concentrate more on research and less on teaching, whilst allowing the University to absorb him over time into full time teaching staff.

Jose's research was in tumour biology and immunology carried out at the St. Justin Hospital, attached to the University of Montreal. At the University of Montreal he was first a position of Scholar of Government of Canada and later as Scholar of Province of Quebec. Being funded by the government agencies allowed him to concentrate more in research and less in teaching duties. After many years, the University slowly absorbed him as a full teaching faculty member (Professor in medical and science streams) in the fields of Immunology, microbiology and virology. He retired as Director of of the Department of Immunology, microbiology and virology.

For many years I would occasionally pull his leg, asking him when his Nobel Prize would arrive. Well, he knew the value of his research and winning the Nobel Prize was achievable in his mind, even though he did not say it himself. He had done research at Institute Pasteur and knew two of the scientists who were awarded the Nobel Prize, soon after he left the Institute. Again, his post-doctoral work was at the Karolinska Institute in Sweden, where they decide on Nobel Prize Winners for medicine, would have given him that touchy feeling for the Nobel Prize.

When he was retiring from the University position in 2017, there was a crowning glory bestowed upon Dr. Jose Menezes, by the Canadian scientific community by inducting him into the Canadian Academy of Health Sciences. This is the highest honor granted to Canadian scholars and obviously it is reserved for a very select group of individuals. He is still the first and only person of Goan origin to be inducted into the Canadian Academy of Health Sciences. If I may add, I am proud to be the nephew of such a man.

CHAPTER 10

The PEREIRA Family

At the start of this chapter, I will admit that my knowledge of my in-law families, the Pereira family (my father-in-law Dr. Francis Xavier Pereira) and the Menezes family (my mother-in-law Phoebe Blenure Menezes) may not be as good as that of my ancestors from the Moniz and Menezes families.

A good deal of the stories about the Pereiras is derived from my many face-to-face sit-down chats with ti Marta (the youngest of the F.X. Pereira siblings, Marta Pereira) and a few cousins. To compensate, I have received a better feed-back from a few of Pereira side cousins than the Moniz/Menezes sides.

Having said that, with all the research work and time I have put into it, I have become a pretty good source of information on Pereira (F.X. Pereira) and Menezes (Phoebe Menezes) families and their ancestry. Most of it is included in this book.

Marta was unmarried and lived in the Margao house, with her parents, Epifanio Pereira and Maria Aurora (Valeriano Barreto) Pereira. Also part of the household were Epifanio's unmarried sister Etelvina and upon his retirement, his brother Mgr. Aniceto Pereira, known to the family as Pati, which is a short form of Padre Tio in Portuguese.

Marta had an uncanny capacity of remembering how any of the near and far relations was connected to our families. She remembered all the important dates, pertaining to various generations of her family members, including births, first holy communion, marriage. I was very impressed with her amazing memory. I tried enquiring about this amazing memory of ti Marta, with one of her older nephews, who knew her well. His interesting but funny response was that "there are a few spinsters around like her, who have this kind of memory."

On my many trips from Canada to India on average every 2 to 3 years over a period of forty years that I knew ti Marta, I would probe into the Pereira family relationships and other news. And I don't remember Marta ever not having an answer to my enquiries. After her death, it dawned upon me that her conversations with me never touched on related stories, or gossip or conjectures.

Now that some, and I repeat some, of the genealogy information is available through the Geni.com website, I can confirm that I have yet to come across any ancestral link that is at odds with the information handed down to me by Ti Marta. On the other hand, she provided me with data, not yet available through geni.com website. Thank you Ti Marta!

The Pereira family hail originally from the seaside village of **Benaulim**, approximately 11 km from Margao, normally a 20-minute drive. My search through various pertinent documents, tells me that they moved to Margao, approximately 1870- 1875, when the first part of the Margao residence was constructed.

It was Joao Batista **ANICETO** Jose Pereira (1833-1878) and his wife Maria Cristina **JOSEFINA** da Cunha (1848-1925) who made the move from Benaulim and put down their roots in Margao, at the location where their descendants were to live till circa 2005. I deduct that Aniceto and his brother Sebastiao Vicente Pereira came to a fair division of their ancestral Benaulim property, with the latter buying out Aniceto.

With the proceeds of his share of the Benaulim property, Aniceto and his wife Josefina bought a plot and built the original part (back side of the final structure) of the Margao house. Aniceto and Cristina ended up being the sole proprietors of the property, in the Tembim subdivision of Margao.

The Pereira residence is just 5 minutes walking distance from today's city centre, and on the main street bringing vehicular traffic from the north of Goa to city centre and proceeding further south. On the other side of the street are the Hospicio or the old, main city Hospital, and the Margao city Catholic cemetery, where you will find two monuments holding the mortal remains of some of our ancestors.

As part of the Benaulim property division, Aniceto's brother, Fr. Francisco Xavier Pereira, (1844-1913, age 70), ended up with a small land plot, known as Boglampedda, situated in Benaulim with its south border adjoining Varca village. This property, was willed to Mgr. Aniceto Pereira, by Fr. F.X. Pereira. It would produce enough rice, coconuts, chillis for family's needs for the year. This property was then inherited by daddy, Dr. F.X. Pereira and it was sold in 1964 for INR 17,000. These funds were entrusted to Marta, for the household expenses.

Fr. Francisco Xavier Pereira, was ordained at age 23 and spent close to 25 years as a missionary in Calicut, Kerala. When he returned to Goa, he took up the chaplaincy of the Monte Chapel, on top of hill opposite the residence and behind the Margao Hospicio complex. This lasted approximately another 25 years.

The chapel has a long history with the residents of Margao city, in particular during the Lent season and Good Friday.

As is the custom in many predominantly catholic villages in Goa, including all the villages our families are connected with, the Lent season was a busy time for the chapel. The lent celebration would culminate with the service at the Monte Chapel in Margao, with the Good Friday re-enactment of the Crucifixion of Jesus Christ. This service has a deep, spiritual meaning to catholic population in Goa. It is always a 3 pm service and most devotees make an effort to attend it.

Besides the special services during the Lent season, Sunday mass was celebrated on regular basis. Over the years many weddings and baptisms were also celebrated at this Chapel.

Besides the Monte Chapel, the only other structures at the plateau site were the buildings of the TB Hospital. This location for the TB Hospital must have been chosen for being on the top of the hill, and thus not only airy, but also secluded enough from the larger population.

Fr. Francisco Xavier Pereira left a will drafted in 1895, It is through this will that I was able to connect Aniceto and Fr Francisco Xavier to their brother Sebastiao Vicente. Interestingly, also mentioned in the will is the name of their brother Anselmo Pereira, whose whereabouts at the time of the will had been unknown for over 25 years. If it was not for this will, this part of the Pereira family, would go unmentioned by me.

Even though Marta spoke to me about the Boglampedda property in Benaulim, she never mentioned Sebastiao Vicente's side of the family tree. My guess is that she did not mention it, because this was the inherited property of Fr. Francisco Xavier Pereira, who through his will gifted it to his nephew Mgr. Aniceto (Pati), on condition that he would offer masses for his soul, upon his death, and also would take care of his own sister Etelvina. It is my recent search through the old family property papers or wills (handed down from ti Marta), which brought to light the existence of Sebastiao Vicente. This is an example of Ti Marta's attitude of sharing family stories with me: if I did not ask a pointed question on a specific topic, she would not go there, even though in this case, in my mind, this information was very important, and she would have known I would have been very much interested in it.

I mentioned earlier that there are two monuments holding the mortal remains of some of our ancestors.

One crypt is a standing monument, located within the roofed structure, up front and containing the remains of Aniceto Pereira's spouse Josefina da Cunha Pereira, Fr. Francisco Xavier Pereira and Marta Pereira (her bones transferred in 2018). The writing on the monument says "Jazigo da Familia Pereira, Aqui jazem os restos mortaes de Pe. Francisco Xavier Pereira ……e de Josefina da Cunha-Pereira". Translation: Family Tomb of Pereira Family, Here rest the mortal remains of Fr. Francisco Xavier

Pereira ……and of Josefina da Cunha-Pereira". Now Marta's mortal remains are also resting in this crypt.

The other monument is a tombstone located outside the roofed structure near the cemetery wall along road towards the hill. This crypt was dedicated by Dr. F.X. Pereira and Marta Pereira in honor of Mgr. Aniceto Pereira (Pati) and to hold his bones. Ti Aniceto's (Daddy F.X Pereira's brother) wish was for his bones to be transferred to one of the Pereira family monuments. At the request of Ti Aniceto's children, not long before her passing, ti Marta gave her blessing for Aniceto's bones to be placed in the same tombstone as Pati's.

The writing on the Pati's tombstone says "A Inolvidavel Memoria de Mgr. Aniceto M.J. Pereira, 16-10-1871 …30-11-1961, Tributo dos seus sobrinhos Dr. F.X. Pereira e Marta Pereira. Translation: To the Unforgettable Memory of Mgr. Aniceto M.J. Pereira, 16-10-1871 …30-11-1961, Homage from his nephews Dr. F.X. Pereira and Marta Pereira". On this monument there is also a headstone with Portuguese inscription, whose translation is "I am the resurrection and the life; he who believes in me will live even if he dies, and everyone who lives and believes in me will never die. If you are good, Jesus will give you eternal rest". I believe this inscription comes from John 11.25.26.

The original residence built by Aniceto and Josefina, underwent major upgrading and additions in 1896, under the tutelage of Fr. Francisco Xavier, upon his return from his mission work in Calicut. It was further modernized with new tiling, in 1938, in preparation of Pati's home coming upon his retirement.

The prime urban location of our residential property became a desirable spot for further development, just like a few of nearby residences. A six-storey L-shaped building, has replaced our old residential home.

The construction of the new building took approximately 5 years to complete and was ready for occupation in 2011. It is a multi-use building, with shops on the ground floor and the first floor, office units on the first, second and third floors, and living quarters (apartments) on fourth, fifth and sixth floors. The longer side (Wing A) is facing the main street and the shorter side (Wing B) is facing the Bernardo Costa Road. The new mixed used building is now known as **Pereira Plaza**. I hope this naming of the building will perpetuate the Pereira family name for many more years to come.

The original idea of some type of development of our property, had been discussed and proposed, a few years prior to the actual construction, by a different developer. Marta, who had lived in this place her whole life, requested daddy, Dr. F.X. Pereira, and mummy, Phoebe Pereira, that they undertake such a development after her death, and the request was granted.

After the deaths of mummy and daddy, and when a new development proposal was brought forward by a different developer, Reliance Builders, Marta agreed to move to a temporary place until the project was completed. This move was tough on Marta who told me she was doing it with a "heavy heart".

Marta was a smart lady and I believe that she agreed for the redevelopment on our property, because she was getting older and she was more interested in looking after the interest of her nieces who were all non-residents of Goa (Marjorie in Mumbai, Yvonne in the USA, and Ethelwyn and Maria Aurora in Canada). She could take good care of her nieces' interests when she was alive. She was perfectly right and, in the end, as per expectations, it all ended well for the nieces and their families.

Marta was also comfortable going through this major upheaval because she had her nephew Cesar Menezes (Ofelia's son) giving her both moral support and dealing with all matters related to her move. Cesar Menezes did a very commendable job, in negotiations on family's behalf with the developer, and in my opinion always kept uppermost our interests (of his cousins) and resisted bending to the developer's advances, for his own benefit. For example, when the developer tried to lump Marta's share of 1/24 with F.X. Pereira's 20/24, Cesar and Marta were adamant against it, and negotiated for Marta to get her own apartment, and that too on the second floor (B-101 on Wing B). We are very thankful for Caesar's services.

Once, when I sat down with Caesar discussing matters related to the new development, I happened to mention, that F.X and Phoebe's children, had a sentimental attachment to the Pereira residence. Caesar's off the cuff response was "Oh, I have more sentimental attachment to this house than they do". Knowing what I know now, I agree with Caesar that Ofelia's, Julieta's and Clarissa's children did in fact have a sentimental attachment to the house, at least as long as their grandmother, whom they loved very much, was still alive. Let us not also forget that some of them were born in that house.

During the construction of the structure, Marta spent five years in a rented place nearby. In her own words, she was also blessed that a Fr. Godinho, from the Pilar Society with an office close by, would take the time to visit her and celebrate mass at her place, on a fairly regular basis. Fortunately she also enjoyed her newly completed apartment at the Pereira Plaza, for four years. She had a peaceful death at the same location where she was born and spent all her life.

Through Marta, I was privileged and lucky to access a Pereira family tree study, Mgr. Aniceto (Pati) had commissioned through an outside source. Thank God I had taken down the information on my own notebook, as later on, as per Marta, one of the cousins who borrowed it, claimed he never took it from her and its whereabouts are unknown. I trust Marta's memory, which was intact till her last day on earth.

The Pereira family tree can be referred to, in the Appendix. An interesting piece of information from the above-mentioned work on the Pereira genealogy is that they identified existence of three priests in the family prior to 1758. Then in the next century 1758-1867, The Pereira family produced 15 more priests, the last of that period being Fr. Francisco Xavier Pereira.

Then the family was blessed with the birth of Aniceto do Menino Jesus Pereira (Pati) in 1871, who was ordained a priest in 1896, and who acted as the Patriarch of the family, besides having had a very illustrious and successful priestly career in Mumbai and Matheran. He was the main counselor and financial supporter to all his nephews and nieces.

From the available historical records (family tree), it is interesting to note that, going back at least five generations, Pereira men married women from Benaulim and farther villages of Curtorim and Raia. This is not surprising, as there are many relationships built on marriages between the villages of Curtorim, Loutulim, Raia and Benaulim.

Aniceto (1833-1878) **and Josefina** (1848-1945) had three children: Estela Estefania ETELVINA Pereira (1865-1948, age 83), Pascoal do Rosario Roque EPIFANIO Pereira (1868-1939, age 71) and ANICETO do Menino Jesus Pereira (1869-1961, age 91). Aniceto, the father, died of a stroke, at age 45, leaving three children aged 13 to 7.

Etelvina was deaf-mute from childhood, and remained unmarried. She devoted her life in helping with the household chores including raising of her nephews and nieces. I understand she had a special affection for daddy F.X., and later in life was really focused in leaving her share of the property and her belongings to him. Whenever family members came visiting, Etelvina would go around with all her gold possessions, hidden in her dress, lest somebody stole them from her. Her mind was already made up, when the time came to finalize her will; they showed her the photographs of her nephews Aniceto and Francis and she promptly selected Francis's photograph.

Epifanio was second of the three children. His father Aniceto had passed away when he was 10. Under close watch of his mother and granduncle Fr. F.X. Pereira, he excelled enough in the undergraduate studies to be admitted into Goa Medical School. However once away from home he was apparently more interested in having fun than studying and failed for two consecutive years. The family then decided to cut off his financial support as a medical student.

Upon returning home, he worked at Banco Montepio, a bank based in Portugal. This was the only employment job he held. Around 1918, on the aftermath of the Spanish flu, Montepio bank ran into financial trouble, and Epifanio lost his job. He was 51 years old at the time, and did not pursue a gainful employment after that.

Monsignor Aniceto do Menino Jesus Pereira (1871-1961), was known within the family as **Pati**, or at least that's what ti Marta called him. I believe some of his grandnephews called him PaTio.

I dare say that, in the first half of the twentieth century, he single-handedly was the guiding light for all his nephews and nieces within the Pereira household. I have read and heard nothing but good things about him, both as a priest and as the granduncle. Ti Marta never spoke to me about Pati's priestly career and his impressive achievements both as a pastor and a capable builder and administrator wherever he was posted in the Greater Bombay Region Archdiocese. For that matter, neither did she venture into talking about any family members unless I asked her specific questions on a family member or a relation.

On the basis of his title of Monsignor, and the big, imposing portrait of Pati in the main hall, and the high respect and esteem ti Marta held for him, I deducted he must have been an influential person in the family and deserved all the respect and accolade. The more I was trying to learn about daddy and his siblings, the more I would see his input into their lives and careers.

Ti Marta had safeguarded a copy of the church magazine Angelus, of May 1940, in which, on the occasion of Pati's retirement as Vicar of the Gloria Church, Byculla, Bombay, there is a tribute to Monsignor Aniceto do Menino Jesus Pereira and a good review of his full sacerdotal career. When I went through this issue of Angelus, I learnt a lot about his life as a pastor and as a very capable administrator.

In the three churches he was posted as Vicar, he practiced with ease the roles of a builder, financial manager and spiritual pastor. It is undoubtedly important for the future generations of Pereiras to know the service record and the achievements of this fine priest, who not only was a trusted counselor to his family, in particular to his nephews and nieces, but also was recognized by his parishioners and the Catholic Hierarchy. I have summarized pertinent data from the Angelus magazine in the paragraphs that follow.

"On completion of his studies at the Seminary of Diocese of Daman (then part of the Portuguese Territories of Goa, Daman and Diu) he was ordained on September 27, 1896 (age 25) and posted as Assistant Pastor at Gloria Church, Byculla, Mumbai.

Why did he choose Daman? It took place through a favor from Mr. Loyola Pereira from Benaulim, who in turn knew a Mr. Francisco Rodrigues, from Mumbai, and who had his contacts at the Daman Seminary. He promised to look after him, including financially, whilst in the Daman Seminary.

"Bubonic plague had broken out in this city (Mumbai) that very year and month. People were fleeing from the city panic-stricken to their native places….. People were dying by the dozens every day. Fr. Aniceto was then young, hale and hearty. He knew no fear. The Parish-priest was an aged man; he prayed that the scourge may pass away from the parish and the city. Fr. Aniceto took up the task…. He was busy visiting the sick, burying the dead, and likewise attending to their temporal needs wherever and whenever necessary."

As an aside, standing in the frontlines against these deadly diseases were doctors and health workers who risked their own lives to save others. One such medical practitioner during the Bubonic Plague in Mumbai, who risked his life was Dr Acacio Gabriel Viegas, (from Arpora, Goa) who is not only credited with the discovery of the outbreak in the city which helped save many lives, but also the inoculation of nearly 18,000 residents despite serious risks to his own health. (J Clement Vaz in his book titled 'Profiles of Eminent Goans, Past and Present', 1997.). The plague ravaged India seriously for two decades and sporadically thereafter from its outbreak in Mumbai city in August 1896, took at least twelve million lives and probably many more.

Another person of interest who was a medical practitioner and was very active in the medical field during the plague, was Dr. Jose Luis Pinto do Rosario, originally from Porvorim Goa, and himself an expert in contagious disease medicine. He was planning to move away from India to England with his family, when he unexpectedly passed away. At the time he was posted in Belgaum. There was a cholera outbreak in a nearby region. Dr. Pinto travelled there to help, where he supposedly had a major heart attack and died. His grandson is Geoffrey Pinto do Rosario, married to the younger Maria Aurora Pereira (F.X.'s daughter).

"After 8 years at Gloria Church, he was transferred to Matheran, as Vicar of the Holy Cross Church, where he worked with the same earnestness for a period of 13 years, till 1917. This is when he was brought back to Mumbai as the Vicar of Church of Holy Cross, Parel. Here during 13 years of his Vicarship, he completed the construction of the new Church, consolidated its finances, purchased some ground for the church compound, founded the parish school, without ever neglecting the spiritual as well as temporal good of his parishioners"

His final posting was back where he first started, the Gloria Church in Byculla, and he took charge of this large parish and its 10,000 souls. A lover of children, he devoted much attention to their religious formation. In 1933 he established the Children's Eucharistic Crusade. He instituted a Children's mass on Sundays at 7:30 am. He took upon himself, the task of instructing children during mass, until illness prevented him from doing so.

"There is a long list of achievements during his Vicarship of Gloria Church, and before his retirement: he undertook major refurbishment of the Church, instituted tight financial management, paid existing church debt, gave relief to poor children by way of reduction of fees and made partial debt payment of the Antonio de Souza High School, of which he was ex-officio Director."

We all have our weak points. Fr. Aniceto's weak point was his desire to be in control and manage everything that he believed was part of his parish. There is an account, where he may have overstepped his authority as expressed about him by the well-known educationist, Prof Aloysius Soares, who was the Principal of the Antonio Souza High School, and appointed to the post before Fr. Aniceto took over the vicarship of Gloria Church.

With a designation of Director, Fr. Aniceto believed he could impose his wishes on the workings of the school, which led to major disagreement with Prof. Aloysius, who threatened to resign and there was a bit of a fracas, solved amicably through setting up of a committee to deal with the matter. (Aloysius Soares "Down the Corridors of Time", Vol 1: 1891-1948, pp 115)

For health reasons, Fr. Aniceto decided to retire in May 1940. His work was well appreciated by the Holy Father, who, on the recommendation of the Mumbai Archbishop, bestowed on him the title of Monsignor and made him a Privy Chamberlain to His Holiness the Pope, in his own right.

At the farewell public demonstration Mgr. Aniceto said "that his principle had always been that the priest was in the parish for the benefit of the people, and not the people for the benefit of the priest".

Even though his failing health was mentioned as the reason for retirement in 1940 at age 69, Pati lived another 20 years and was 90 at his death.

As I said earlier Pati loved children. But to his grandnephews coming visiting, Pati, with his long flowing white beard, projected an aura of seriousness and holiness. However, they would soon find out at the dining table, he was not as serious as he looked.

Epifanio (1868-1939, age 71) married **Maria Aurora** Valeriano Barreto (1877-1957, age 80) from Raia, on January 30, 1904. Maria Aurora's parents are Joao Martinho Valeriano Barreto form Raia and Ludovina Quadros (from Loutulim). They had eight other children, six male, including three priests, and two female. From the Valeriano Barreto side of the family tree, Maria Aurora's children have eleven first cousins (Valeriano Barreto and Pereira) and her grandchildren have lots of second cousins, Barreto, Pereira, Faleiro, Andrade, Barbosa, Wiseman Pinto, now spread all over the world.

Ludovina Quadros is a fifth-generation descendant of Manuel Quadros from Loutulim and Joana Benedicta de Noronha of Margao. After traveling in late 1600s to (Portuguese?) East Africa, Manuel Quadros returned with "riches", which added to the family's existing wealth. He was pious and charitable and spread his wealth, helping the poor, and supporting charitable activities and instituted pious societies. He perpetuated the memory in as many perpetual cemetery graves (Loutulim and Pilar), as was the craze in those days. (This information comes from the "Register for Manuel Antonio de Quadros", prepared by Pedro do Carmo Costa, and distributed by Berardo Pinto Pereira).

As an aside, Ludovina's sister, Ana Leticia Filomena Quadros, married in Piedade (Divar) to Antonio Xavier Gomes Pereira. Their granddaughter Margarida married Eufemiano Alvares (architect) of Loutulim. Their son Manuel Alvares married Wilma D'Souza, sister of Ralph D'Souza, married to Yvonne Pereira, Ethel's sister.

Epifanio and Maria Aurora had seven children:
Ofelia P. Menezes (1904-1980, age 76, married 1927),
Julieta P. Cota (1906-1963, age 57, married 1931),
Aniceto Pereira (1909-1988, age 79, married 1940),
Clarissa P. D'Souza (1912-1998, age 86, married 1933),
Francisco Xavier Pereira (1914-1999, age 85, married 1945),
Jovita P. Pinto Pereira (1917-1998, age 81, married 1942)
and Marta Pereira (1919-2015, age 95).

Ethel and her siblings have only vague remembrances of Pati and their grandma, who to their cousins was Mama. But some of their cousins, who are older than my sisters-in-law, namely brothers Aires, Joe and Fr. Albert Menezes, shared their reminiscences as kids and youth visiting Mama's house.

I had already summarized what they shared with me, until **Fr. Albert** was kind enough to write it down himself. After I read his notes, written so beautifully, I decided not to reinvent the wheel. Here it is, with one paragraph in italics my own.

Fr. Albert's write-up on the Pereira Household during his Younger Days

"To me, PaTio was a good exemplar of what a good Jesuit was *then* considered to be: strict, stern, going by the book, acetic, hard-working, learned, and holy, with his physical appearance highlighting these traits: gaunt, pale-bordering-on-crimson faced, grey haired, high cheek boned, with deep inset eyes, and well-trimmed and pointed beard.

"There are two painted full portraits of him still on display, in the Hall at Mama's place and in a staircase well at Gloria Church in Byculla, that bear out this description, though in them, drawn up some eighty years earlier, he appears a little more enfleshed.

Any relative, ancient of days or a tiny tot, on entering Mama's place, had to go to PaTio to pay his respects and receive a blessing, a courtesy also extended to Mama but without consequences if that was not done.

To do that, one entered the house from the top end of Rua da Bernardo Costa, passed by the Chinese wood and painted canvas screen that was meant to partially block the view of the large dining hall and meeting place, and by the north end of one bedroom was escorted usually by Tia Marta to PaTio's room where he spent most of the day.

He only came out of it to go to the traditional "loo" (toilet) that on lower levels was the domain of pigs that predictably ended up as good pork. He also did so to go to the bathing room which had a feature that was rather unique: outside it was a huge *bhaan*, a big size copper vessel that was heated up by heaps of dried leaves gathered regularly from the fruit garden outside. It was tilted in such a way that its head could go through the hole made in the wall of the bathing room, so that one inside could scoop out with a *tambio,* a small copper vessel, hot water from it sufficient to pour into already partially filled buckets of ordinary water so that it could be as warm as needed for a good scrub.

Be it noted that the water used was not really ordinary. It came from an amazing well, at the corner of the bathing room and kitchen, with not too long a rope to pull up the *bindul (copper vessel)*, and its water was always clear, and always at the same level, throughout the year.

PaTio also left his room to say his daily private Mass in a corner room, just beyond the Oratorio (home little chapel big houses had). He had Rome's special permission say the mass at home, since he had retired from Gloria Church. Each morning, Tia Marta would prepare the altar and have the missal, liturgical vessels, and vestments laid out in their proper places, and then move off to make the necessary responses in Latin from a distance, not ever coming close to the altar like any altar boy would do. PaTio said Mass in Latin, with due devotion and composure.

Then he shuffled off to the dining table for breakfast, together with the usual attendants at Mass: Mama, Tia Marta, and *Mana* Magdu (brought up as an orphan in the Pereira family, and in later life considered an aunt, and loved immensely by all). Once the chore of seeking *bemŝao (blessing)* from PaTio was completed, the young ones rushed to seek the same from Mama.

Mama was, it can be said with due respects to Our Lady, the sweetest and kindest person that ever lived or will live on this earth. After ruffling the hair or patting the back of the child, she'd reach into her *pothi* (apron with a pocket) hung round her waist and give from it some sweets and or a coin or two to buy a good-sized sugared cashew nut *laddoo* from Babloo's *posro (little shop)* at the tapering end of the property. And most of the day, she would be in her *altair* (armchair or rocking chair), either seated on the front verandah or praying the rosary or just still before the large painted and statue filled Oratorio.

I know many descendants from her Valeriano Barreto side, including my own sister-in-law Maria Lurdes (Barreto) Moniz, and they can smother you with their etiquette, kindness and love. I would not be surprised Maria Aurora had the same traits.

PaTio would be in his room, reading the breviary at the appointed times, scanning through the daily newspaper *O Diário*, and methodically going through the spiritual books that filled many cupboards, with no loosening of his straight posture or of his serious demeanour.

His self-possession and imposing presence and topmost position in the family hierarchy made him the regular occupant of the main chair (head of the table) at all the functions at Mama's.

With the heads of families around him, his conversation was easy and pleasant, but it could never be interrupted by the noise or complaining cries of the children playing around. That's because in those days, when elders were around, the children could only be seen but never heard.

PaTio, Mama, and Tia Marta presided over the Rosary recited daily, before the Oratorio, and it seemed to go on interminably because the additions of many litanies and 3 Our Fathers and 3 Hail Mary's for various intentions, and it was escaped / avoided by many staying visitors if they had any excuse, no matter how weak, to be somewhere else during the half-hour starting at 8:00 pm.

When PaTio was at Mama's, everything was regimented, and that was never objected to, since the loving concern of the trinity of PaTio, Mama, and Tia Marta was something that was always taken for granted. They implanted strong archetypes into the psychological makeup of those privileged to have been under their influence."

END of Fr. Albert's Write-up.

The Margao Pereira home was a gathering place for cousins coming from all over Goa. They remember playing games, eating plenty of mangos and going to the beach in Colva, from this house.

Through discussions with cousins, my general impression on the uncles and aunts is of a family that got along smoothly with no true negative vibes. Ofelia and Marta were considered the more serious and disciplinarian of the lot and Julieta and Clarissa the more easy going and fun to be with.

Ofelia being the eldest and also a teacher was looked up by her siblings with love and respect. They got along really well. It helped that Roque, being a doctor, was a "doctor in the house" for the siblings. Their brother, Francis graduated as medical doctor in 1943 and he always practiced medicine in Mumbai.

It happens that Ti Roque's niece Maria Helena Quadros married my eldest uncle Riario Moniz, who lived in Mazagon, Mumbai. I used to hear stories about Ti Ofelia and Ti Roque (The Menezes) from my first cousins, when they used to come down to Goa on their summer holidays. Normally the stories revolved about how they were afraid of the discipline and toughness of Ti Ofelia and Ti Roque.

One of the funny things narrated was this episode at the dining table in the Menezes house, where potatoes was one of the servings. My cousin Egidio, did not particularly like to eat potatoes. But he was afraid to say so to ti Roque and Ti Ofelia. Thus, when he was served potatoes he decided that he would eat his potatoes first, and then the rest of "good food". Ti Roque, mistakenly thought Egidio really liked the potatoes and he would refill his plate, and this dance went on, to the chagrin of his cousins, who would love to have more potatoes and were getting neglected.

I met Ti Ofelia for the first and last time in 1975 when I got civilly married to Ethel and Ti Ofelia came visiting us at the Pereira residence in Margao. I thought she was nice to me. Coincidentally, it happened that Egidio also dropped in to see me. Ti Ofelia had been told by Egidio's dad (my uncle Riario) that he had a girl-friend in Pune. When Ti Ofelia congratulated him on his girl-friend, Egidio says "no aunty she is not really my girl-friend". And Ti Ofelia, thinking he was lying to her, let him have it. To me it just confirmed there and then, all that I had heard about the "tough ti Ofelia". To my bad fortune, that was to be the first and last time I would meet Ti Ofelia.

Fr. Albert Menezes, S.J., the sixth of Ofelia's eight children, at my request, has written beautifully about his parents and the Menezes clan. Even though it is a bit longer than I was expecting, I am going to incorporate it here in "almost" its entirety, with my additions, shown in *italics*.

OFELIA AND ROQUE MENEZES and Family
by (Fr.) Albert Menezes

"My mum was known as Ofélia in Goa and as Ophelia everywhere else, and it is from her that we got to know how she got to know Roque on some trip on which both their gender gangs separately happened to be in Goa for some holidays. They met while returning by train to base, the young lady teachers to Mumbai, and the medical students to Pune.

There is still a sepia tint photograph of the time before they tied the knot: the tall and handsome Roque sitting crossed legged on a Victorian chair, while petite Ophelia's superimposed image hovers behind, as if he is thinking about her the whole time. It's not known who led them up the aisle of the Holy Cross Church in Lower Parel on 29 January 1927, for the vows made "till death do us part," but we do know that the Officiant was Fr Aniceto Pereira, the Parish Priest, Ofelia's paternal uncle. The witnesses were Herculano D'Sa and Manoel Francisco Colaço.

Since nowadays it is always "ladies first," Ophelia will be the first to be profiled. Ofelia was born to Maria Aurora and Epifanio in Raia, Salcete, Goa, following the old custom by which Maria Aurora went to her maternal house, for the delivery of the first child. Ofelia grew up in the cherished home of the Pereira family and all those who married into it.

Because of the thrill of her being the first born, they heaped on her nine names, not counting the surname, and Ofelia was only her fifth one! Four girls and two boys (in order: Julieta, Aniceto, Clarissa, Francis, Jovita, and Marta) followed her, and all raised great families. Only the last one remained a spinster, taking care of her mother and uncle priest. She was thin as a reed but sharper than any knife in interactions, well mellowed in adult life to be a very respected *materfamilias* and the last to die among them.

It can be supposed that Pe Aniceto took his niece Ofelia after the customary initial studies in Portuguese to Mumbai for some bit of company and for education in English with the Franciscan Hospitaller Sisters, in Prabhadevi, Dadar, and then in Mount Mary's at Bandra. At the dinner table at home so often we heard stories of her stay in Matheran with Pe Aniceto during the holidays, like of both going out for a party only to find, on the way back at night, panthers and tigers lying athwart the road, able to be shooed away only by the striking of a match.

She continued to be under the simultaneously strict and kind surveillance of Pe Aniceto till her matriculation and her first years as a teacher in Antonio de Silva's Primary School. After marriage she accompanied Roque to be with him during the final stretch at the Pune Medical College to obtain the LCPS which enabled him to practice medicine. They stayed in the home of the affectionate Mr and Mrs Andrews where their eldest was born, Arthur, named after their great patron, Dr Arthur da Gama; the Andrews had set up a shrine in honor of St Anthony at which "St Anthony's Bread" continues to be distributed since their time till now; Mrs Andrew continued to be in close touch with us till as late as 1966.

My dad came from a culturally different background from that of my mum, more immured in Konkani and local "native" dress codes, without the sophistication that Portuguese speech and town-living that had crept into the Margao inhabitants—the men and women of one set were comfortable in Western dresses and suits; the women of the other set showed themselves off in their elegant festal *todopes* and their men were at ease in their banians and khastis when having their evening *kottees (shot)*.

Roque was brought up in the part of the village of Fatorda that bordered Margao where the Old Market was situated, and where his father, Piedade Xavier, had his General Merchandise shop. Piedade's father himself had a wine importing agency.

It must have been Piedade's well known reputation for honesty and for delivery of genuine goods that must have permitted the Pereiras to be connected with the Menezes. He had married Conceiçao Madeira from Manora, part of Raia, and adjacent to Kirbat which belonged to Nuvem.

It was in Kirbat eventually, especially after a house was built there in 1937 to mainly store the harvested rice and fruits, that we made our home which also became a magnet for all our relatives.

There is one mystery though, about my dad's ancestry, which now seems almost impossible to unravel. It is clear that they originated in Loutulim, in one of the Menezes families there. And this was taken for granted by, until my aunt, Tia Marta, told me, a couple of years before she died that, from what she knew, my grandfather, and his siblings, were children born in a Hindu family there, but their parents died in a plague and, at their request before dying, the children were taken over as orphans by a Menezes family which made them converts and bestowed on them their surname.

I understand Piedade would receive visits from time to time thereafter from his Hindu cousins, with "xhendi" (pony tail) from Karwar, resulting in subsequent gossip from the locals. Other than the fact that Piedade may have been an adopted child, we must not forget that our Christian ancestors were all once Hindus, converted in the late sixteen century or first half of seventeen century.

Those that could supply reliable data are now all dead, and facts about which Menezes family it was that supplied the patronymic are not possible for me to dig into. I still regret that I did not set to do the necessary research about it immediately.

Piedade and Conceiçao had 8 children, and my dad was the fifth (preceding him were Rosarinho, Espiciosa married in Fatorda (Quadros), Ermelinda married in Chandor (Pereira), Flaviano who died at 15 in a cholera epidemic; following him were Claudina married in Verna, Miguel who lived in Bangalore and married a wonderful Tamilian lady, and Isabel married in Solva (Coelho); and they were all well settled.

My dad, due to circumstances not known, after initial studies in Portuguese, was placed in the Arpora English School in Bardez, the first of its kind in Goa; midstream, he was sent to Belgaum to complete his matriculation at St Paul's, a Jesuit school, and worked in some capacity in the Central Telegraph Office in Mumbai

Story is told that Dr Arthur da Gama, who was based in Pune, met Roque at Central Telegraph office and finding out he hailed from Goa, tried convincing him on more than one occasion that he should give up the work at the telegraph office, and become a medical doctor.

Roque explained to Dr. da Gama he could not afford pursuing a medical course to which Dr. da Gama assured Roque that he did not have to worry about the school fees and other costs, as Dr. da Gama would take care of them. Roque finally agreed, under condition Dr. da Gama, would also pay for a close Goan friend, Antonio Sequeira working at the same telegraph office. And Dr. Da Gama agreed.

He joined St Xavier's College where, the Principal, Fr Blatter, in his heydays, at College social functions had girls sitting on his thighs, waiting to be launched out to the dance floor to be picked up by guys like my dad. After Inter-Science he was able to gain entrance into the Pune University Medical College, with the benefit of being, like other young Catholic students, under the aegis of Dr Arthur da Gama living at Synagogue Street.

Roque did his Licensurate in Medicine through the Army School (during WW II) and worked for the Army for a couple of years. Years later I used to meet with elderly male and female doctors who used to convey the excitement of their student social life in Pune centred round dad and his chums.

Dad was almost six feet tall, lean, well boned, and even in old age, imposing. He was good at games. He had an excellent tenor-baritone voice and though he could not read music, he used to play the guitar and the violin, the latter invariably at the many *ladainhas* sung. Dad and mum would later be often called upon to lead the *mando* with dad most often on the *ghumott*, leading the singing. Aires (and Teresa) and Joseph continued with the mando singing tradition.

In Loutulim, Roque was able to try his hand at composing Mandos, under the tutelage of the great Goan mando composer Torquato Figueiredo (1876-1948). One composition that I know of, is the beautiful mando for the wedding of his niece Elena Quadros and my uncle Riario Moniz, in 1954 "Suria Uzvadd Fankarolo", meaning "The light has blazed with the sun"

It is noteworthy to mention that Arthur took violin lessons initially from Torquato Figueiredo. Arthur and Caesar also took violin lessons from the famous Goan classical music composer Prof. Michael Martins in Panaji, Goa's capital city.

In the '70s my mother went to consult with the famous specialist, Dr Raheja, for her diabetes and he spent most of the time recalling the many enjoyable events in the company of dad when they were in the same medical school. The closest friends to dad and mum were dad's Pune companions, Drs Manu and Marcy Sequeira, and whether in Goa or Bombay, they were frequent visitors at our home.

The first part of the family history began in Goa. For a growing family like ours there was nothing to go by except an inherited property and some small fields and coconut *baands* in Seraulim. My dad started his practice in Loutulim from the house in which Caesar was to be born and which later became an *Albergue*, sort of a home for old people; we then moved to a permanent residence belonging to Mr Eufemiano Alvares (later to become, with its hilly environs, a "must see" tourist spot in Salcete: The Big Foot) in which were born Aires, Louis, and Joseph.

After the marriage of Eufemiano Alvares, the Menezes family had to move about a hundred meters away, to a house opposite that of a very good friend of the family, Mr. Basilio Barreto, and that is where I, Albert Maria Piedade, was born. My names all came from famous Lotlikars: Fr Albert Mascarenhas, Maria Faria, and my grandfather Piedade, whose name was also given to all my siblings.

I do not know the exact reasons which made my dad transfer his practice to Verna and then to Rachol, but my guess is that it was to improve his earnings. There was never ever any conflict between my parents except on dad not bringing in sufficient earnings to support the family.

All her married life, my mum never operated from any bank account. And in my life, I never saw my dad charge his patients; he accepted whatever they gave. Besides, because of the company of the elite he kept in Loutulim, quite often an unexpected visit of my mum, with a few kids in tow, would find him bidding at poker when he should have been out seeing his patients.

The shortage of money in the family may have shortchanged Aires' educational aspirations. He completed studies only to Grade 6, whilst all his siblings completed college education. He was good at trades, initially making buttons, then tailoring and then as an artist. At a very young age he was already bringing in money and contributing to the family finances. I understand that through his natural gifts and hard work, he was very successful building a successful and profitable business.

When I was first introduced some years ago to Mario Miranda, the famous cartoonist, he said: "You are Dotor Roque Menezes' son?! He and my father were famous *jogadores (card players)* in Loutulim!"

I now continue with what I can personally vouch for about the main happenings in our family.

I, born in the last quarter of 1939, remember nothing about anything till about the beginning of 1943, in Rachol at Costa's house not far from the Rachol Seminary of which my father was the official physician. The house was isolated and the spaces around were wide, and there was no end to the howling sounds of foxes and hyenas nearby and to the croaking of frogs during the monsoon months at night and to the slither of snakes all the time.

It is there and also in Kirbat that I had the good fortune to be in proximity with wild life (tigers and panthers were often killed in Kirbat and also at my aunt's place in Solva, Raia), to know about how the ground and seeds were prepared for planting and see the green fields turn brown for harvesting, and how the ponds were emptied for catching fish, just before the monsoons began, and how coconuts were de-husked by pointed spears and their flesh set out into the sun to be dried and browned into copra which would later be ground to extract oil. That's why I much prefer the hills and freshwater streams than beaches for holiday loitering.

I thank my stars that I was city bred but not city born. While I was in Rachol in the company of Dad, taken good care of by his unmarried cousin, Maria Augusta, *Mana*, my Mum was in Panji, teaching in People's High School, a rare English medium school; Arthur was studying at the Lyceum, and both he and Caesar were learning the violin with Michael Martins and playing in his orchestra; Aires, Louis, and Joseph, all armed with *Segundo Grau*, were now in the People's High School (and also taught how to plunk at the piano by Michael Martins).

On weekends, Dad and I would go to Panji most often by launch (ferry boat) and return on Monday mornings by *caminhao* (bus) via Borim bridge. And I remember that once with Maria Augusta *Mana* the trip from Rachol to Panji was made in a *patmari*, a sailing boat, which left the Zuari estuary at Marmagoa and then went up to enter the Mandovi one.

I didn't know what it was all about, but everybody was excited about one particular trip to Panji, and I noticed that many at home tried hard to make me very happy, visiting the dentist clinics of two cousins and entertaining me on the dentist's chair, and I lapped up all the fuss. There was a lot of movement in the house and suddenly I heard the painful cries of my mum that were followed by a massive howl of a baby.

That was on 5 March 1943 when my brother, Roque, was born and sometime after that I remember his baptism in the Panji Church and after that followed a whirl of events too many to remember that ended with a new era for the family: a farewell to Panji and Margao and Kirbat and to all the many family gatherings at uncles' and aunts' homes and especially those at Mama's and Tio Agostinho's and Tio Jose's and a momentous migration to Mumbai, India!

My parents were both educated in (British) India and they knew the value of English education; the higher education in Portuguese was restricted to the Lyceum and medicine at the Goa Medical School; for other disciplines one had to go to Portugal where, as they said in Konkani, *"te ped'der zatole"* ("they will get spoilt").

Plans were therefore made to migrate to Mumbai with the help of a rich in-law nephew of dad's but he suddenly died in May and all that was arranged to be in Mumbai at the start of the academic year was cancelled.

There was new planning, helped by the availability of a decent flat of my mum's brother, Aniceto, who was quartered as a naval officer in Byculla, and so we all piled into a train and set off via Collem and Castlerock to Londa from where another steam train took us via Pune, terminating at Victoria Terminus (VT in Mumbai) just before noon of 25 October 1946, the day I completed seven.

The biggest snag was getting us into school when almost half of the academic year was over; it was dissolved by two angels who got us into the matriculation St Mary's School (different from St Mary's across the road which had a Cambridge syllabus): one was Mr. C.J.V. Miranda, then the most famous police officer in the city (and later a cherished Police Commissioner) who personally accompanied us to put in a good word for us with the school authorities. C.J.V. Miranda was a first cousin and close friend to Ti Phoebe, Ti Francisco's wife.

The second angel was Fr Thomas Molina SJ who was the soul of kindness. He gave us a benign look and in a few minutes he had placed five of us in different classes, from Caesar in the Matriculation till myself the youngest: he must have not checked my birth date but looking at my height he put me into "Senior Preparatory," and that was a lucky mistake for I finished my SSC a year earlier than I should have.

We were 8 boys in the family, but it was never felt that we were "one too many." The last one to be born, and the only one in Bombay, was Vasco, in January 1948, and there is still a family photograph with mum nestling him in her arms. That year, for reasons not remembered, only my cousin, Lucy Coelho, and I went to Goa for the summer vacation.

One night there I dreamt of a white coffin wafting up and breezing through the clouds in the skies. On an April day, in Mama's house, Tia Marta broke to me the news that Vasco had died. Later I got to know that dad, on consulting some of his friends of the medical fraternity, was told that there was perhaps no need to vaccinate the baby for smallpox which was raging in the city; he was told only not to take the baby out of the house. Vasco was never taken out and yet he got the worst type of small pox possible and died almost immediately; his body was taken in a horse *gharry* by dad to be buried at Haines Road Cemetery.

When Lucy and I returned from Goa in early June, and Mum met us, I saw my mum cry so bitterly and for so long. I had never seen her cry so much.

Dad did not like being in Mumbai but he couldn't help it and fortunately he was appointed the Medical Officer of the well-known engineering firm, Garlick & Co. It was very easy for dad to get to and back from work because of a convenient tram service from close-by Keddy & Co to Mahalaxmi where his work place was located. He bravely bore the din in the factory but seems to have been well respected by the workers, and its General Manager, Mr. Knock, an Englishman, often came over for long chats with him.

He retired in the late '50s but acted as a locum doctor in a few private clinics, but as soon and as fast as he was able to get away from Mumbai he did; that was once the family moved from New Nagpada to Vile Parle East, and put up on the ground floor of the newly built one-storey building, newly constructed by the Motivalas, friends from Byculla days. In the early '60s, he and mum returned to Kirbat and only returned to Mumbai for an occasional visit.

It was only sometimes that we had a full time cook at home in Mumbai and so mum had to be a housewife, having to control the boys and do the cooking which, though she was quite good at it, she detested. But she loved knitting and crochet work, which she did during her free time whenever she was not reading, which she also loved to do.

She and all of us were very blessed by having Lucy, Ubaldina (now a Franciscan Hospitaller Sister), Palmira (died of typhoid in Byculla when barely 18) and later Rosario and Peter, our Coelho cousins from Solva, staying with us for studies and also work; we boys were extremely lucky to have the three female cousins with us for otherwise our upbringing in an all-male setting would have lacked something vitally essential. They and Rosario and Peter were as good as any other sister or brother would have been, and dad and mum dealt with them as their own children, and no difference was made. Till today the relationships remain very close.

Arthur married Olive in 1958 but after the birth of their Pia and Monica, they had to go to England. Arthur transferred from Ciba's in Mumbai to Ciba's in UK, for surgery to deal with the hole-in-the-heart that he was born with and now gave trouble, and that necessitated that mum accompany them to Horsham and return only after Arthur had fully recuperated.

Thereafter mum was always in Goa with Dad, but both were in Mumbai for Louis' and my ordination on 25 March 1966 and 15 March 1969 respectively, and both occasions were great opportunities for the gathering of the Menezes and Pereira families.

It was a few days after my First Mass that dad called all his sons together at Caesar's family quarters in Sion to finalize matters about the family property.

With mum present, dad asked each of us what one wanted. Arthur and Roque said they didn't want anything since they intended to be permanently abroad; Louis and I, naturally, didn't require anything either; Caesar, Aires and Joseph said they'd accept whatever was given.

Dad gave our dear cousin, Jorge Quadros, powers of attorney who saw to it that all we had said was notarized and dad sold his property to the three who had families in India for a very nominal sum and so it was that, after his and mum's death, there would absolutely be no family property problem. I take my hats off to dad and mum for that.

It is not to be wondered that all through their adult lives they were both highly esteemed and respected, much consulted by family and friends, despite the fact that dad was hot-tempered, though equally quick to cool down; and mum was straightforward and fair, without a drop of self-pity in spite of the inevitable hardships she had to bear because of economic reasons.

Dad took ill after his 75th birthday on 15 September 1974 and many doctors readily attended to him, but he died on 8 October after I was beckoned home by Manec Cotta, a dear cousin, from the Nuvem Church where I had gone to say Mass in the evening; present at the bedside too were Caesar, Aires, and Joe and their wives. It was a peaceful death, with nobody distraught, and the Mass and Funeral on the next day was well attended by innumerable relatives and close friends.

Mum suffered most of her adult life, from diabetes, which ran in her family. She was careful about diet and did her walks, but gradually, in her 75th year, she began to feel weak and became slightly dark in the skin. The problem was not, it was discovered, diabetes but infection of the kidneys. The surgeon at Dr Shirodkar's Hospital on Cumballa Hill operated on her on 11 May 1980, only to find that she had 3 kidneys! Whatever was infected was taken away and the operation was decidedly successful. But that night, around 3:00 am, she had a massive heart attack and that was it. We, the Menezes brothers, could not have had more or better than what Roque and Ophelia gave us, and none of us can say that we achieved greater things than they did." ***End of Fr. Albert's Write-up***

Julieta do Sagrado Coração de Maria Pereira e Cota (1906-1963, age 57). She married Sebastiao Cota from Loutulim, in her early 20s and had her first child, Maria in 1932. They had seven children in all, including Fr. Mariano, Maurelio, Manecas, Miguel (Miquito), Fr. Antonio (Tony) and Maria da Graça (Gracinha) Cota das Neves Sequeira

Fr. Mariano (1934) was my Prefect at Saligao Seminary where I joined in 1957, and he probably was a recently ordained priest. All the boys, except Manecas, attended Seminary, but only Mariano and Tony became priests. Going to the Seminary may have been influenced, as they were growing up, by having a grand-uncle priest (Conego Cota) in the house.

The Cotta children are musically gifted with good singing voices, which they have put to good use in their priestly profession and in case of Maurelio and Miquito through singing as a profession.

I am told that ti Julieta was a fun person to be around. She was struggling with diabetes and in one of her health-related episodes, her life came to an unexpected early end, at age 57, just six years after death of her own mother, and with the youngest of her seven children only five years old. Supposedly the doctors were treating her for diabetes when the health issue at hand was a different one.

The Cota family were staying with Marta, in the Pereira residence at the time of Julieta's death. They had moved to Margao from Loutulim, for the sake of children's education, and after the recent deaths of Pati and their mother, Marta agreed to accommodate the Cota family.

(Cpt) ANICETO PEREIRA (1909-1988, age 79)

Born in Margao on 19 April 1909, Joao Batista Aniceto must have been named after his grandfather, even though his dad's brother, Pati, was carrying the same name. As I am writing on the Pereira family, I have to be careful that the reader does not mix up one with the other.

Whenever I had an opportunity to talk to family members or outside the family circle, the first thing that people would say is that Aniceto was fun to be around, and he liked to party, probably like his father Epifanio, in his younger days. The latest (2018) account, came from Filomeno Almeida, who himself was in his nineties, when we met.

Filomeno Almeida's mother and Aniceto are second cousins via the Valeriano Barreto side of the family, but I do not know if they knew the family connections then. Filomeno having excelled in his Engineering graduating class at the Pune University, and gone through the all-India competition, was posted in New-Delhi for a short while before he migrated to the USA, where, after doing his Ph.D., he became a lecturer and later Dean of Engineering at University of Detroit.

Filomeno, is a nephew of Ricardo Miranda, and was pleased to know Ethel was Aniceto's niece, and I could tell from his facial expression he was happy to reminisce the many parties and fun outings he attended at Aniceto's house in New-Delhi. Ti Marta, also recounted to me that when he came down to Goa, there were comings and goings galore from his friends. But she added, he would pay for all the expenses.

Aniceto was brought to Mumbai by Pati. His first job was at Excise Department, whilst at the same time he was trying to upgrade his education through college. Pati, who was about to retire in 1940, seeing that ti Aniceto, now close to age 30, had not completed his degree, suggested he join the Officers Training School in Bengaloru.

He married his first cousin Maria Alicia (Alice) Pereira, (i.e. Maria Aurora's niece) in 1940 and they both travelled to Bengaloru. He was commissioned in 1942, the same year their oldest child Churchill Aniceto Pereira was born. Aniceto and Alice had five children, Churchill, Janet P. Fortes, Indira P. Pimento, Orlando and Oscar.

He was posted in Mumbai till 1946 and lived in Byculla. His transfer out coincidentally came at the right time when Ofelia and Roque, with their family, had made arrangements to move to Mumbai.

As Albert Menezes recounts "Before going to his new posting, U. Aniceto, to our eternal gratitude, transferred his flat to dad's name, but for a few weeks his family and ours lived together, on the second floor of the Aga Khan Building at New Nagpada Road opposite the Police Hospital, with the Nagpada Police Station and the still famous Sarvi Restaurant at the other end of it.

We always looked forward to his visits and listened in awe to his naval and political stories which, without embellishments, were always exciting. "

Aniceto regularly rose in rank, transferring from one naval base to another, and eventually to New Delhi.

He served as Staff Officer, Cabinet-Secretariat-Military Wing in New Delhi between 1948 and 1950, where he got to know the first Prime Minister of India, J. Nehru. He was also Secretary to the Chiefs of Staff Committee, The Defense Committee and the Defense Minister's Commission.

A logistics expert, he was appointed Fleet Supply Officer to the Indian Navy, and then became Deputy Director-Supply, both posts at Naval Headquarters.

Promoted to the rank of Captain on July 23, 1953, he was appointed the Naval Secretary, becoming the first Indian appointed to the post, i.e. post-independence.

He retired 19 April 1959 (at the then superannuation age of 50) as the Head of Naval Pay Office, responsible for payments of salary and allowances to all officers and sailors of the Indian Navy.

Aniceto was among the first Goans to attain the high naval rank, and in the Goan community or Naval community everybody knew Cpt. Pereira. He settled in Colaba, Esperança Building, Mumbai, and for many years he was an important and respected administrative hand in the Mumbai Archdiocese office next door. Aniceto passed away at age of 79, on 02 June 1989.

Clarissa Pereira De Sousa (1912-1988, age 86). Clarissa was the fourth of seven children and two years older than Ethel's dad (my father-in-law) Francis. I understand that besides the kinship, he had a special fondness for this sister. She passed away close to year and half before Francis, but the family chose not to inform him about it, as his health was not that great at the time.

Clarissa married Jose Joaquim de Souza (1893-1969, age 74) from Dogrim, Mandur, at age 21. They went on to have 10 children; the oldest Celina de Souza Soares, (1934-2021), being Clarissa's first child, was born at the Pereira house, as was the custom of the day.

Celina, whom I have known to be always cool and sweet, married Adv. Antonio Maria Venancio Soares, and they had ten children of their own. Through her ten children Celina has 23 grandchildren. An interesting point of information is that each of Celina's 10 children, except one, is conversationally known with a nickname.

Here is part one of the write-up from Clarissa's son **Oscar de Sousa** (Portugal). Part two of his write up is presented in the chapter "Our Family Emigration from India".

"I am Óscar Conceição de Sousa, born in Goa in January 1941. I am the son of a large family of ten siblings, five girls and five boys. My father also adopted another girl who joined the family. My parents are: José Joaquim Lázaro Tomé Nascimento de Sousa, who died in 1969; my mother Clarissa Ludovina dos Reis Pereira, who died in 1998.

My father's family came from Aldona. My paternal grandparents David Januário de Sousa and Maria Estella Pereira had to move to Dongrim, Mandur, a village in the municipality of Ilhas, between Goa Velha and Velha Goa as my grandfather was hired for the post of the "escrivao" (head clerk) of the Comuninade of Carambolim.

My grandparents' family consisted of eight children, six sisters (one of whom, a twin to the youngest brother, died at birth) and two brothers. My grandfather became a widower shortly after the birth of his last child. The older sister who was a spinster, became the caretaker of the Dongrim's house till she died.

The other four sisters married early and left the household, one married in Aldoná and the other three in Salcete. My father was the last to get married on April 29, 1933. He bought the Dongrim house. My father's other brother followed the priestly vocation. My father studied at the Portuguese primary school and completed his formal education by attending High School in English in Arporá.

My mother hails from Margao and comes from the Pereira household. My mother went to primary school and attended high school in English in Mumbai.

After getting married, in order to support the family, my father opened a store, Casa Juka, in Panji, next to the Government Palace. The store mainly carried products for ladies of the middle and upper middle class. In order to facilitate their children's studies, the family moved from Dongrim to Panji, renting a house in Fontainhas just below the Lyceum. In the period between the two wars, my father went to work in the Persian Gulf, in order to earn money to invest in the store, delegating the responsibility of managing the Casa Juka store to a nephew. He returned for good to Goa in 1938, before the Second World War.

Contrary to what happened with most of the rest of the family (from my uncles to my cousins), my parents opted to provide their children with education in Portuguese, until the date of annexation of Goa, by India, in December 1961. After primary school, all of us enrolled in the Lyceum school which coincidentally was right there next to the house where we lived.

While we were in Panji my parents also enabled us to learn music and to play an instrument by hiring a teacher who came to the house. Most of us learned the violin that I continued to play after arriving in Portugal and even completed the exams of the Lisbon Conservatory General Course. As for studies, I went to primary school until I was 10 years old and entered the Seminary in Goa. (*End of Oscar de Sousa's write up Part I*)

Oscar's siblings are: Carlito m Fania, Clelia m Aires Mascarenhas, Oscar m Cynthia, Maria Angela m Luis Vaz, Mario m Lynette, Fatima, Olavo m Carmen, Bernadette m Merwyn Lopez, and Edgar m Celia Barneto

Maria **Jovita** dos Reis (Pereira) Pinto Pereira (1917-1998, age 81). Jovita is the sixth of the Epifanio and Maria Aurora's seven children. A few times

I met her, she was calm and soft spoken. Being close in age to Marta, she came visiting her often.

She married Antonio Vicente Pinto Pereira in 1942, and their only child Berardo Pinto Pereira was born in September 1943. To her bad luck, her husband passed away in 1960, at a fairly young age of 47. Jovita was 43 and Berardo was 17 when his father died.

With the proceeds from their property in Benaulim, she managed to support Berardo's pursuit of his studies in Portuguese in Panji. Later on he joined the Seminary in Poona. He did not complete his seminary studies towards priesthood.

From the website Geni: "Berardo had an illustrious student career culminating in winning the President of India Gold Medal at the M.A. in Personnel Management. He was well studied with a baccalaureate in Chemistry, and Masters in Education and in Philosophy. Hailing from the village of Benaulim in Goa, he was well known as an author, poet, management guru and finance wizard."

I understand Berardo was a party man, and was fun to be with. When he was in Mumbai there were many get-togethers with him, that cousins remember fondly.

I remember Berardo sending me a link to the web site to access a new work of his poetry works. I was very impressed with the high literary level of his work, after all these years after he moved on from Portuguese studies. In fact, I had to refer to a Portuguese dictionary, more than once, even though my own Portuguese language capability is strong, on account of my six years of Seminary education in the Portuguese medium.

When Berardo was hired by Mittal Steel, as Personnel manager for their steel mill in Trinidad & Tobago he and his wife, Dr. Lexley, along with their three children, moved to Trindidad and made this island state their new home.

Jovita stayed back in Goa until 1997 when she was convinced to move to Trinidad & Tobago. She did not like it there and when she returned on a trip back to Goa, in August 1998, she was dreading to go back. She was putting up with Marta, when she had returned and suffered a heart attack and did not survive.

Berardo's intention was to spend part of his retirement days in Goa and to that effect, he had been upgrading his house in Benaulim. He did not get to complete the home renovation, as on one of these trips, during monsoon season of 2007 in Goa, he had a massive stroke and passed away within a couple of days, at age 63. Coincidentally I arrived in Goa, the same day he passed on. On his funeral day, the rain was so incessant and heavy, I was basically wet from head to toes, even under the cover of an umbrella.

I had not met Berardo, but I had corresponded with him and spoken to him on multitude of occasions, and I was looking forward to get to know him in person. But it was not to be.

Berardo was responsible to get his hands on a genealogy work, prepared initially for a Mr. Manuel Antonio de Quadros, circa five generations ancestor of Ludovina Quadros Valeriano Barreto, mother of Maria Aurora Valeriano Barreto Pereira who married Epifanio Pereira.

Berardo then put in lot of effort to expand this work to cover the extended branches of the Pereira family, up to 2002. He put the work together in a bound volume, copies of which he distributed widely, now being used as reference by our cousins. I would say Berardo's reference work, and the Genealogy or family tree completed by Fr. Luis Menezes, the latter included in this book, compliment each other and together form good or fairly complete references to the Pereira Family ancestry.

Marta Marcelina Caridade Pereira (1919-2014, age 95).

Marta was the youngest of the seven siblings. She was petite and thin, and for close to forty years that I had known her, she looked frail. Looks can often be deceiving. She followed a regimented diet and health routine, such as taking B complex injection at fixed intervals. A few months before her death, she told me that "everybody thought I was a weakling, but look now, I have survived them all".

Marta was a pious and serious person, to the point that she did not have or want to have a radio or a TV in the house, even though we offered to buy it for her. Mummy Phoebe, spent years trying to convince her to get a telephone at home, so that they could keep in regular touch with her; instead Mummy and Daddy would telephone the neighbour's place and they would then go and fetch her to take the call. I am sure it was on account of saving on the monthly telephone bills. By the way, this kind of good neighbourliness was more of a rule, rather than an exception, in good old days in Goa.

Speaking of her piety, in 2011 when we were in Goa visiting her, our grandson Ethan, who was two at the time, and his parents, Celine and Russell, had joined us. Marta liked Ethan, who in turn would try to needle her by purposely picking up her rosary, which she would keep in a certain place. One day we saw him walking behind her, imitating her walk and mumbling to himself (imitating her saying the rosary).

In her final years, all her contemporaries were dying one by one, and she was one of the last to go from her social group and age bracket. At this stage in life, she would often wonder out aloud, why God had still kept her in this world.

I never heard her tell a joke, and for that matter nobody in the family dared tell one, out of respect for her. But on our last visit, approximately a year before her death, she shared the following joke with me.

"A person named Joseph, would attend the morning mass every day without failure. Then his 90th birthday arrived, and the family celebrated it in style, including having a special celebratory mass for him. After this day, Joseph stopped attending the morning mass. The parish priest noticed his absence and after a couple months decided to pay a visit to Joseph at his home and knocked at his door. The priest enquired about his health and why he was not seeing him at the mass, as he used to do. Joseph responded. "I have been going to the house of God, praying every day for a while to take me to be with him up there, and he has forgotten me. So, I gave up coming to his house".

When Pati (Mgr. Aniceto) retired in 1940, and moved to Goa, he put her in charge of managing the household and that meant taking care of three elderly people: her mother, Pati and Mana (Magdu). She was 20, and she told me "do you know how much responsibility that was? It was a lot of tension for me." Well, from what I know she did a fabulous job. Her mother and Pati passed away 17 years and 21 years later respectively. Magdu died in early 1980s.

Marta was the sole Pereira member left to reside in the family residence for over 50 years. After the erection of the new building, the Pereira Plaza, was completed in 2011 in the place of the old family residence, she moved in into her own apartment and lived there for 3 years before her death.

For the last 40 years of her life, Marta was blessed to have the same house maid Josefina Fernandes, (Josefine to us all) who was trained by Marta well and they became good companions for each other. We all (F.X. Pereira's children) loved Josefine, and to this date, we care for her wellbeing and keep in regular touch with her.

Marta taught her to cook, and Josefine cooked delicious dishes which we all loved. Ti Marta told me she herself never cooked or worked in the kitchen. Marta thoroughly looked after Josefine's well being, such that no matter what happened to ti Marta, Josefine's future was looked after. For the services rendered and dedication shown to Marta, Josefine deserved the personal attention she received from Marta.

Marta taught her to save most of her earnings in fixed deposits at the bank, so that at her death, Josefine was financially well grounded. Marta arranged for Josefine to get her own ration card and assured that she would also receive the monthly Government allowance of INR 2,000, for which she was eligible, after age 65. Marta also paid special attention to Josefine's health (in particular diabetes), and an early morning walk became part of Josefine's daily routine.

Marta kept herself busy with crochet. She was very adept at it, and over the years, she would take orders, and earn some pocket money. A few of her family members were also beneficiaries of receiving her crochet works, as gifts. We received a few pieces, the principal being a bed cover.

Another facet of life, Marta was good at, was match making. The people involved would be relatives and friends. I know a few she has successfully brought to fruition, and I am sure she has had her hand in few more.

Marta put her organization and disciplined approach to good use, and we have lot to thank her for it. She had all her own affairs in good order, as did the Pereiras going back at least 200 years. She had every document possible well guarded, so that when the time came to sort out any household or property related matters, she had the original documents needed by the lawyers, the builders or municipal authorities.

(Dr.) **Francisco Xavier Pereira** (1914-1999, age 85), known to his siblings as Francis, to his nephews as Ti Chico, and to outsiders as F.X. or Dr. Pereira, is Ethel's dad. F.X. along with his wife Phoebe Menezes, make up one half of the families (Ethel's side) whose stories this book is all about. The other half is the Moniz and Menezes families on Emano's side.

Right from his childhood, Francis was a quiet lad, and unlike most young men, he was happy to get hold of good book and sit reading it in the living room. They have a Konkani saying for it, "ghor mazor", or house cat.

He appeared to be following in Pati's footsteps and was studying for priesthood, again at the Seminary in Daman, where Pati did his formation. He completed his Philosophy studies, and was probably about 2 years from priesthood.

Then he decided that priesthood was not for him. When Francis informed Pati, about his decision, he was asked him what did he want to do with his life. Francis said "I want to be a medical doctor". Pati supported his decision and by 1943 he had completed his medical graduation and internship. His first job was at Kemps Pharmacy

Maria Blenure **Phoebe** Menezes (1917-1998, age 80) and Francis married on April 22, 1945. Phoebe, who had a good job at Firestone, and Francis had been in courtship even before he had completed his Medical degree through KEM Medical School, University of Mumbai

Phoebe, who never missed a chance to help others, used her position as Executive Secretary to the Managing Director at Firestone, to put a good word and help many Goans to get employment within the company.

Francis and Phoebe lived with Phoebe's mother for the first few months of their married life, before they moved in with Llewelyn (Loyola) and Aida Pacheco family in Byculla. It is worth a mention that Loyola Pacheco's grandson Kevin Pacheco, has married my eldest brother Loyola's daughter, Rochelle Moniz.

The Pereira-Pacheco friendship lasted till the end. Just a few months before daddy died, I was down in India. Daddy was bed ridden and he would hardly respond to our communication with him. There were two instances where he surprised me. My brother Loiola came visiting in Byculla. When I announced to daddy that my brother Loiola was there to visit him, he responded "Loiola Pacheco"? The old memory and affection was still there!

A similar situation happened when Vernon Miranda (C.J.V. Miranda's son) dropped in to visit daddy, Marjorie and me. When I announced his presence, daddy's tongue suddenly freed up, saying "Nice to see you Vernon after a long time. What brings you here?" His old memories of people, were still there.

In 1948 Francis and Phoebe would buy (through pagdi) their own flat for INR 2,000 at 17 Habib Park, on Clare Road, where they raised all their children, and lived all their lives. In mid 1960s the adjoining flat came up for sale, for INR 16,000 and the Pereiras added it to their existing premises. I have given the prices paid for the flats, so that there is a marker for property prices over time, for future reference, regarding real estate price inflation in Mumbai.

Under the pagdi system, introduced decades ago, the rent the tenant pays is nominal and the tenant is a part-owner of the house but not the land. The tenant also keeps paying the rent till he has not sub-let the premise. This tenant or part-owner could also sell the property but a portion, about 30-50 per cent of the gross amount had to be paid to the real owner.

Their first trip to Goa for Francis and Phoebe, as a married couple, came in September 1946, on the occasion of Pati's First Mass Golden Jubilee (Sept 27, 1896-1946). I am told, there was an expectant excitement, among the young nephews in Goa, at the prospect of seeing Ti Chico's bride, for the first time.

One of these nephews told me, that when he laid his eyes on Phoebe, as she was getting out of the car, he couldn't believe his eyes. He said to me "what a beauty ti Phoebe was!" By the way, many of the nephews could only look from far as they were suffering from smallpox.

The family was celebrating Pati's birthday on October 16, the day Francis came down with high fever. Francis was under the care of Dr. Antonio Colaco and then Dr. Antonio Dias, the Director of Surgery at the Hospicio. Two weeks passed by, and the fever would not go down and he even threw up some blood. The initial diagnosis was typhoid and then changed to Peritonitis, which is inflammation of the peritoneum or the lining of the inner wall of the abdomen.

On December 1, the doctor told Phoebe, that Francis' end was near and word was sent to his sisters about it. All sisters came over with black dresses ready for the bad finale. Then on December 3, Dr. Antonio Dias, during his examination, felt a lump on Francis side and with the help of a syringe found puss from an abscess on the liver.

Francis was operated immediately and the operation was a success to family's great relief and joy. If you believe in miracles or by coincidence, December 3, is the day Goans, both Christians and Hindus celebrate the feast day of St. Francis Xavier, Patron Saint of Goa, (Goencho Sahib). On this day thousands of people from all over Goa, flock to Old Goa, and pray at the Basilica of Bom Jesus where St. Francis Xavier's venerated body lies.

Phoebe returned to Bombay soon after, as she had to report back to her job. Francis followed her only in March.

Phoebe was the front person, the talkative one and a ball of unbridled energy. Even at age 80, she would go up and down the two levels of staircase in their building, to get some snacks or whatever, when a younger person in the house could easily have done it.

Phoebe made up for her husband's extreme quiet nature and embraced her husband's side of the family with unending enthusiasm. She was loved by everyone in particular her nephews and nieces. Those coming from Goa, whether family members or just good friends, were treated to her magnanimous nature and ever readiness to accompany them into town for shopping.

Francis was quiet and happy to be left alone. His DNA was that of husband and father bringing the bread home, always cool, who believed in doing what is right. He was also very proud of his brain power and smarts. I heard him say he had brains, even in his toe nails.

His pleasures were a daily glass of Whiskey (Indian Whiskey) in the evenings, a smoke after meals and playing cards with their circle of close friends on Sundays.

When his daughters were visiting from abroad, it was an opportunity for him to have a second glass of whiskey with sons-in-law accompanying him, to the chagrin of Phoebe. This son-in-law, would not join him, and he said that I was no fun! By the way, Phoebe would take a sip or two from his glass and then make faces, as she did not enjoy it, but that was her way for Francis to consume less whiskey.

Playing cards was a serious pass-time and the Pereiras and their friends would meet once a week or at alternate week at each other's homes, with drinks and food provided. In fact, Daddy would play Uffa cards game with our son Francis, then 7 or 8, and daddy would take it very seriously even with the junior Francis. Mummy would say to daddy, "Francis let him win no!"

Towards his final years, Francis had contracted emphysema, probably as a result of his smoking, even though he was only a moderate smoker. That did not stop him from continuing to smoke. I heard him say that he "took care of the kids and the family, and in his final years he was not going to forgo one of his few pleasures"

In 1950, an opportunity arose for Francis to set up his own clinic, near Byculla Bridge, a location not too far from where they were living, and it turned out where eventually they bought their flat. The seller was a patient of his, and who was in arrears in rent payment and would otherwise lose possession of the place. The asking price was INR 4,000. This was soon after they had bought the Byculla flat. They closed the deal with INR 2,000 of their own money and the balance a loan from Phoebe's mother.

Francis and Phoebe had five children: (Dr.) Marjorie (1948), who remains unmarried, and continues to live in their Habib Park flat, after Phoebe and Francis passed away in 1998 and 1999 respectively; (Dr.) Yvonne Pereira D'Souza (1949) (married Ralph D'Souza, with family roots from Moira, Goa); Ethelwyn Pereira Moniz (1953) (married Eufemiano Moniz, with family roots from Curtorim, Goa); Francisco Pereira (1954-1957); Maria Aurora Pereira (1959) (married Geoffrey Pinto, of Pinto Rosario family roots from Porvorim, Goa).

Marjorie stayed in India, whilst the other three migrated to North America: Yvonne to USA, and Ethelwyn (Ethel) and Maria Aurora (Maria) to Canada.

In 1980 Francis and Phoebe came to visit us in Canada. Actually, they were sponsored to come as landed immigrants (permanent residents) to Canada, only to facilitate immigration for Maria Aurora, and they had no interest in settling down in Canada. After a short vacation here and then a visit to Yvonne in the USA, they went back to India. Daddy told me he hated flying and had nightmares about this whole ordeal. Mummy returned in 1985, to help Yvonne on the occasion of the arrival of her third child, Andre.

The Pereiras went through a terrible time, when their three-year old son, Francis, also known affectionately as Babulucho, got hit by a BEST bus, and died instantly in 1957. The servant boy looking after him got distracted and young Francis supposedly seeing family friends across the street, darted across the road.

Everyone was devastated, and most of all daddy, who I understand, was never the same again. Daddy Francis' mother passed away a few months later, in the same year. When the post-man came to deliver the telegraph, he said to Daddy, "I have some sad news for you;" daddy's response was "I have just lost my son, and there can be no sadder news than that."

Dr. F.X. and Mrs. Phoebe Pereira and Baby Francis' remains rest in the family grave at the Catholic Cemetery at Haines Road, Mumbai. Baby Francis has a special pedestal with the following inscription.

In Ever Loving memory of Baby Francis Xavier
Beloved Son of Dr. and Mrs. F.X. Pereira
Born 15th December 1954
Died 3rd November 1957

Silently at dusk came the divine gardener
And plucked from our garden the sweetest flower
We see not your smile, we hear no voice
Which for three years our hearts did rejoice
On hope we live, Babulucho dear, that sooner or later
In your heavenly home, we will join you forever

Tribute of love from Your sorrowful parents and sisters

Yes, he is still remembered on his special dates and through a beautiful photograph.

When our son was born in 1990, we decided to give him the name Francis. When I called to convey the news of the birth and our decision to name him Francis, I heard protestations from mummy, saying it was not a lucky name. Remember Babulucho's name was Francis. I told them I did not believe in such things, and we went ahead with the name.

After Phoebe's death, I heard from so many people, who were grateful to her for helping them. Many of the requests would be favours at Customs, knowing the family had good contacts at the time, with a few senior customs officers. More than once, I am told, she would even wait at the Mumbai docks for hours, for the ship to arrive from East Africa.

I picked up a part of the wording on the mass card on the occasion of one week's remembrance, for Phoebe as it is better than I can articulate.

Happy, smiling and always content
Loved and respected, wherever you went
To a beautiful life, came a sudden end
You died as you lived, everyone's cherished friend

Francis was a genuine and gentle spirit. He was a good son and a responsible son, and acted as one all his life. As soon as he started working as a medical doctor, Francis dutifully and regularly remitted funds to support his mother to her final days. All the maintenance costs for the Margao house, were also borne by Francis from prior to and after Pati's death.

He continued to pay for all the expenses related to the maintenance of the Goa residence, and support payments for Marta. Phoebe supported him fully on this matter, and they were always a team. In fact, the last ten years of their lives it was Phoebe who had taken over this task. Francis's children and their spouses made sure this support and maintenance for ti Marta, the house and Josefine, continued and were enhanced.

In 1997 Ethel convinced mummy and daddy to accompany us to Goa, as they had not been there for many years and they had not seen many family members for a while. I can think of Ti Clarissa, to whom daddy was close to in age and had a special fondness.

As expected, daddy was reluctant to come down to Goa out of fear of flying. The short but bumpy ride due to monsoon weather did not help.

I am positive that their final trip to Goa was a truly heart-warming experience for mummy and daddy, his siblings and relatives. We also had an opportunity to celebrate Mummy's last birthday (July 28) with singing of Ladainha (Litany) and a modest party at home with all family members of their generation present.

In hindsight this trip to Goa was timely. In the years 1998 and 1999 we had more than our fair share of deaths in the family: Clarissa (February 1998); Cajetan (C.J.V.) Miranda (mummy's cousin and close friend) (April 1998); Phoebe (June 1998); Jovita (August 1998); F.X. Pereira (July 1999); Arthur Menezes (March 1999); Cesar Menezes (September 1999). The latter two are Ti Ofelia's eldest sons.

Many within the family were of the opinion that Phoebe should get herself checked up for what was suspected to be jaundice. After a lot of prodding, Phoebe finally relented and had a biopsy done on June 30. The same evening, she breathed her last at home.

Daddy, who by this time was partially bed ridden, lasted exactly another year. Marjorie should be credited for being his sole and devoted care giver for that period.

I would like to share with you a tribute from one of our cousins, Vernon Miranda, to Francis and Phoebe, who would have been delighted to hear it. "Phoebe and Francis were very special people. Dr. Francis was a man of very few words but a very noble human being. Phoebe was a very lovely person at heart and her warmth, sincerity and affection, which she showered on one and all, was beyond what words can describe."

"Words are inadequate for me to describe the great affection, love and respect we have for this lovely couple, who you are fortunate to have as your parents-in-law. They brought up four lovely daughters for whom we have much affection".

"We all are now at a stage in our lives where we take delight in our children and grandchildren. We have reaped the benefits of all the good deeds and traditions our respective ancestors have left behind for us."

At the personal level, I still remember Francis and Phoebe as in-laws from heaven: always supportive and never a word about how to raise our kids, or anything we did or did not do. The gist of the only thing Daddy ever asked me, through a note he wrote to me, when I married Ethelwyn, is "to take good care of my little girl. She has always been close to me. She has decided to marry you and move to Canada. And I respect her wishes." I took my father-in-law's words seriously and I believe I have done my best to fulfill his wishes. I used to send messages about it to daddy with people going from Canada to Mumbai, partly as a joke and partly to reassure him. I hope at least one of those messages reached him.

Francis and Phoebe were way ahead of their time, in never interfering or volunteering their advice on how to bring up their grandchildren. Even with Francis and Phoebe showing us the way, we have not really learnt from their example, as we do not miss an opportunity to give our advice to our children, which even if well intended, is probably not always welcome.

I am truly amazed at Francis and Phoebe's confidence in our abilities to manage our life, in particular their grandchildren. I have watched these matters in many other families when I was growing up in Goa. I do not have to go too far. My own mother had all kinds of advice for us, when she came visiting in Canada: your kids have too many toys even though all toys were either company Christmas party gifts or bought at garage sales for pennies on the dollar; you are not feeding your kids enough (because Celine was a premature baby, in my mother's head she was a weakling).

As of this time of writing, I asked myself, how do I remember Francis and Phoebe, my in-laws. I remember Daddy as a man of extremely few words. French philosopher Blaise Pascal said "all humanity's problems stem from man's inability to sit quietly in a room alone." Daddy did that his whole life from his young age in Margao to his life in Mumbai I wish I had twenty percent of that virtue.

I remember Mummy for being the most unselfish person I have known, which earned her a special kind of love from all her nephews, nieces and anybody who knew her. Another thing that reminds me of her is her loving habit (but at the same time annoying to me) of adding food in my plate, even under my protestations. This would also irritate daddy, who used to say to her, "if he is telling you not to add food in his plate, why do you do it." And this comes from a man of very few words. I know mummy meant well, and it is not an uncommon habit amongst many old time Goan ladies.

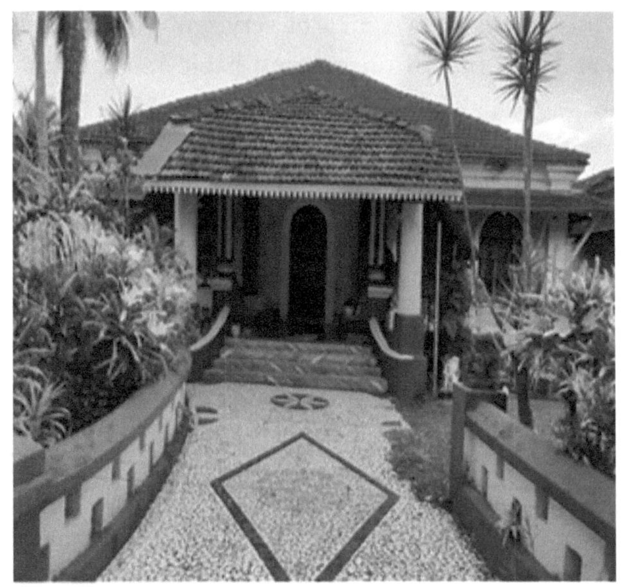

The MONIZ (Menkar) House,
Maina Curtorim, 2022

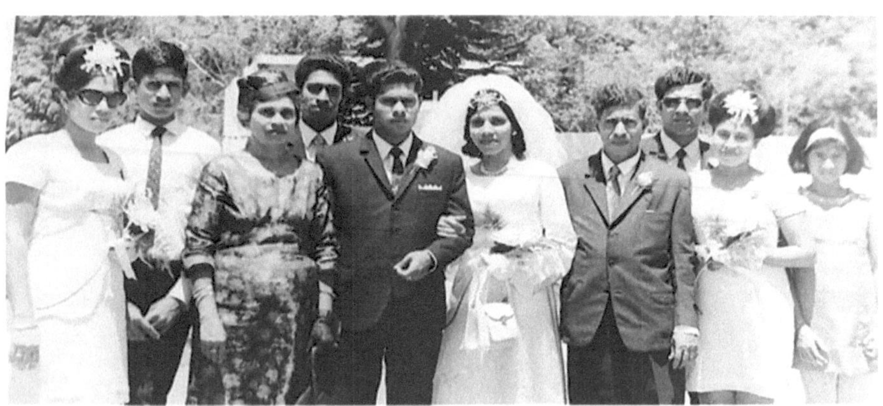

1970: Loiola and Benildes Moniz Wedding
Violeta, Flaviano, Marcelina, Eufemiano, Loiola,
Benildes, Caetano, Heriberto, Blanche and Serena

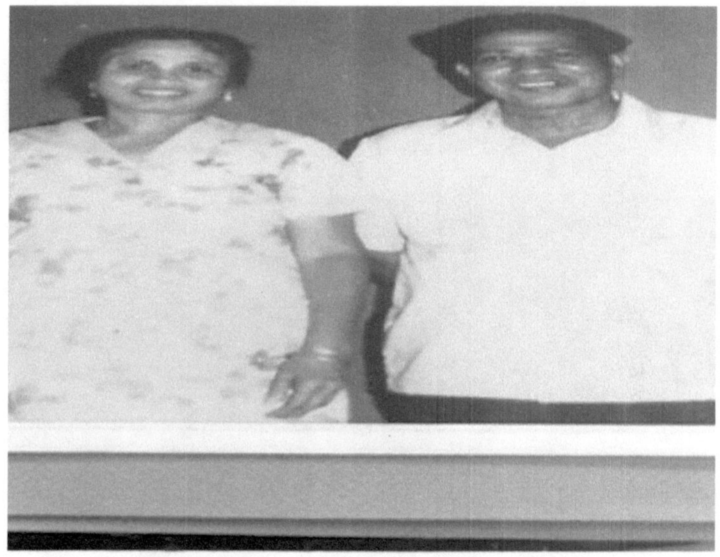

Marcelina & Caetano Moniz, 1975

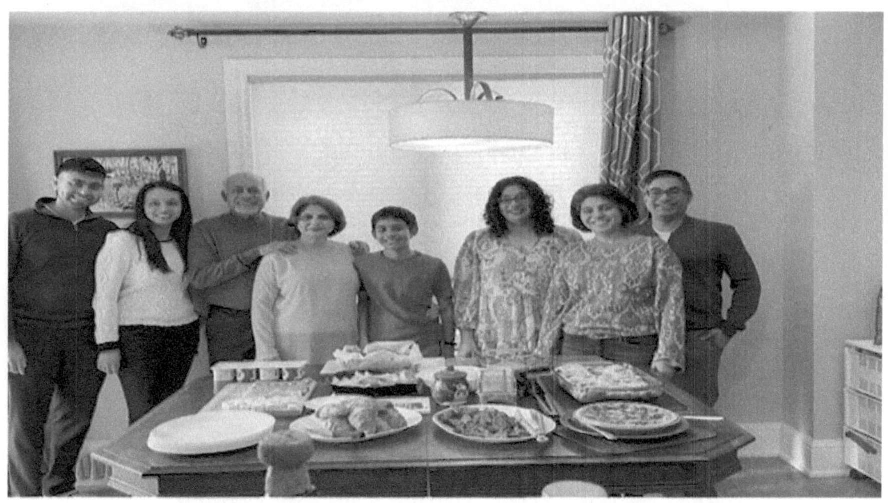

January 2024 Ethel and Emano's Family: Francis, Kimberley, Emano, Ethel Moniz, Ethan and Celine and Russell de Souza. Larissa Moniz standing between Celine and Russell.

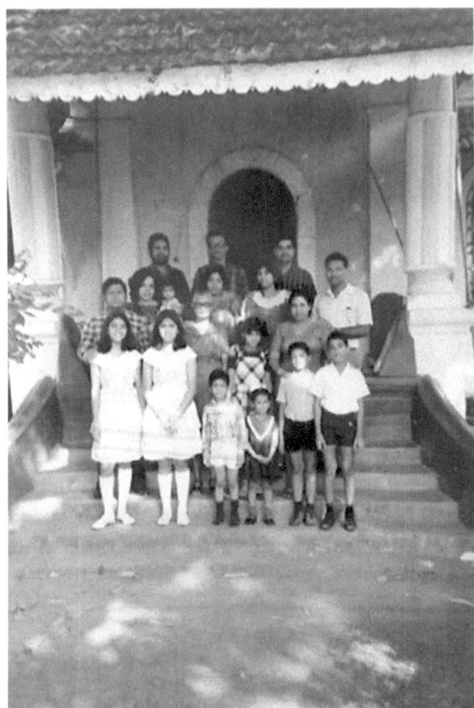

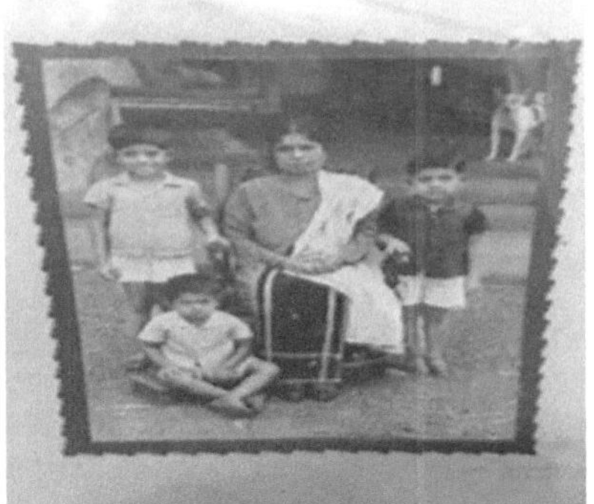

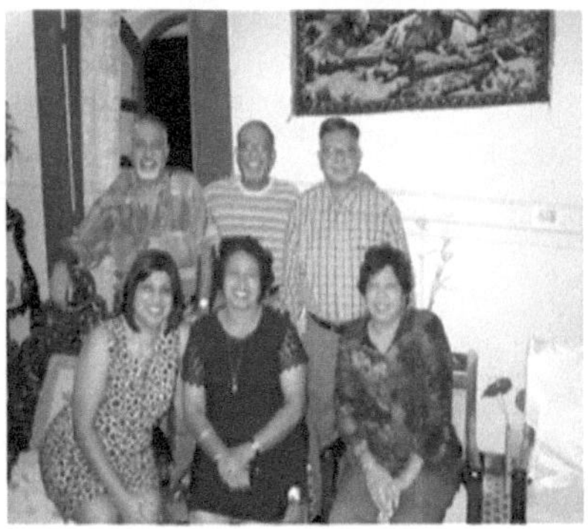

1951 Top Right L to R: Loiola Grandma
Cecilia, Heriberto, Front Eufemiano

2011 Right Bottom Photo: Siblings- Front Serena, Blanche,
Violeta, Back: Eufemiano, Heriberto and Loiola.

1991 Top Left Photo at Moniz House in Maina.
From Back Row:
Flaviano, Albino, Belrosario,
Middle Row: Loiola, Benildes holding Danielle,
Marcelina, Violeta, Serena, Blanche, Placido
Front Row: Michelle, Rochelle, Pierre, Nadia, Muriel, Olancio, Ashly

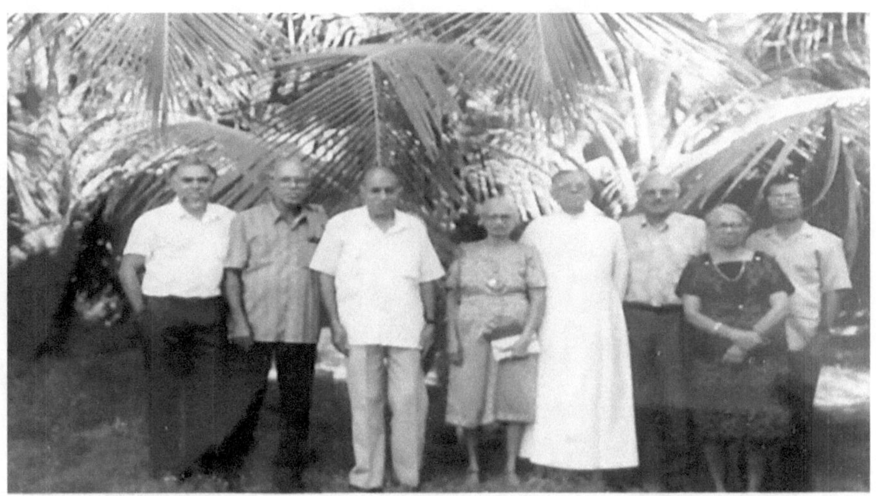

1980? Top Photo-The Menezes (Godd) Siblings, Left to Right: Jose, Constancio, Carmo, Marcelina, Fr. Rosario, Francisco Xavier, Albertina and Lourencinho

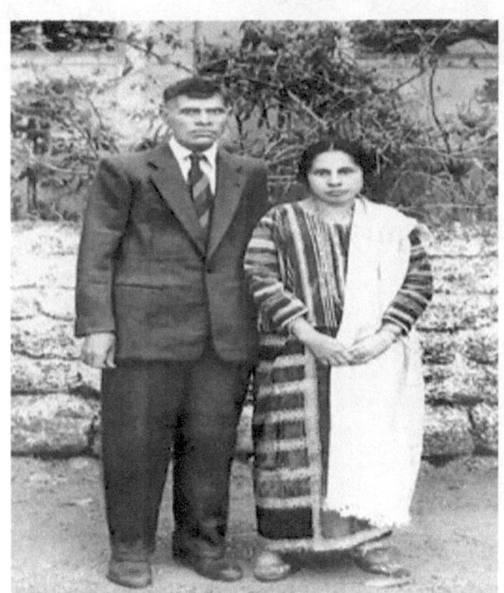

\1960? Above: Caetaninho and Maria Menezes, my Grandparents "Godd"

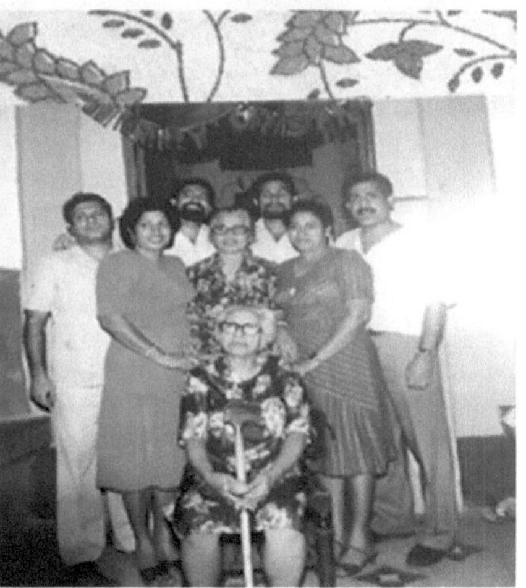

1975? Above: back to front, left to right: Loiola, Eufemiano, Flaviano, Heriberto, Violeta, Mae (Marcelina) Blanche and Xamae (Maria)

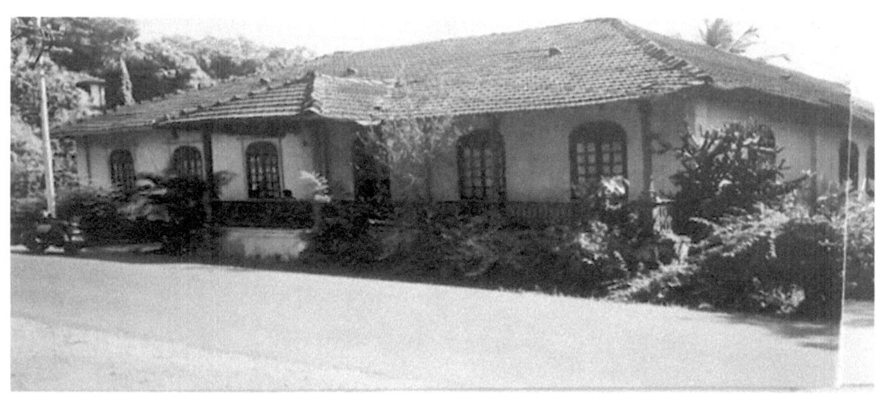

The PEREIRA House in Margao mid-1800 to 2008

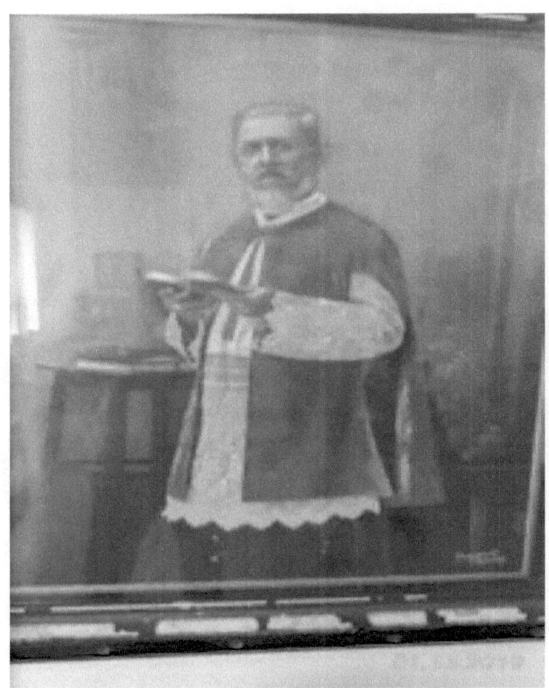

1938 Msgr. Aniceto Pereira, brother to Epifanio
Pereira and Mentor to F.X. Pereira and siblings

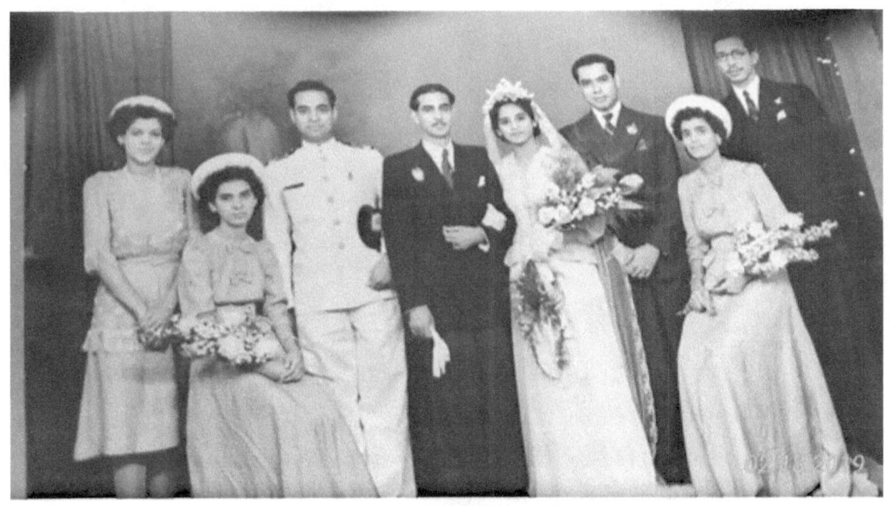

1946 F.X. Pereira and Phobe Blenure Menezes Wedding.
From L to R: ???, Marta Pereira, Aniceto Pereira, ???,
Nina Menezes, Grevi Menezes

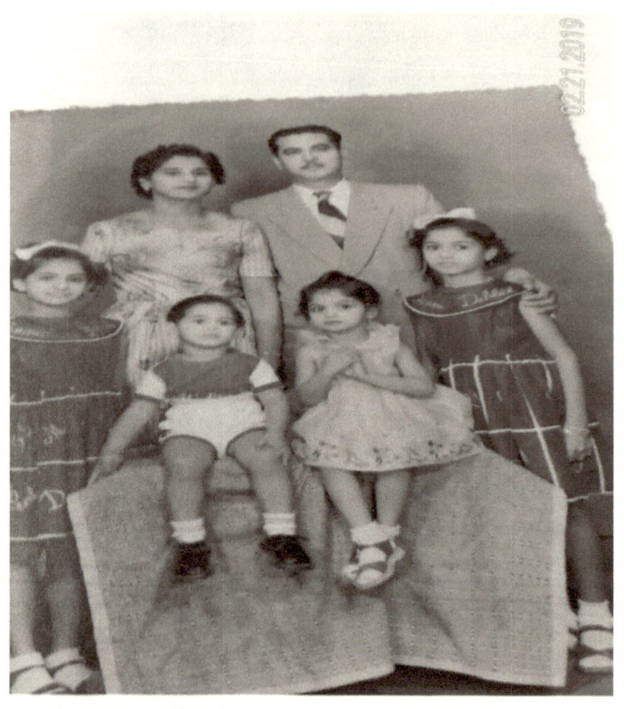

1956 Above: Phoebe and F.X. with L to R: Yvonne,
Baby Francis, Ethelwyn and Marjorie.

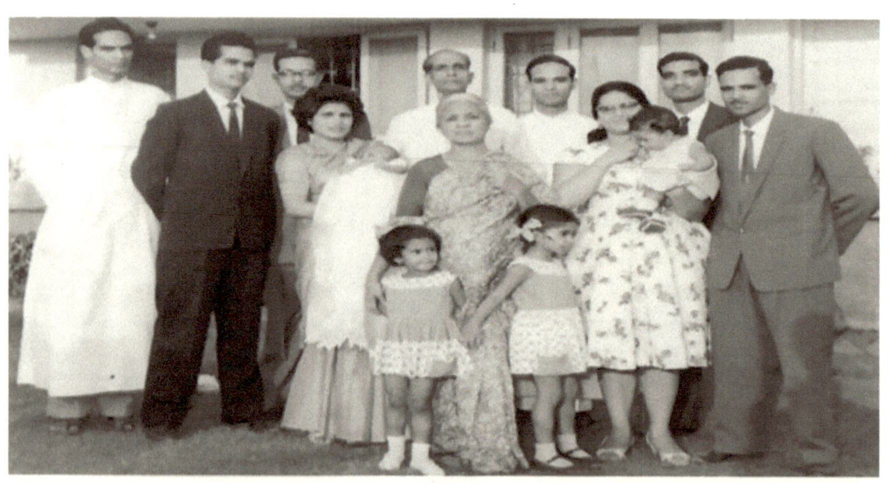

1962 – Roque and Ofelia Menezes Family
L to R: Fr. Albert, Roquito, Cesar, Anita holding Sunita, Roque,
Ofelia, Fr. Luis, Teresa holding Flavia, Joseph, Aires.
Missing Arthur: Monica and Pia in front

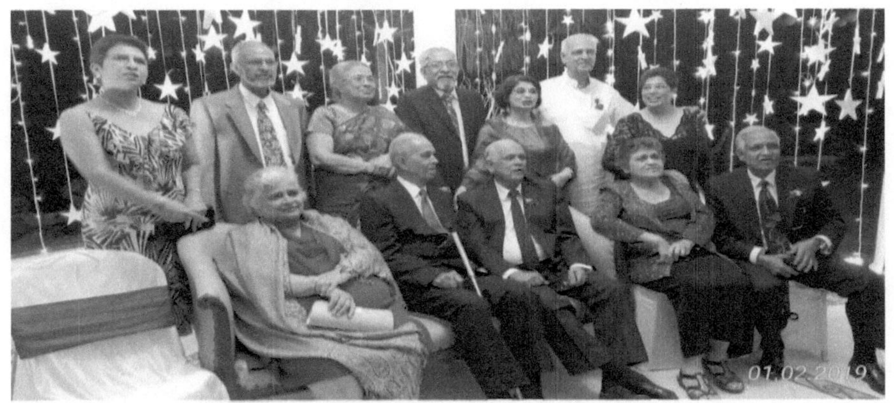

2019 First cousins at Sunita and Michael
D'Souza's daughter Larissa's Wedding
Back Row L to R: Bernadette, Edgar, Clelia,
Mario, Ethel, Fr. Albert, Leah
Front Row: Theresa, Maurelio Cota, Aires, Toni and Joseph

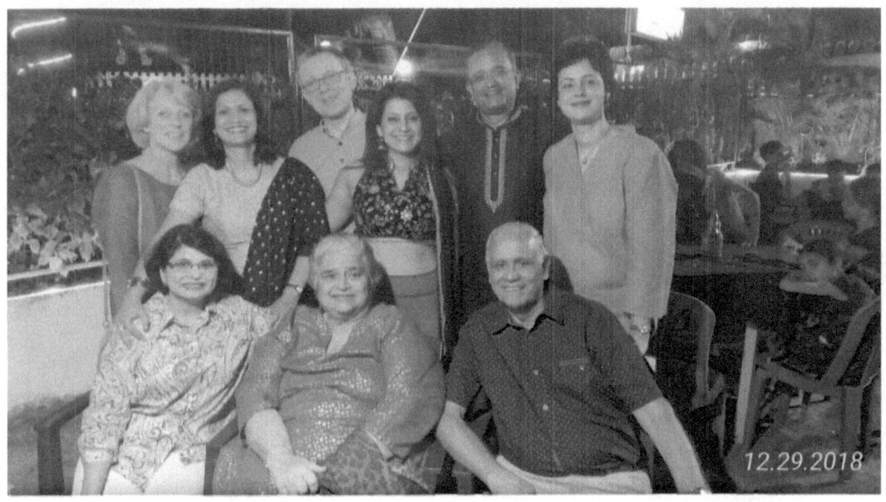

2019 Above Photo: Back Row: Monique Demortier Menezes,
Flavia Menezes Pereira, Paul Henri-Renard, Priya and
Savio Menezes, Johanna Menezes Henri-Renard.
Front Row: Ethel Pereira Moniz, Theresa and Aires Menezes

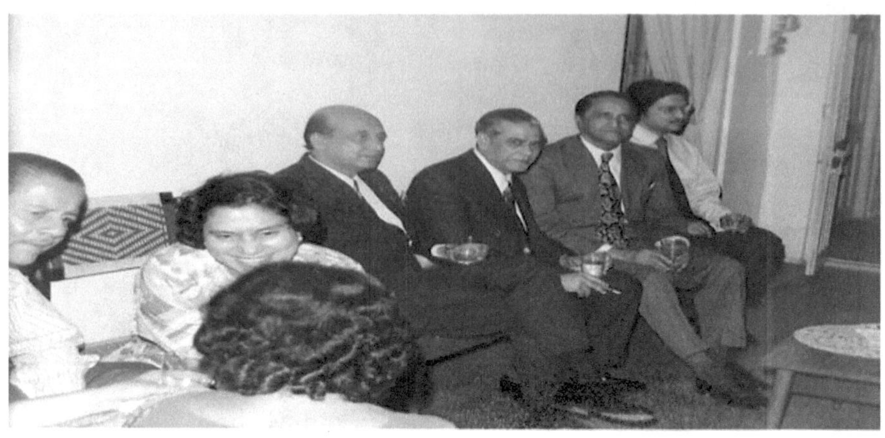

1975: Engagement Occasion of Ethelwyn Pereira and Eufemiano Moniz
Top: Christopher and Edith Soares, Bob Tellis, F.X.
Pereira, C.J.V. Miranda and Cecil de Cruz
Bottom: L to R: Lino Misquita, and Monizes (Benildes,
Belmira, Carol, Joaquim and Maria E and E, Jeanette,
Helena and Riario Moniz, Ralph, Loyola and Lira)
(Belmira is Lino's sister and Carol is Lino's wife)

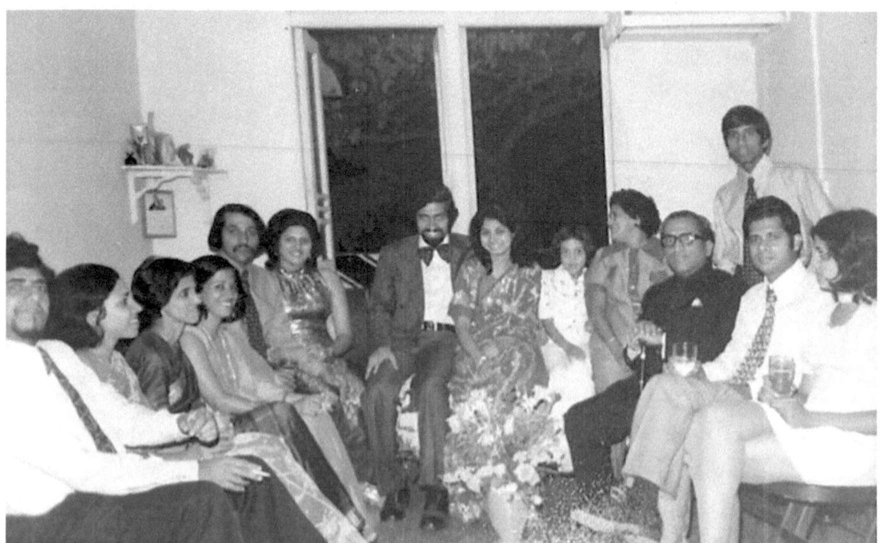

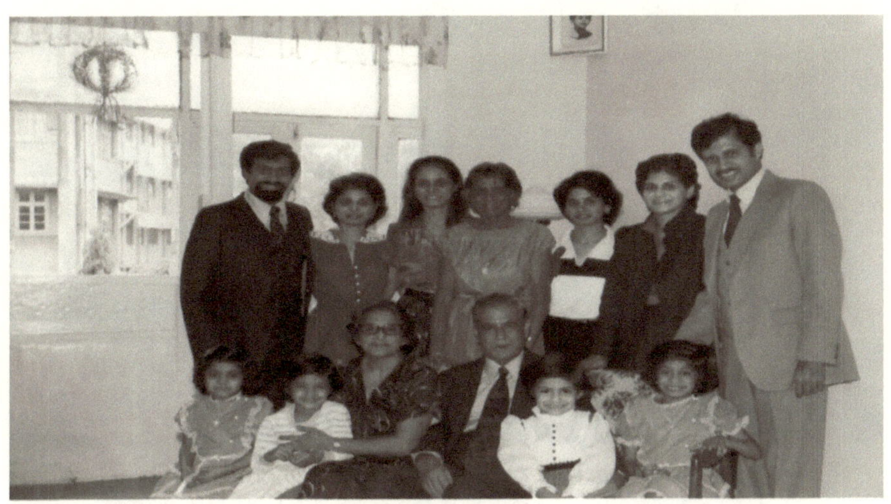

1983 L to R
Rear: Eufemiano, Ethelwyn, Marjorie, Nina Menezes,
Maria Aurora, Yvonne and Ralph D'Souza.
Front: Larissa Moniz, Marise D'Souza, Phoebe and
F.X. Pereira, Simone D'Souza and Celine Moniz

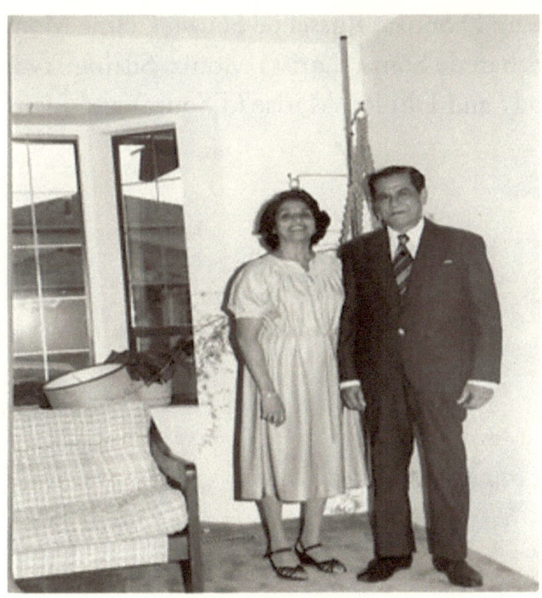

1980 in Vancouver
Phoebe and F.X. Pereira visiting the Monizes

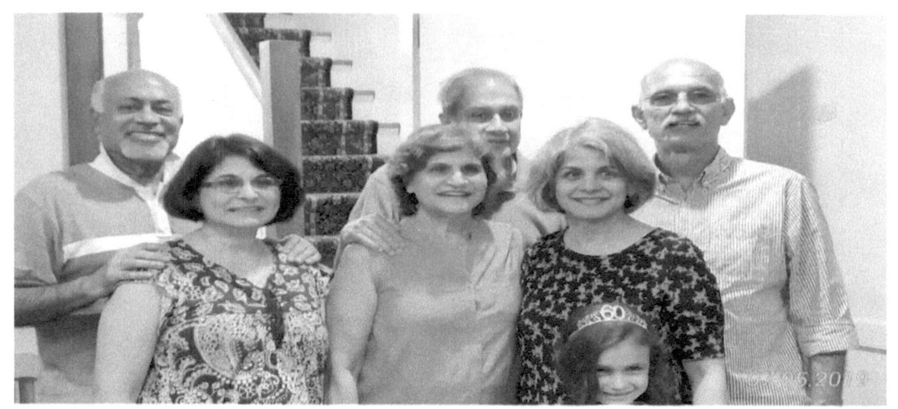

2019 Get-together of Yvonne, Ethelwyn and Maria
Aurora's families at Cornell USA, to celebrate Maria"s
60th Birthday. Kiera Brody in front of Maria.
Bottom Photograph: L to R. <u>Rear Row</u>: Michael Brody holding
son Ryan, Ralph d'Souza, Geoff Pinto Kyle< Casey Butterly, Kyle
and Alexandra (Ali) Pinto, Francis Moniz, Ryan and Anna Pinto.
<u>Front Row</u>: Simone d'Souza Brody with Luke B, Maria Aurora,
Rita and Andre D'Souza, Russel de Souza, Celine Moniz de Souza,
Ethel with Ethan de Souza, Larissa Moniz. Sitting: Yvonne holding
Kiera Brody and Dhillon Marise (d'Souza) and Liam Butterly

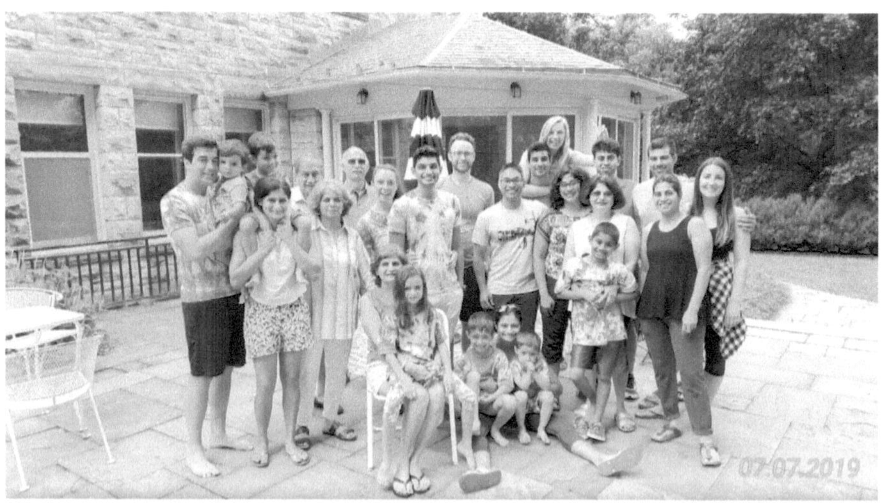

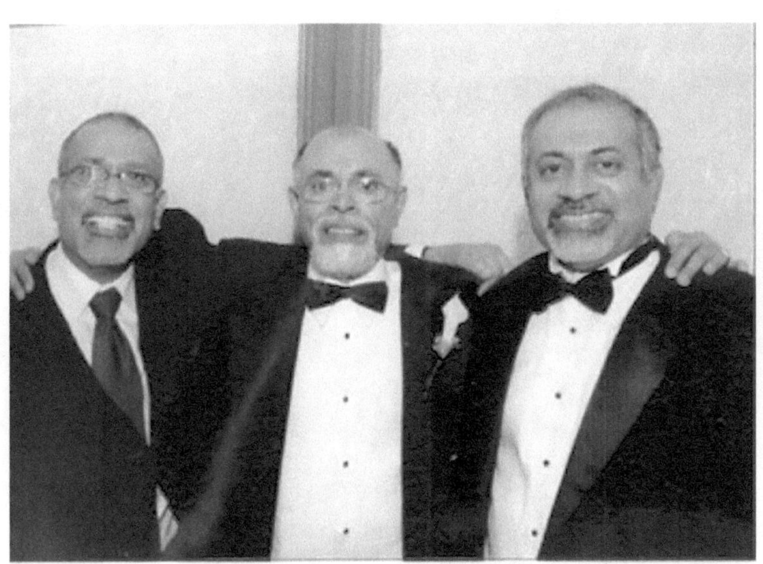

2014 Photo
Heriberto Moniz, Our Uncle Jose Menezes, Eufemiano Moniz
Bottom Photo

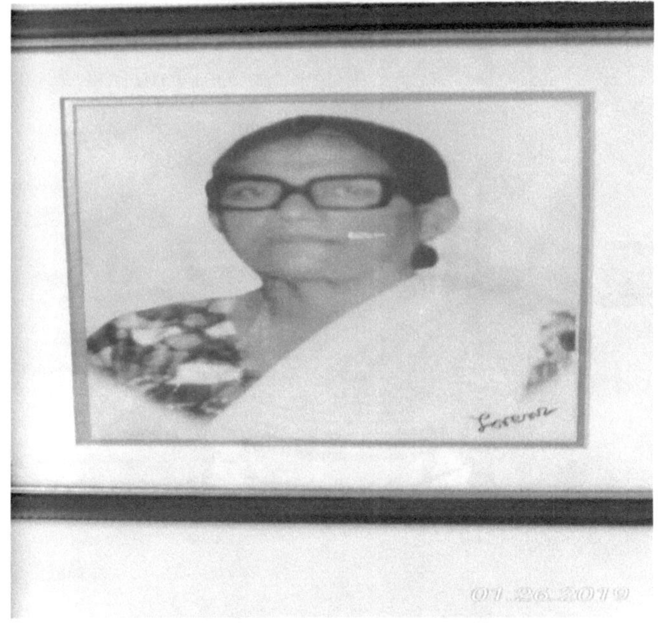

Rosa Maria (Menezes) Sardinha

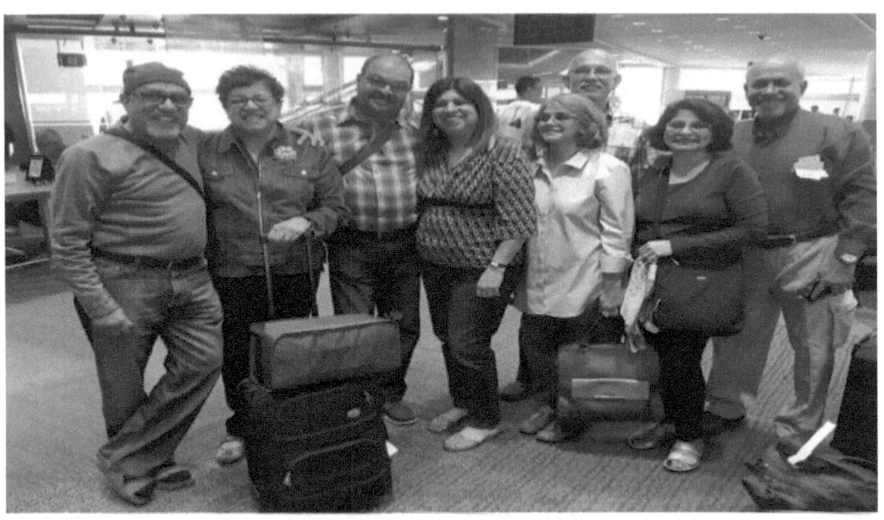

Above: May 2017 -Trip to China. L to R Heriberto and Maria Lurdes Moniz, Belrosario and Serena Diniz, Maria Aurora and Geoffrey Pinto, Ethelwyn and Eufemiano Moniz

Below: 1920. L to R – Ryan, Maria and Geoffrey Pinto, Kimberley and Francis Moniz, Larissa, Ethelwyn and Eufemiano Moniz

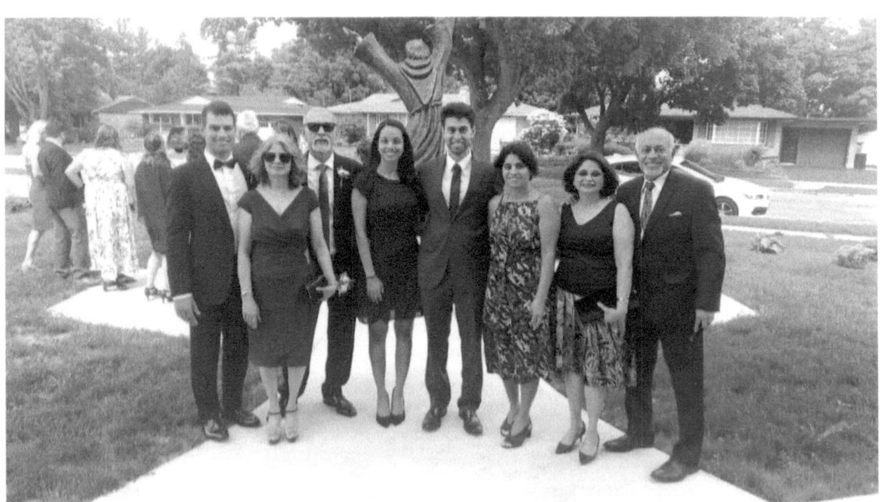

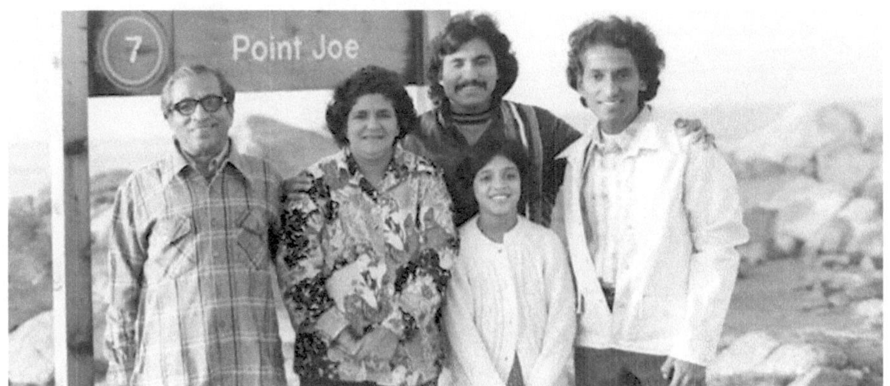

Top: mid 1970s Riario, Helena, Avito,
Jeanette and Fr. Joe (in California)

Bottom: 1981 at Curtorim House– Back Row: Tony, Joaquim,
Fr. Joe Front Row: Avito, Carol, Helena, Egidio and Jeanette

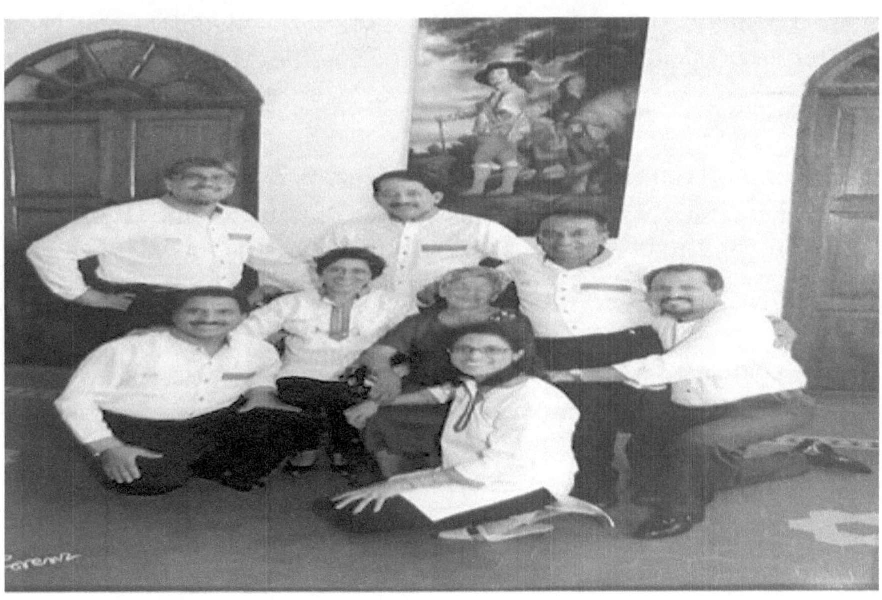

C H A P T E R 11

MENEZES (PHOEBE MENEZES PEREIRA) Family

Compared to the three big families we have talked about in the previous three chapters, including siblings and nephews and nieces from the F.X. Pereira side, Phoebe's side is no doubt much more limited in numbers.

Besides her own two siblings, Phoebe had two sets of first cousins: Cajetan (C.J.V.) Miranda (Phoebe's close friend too, confidant and go to person) and his sister Miquelina Lourenco. Phoebe's mother and Cajetan's mother are sisters.

The other set of cousins was: (Dr.) Mario Menezes, Zelma Menezes da Silva; three other Menezes siblings are the children of Luis Caetano Gonzaga de Menezes (1864-1937). Luis Caetano and Phoebe's father Antonio Vicente are brothers and thus their children are first cousins.

Phoebe's parents are Antonio Vicente Fortunato de Menezes (?1877?-1935, age approximate 60) from Magilvaddo, Raia and **Filomena** Carmelina Joaquina Fernandes (circa 1880-circa 1963) from Curtorim. The father worked at the Bombay Post office and the mother was a housewife, supplementing house income doing mid-wife jobs. They lived at Byculla Chambers, not too far from the Byculla Railway Station and the old vegetable open air market.

The money was not plentiful, but sufficient for the household expenses including education of the children. After Antonio Vicente died suddenly in 1935, during a vacation visit to Goa, money was in short supply in the household.

They had three Children: Anthony **Grevy** Menezes (1912-1992, age 79), **Nina** Menezes (1914-1998, age 84) and Maria Blenure **Phoebe** Menezes Pereira (1917-1998, age 81).

Nina, who stayed unmarried was a fun-person to be around. She was artistic, well dressed, and left good memories with her nieces. She is remembered for dressing them up, playing with them, doing little things like entertaining them and dancing with them.

She had joined the JJ School of Arts, but had to drop out, upon death of her father, in order to help financially at home, in particular as Grevy was pursuing the law degree studies. She liked to be independent, and had a bit of a "short fuse" and thus not one to take advice from others, except maybe from her brother Grevi.

After passing of her mother, Nina found herself a place in Bandra, near Mehboob Studios, where she would keep boarders to create an added income. After many years at this location, a real estate agent, who had befriended her and she came to trust, convinced her to sell the place in Bandra and move further north. I understand the thinking was, you get more money for your place in Bandra than the cost of the new digs further north, and you have surplus funds towards retirement expenses.

Nina made the move twice (to benefit the real estate agent?), until she was too far for mummy to even visit her. I believe it was Andheri North, in a brand new development, where there was not even adequate transport. Mummy would send a good family friend Pascu Colaco, himself an older gentleman but physically in good shape, to go and enquire about her. Somewhere during the multiple moves the real estate agent, made herself the beneficiary of Nina, which mummy made her change.

At her new residence, Nina used to receive regular visits or check-ups from the nuns in the area who used to take holy communion for her. In one of those visits, she was found dead, a few days after her death. It was just a few months before mummy passed away.

Grevi, also known as "Tony", became a lawyer and after a few years of practicing law in Mumbai, joined the Government of India's Foreign Service Department in 1948.

Grevi's first posting in September 1948, was in Brazil, as India's South American Commissioner of Commerce. Then in the 1950 -1958 period, various assignments followed, each approximately of two-year durations, as First Secretary of the Embassy in Rangoon, Burma, Joint Secretary at External Affairs in New Delhi, First Secretary of the Embassy in Paris, France and Jakarta, Indonesia and again Joint Secretary at External Affairs in New Delhi.

Grevi was then appointed as the Consul General of India in Hanoi, Vietnam (1958-1960) and San Francisco, California (1960-1962).

Grevi was promoted to Ambassador level position holding these posts between 1963-1971 in Nom Pen, Cambodia and Dublin, Ireland. He retired from diplomatic corps in 1971, after 23 years of service in the Indian External Affairs Department.

As you would expect, Grevi's mother and sisters were very proud of their son and brother, for his achievements in the Indian Diplomatic Services, even though they rarely saw him and his family.

After his retirement from the Diplomatic services, Grevi worked as a lawyer at Indian Supreme Court till his vision failed him in 1990. He was placed in a nursing home in Bengaluru in early 1992, but he passed away soon thereafter.

I corresponded with ti Grevi on a regular basis, after I married Ethel, in 1975, even though I had never met him or even seen a photograph of him until after his death. He enjoyed our regular correspondence but the correspondence with ti Grevi stopped when his eye sight was failing him.

A combination of being away on diplomatic service duties all over the world, and lack of effort on his part in keeping in touch with his own family, resulted in his nieces hardly knowing their uncle. I believe he came to that realization, when he counseled Maria Aurora and Geoff, in 1989 when they visited him in New Delhi. He told them "do not neglect your own family, the way I did."

Grevi married Thelma Alvares and they had two daughters, Geeta Alvares Menezes (1952-2017) and Nisha Alvares Menezes (1955-1989).

At ti Grevi's suggestion I wrote to Geeta and Nisha, as he told me they would happy to receive correspondence from me. I never heard back from them.

Years later I met **Geeta** once, when she came visiting us in Canada. She was visiting Yvonne and family, in New York City and accompanied them for a week's vacation. She died in 2017.

When I met Geeta, her younger sister **Nisha** was no longer among the living, having died at age 34.

Thelma, who had a long history of cardiac problems and surgeries for it, died, after suffering a major heart attack on the news of her daughter Nisha's death.

Cajetan (C.J.V.) Miranda (1911-1998, age 87)

As far back as I can think, I felt great pride, when any Goan excelled in life, in particular when they were holding high positions in the public or private sector.

For example, when I was studying Engineering in Mumbai between 1966 and 1970, Cajetan Miranda, who was the super cop in the Mumbai / Maharashtra State Police services, was frequently in the news of the evening English language tabloid, and from his name I assumed he was a Goan. His daughter Carmen, an accomplished pianist, and trained in Vienna, was later also in the news from time to time each time she had a recital. I am not sure, whether I had connected them then, as being father and daughter. Another name in the news at that time was Commissioner Julio Ribeiro, posted in the area covering Matunga, where my Engineering College, VJTI was located.

Each time I would read about them on the evening newspaper, I felt a touch of pride. I never expected that one day I would be part of the Pereiras' or Phoebe's extended family. My mother-in-law Phoebe and Cajetan are first cousins, as their mothers are sisters and that too hailing from Curtorim, the place of my upbringing.

Move forward to April 9, 1975, the date of my engagement to Ethel and a reception at her house in Byculla, when I met Uncle Cajetan. I don't really remember whether I was awestruck or just very happy to meet Cajetan, my hero of so many years. I hope I contained my excitement in meeting him, but we corresponded regularly, and visited with the Miranda family each time we went down on vacations to India.

All these years, my admiration for Uncle Cajetan, was on the basis of a broad knowledge of the position he had attained, and after my marriage to Ethel, on the basis of their close family bonds. Only recently upon digging for information on his professional achievements, did I gain greater knowledge about this principled man and his brilliant career and meritorious awards.

Would I have been intimidated, if I had known all that prior to now? Probably not, as both through my written correspondence and face to face meetings, he was a gentleman, showed genuine interest in our lives and made us always feel at ease.

Cajetan and Phoebe, were not just first cousins. As kids, they spent lot of time together under the same roof at Phoebe's place in Byculla, during the summer school breaks. They were good pals. Their friendship only grew with time, and Phoebe would not hesitate to call her cousin for advice or help, on police matters or otherwise, not for herself but for neighbors and friends who knew of this connection. That is Phoebe for you.

Cajetan's position and good name in the police services enhanced respectability of the Goan community in Mumbai I understand that because of his influence, functions such as Catholic Gymkhana, would get better police protection.

He did not forget to help family when he could. As you have read earlier, through his good word, Ti Ofelia's children got admission at St. Mary's, Mazagon, in the middle of the school year, and they did all their schooling at St. Mary's free of the school fees.

It was not all an easy life for Uncle Cajetan. His father died young, leaving two small kids, Miquelina (1904-1986) and Cajetan (1911-1998) and wife Maria Herminia (1885-1970) to fend for themselves in Loutulim.

Cajetan's mother left the kids back in Loutulim, and moved to Mumbai. She upgraded her education and took up a job at Thane Jail as she was getting living quarters to go with the job. She then sent for her children. Thus, Cajetan had to take the train daily to attend school in Bombay proper (St. Francis Xavier School, Fort, Bombay).

Cajetan graduated from St. Xavier's College, with high marks and his first job was teaching at St. Xavier's College. As he had promised his mother he would look after her once he was employed, he then requested her to retire from her job as the Thane jail warden. In the early 1940s he joined the civil service as a young police officer and had a meteoric rise in that line of work.

I relate to the above true story that education is the road to opportunities. It fits in well with the theme of the stories of progress of our families in this book, in the last one to two centuries, when higher education was not readily available to most, in particular if you were female or grew up in rural /agricultural villages. Maria Herminia, is the greater hero building Cajetan's character to excel in the face of added adversity.

Uncle Cajetan's achievements in the public office, easily qualify him as one of the eminent people within the family. More about his professional career can be found in the chapter that follows on Eminent and Meritorious Members within our Family.

CHAPTER 12

Eminent and Meritorious Members Within Our Families

I referred to Merriam Webster dictionary for the formal meanings of meritorious and eminent, to see which would the more appropriate adjective to apply to some members of our families. "Meritorious as an adjective, e.g. meritorious service tells me it is "deserving of honor or esteem". There is a further explanation: "People who demonstrate meritorious behavior certainly "earn" our respect". "Eminent: famous and respected within a particular sphere or profession; standing above others in some quality or position."

My intention is to celebrate the achievements of select family members who have excelled in their fields and have been publicly recognized as such. I have my personal heroes within our families, because they have impacted my life and that of others in a special way.

It is quite natural to hold our parents or at least one of them as our most admired people in our lives. They have nurtured us, they have built our characters through example and they have supported us every step of our lives. They were there, as we pursued our careers, more often than not, through financial sacrifices. And there is nothing wrong in that thinking.

Then there are others in the family, who in one way or other, have impacted our lives in a super-normal way. When you look back, you know they have left a lasting impression on you. On my own family side, for me, three names jump to the top: my Xamae (maternal grandmother), Riario Moniz (paternal uncle) and Rosa Maria Sardinha (mother's first cousin). On the Pereira side I would suggest Pati (Mgr. Aniceto Pereira) and Phoebe Pereira.

What this chapter reflects, is my attempt to identify those in the family who have proved that some of us are "more equal" than others. These are the people, who through public office or scientific pursuit, have distinguished themselves, and by association have brought lasting "honor" and "pride" to our families. Some people may not agree with my selection criteria, saying that every priest, every doctor, every scientist (Ph.D.), every lawyer, every teacher, and every other professional within our families, should make into this list. We all have a right to our own thoughts on this.

The majority of people honored herein are direct blood descendants of the four families who are the subject of this book. At the end of this chapter, I brought in two sets of families, the Pinto Rosario and Majumdar, who find their place in this group via marriage.

Mgr. Aniceto Pereira
C.J.V Miranda IPS, Commissioner
Aniceto Pereira, Cpt
Grevi Menezes, ICS Ambassador
Gilbert Menezes, Commodore (ret)
Francisco Xavier Menezes, Governor
Constancio Menezes, Dir. Of Agriculture, Goa
Dr. Jose Menezes, Fellow Canadian Academy of Health Sciences
Francisco Sardinha MP, Indian Parliament
Enio Pimenta, MLA, Goa Legislative Assembly

Monsignor Aniceto do Menino Jesus Pereira (1871-1961)

Connection: Epifanio Pereira's brother and de facto family Patriarch
Ordained: 19th September 1896
1896-1904: Assistant to the Vicar of Gloria Church, Mazagon, Mumbai
1904-1917: Vicar of Holy Cross Church, Matheran, Maharastra
1917-1932: Vicar of Church of the Holy Cross, Parel, Mumbai

1932-1940: Vicar of Gloria Church, Byculla, Mumbai
1940 Appointed as Monsignor and Privy Chamberlain in his own right
1940 Retired and moved back to his house in Margao, Goa

In every posting Mgr. Aniceto Pereira dedicated himself to true service of his parishioners' spiritual and temporal needs, including being attending to his flock through the bubonic plague that had just broken out the same month and year of his first appointment at Gloria Church.

Besides attending to the spiritual needs of his parishioners, Mgr. Aniceto's work concentrated in three areas: children's education, including providing free education to needy families; building new or adding to church properties and even more important retiring any debts the churches were carrying before he was posted there.

At every posting Mgr. Aniceto received abundant appreciation and gratitude from his parishioners. Eighty years after his retirement, there is still a big portrait of him hanging at the Gloria Church.

C.J.V. Miranda (1911-1998, age 87) IPS, hails from Loutlim, Salcete, Goa.

Source: "Profiles of Eminent Goans", a St Xavier's College Publication, pg 290-291
Connection: Phoebe Pereira's First Cousin

After a brilliant academic career, he became a Fellow in English and French of St. Xavier's College, Bombay, when he also did a stint in teaching.

He had the unique privilege of being the matriculation teacher (French language subject) of Miss Indira Nehru (Gandhi), daughter of Pandit Jawaharlal Nehru, who as Mrs. Indira Gandhi became the prime Minister of India.

Thereafter C.J.V., as he was popularly called, joined Government Service and as a young police officer made his mark as one of Mumbai's ablest detective officers. His daring exploits in some of the sensational cases of his time, earned for him wide acclaim from the public and the press.

The then Chief Justice of Mumbai High Court, Mr. M.C. Chagla and Justice B.P. Gajendragadkar (later Chief Justice of India) observed in their judgment in a case in which C.J.V. had spurned the biggest bribe known in history, thus: "We in Mumbai, are justly proud of our police force and the high reputation that the force has earned, for ability and integrity is largely due to its possessing officers of the caliber of Mr. Miranda".

In 1949, C.J.V. Miranda was selected for the Indian Police Service (IPS) (All India Service) by the Union Public Service Commission, where exciting and dangerous events, which he always handled dexterously, highlighted his career. He held assignments in all the important cities of the former Bombay State and in the present Maharashtra State (Surat, Ahmedabad, Nagpur and Pune) and throughout was known, respected and feared for his clean and efficient administration.

His outstanding work attracted the attention of the Central Bureau of Investigation, New Delhi, and he was twice invited to join it but circumstances beyond his control compelled him to decline the offers. His last assignment in the Police, after being the Chief (now designated Commissioner) of the State Criminal Investigation Department, was as Director of Anti-Corruption Bureau (a post at present held by an officer of the rank of Director General of Police).

During his scintillating tenure of three years the A.C.B. struck terror in the hearts of smugglers, and as a result of his anti-smuggling drive the Government exchequer was substantially enriched.

As dynamic officer of proven administrative talents C.J.V. Miranda became a legendary figure amongst the police personnel for his untiring efforts on their behalf, which he manifested by building welfare centers, maternity homes, recreational halls, children's parks, and above all, police colonies in the key centerss of Pune and Nagpur, holding over thousand families. He was responsible for the construction of the beautiful Police Commissionarate building in Pune.

A much-decorated Police Officer, C.J.V. Miranda was awarded the Indian Police Medal for conspicuous merit in 1948, the Police Medal for long and meritorious services in 1963 and the President's Police and Fire Services medal, the nation's highest police award for distinguished service in 1967.

Blazing a trail of glory, he retired in 1969, but in recognition of his long and yeoman services to the Nation, he was appointed on the very day of his retirement, as a member of the prestigious Public Service Commission – the first police officer to be so honored.

C.J.V. had also been a gifted public speaker at meetings of the Rotary and the Lions Clubs and on All India radio; at official and other social functions his voice had invariably elicited attention and appreciation.

He has interesting publications to his credit, one of which is the Maharashtra Anti-Corruption Manual of Instructions - a handbook that is kept constantly at hand for consultation - to A.C.B officers. It received approbation from judicial authorities, including an ex-chief Justice of the Supreme Court of India, some High Court Judges and special judges all over the country entrusted with the duty of trying cases involving corruption.

C.J.V. Miranda died in April 1998. In their funeral orations, the Auxiliary Bishop of Mumbai, Bishop Ferdinand Fonseca and 'Supercop' Julio Ribeiro heaped lavish praises on Mr. Miranda.

Bishop Fonseca extolled his uprightness and incorruptibility. Mr. Ribeiro described him as an idol for police officers. He also referred to Mr. Miranda's great concern for the poor.

Mr. Miranda was buried with full police honors at the Haines Road Cemetery, Mahalakshimi.

At the well-attended funeral, people from all walks of life got together to pay their last respects, including top serving and retired police officers, as well as common people, whose lives he had touched.

Gilbert Menezes (1943-) Commodore, Retd. Indian Navy, VSM.

Connection: Gilbert's Dad and Phoebe Pereira are first cousins
Joined the National Defence Academy as a cadet- 1960
Commissioned as a Sub Lieutenant- 1965
He volunteered for Submarine Service in 1967, trained in the Soviet Union and served on submarines for almost 28 years.
Commanded 2 submarines, Kalvari and Khanderi and later commanded a large frigate, Taragiri.

I am told that on his inaugural trip as commander of Kalvari, when he arrived in Mumbai, he was greeted upon arrival by then India's prime Minister Jawaharhal Nehru, with Cpt. Aniceto Pereira (Ret.) also being present. A few of Pereira side family cousins were there too.

Gilbert graduated from the Royal Navy Staff College at Greenwich UK in 1967 and from the National Defence College, Delhi in 1990.

Gilbert was awarded the Distinguished Service Medal (VSM) by the President of India.

Gilbert retired as a Commodore in 1993.

Post retirement, Gilbert joined Ericsson Telecom Co, Sweden in 1998, worked as a Project Manager in India, Brazil, USA, and Africa, before retiring in 2002.

Gilbert is now settled in Seraulim Goa with his wife Maria Julieta (Julosha) Barreto.

Joao Batista ANICETO Pereira, (1909-1988) Captain, Indian Navy

Connection: Aniceto and F.X. Pereira are brothers

Joao Batista Aniceto Pereira (1909-1988) joined The Officers Training School in Bangalore in 1939 and was commissioned in 1942.

He was posted in Bombay till 1946 and lived in Byculla.

Aniceto regularly rose in rank, transferring from one naval base to another, and eventually to New Delhi.

He served as Staff Officer, Cabinet-Secretariat-Military Wing in New Delhi between 1948 and 1950, where he got to know the first Prime Minister of India, J. Nehru. He was also Secretary to the Chiefs of Staff Committee, The Defense Committee and the Defense Minister's Commission.

A logistics expert, Aniceto was appointed Fleet Supply Officer to the Indian Navy, and then became Deputy Director-Supply, both posts at Naval Headquarters.

Promoted to the rank of Captain on July 23, 1953, Cpt. Aniceto was appointed the Naval Secretary (Delhi) becoming the first Indian appointed to the post, i.e. post-independence.

He retired 19 April 1959 (at the then superannuation age of 50) as the Head of Naval Pay Office, responsible for payments of salary and allowances to all officers and sailors of the Indian Navy.

Upon retirement Aniceto and family moved into the Esperança building, adjacent to the Holy Name Cathedral, in Colaba, the seat of the Archbishop of Mumbai. I understand that Aniceto, was a strong contributor of his administrative skills both to the Archbishop and the cathedral.

Anthony GREVI Menezes (1912-1992), Ambassador, Indian Diplomatic Services

Connection: Phoebe Pereira's brother

Lawyer by profession, joined the Indian Diplomatic Services, in the Ministry of Foreign Affairs, in 1947, rising to the position of Ambassador, before he retired from the diplomatic service in 1971.

After retiring from the Diplomatic services, worked as Supreme Court lawyer for over 20 years.

Founder of the Indian Christian National Congress Party.

Foreign Postings
1948-1950: Brazil, Indian Embassy, Commissioner of Commerce S. America
1950-1951 Burma: First Secretary, Indian Embassy in Rangoon, Burma
1951-1952 New-Delhi: Assistant Secretary, Ministry of External Affairs
1953-1955 Paris: First Secretary, Indian Embassy, Paris France
1955-1957 Jakarta: First Secretary, Indian Embassy, Jakarta, Indonesia
1957-1958 New-Delhi: Assistant Secretary, Ministry of External Affairs
1958-1960 Hanoi: Consul general, Hanoi, Vietnam
1960-1962 San Francisco: Consul general, San Francisco, California
1963-1965 Pnom Pen: Indian Ambassador to Cambodia
1968-1971 Dublin: Indian Ambassador to Ireland

Ref The Times of India Directory and Year Book Including Who's who, Bennett, Coleman & Company, 1964 p. 1167

José P.C.A. Menezes (1939-), Eminent Scientist, Member of Canadian Academy of Health Sciences

Connection: Brother of Marcelina Menezes, mother of Eufemiano Moniz

Jose is my mother's youngest of eight siblings. He graduated from veterinary medicine in 1963, from University of Perugia, Italy, having transferred there from the University of Lisbon, Portugal. That was no surprise as he showed great love for his domestic animals, principally the buffalos and poultry. A good pastime when he was on vacations from his Lyceum studies was to have cock fights with neighbouring friends' rooster. He did not practice Veterinary medicine but pursued academic research in the field of tumour biology and immunology.

His scientific accomplishments, scientific papers and awards number over 400 and I have done my best to give a concise summary of the here.

When he was retiring from the Department of Microbiology in the Faculty of medicine of Montreal University (2007) he was recognized for his career achievements by being inducted as **Fellow of The Canadian Academy of Health Sciences**. This is the highest honor in the field, and bestowed on very few practitioners in that field. To my knowledge he is the first Goan (and the only one to date) to achieve this honor.

Educational Background:
1958 Lyceum (Sciences) "Liceu Nacional de Goa", India
1963 D.V.M., Faculty of Veterinary Medicine University of Perugia, Italy
1965 "Diplôme de Bactériologie" Pasteur Institute, Paris, France
1967 M.Sc., Microbiology and Immunology Faculty of Medicine, Univ of Montreal
1971 Ph.D., Microbiology and Immunology Faculty of Medicine, Univ of Ottawa
1971-1973 Post-Doctoral at Karolinska Institute, Sweden
1973-1978 Scholar of the Medical Research Council of Canada (At: University of Montreal)
1978-1985 Senior Research Scholar of the "Fonds de la Recherche en Santé du Québec" (At: University of Montreal).
1984 Astra Research Award in Herpes
1996 J.-Louis Lévesque Foundation Award in Immunovirology
2006 Special 40-year membership Certificate presented by the American Society for Microbiology for "dedicated service to the Society, and in recognition of contributions to Science"
2006 Fellow, Canadian Academy of Health Sciences
2007- Emeritus Member, American Society for Microbiology
2007- Emeritus Member, American Society for Virology
2007- Emeritus Member, New York Academy of Sciences
2008- Emeritus Fellow, Canadian Academy of Health Sciences

Faculty and Related Positions:
1966 Lecturer, Department of Microbiology and Immunology
Faculty of Medicine, University of Montreal
January - May 1966
1973-1977 Assistant Professor,

Department of Microbiology and Immunology
Faculty of Medicine, University of Montreal
1977-1981 Associate Professor,
Department of Microbiology and Immunology
Faculty of Medicine, University of Montreal
1978-2007 Director, Laboratory of Immunovirology Pediatric Research
Center, Ste-Justine Hospital and University of Montreal
1981-2006 Professor, Department of Microbiology and Immunology and
Pediatric Research Center, Faculty of Medicine, University of Montreal.
2002-2008 Head, Viral, Immune Diseases and Cancer Program
Ste-Justine Hospital Research Center – University of Montreal
2007- Professor Emeritus University of Montreal, Faculty of Medicine

Research Interests:
- Viral Immunomodulation, Immunosuppression, and Cytokine Gene
Activation.
- Cellular Effector Mechanisms in Anti-Viral Immunity.
- Immunobiological Effects of Viral Glycoprotein Gene Expression.
- Development of Novel Immune Reconstitution and Immunotherapeutic
Approaches.
Authorship or co-authorship of over 400 scientific papers.

Francisco Xavier Menezes (1929-2006), Provincial Governor, Angola

Connection: Brother of Marcelina Menezes, mother of Eufemiano Moniz
1951- Dip. Commerce, Delhi University
1951-1954- Administration Course of Portuguese Overseas Territories
1955-1968 Posted in TIMOR as Civil Administration Officer, then
promoted to Administrador of Districts of Baucau and Emera.
1968-1971 Mayor of Capital city of Dili and Director Tourism, Timor
1972- 1975 Transferred to Angola as Deputy Governor of province
of Melange. Then transferred as Governor to South-east province of
Cuando-Cubango
Returned to Portugal due to sudden independence of Angola and
withdrawal of the Portuguese Army.
1975- Voluntary Retirement from the Portuguese Overseas Duties

1978-1995 Sociedade de Construcoes Soares e Costa, a large construction company in Portugal, Human Resources Manager.
Author of two Books: "Genese da Cultura Luso-Timorense" and a book of Poems "Timor Uma Paixao".
Francisco Xavier Menezes used to say "Goa é meu amor, Timor é minha paixão"- Goa is my love, Timor is my passion.
1968- Post Graduate Studies (Master's Degree program) in public administration, anthropology and sociology. Was awarded the "Infante D. Henrique" prize by the Universidade Tecnica de Lisboa for the best paper presentation.

Constancio Xavier Menezes (1932-2019), Director, Department of Agriculture, Goa

Connection: Brother of Marcelina Menezes, mother of Eufemiano Moniz
1954- Graduated with Degree in Agriculture, University of Belgaum, India
1955-1958 Officer in Charge (Agrônomo), Diu (a Portuguese territory)
He had further postings as shown below (time frame unknown)
Officer in Charge (Agrônomo), Pilerne, Bardez, Goa
Officer in Charge (Agrônomo), Margao, South Goa District
1988-1992 Director, Department of Agriculture, Goa
1993 Retired
After retirement, he worked part time as property settlement consultant to individual property owners.

Cosme Francisco Caetano Sardinha (1946-) MP for South Goa, Lok Sabha, India

Connection: Eufemiano's cousin, our mothers are first cousins.

In his own words.

"My political career started when I, along with many others, worked tirelessly to prevent Goa's merger into Maharashtra, when the Indian Government held the 'Opinion Poll', on January 16, 1967.

After that, I worked for two consecutive terms to help Mr. Erasmo Sequeira get elected as Member of Parliament, representing South Goa. In 1972, the people of my village requested me to contest the Panchayat elections and I got elected. The members of the Panchayat committee elected me as the Deputy Sarpanch while Mr. Caetano Moniz (Eufemiano's dad) was elected as the Sarpanch of the village.

In **1977**, when Adv. Eduardo Faleiro contested the Lok Sabha elections for the South Goa parliamentary seat, under the Congress Party banner, I was kept in charge of the Curtorim constituency. Eduardo Faleiro won the elections. Soon after, in the same year, there were assembly elections and I was offered the Congress Party ticket to contest for the Curtorim constituency assembly seat. When the election results were declared, I was elected for the first time, but our party was in the opposition.

The assembly was dissolved in 2.5 years and soon thereafter there were fresh elections. I again contested and won on the Congress party ticket and this time the Congress party got a majority. I was elevated to the rank of a Cabinet Minister in the government headed by Mr. Pratapsingh Raoji Rane. Thereafter, I won four more elections and served as a minister for five terms, managing most of the important portfolios.

During my tenure of six terms in the Goa assembly, I have had the honor of being the Chief Minister of Goa from November 1999 to October 2000, Leader of Opposition from 2000 to 2001 and Speaker of the Goa Legislative Assembly from 2005 to 2007.

I have also been elected as a Member of the Indian Parliament (Lok Sabha) for four terms. In my third term (2009-2014) I was elected as the Chairman of the Estimates Committee of the Lok Sabha and held the prestigious post for 5 years. I was also on the panel of speakers of the Lok Sabha for 5 years. In 2013, I had the honor of representing India at the World Health Organization (W.H.O.) as a permanent member for one year.

The same year, the Congress Party deputed me to represent India at the Conference of Socialist Countries of the World in Portugal as the Keynote Speaker.

At present, I am serving my fourth term as Member of Parliament, Lok Sabha, from the Congress Party, representing South Goa parliamentary constituency. The general elections were held in May 2019"

Enio Pimenta (1923-1994) **Freedom Fighter, and MLA, Curtorim Constituency**

Connection: Eufemiano's cousin.

Submitted by his daughter Melba Pimenta.

Enio Pimenta was a prominent Goan Politician, Freedom Fighter, Journalist, Editor, Educationist, Nationalist, Konkani language Protagonist and a visionary who lived his life in service to others, He was born on December 26th, 1923 in the village of Curtorim. He completed high school in Portuguese medium at the Lyceum, and earned his B.A. from Bombay University. He married the love of his life and was a wonderful father to six sons and one daughter.

He played an active role in the Goa Liberation Movement. As a young adult his activism was inspired by Mahatma Gandhi's Quit India Movement in 1942, He was arrested in Margao, Goa during an uprising (morcha) against Portuguese colonial rule. He uprooted his family and moved to Mumbai to safely continue his fight. He wrote editorials in the daily newspaper called "Goenkar" and was a founder member of Konkani newspaper "SOT". He channeled his views and successfully highlighted the oppressive rule of the Portuguese government through this avenue.

Enio Pimenta played a stellar role in protecting Goa's identity and preventing the merger of Goa with Maharashtra during a referendum held in 1967 famously called "Goa Opinion Poll".

After Goa was liberated in 1961, Enio Pimenta was elected the First MLA to the Goa Legislative Assembly, from Curtorim Constituency under the United Goan Party. During his term in office, Enio Pimenta founded the first English school in Curtorim, St Xavier's Institute. He was founder chairman of Curtorim Service Cooperative Society as well as a founder member of Curtorim Education and Welfare Foundation. He was also instrumental in setting up Curtorim Primary Health Centre in addition to many other accomplishments to better the lives of Curtorkars.

On March 25, 1994, Enio Pimenta said goodbye to his loving family and his beloved GOA. To honour the memory of Curtorim's first MLA and Freedom Fighter, the road from Maina to Macazana has been named "'Enio Pimenta Road".

Dr Jose Luis Pinto do Rosario, Epidemiologist and Vaccine Expert

Connection: Grandfather of Geoffrey Pinto married to Maria Aurora Pereira

Dr. Jose Luis Pinto do Rosario's family hails from Porvorim-Bardez, Goa, where the family is well known to this date.

. 1920 - Medical and public health degrees in Edinburgh and Glasgow.
. 1920 - Joined the Bombay Presidency's Public Health Service in 1920
. 1926 – Director, Vaccine Institute, Belgaum
. 1930 - Director of Public Health in Poona

Dr. Pinto do Rosario "was not just an expert epidemiologist, he was a forefront fighter of plagues and epidemics - viral epidemics and cholera broke out frequently at the time -- in west India. At any given time, he had a million vaccines ready to be despatched to any part of India, even abroad.

Dr Pinto do Rosario was director of Government Vaccine Institute in Belgaum, where he suddenly and prematurely succumbed to a massive heart attack, at a rather premature age of 52"

Ref: Writer-author Valmiki Faleiro with excerpts from out-of-print book *Patriotism In Action: Goans in India's Defence Services*, *Goa,1556, 2010* *(ISBN: 978-93-80739-06-9)*

Three of his sons joined the defence services of India as Commissioned Officers, each in the Army, the Navy and the Air Force, Cpt. Norman Pinto, Rear/Adm. Fausto Pinto and Air Vice/Marshal Elrick Pinto respectively.

Fausto Antonio Pinto do Rosario (1918-2004), Rear Admiral

Connection: Father of Geoffrey Pinto married to Maria Aurora Pereira
Graduate of Grant Medical College
1962-1964 Naval Attaché, Indian Embassy, London, U.K.
1976 Founded Marine Medicine Society to further the subject of Underwater Medicine and Hyperbaric Medicine.

Over the years the ambit of the society has grown with the addition of fields like Nuclear medicine, Aviation Medicine, Human Machine Interface and Safety in the Naval environment, etc.

Erlich Wilmot Pinto (1921-1963), PVSM, Air Vice/Marshal

Connection: Uncle of Geoffrey Pinto married to Maria Aurora Pereira

Air Vice Marshal Erlic Wilmot Pinto, PVSM, was an Air officer in the Indian Air Force. He was the Air Officer Commanding-in-Chief (AOC-in-C) Western Air Command when he was killed in an air crash in Poonch. He served in the IAF from 1940 until his death in 1963.

Erlick rose through the ranks starting from Flight Officer (1942) to Air Vice-Marshal (1959).

Erlick, was the theatre air commander commanding the air operations during operation Vijay for Annexation of Goa, December 18, 1961.

His directive was to assist the land forces in the attainment of their objective with the use of minimum force. The risk of casualties to the civil population in air ops was inherent. As a result of meticulous planning by Air V/Mshl Pinto and efficient coordination, the air ops in the three enclaves were carried out most successfully, with only two targets being bombed: The Radio transmitter and the Dabolim Airport strips..

Battles/wars: World War II, Annexation of Goa
Service/branch: Royal Air Force, Indian Air Force
Rank: Air Vice Marshal (at death)

Years of service: 1940–1963

Capt Norman Pinto do Rosario

Connection: Uncle of Geoffrey Pinto married to Maria Aurora Pereira
Joined Army Dental Corps
Dental Surgeon to the President of India and Dental Advisor to the
Government of India.

K.K. Majumdar (1913-1945) Wing Commander

Connection: Karen Menezes' husband Rohan Lobo's Grandfather

1933 Joined the newly formed Royal Indian Air Force, 3rd batch

Saw action in the North West Frontier province in the Indo-Afghan tribal
engagements and throughout World War 2.

First Indian to attain the rank of Wing Commander,

Won the Air Force's highest gallantry award (the DFC or Distinguished
Flying Cross) twice: first for the Burma Campaign, and then for his efforts
in the Normandy campaign.

He is the only Indian to have been awarded the DFC and bar; in the 90
year history of IAF, he remains the most highly decorated officer.

1945 Killed in air crash in WW II theater.

But for his untimely death, there is general consensus among both his peers
& historians that he would have been the first Indian Chief of Air Staff of
independent India's Air Force.

Addendum: K.K. Majumdar's grandfather, **W.C. Bonnerjee** was first ever
President of the Indian National Congress (precursor of today's Congress
party) in 1885.

C H A P T E R 1 3

Our Village Culinary Heritage

Goan Christians adapted and often were forced to adapt to cuisine imported by the Portuguese who arrived in India in 1498 and stayed till end of 1961. Nobody called it that, but it was a classic Fusion cuisine of western and Indian cuisines.

The Portuguese were instrumental in introducing the CHIILI plant to India. The Christian population was also introduced to eating pork meat and use of vinegar. In my opinion a great non-vegetarian fusion cuisine, Luso-Indian cuisine, was born over 300 years back and it still thrives. In the last half century, some of these dishes have been adapted by non-Goan chefs world-wide.

Today we live in a world where globalization is a fact of life. Going back half a century, we as a family have been part of this greatly increased global trend of migration of people, in particular from the developing world to the developed world. People have brought along their native cuisine and have shared it with the local population of their adopted countries.

In truly cosmopolitan places like the Greater Toronto Region (GTA), which has been my home for the last 35 years, you can find places or restaurants that cater to the cuisine of almost every corner of the world or nearly so. Such public eating places are supplemented by small scale preparation and sale of foods from home by individuals, principally ladies, who fill in the demand for the ethnic foods.

Goan diasporas in major cities in Canada, Australia and the UK, have access to typical Goan food prepared by entrepreneurial individuals and occasionally restaurants, catering to Goan and local cuisine.

For example, in the GTA there are many individuals who will supply a variety of Goan foods, ranging from Goa sausages, to all kinds of typical Goan delicacies such as vindalho, sorpatel, xacuti and a variety of pickles. In this chapter when I mention Goan food it alludes to food preparation by Christian Goans.

Goa sausages, along with Cashew Feni, are unique to Christian Goans, not only in Goa but also the Goan diaspora anywhere in the world, who are the first generation emigrants from Goa. Goa sausages are commonly known as "choris" from the Portuguese "chouriço" or its Spanish name "chorizo". Choris was introduced to the area by Portuguese, but Goans have given it its own very Southern Indian twist with addition of local coconut toddy vinegar, which along with red chillis, gives it a unique, tangy flavour. Choris is a good deal spicier than the Spanish chorizo or the Portuguese linguiça.

In the days of lives of our parents and ancestors in the village, most folks prepared their own sausages, normally twice a year. My generation was probably the last one, to experience this home sausage making routine. The process involved cutting the pork meat (a little fat content was always a must), salting it abundantly and kept under heavy weight, to dehydrate the meat for approximately two or three days. This is followed by marinating the meat with prepared ground spice masala for three to five days, The next step would be to fill the meat into casings and tie links in approximately 5 cm (2 in) lengths. Now-a-days it is a rare home that goes to trouble of making choris at home. Instead, most people buy the readily available market variety, where individual sausage link looks more like a large Rosary bead.

The freshly made sausages were first dried out in the sun and it was a task for us kids to take turns keeping an eye on them against attacks by crows or other roaming animals. These sausages were then smoked on a wooden pole hanging over the wood fire which was the only way all households cooked their food.

The most common way to prepare the choris for the table was plainly with a good ammount of onions (quartered) and a few potatoes diced in small cubes. This was an accompaniment to the regular fish curry. The sausages came really handy during the monsoon season, when fresh fish from the sea was not readily available. Other common uses for choris would be to enhance the flavour of "Goan Stew" or with pulav (arroz).

Now-a-days one of the most common items using the Goa sausage is "choris-panv", which is a small freshly prepared bread stuffed with cooked sausage meat. Choris-panv is widely served in take-out or street food in Goa, Mumbai and even at picnics here in Canada, as one of the items on the guest welcoming plate.

When India's first Prime Minister J. Nehru, paid his first visit to Goa, upon its liberation from the Portuguese, he said in his speech that Goans are renowned as great cooks and musicians. He meant it as a compliment, but it was not appreciated by the Goan elite.

Folks from our parents' and grandparents' generations did not have written down recipes. First of all they cooked and baked by approximate measures. The cooking "recipes" were learnt in the kitchen by word of mouth and by watching your elders in action. Also it should be remembered that most of these folks' (women) literacy was minimal.

I remember watching the great Goan chef of the day Salvador in action. He happened to hail from our village, and was recognized and in high demand from Panaji to all over South of Goa. He was the chef of choice at weddings and other receptions, including those given by the Portuguese Governor in Panaji. I believe the occasion was my older brother Loyola's wedding. In those days the wedding reception menu was kind of standard: a plate of appetizers (croquettes, forminha, a meat patty, etc.), "caldo" or soup served in a tea cup, and the main dish or plate made up of pulav, Goan stew and slice of bread and another item or two. Salvador came over and once informed about the expected number of guests, he rattled off the top of his head, the list and quantities of ingredients needed for each of the dishes planned for the reception. Amazing!

In this day and age one can search for a recipe simply by "Google"ing it. Thus, having a chapter on our village food or Goan cooking may appear unnecessary.

However, food and cooking is an important part of our cultural heritage. I have therefore made an effort to collect a few recipes which I believe reflect our village typical cooking I grew up with, and which I believe has evolved and has been passed down over the last century.

After close to fifty years in Canada, when a family member (particularly my sisters Blanche and Serena, and my cousin Chrysann) prepares a dish typical of our village cuisine, I see myself transported back to the days of my youth. There must be a little corner in our brains, which never forgets the particular taste of those dishes our folks prepared both on day-to-day basis, such as rice and curries (mainly fish, but occasionally chicken), as well as dishes prepared less frequently, such as Xacuti, Vindalho, Sorpotel or my favourite dish style of preparation, we have called Randlolem. The principal criteria in choosing the recipes in this chapter, are those that remind me of foods of my childhood, hence "typical" home cooking.

I have been coaxing a few family members to make a contribution in the form of recipes, such that this Chapter would reflect a broader family input and as a result, as genuine cuisine as we grew up with. Even good cooks in the Moniz and the extended family didn't feel comfortable in going to the extra effort of writing down the exact quantities of ingredients. I am glad to point out that the current generation of the Monizes including the extended family, both male and female, is for the most part, more than handy in the kitchen. For example, it is more of an exception that, when we regularly talk on the phone, my siblings and I do not share news of our latest cooking exploits, or at least ask each other "what did you have for dinner?"

Writing down recipes, I believe, started with women of my generation (including my wife), who having pursued University/College education, had spent less time in the kitchen. Also they could write. Thus, they have taken the trouble to stand by the cook in the kitchen, jot down the ingredients and procedures and create recipes out of approximate quantities our family members were used to.

I currently observe that many members of the generation that has followed my generation (our own children, nephews, nieces and cousins) principally those living overseas, are good in the kitchen and relative to the earlier generation they feel lot more comfortable and ever ready to try new dishes. Through the WhatsApp groups, cousins are sharing food recipes of Goan and non-Goan style food recipes.

At this junction, I would like to give a shout or mention to Danielle Moniz Mascarenhas, who has her own Goan/Indian cooking blog, Danielle's Cooking (https://thedaniverse.wordpress.com/), where she has collected a wide array of recipes from Goa/India.

My aunt Ti Albertina's cooking and baking was without parallel. Without bias, my sisters, Violet, Blanche and Serena, have turned out to be very good cooks, and I suppose this is due to both the natural village cooking exposure and added influence of my maternal aunt ti Albertina's proficiency. Blanche, having been closest to ti Albertina, comes closest to have absorbed Ti Albertina's skills in the kitchen, and thus she is the family cuisine "consultant", when we want to recreate the "heritage cuisine" of our villages.

Every person submitting the recipes for this book, has been acknowledged. I would like to make special mention of Chrisann Misquitta Barnetto, daughter of Carol (Moniz) Misquitta and Lino Misquitta, who lives close by to us and whom I have come to know well. In my opinion Chrisann, besides being a good cook in her own right, has captured and organized recipes she learnt from her grandmother, our dearest aunt, Ti Helena, whose cooking we loved when we would occasionally visit ti Riario's family at Degamwalla Chambers, Mazagon, Mumbai. Chrisann probably has collected the full range of recipes that reflect the good old village cooking style and taste. She basically offered to share with me any recipe she has and I would like to include in this book.

I have taken up her offer and included a few of her food recipes. My aim in presenting a few select Goan dishes in this book is to protect, maintain and pass on our own village cuisine identity.

The populations in the villages in question were predominantly Christian and our cooking was therefore significantly influenced by the Portuguese, not only being non-vegetarian but also the presence of vinegar and other acidic ingredients.

Before the nineteen seventies, the village folks consumed vegetables mainly during the monsoon season, when people grew their own vegetables on their own property, or grown for sale by local individuals. In the non-monsoon times, availability of vegetables (brinjal, spinach) was much more limited.

I have however made an effort to include a few vegetable recipes (typical vegetables grown in Goa, during the monsoon season). This entire section of vegetable dishes, was made possible through contribution from Benildes Coutinho Moniz, my older brother Loiola's wife. I wish to thank Benildes (Coutinho) Moniz, Chrisann, Heriberto, Blanche, Serena, Maria Lurdes, Ethel and Michelle (Moniz) Rebelo, for their inputs.

The recipe collection in this chapter includes principally non-vegetarian dishes of fish and pork and to limited extent chicken, all readily available in the village environment. Goan baking recipes have two principal ingredients: the coconut and eggs, again, ingredients readily available to common folk.

The typical diet of Goan Christians in the villages was rice, curry and fish. For people with the means, chicken, pork and beef, in that order, were the choices available. Pork and beef were available once a week, at least in my village of Curtorim.

Goan cooking is at its core, a **sweet and sour preparation**, and this is what differentiates Goan cooking from most other cuisines, including the Indian cooking. The spiciness comes from pepper, red chili (Kashmiri chili is preferred for its mild heat and bright red color) and green chili (the spiciest being the small pir-piri, locally known as "putkepar"). The principal ingredients (spices) used are onions, garlic, ginger, cumin and turmeric and pepper. The sweetness is derived from addition of coconut. The sourness is derived from addition of vinegar, tamarind and kokum. The holy grail of the Goan cooking is to find the right balance of sweet and sour level.

When it comes to baking, coconut is omnipresent. More often, coconut is added in the grated form, in particular for making various snacks to accompany the afternoon tea (merenda). The four main ingredients in the iconic Goan sweet, Bibinca, the multilayered cooked pudding style sweet, are coconut milk, egg yolks, sugar and flour along with some nutmeg.

Useful Pointers

Typical old style Goan cooking has a sweet and sour base.

Local village cooking has been learnt through word of mouth and experience. Therefore, one has to adjust the quantities of spices, in particular the chili, to your taste and heat tolerance. The desirable chili pepper is "Kashmiri Chili" both for its deep red color and medium heat level. To go with the sweet and sour theme, where there is chili, adding a pinch of sugar does its trick.

Recipes given herein assume use of Kashmiri Chili and medium to low heat green chili. You will need to make adjustment to match your spice heat tolerance. You can always add more of the spice to suit your taste.

When a curry (and some other gravy dish) nears completion, addition of a whole, slitted green chili, will enhance its flavor.

Flavor of dishes with red chili and vinegar can be enhanced with addition of a teaspoon of sugar.

When spices are not available in powder form. you can conveniently use the cheese cloth to bundle spices such as cloves, cinnamon stick, cardamom, and remove the bundle out, when cooking is completed. This avoids grinding these spices into a paste.

Even spice experts can't seem to agree on an exact ratio to rely on when substituting the ground spices (you buy at grocery shop) for the whole spices called for in a recipe. I read somewhere that the general rule of thumb is a measured amount of whole spices will fill about 70 to 80 percent that volume when ground. Because the recipes that follow do not follow one set of measurements, the following table of convenient conversion of spices is my attempt to simplify these recipes a little bit.

Convenient conversions of spices and measures

Water: 1 tsp.=5 grams appr.
Garlic (1-2 medium cloves = 1 tsp minced)
Garlic (2-3 medium cloves = 1 tsp. paste)
Ginger (1 inch (2.5 cm) fresh piece= 1 ¼ tsp. ground or paste)
Cumin 1 tsp. cumin seed=1 1/4 tsp. ground
Cinnamon Stick = ½ tsp. powder
Cinnamon Stick 3 inch= 1 tsp. powder
Cloves: 1 tsp. whole cloves=3/4 tsp. clove powder
Cloves: 3 whole cloves = ¼ tsp. ground
Cardamom: 1 pod=12 seeds; 1 tsp. seeds=1/2 tsp. ground
Kashmiri Chili (dry) 3-5 = ½ -1 tsp. powder
Kashmiri Chili Substitute: smoked paprika and cayenne, 3:1 ratio.
Turmeric: in most recipes Curry powder substitutable
1 Lemon= 2-3 Tbsp juice; 1 Tbsp lemon zest
Onions: 4-5 medium=1/2 kg=1 lb+
Tomatoes=5 medium=1/2 kg=1 lb+
Coconut (large): 450g or 5-6 cups grated; 1 c undiluted coconut milk
Coconut (medium): 3-4 cups grated; 1 cup=76g

Common Food Measurements or Conversions

1 Tbsp=3 tsp.; 4 Tbsp=1/4 cup; 1 dash=1/32 oz
1 Cup= 8oz=237 ml = 16 Tbsp
¼ Cup=50ml =4 Tbsp
1 tsp.= 5 g Water
Flour (all purpose): 1tsp= 2.6g, 4 c= 1 lb=450g
Sugar (granulated): 1tsp= 4.1g, 2 c= 1lb=450g
Icing Sugar: 1tsp= 2.5g, 3 1/2c=1lb=450g
Sugar (granulated) 1C= 1 ¾ c icing sugar
Butter: 1tsp=4.7g, 1 cup=225g=1/2 lb=2 sticks

Important Note: The recipes included in this chapter were submitted by different individuals, and I have presented them without significant editing, both for the sake of authenticity and the effort which would entail on my part. I have learnt that even within our family members, there are minor differences in spices that go into specific dishes. You may also not find uniformity in measurements of ingredients, for which I apologize.

You can avoid need for grinding the spices, by using the spices in powder or pre-ground form, as per approximate convenient conversion of spices given earlier in this chapter.

Recipes for Vegetables by Benildes (Coutinho) Moniz

VIR VIR VEGETABLE (Long Beans)

Ingredients

Vir Vir- 300gms

Onions, medium- 2

Mustard seeds- 1/4tsp

Coconut, grated- 1/2 cup

Green Chillies, chopped fine- 2 /
as per taste

Pepper powder (optional)- pinch

Turmeric Powder (optional)- pinch

Water- ½ cup

Salt- to taste

Oil- 1-2tbsp

Wash and cut the vegetable into fine bits.
Saute the onions in oil, add the mustard seeds.
Add in the vegetable, stir well and let it cook on medium flame
Add the water, green chillies, turmeric, pepper and let it cook
When almost dry. add the coconut and salt
Stir, let it dry completely

GOSALIM VEGETABLE (Chinese Okra)

Ingredients

Gosalim (about 9-12 inches long)- 3
Oil- 2-3 tbsp
Green chillies, finely chopped- 1-2
Onions, medium- 2
Prawns- ½ cup
Coconut, grated- 1/2 cup

Peel the sharp ridges of the gosalim, wash and cut into small pieces
Saute the onions in oil, stir in the prawns, add in the chopped vegetable
and mix, no need to add water
Add the green chillies and cook on slow fire
When almost dry, add the coconut and salt and let it dry completely

BENDHI VEGETABLE (Indian Okra, Lady Fingers)

Ingredients

Bendhi- 300gms

Oil- 2-3tbsp

Onions, medium- 2-3

Tomato, chopped fine- 1

Goan Palm (or apple cider) Vinegar- 1tsp / Bindi (kokum) Solam- 4

Turmeric powder- 1/4tsp

Cumin powder- 1/4tsp

Pepper powder- pinch

Garam Masala- pinch

Kashmiri Red Chilly powder- ½ tsp

Salt- to taste

Coconut, grated (optional)- 1tbsp

Wash, dry and chop the bendhi fine

Saute the onions in oil, add in the tomatoes and fry a little

Add in the bendhi, vinegar or solam

Stir fry on low flame, adding the spices and salt

Cook on low flame until the bendhi cook, while stirring in between or it will stick to the pan

Stir in the coconut just before you turn off the flame

Stuffed Padwal (Snake Gourd)

Ingredients

Padwal (snake gourd)- 2, thick, 10" each

Prawns, med size- 1 cup / 45 nos.

Coconut, fresh & grated- 1 cup / 80gms

Cinnamon- 1/4 inch

Cloves- 3

Green Cardamom (Elaichi)- 1

Vinegar- 1tsp

Salt- to taste

Water- as required

Ginger- 1/2 inch

Garlic- 5 flakes

Peppercorns- 5

Turmeric Powder- 1/2tsp

Cumin Powder- 1/4tsp

Onion, small, chopped- 1

Green Chillies- 3

Scrape off the skin of the padwal & scoop out the inside & discard. Wash and clean the padwal & cut into finger-sized pieces

Boil the padwal with some water & salt until soft. Approx 8 mins. Set aside

Boil the prawns with little water. Add in the cinnamon, cloves, green cardamom & vinegar. Approx 5 mins. Set aside

Fry the chopped onion until golden

In a mixer, add the green chillies, ginger, garlic, prawns, coconut, turmeric powder, peppercorns & fried onion. Grind to a fine paste, without water

Now stuff the padwals with this prawn paste until full. Do not over-stuff. Fry on medium heat, Fry on medium heat, making sure all sides brown well.

Stuffed Karela (Bitter Gourd)

Ingredients

Karela (bitter gourd)- 2, thick	Water- as required
Prawns, med size- 1 cup / 45nos.	Ginger- 1/2 inch
Coconut, fresh & grated- 1 cup / 80gms	Garlic- 5 flakes
Cinnamon- 1/4 inch	Peppercorns- 5
Cloves- 3	Turmeric Powder- ½ tsp
Green Cardamom- 1	Cumin Powder- ¼ tsp
Vinegar- 1tsp	Onion, small, chopped- 1
Salt- to taste	Green Chillies- 3

Scrape off the skin of the karelas. Wash, and boil in water, with a dash of salt until slightly soft

Remove, cool and slit the karelas and remove the seeds

Stuffing Preparation Method #1

(Goan Stir Fried Shrimps Recipe# 10 below)- South Goa

½ kg fresh Prawns
(shelled, deveined & washed)
3 med. size Onions (finely chopped)
Coconut, fresh & grated- 1 cup / 80gms

3 tbsps. Goan Rechado
Masala
3 tbsps. Cooking Oil
Salt to taste

Marinate fresh prawns with 1 tbsp. masala paste for 10 mins.
Heat cooking oil in a pan on medium heat (wok works well)
Add marinated prawns, 2 tbsp masala paste & stir fry on medium to high heat for 3 mins.
Keep aside in a bowl.
To the same pan/wok add onions and stir fry for another 2 mins on medium to high heat.
To this add the prawns from the bowl & again stir fry & toss for another 3 mins.

Stuffing Preparation Method #2

Boil the prawns with little water. Add in the cinnamon, cloves, green cardamom & vinegar. Approx 5 mins. Set aside
Fry the chopped onion until golden
In a mixer, add the green chillies, ginger, garlic, prawns, coconut, turmeric powder, peppercorns & fried onion. Grind to a fine paste, without water.
Now stuff the karelas with the prepared prawn stuffing until full. Do not over- stuff. Tie the karela with a string to avoid stuffing coming out..
Fry on medium heat, Fry on medium heat, making sure all sides brown well
Remove once browned & serve hot.

Non-Vegetarian and Baking Recipes

1. Pulav or Pilaf (Emano Moniz)
2. Goan Shrimp Curry (Danielle Moniz Mascarenhas)
3. Chicken Curry (Chrisann Misquitta Barnetto)
4. Chicken or Fish or Curry (Emano Moniz)
5. Chicken Xacuti (Chrisann Misquitta Barnetto)
6. Chicken Xacuti (Melgoans)
7. Fish Randlolem (Blanche and Emano Moniz)
8. Recheado Masala (2 recipes)
9. Recheado (Stuffed) Mackerels
10. Goan Stir Fried Shrimps (Blanche and Heriberto Moniz)
11. Shrimp Patties (Almona) (Chrisann Misquitta Barnetto)
12. Shrimp Patties (Maria Lurdes Barreto Moniz)
13. Ambtto (Mango) Curry (Blanche Moniz Viegas)
14. Pork Vindalho (Blanche and Heriberto Moniz)
15. Pork Vindalho (Melgoans)
16. Fish Ambot Tik (Sour and Hot) Curry (Blanche Moniz Viegas)
17. Solantulem (Blanche Moniz Viegas)
18. Add Mas (Pork Meat on Bones) (Heriberto Moniz)
19. Pork Soi Mirem (Heriberto Moniz)
20. Pork and Okra (Blanche Moniz Viegas)
21. Pork Assado (Blanche and Ethel Moniz)
22. Presunto (Blanche and Ethel Moniz)
23. Pork Torrado (Blanche and Ethel Moniz)
24. Fish Caldinho (Serena Moniz Diniz)
25. Goan Wedding Stew **I** (Maria Lurdes Barreto Moniz) and **II** by (Blanche M Viegas)
26. Beef Croquettes (Michelle Moniz Rebelo)
27. Bibinca (Heriberto Moniz)
28. Bolinhas (Serena Moniz Diniz and Joyce Fernandes)
29. Bhatica (CLR Group)
30. Kul Kuls (Benildes Coutinho Moniz)
31. Patoleo (Serena Moniz Diniz)
32. Goan Wedding Cake (Anonymous, modified by Emano Moniz)
33. Caramel Custard (Emano Moniz and Maria Lurdes Barreto Moniz)

34. Caramel Bread Pudding (Michelle Moniz Rebelo)
35. Bolacha (Joyce Fernandes and Blanche Moniz Viegas)
36. Doce (Blanche Moniz Viegas and Joyce Fernandes)
37. Godxhem (Blanche M Viegas and Danielle Moniz Mascarenhas)

282

1 PULAV or PILAF (Arroz Refugado)

Emano Moniz

Ingredients

2 c Basmati Rice (give 3-4 washes)
2-3 tbsp olive oil or vegetable oil
2 tbsp bacon fat (optional; it enhances the taste greatly)
2 medium Onions finely chopped
1 medium tomato finely chopped (optional)
1 stick Cinnamon
2 Bay leaves
4 cloves
2 green cardamom
1 10g chicken bouillon cube
1 tsp. salt

Method

Sauté the chopped onions, (browning onions enhances the colour of pulav).
Add the tomato and sauté 3 minutes.
Add remainder of ingredients and bacon fat and cook for3 mins.
Add 4 cups of water (boiling water will accelerate cooking time).
Taste for salt.
Add washed basmati rice and cook at high heat. Once the mixture comes to full boil, lower the heat to low and cover and cook for approximately 12-14 minutes.
When rice is cooked, aerate the cooked rice with a fork, adding some extra virgin olive oil on the top, to enhance the flavor.
Notes: You can add one or two whole eggs (in shell) after adding water and top the pulav with sliced eggs when serving.
When serving pulav, you may top it with olives and or cooked chouriço.

2 GOAN SHRIMP CURRY

Danielle (Moniz) Mascarenhas
Minor Modifications by Emano

Serves 8-10

Ingredients

Tamarind –small ball (1/2 tsp paste)
Onion 1 and ½ large (2 med) - finely chopped
Salt to taste
Prawns -20 medium size, more if desired for added flavour
Dry Kashmiri Chillis 3-5 (1 tbsp. powder)
Coriander Powder ½ tsp.
Cumin seeds 1 tsp. (1/2 tsp. powder)
Turmeric – 1tsp
Garlic 6-7 cloves (appr 3-4 tsp. or 1-1 ¼ Tbsp)
Tomato Paste 1 tsp
Coconut Milk 200 ml
Green Chillis – 2 (more or less optional)

Method

1. Soak the tamarind in water. Set aside
2. Press & mix the onions with salt. Keep aside
3. Make a paste: Kashmiri chillis, coriander seeds, cumin seeds, turmeric powder, garlic and tamarind water into a very fine paste
4. In a pan, on medium flame, add in the ground paste, onions and thin coconut milk.
5. Rinse the mixer with water and add to the pan. Keep adding water, until you get curry of desired consistency.
6. When it nears boiling, add the prawns and the green chillies
7. Boil the curry on medium heat for 5 minutes
8. After 5 mins, the prawns and onions are cooked and the curry is ready.
9. Add the thick juice. Bring the curry to a boil again, and turn off the fire.
10. Serve hot, over rice, with fried fish and pickle

Tips

This curry tastes better with time and can be left in the fridge for up to 10 days. Just heat it (not boil) before serving.
Adding ½ to 1 chicken cube enhances the flavour. Add ½- 1 tsp sugar.
Consider adding a semi-ripe mango seed (kato) also to enhance flavour.
Watch out for salt level.

3 CHICKEN CURRY

(Chrisann (Misquitta) Barnetto – Helena Moniz's Recipe)

Ingredients

1 full chicken cut into medium size pieces. (1 kg)	1 Tsp turmeric powder
2 medium size onions	1 Tbs chilli powder
5-6 cloves garlic	1 can of coconut milk.
1 small lemon size tamarind ball (1/2-1 tsp paste)	½ tsp sugar
	2 tsp salt
	1 green chilli (2 if not spicy)

Method

Cut the chicken into medium pieces, apply salt and turmeric powder, and set aside for half an hour.
Soak the tamarind ball in hot water for 5 mins.
In a nonstick pan, heat 2 tbs of oil and add the chopped onions. Fry till translucent to golden brown, adding garlic a minute before adding the chicken. Fry chicken for 3 to 4 mins till color changes. Then add the chilli powder, tamarind pulp, sugar and the can of coconut milk with ¼ cup water.
Cook on medium heat till chicken is done. Taste for salt. Slit a green chilli and add at this time. Boil for another minute. Turn off the fire and enjoy with plain white rice.

4 CHICKEN CURRY OR SHRIMP OR FISH CURRY

Emano Moniz

(8 chicken breast pieces each cut into 3 pieces)

CURRY PREPARATION

2 Med Onions chopped fine. Saute lightly 5 mins then add
4 Garlic cloves chopped fine (1-2 tsp paste) and fry another 3 mins.
Then add and fry for 3-5 mins
2 Tbsp red masala (see recipe elsewhere here)
1 maggie cube
½ tsp tamarind paste (dissolved in little warm water)
½ -1 Tsp coriander powder
½ Tbsp cumin powder
1 tsp turmeric

ADD
1 28oz Tomato can
Take the pan off the fire and Puree all contents
Bring the pan back on fire and

ADD
1 Can of Coconut milk (if light and thick portion: use mainly the light
portion first, setting the thick portion aside to be added towards the end)
If sweeter curry is desired use 2 cans of coconut juice

ADD
Chicken pieces and cook on med to low heat for approximately 15 mins
Then ADD the thick part of Coconut juice just before end of cooking.
Add one green chilli (slit) and 1-2 tsp sugar (?) and salt to taste.
Keep on fire for approx. 2 more mins
Add more chicken cube to enhance flavour if required
Note: (If making shrimp curry and shrimp shells and heads are available,
boil them in small amount of water and add this water along with tomato
can contents)

5 CHICKEN OR BEEF XACUTI
Chrisann Misquitta Barnetto

Ingredients

1 kg chicken/beef	12 cloves garlic
2 tsp salt	1 inch (2.5cm) ginger
1 tsp turmeric	¼ tsp nutmeg
1 full coconut, grated (1 cup desiccated coconut)	6 to 8 Kashmiri chilis
	4 to 5 Green Cardamom
3 tbsp full coriander	1 tsp sugar
1 tbsp cumin seeds	1 green chili slit (optional)
10 cloves	4 potatoes (cut into 1/4 's)
3 medium sticks cinnamon (1 ½ tsp)	

Method

Cut the chicken or beef into medium size pieces, apply 2 tsp salt and 1 tsp turmeric powder and set aside for an hour.

Dry roast the coconut till brown and set side

Roast the coriander, cumin, cloves, cinnamon and cardamom on medium heat for 2 mins and set aside. Lastly roast the Kashmiri Chillis. Grind all the roasted spices to a fine paste with water.

Heat 2 tbsp oil in a pan, add the chopped onions and saute till golden brown. Add the chicken and fry for some time on medium heat. Then add the ground masala, roasted coconut, mix well, add tamarind pulp, 1 tsp sugar and the potatoes.

Bring to boil, and then cook the chicken or beef on medium heat until done. Slit a green chilli if needed at this time. Boil for another minute and shut of gass.

(P.S.) If you are making beef Xacuti let the beef cook half way then add the potatoes).

6 CHICKEN XACUTI
from Melgoans (Australia)

Ingredients

1 large chicken (1 ¼ kg)
salt to taste
one cup grated coconut and 1 tbsp
fresh, diced coconut
1 ½ tbsp coriander seeds
1 dessertspoon cumin seeds
1 tbsp poppy seeds
1 tsp turmeric seeds
8 red dried chillies

1 tsp grated nutmeg
6 star aniseed
2 tsps fennel seeds
1/3 cup oil
2 large onions, chopped fine
6 green chillies, chopped fine
2 tbsp tamarind pulp
3 cups water

Method

Wash, clean and joined the chicken, and then each piece into two. Apply salt and keep aside. In a flat/ griddle, on medium heat brown the grated coconut, and all the spices except the nutmeg, green chillies and diced coconut. You will get a strong fragrance when the spices are done (approx. 3 -5 mins.). Remove from heat and grind this mixture of roasted spices to a paste in the blender/grinder. Heat oil in a pan on medium heat and saute all the ground spices along with the green chillies, and 1 large onion chopped fine. Add the chicken pieces, diced coconut, nutmeg and salt to taste along with the tamarind pulp. Lower the flame and add the water gradually, stir cooking, as you do so in an open pan. After 15 minutes, raise the flame and shake the pan gently. The oil will rise to the top. Remove from fire. With boneless lamb, add more water and simmer on low heat until fully cooked and soft. This could take about an hour unless you are using a pressure cooker.

7 RANDHLOLEM - MILK FISH
Emano Moniz (Blanche's recipe)

In my opinion, this recipe or style of cooking is very unique to our Curtorim families' cooking, and if I may say, one of my favourite recipes. *Even though the recipe given here below is for **fish**, you can prepare **chicken, beef, pork** or even vegetable such as eggplant or brinjal using the same recipe.* You can substitute milk fish with any other fish e.g. pompano, pomfret. It just happens that the first time I made this recipe, I used milk fish.

3 Med Size Milk Fish (cut in steak form and salted)
1 Med-Large Onion finely chopped Sautee onion 3-5 mins.

ADD to Sauteed onion the following

4 Green Chillies (2 if hot) finely chopped   ¾ -1 Tsp Turmeric
2 tsp Garlic paste (heaping)   ¼ tsp pepper
¼ tsp Clove powder   Salt to taste
¼ tsp Cinnamon Powder

ADD
Fish (in layer if required)
COOK on med heat for 5-10 mins approximately
Just before finishing cooking

ADD
¾ tsp Heaping Tamarind Paste, dissolved in 1/8 cup of boiling water. Then add 1/8c Goa vinegar or Apple cider vinegar.
Cook for another 5 mins.
Add little (boiling) water for more gravy.
NOTE: For eggplant: cut the eggplant in cubes and apply good amount of salt and keep aside for ½ -1 hour to draw water. Then wash the cut eggplant and pat dry, before frying in oil to semi-doneness. Set aside. Prepare masala. Then add the eggplant to prepared masala, just as you would do with fish.

8 RECHEADO MASALA #1 (stuffing masala)
Danielle (Moniz) Mascarenhas

Recheado (pronounced as ray-shaad) Masala or 'Jeerem Mirem' is that magical blend of spices found in every Goan household. It's a simple blend of fragrant and strong spices, used to flavour fish, prawns, meat, curries, vegetables and loads of other dishes!

Prepare this masala once in a while, using your handy mixer grinder, and store it in your refrigerator. And whenever you need it, just scoop out some masala and spice up your meals!

Makes: Approx 350gm

Ingredients

Kashmiri Red Chillies- 100gms
Ginger, chopped- 50gms
Garlic- 50gms
Cinnamon- 1.5 inch
Peppercorns- 16
Cloves- 15

Cumin (Jeera) Seeds- 1.5tsp
Sugar- 4.5tsp
Salt- 2tsp
Goa Vinegar / Palm Vinegar- 135ml
Turmeric (Haldi) Powder- 1.5tsp

Method

Soak the tamarind in some water, just covering the tamarind. Crush and squeeze out the tamarind until it forms a thick paste. Soak the squeezed tamarind into some more water and set aside for later use
Transfer all the ingredients into a mixer grinder, except the tamarind
Grind to a thick paste, adding in the tamarind water and paste, gradually
Your masala will be ready when thick and reddish brown in colour
Rinse the mixer grinder with some water and add to the masala
Refrigerate for later use

8 RECHEADO MASALA #2

Helena Moniz submitted by Chrisann (Misquitta) Barnetto

Ingredients

Kashmiri Red Chillies- 100gms
Ginger, 1 inch (2.5cm) piece
Garlic- handful
Cumin 3 tbsp
2 onions
Sugar- 250g

1 big ball of tamarind soaked in
135ml Goa or Apple cider vinegar
Salt- 1 tsp
Turmeric (Haldi) Powder-2 tsp
4-5 green chillis

Method

Chop garlic, ginger, onion, green chilli, cumin and grind with enough vinegar. Then add the whole of tamarind (if using paste adjust) and grind to fine paste.

Add Kashmiri chili powder and sugar and mix well. Add salt and turmeric powder and mix well. Taste and adjust to taste as per above ingredients.

9 RECHEADO (STUFFED) MACKERELS
(RECHAD BANGDDE)

During fresh mackerel season, preparing the fish with recheado masala stuffing, was a welcome change of way of preparing the mackerel. The more common ways would be making fish curry and plain fried mackerels.

6 fresh mackerels
Remove heads, fins and entrails and wash well. Slit fish on either side of the centre bone from head to tail or if desired removing the central bone allowing a bit of the tail bone to remain.
Apply a little salt and keep aside.
Stuff the recheado masala (recipe above) into each mackerel very evenly on either side of the centre bone and fry it in hot oil.
Serve with rice and fish curry.

10 GOAN STIR FRY PRAWNS

(Blanche Moniz Viegas and Heriberto Moniz)

½ kg fresh Prawns (shelled, deveined & washed)

3 tbsps. Goan Recheado Masala

3 med. size Onions (roughly chopped)

3 tbsps. Cooking Oil

1 Capsicum (Green Bell Peper (diced or sliced)

Salt to taste

Marinate fresh prawns with 1 tbsp. masala paste for 10 mins.

Heat cooking oil in a pan on medium heat (wok works well)

Add marinated prawns, 2 tbsp masala paste & stir fry on high heat for 3 minutes.

Keep aside in a bowl.

To the same pan/wok add onions & capsicum & stir fry for another 2 mins on high heat.

To this add the prawns from the bowl & again stir fry & toss for another 3 mins.

Serve hot with fresh bread, hot chapati or steamed rice.

11 SHRIMP PATTIES #1 (Almondegas)

Chrisann (Misquitta) Barnetto

Ingredients

2 cups shrimp

¾ cup coconut

4 medium size onions

1 tsp salt

1 tbs cumin seeds

2 TBS apple cider vinegar

1/ inch ginger

1 tsp sugar

2 pods of garlic

4 Bread slices soaked in milk or water

1 medium size stick cinnamon

1 egg

2 to 3 green chillies

1 TBS olive oil.

1 tsp turmeric

Method

Add 1 tsp salt to the shrimp and steam it with onion, coconut, ginger garlic, green chillies, turmeric, cumin seeds, cinnamon and salt, vinegar and ¼ cup water for 10 to 15 mins till the water dries out. Let it cool. Blend it in the mixer. Remove in a bowl, add the bread slices squeezed of liquid, egg and olive oil, mix well and shape into cutlets. Roll in bread crumbs and fry till golden brown.

12 SHRIMP PATTIES #2 (Almondegas de Camarao)

Maria Lurdes Moniz, Original from Fulu (Barreto House)

Ingredients

1/2 kg prawns	1 tsp cumin
1/2 cup of grated coconut	1 tsp pepper
4 to 5 whole red chilies	2 slices of bread soaked in water.
1 onion	1 chicken flavoured bouillon cube
1 tsp garlic finely garlic	salt to taste

Method

Slice the onion and roast dry in a frying pan.
Add coconut and whole red chilies.
Let it roast well then add garlic, cumin and pepper.
Add chicken bouillon cube along with cleaned, deveined prawns
Let the mixture dry and cool
Squeeze the slices of bread of all the water
Blend the prawn mixture with the slices of bread.
Shape into round patties with and shallow fry.
Enjoy with rice and curry of your choice.

13 MANGO CURRY- Samnsua- Amtto

Blanche (Moniz) Viegas

Note: In bracket below ( ) is for double the quantity I tested.

Ingredients

4 (8) semi-ripe med to large mangos, skinned and cut into thick slices and then chopped lengthwise.
In blender grind
1 (2) onion
1 chunk (1tsp concentrate) of tamarind in water
2 green chillis (3 hot chillis)
4 to 5 tbsp (more if needed) of coconut powder (2 can milk)

Heat oil, add curry (patha) leaves (2 twigs), mustard seeds (1 ½ tsp), pinch of asafoetida (hing), turmeric (1 tsp), the ground masala and fry a bit. Let it thicken up then add mango, little water to clean the milk cans) and cook closed, appr 10 mins. Do not let mango get too soft. When ready add little sugar and one slit chilli.
Ambtto, means sour. If you wish less sour, add little more sugar.

14 PORK VINDALHO #1 (Vindaloo)

Blanche (Moniz) Viegas, Submitted by Heriberto Moniz

2 kg pork, cut and salted (4 tsp)
Grind the ingredients below into a fine paste

16 dried Kashmiri chilies (2½ -3 tsp)   1/2 tsp whole black pepper corns
1 inch piece cinnamon (1/3-1/2 tsp)   1/2 tsp turmeric
1 tsp cumin   1 ½ tbsp vinegar
6 garlic cloves

Mix the pork with above paste and refrigerate overnight or at least a few hours
Saute two medium onions finely diced, till golden brown
Add 1 tbsp garlic paste, 3/4 tbsp ginger paste
3-4 tbsp recheado masala
½ cup soaked tamarind (1 tsp paste, dissolved in hot water, adjust?)

Little (1/2 tsp) cinnamon powder, clove powder, cumin powder, each.
Add the pork with marinade
Add 1 1/2 cups of boiling water and bring it to simmer. Cook on medium-low heat till pork is tender (about 40 mins). Add water as needed.
Add Goa vinegar (or apple cider vinegar) (about 1/4 cup) or to your taste.
Note: You may substitute half of vinegar with tamarind water, for slightly different taste.
Add sugar (2 Tbsp) and Season (salt) to taste
Final product should have some thin gravy consistency, not curry consistency.

15 PORK VINDALHO #2 (Vindaloo)

Melgoans (Australia)

Ingredients

1 kg lean pork, cleaned	1 tsp cumin seeds
Salt to taste	½ mustard seeds
10 dried red chillies/peppers	½ tsp sugar
10 peppercorns	½ tsp vinegar
10 cloves garlic	2 tbsp oil
1 inch piece ginger	½ peg coconut feni
8 cloves	2 medium onions, chopped fine
1 inch piece cinnamon	2 cups water

Method

Cut the cleaned pork into bite-sized pieces. Apply salt and keep aside. Grind all the spices in the vinegar, adding the ½ tsp sugar. Apply the ground spices to the meat and keep aside for 4 hours.

Heat the oil in the pan on medium heat and add the meat. Stir fry the meat for 5 minutes, then add the chopped onion, coconut feni, rest of the vinegar and the water gradually. Cover the pan and lower heat. Stir cook till meat is tender and the oil rises to the top (approx. 30 minutes).
Note: Chicken or beef can also be used in the recipe given for Pork Vindalho.

16 FISH AMBOT TIK (Sour and Spicy)
Submitted by Heriberto Moniz, (Blanche's Recipe)

Fish that makes good ambot tik are: squids, shark, skate or cat fish. Tilapia, Pampano and Mullet also can be used.

Ingredients

Fish about 1kg, cut into steaks, washed and slightly salted
1 medium onion, finely chopped
Tamarind (golf size ball), soaked and squeezed 2,3 times over

2 green chillies slit	1 tsp cumin powder
1 1/2 tsp Kashmiri chili powder	6-8 kokum (binda solam)
1/4 tsp turmeric	2 tbsp oil
3-4 cloves garlic	

Method

Put 2 tbsp canola or coconut oil and saute onion for 3-5 minutes
Tamarind, chilli powder, turmeric, garlic and cumin can be ground or mixed together in a mixer with tamarind water and strained.
1 ½ c Water
As onion turns golden brown, add the above mixture.
Add slit chilis and kokum and 1tbsp Goa vineagar (optional)
Check for salt level adding more salt if needed
Bring it to a boil
Add fish, and as soon as it again starts to boil, fish is cooked
(Adding curry leaves while sauteing onion, gives ambot tik a different flavour and aroma)

17 SOLANTULEM #1
Heriberto and Loyola and Blanche Moniz

1 kg meat, cut with or without bones, wash and salt
Add tamarind water (small ball of tamarind soaked in water)
4-5 kashmiri chillies, broken
7-8 bindda solam (kokum)
1/2 tsp turmeric. Mix all these and start cooking on slow fire, as it will release its own liquid. Cook till meat is semi tender

Then, add the following:
3-4 green chillies slit (mild)
2 med. onions, roughly cut into squares
4-5 garlic cloves
1 tsp cumin crushed

Cook for another 10-15 minutes till meat and onions are done.
Adjust liquid as per your need by adding water or reducing liquid on fire.

17 SOLANTULEM #2
Ethel (Pereira) Moniz

Ingredients

1 kg pork meat (cut up in 2 inch pieces)
4 medium onions (chopped, not fine)
2-4 Dry Chilis broken in half
Kokum (5-6 pieces halved)

Add little Water and cook the meat on medium heat, approximately 30 minutes, until the meat is cooked.
Once meat is cooked dry all liquid under high heat.
A final light browning in a frying pan is optional.

18 ARD MAS - PORK MEAT on BONES

Heriberto Moniz

Ingredients

1 kg pork meat with/on bones
2 medium onions finely chopped
4 garlic cloves finely chopped
1 tsp ginger finely chopped
1 tsp cumin
1 tsp chilli powder

Small ball of tamarind soaked in water (1/2 tsp paste)
Few Kokum (5-10)
Salt to taste (ground pepper ½ the quantity of salt)

Sauté onions till translucent (5 mins)
Add remaining ingredients and continue sautéing for another 3 minutes.
Add the pork meat and cook till meat is cooked.
Add little water if required.
This dish should be wet but not too much liquid.

19 SOI-MIREM

Heriberto Moniz

All measurements are approximate

1 lb salted pork, soaked overnight and rinsed. Cut into pieces, size of your liking

1 1/2 cup grated coconut
4 kashmiri chillies
1 1/2 tsp dry coriander seeds

1 tsp cumin seeds
4 cloves garlic
1" piece ginger

Grind the above with little water to a smooth paste
In a pot over medium heat, add 2-3 tbsp of oil and saute one medium size diced onion.
When golden, add soi-mirem paste and cook for a minute or two.
Add pork, mix well and cook on low heat till meat is cooked.
Add water as to the constituency that one desires.
Note: You may also add 4-5 dry mango solam, if one desires slight tart taste

20 PORK and OKRA

Blanche (Moniz) Viegas

Ingredients

1 kg Pork meat
450 g Okra (fresh or frozen cut into 3cm long pieces)

Apply extra Salt to the pork meat and keep aside for 1 -2 days.
When ready to cook, wash the pork thoroughly and cut in cube form (say 2-3cm). Apply little salt.

2 medium onions (chopped, not fine, and no need to saute)	1 tsp turmeric
3 cm Ginger	½ tsp Clove powder (little more if needed)
1 tsp Cumin powder	½ cinnamon (little more if needed)
6 cloves garlic (chopped)	½ tsp pepper
Tamarind (small ball), soaked in little boiling water	

Cook the meat on medium heat, approximately 20 minutes, adding little water as needed, until the meat is cooked. Approximately 5 minutes before the meat is ready, add okra. Add little salt if needed.

21 PORK ASSADO (Pork Belly Roast)

Blanche (Moniz) Viegas

2 kg Pork Belly cut into 2 inch pieces.
Add 1 lemon juice (3 TBSP) and 1 TBSP vinegar, and
Add the following ground masala: 5-6 green chillies, 2 inch ginger (1tsp), 2 med pods garlic (2tsp paste), 15 cloves (1 1/4tsp paste), ½ tsp cinnamon, 1tsp+ turmeric, 1 med-large onion, little sugar (1tsp) and little pepper.
Keep at least for 24 hrs- keep rotating the meat.
Cook on med to low heat in its juice (do not add any water, water will come out from the meat) till all liquid is dried up.
Fry when required. When frying is completed add ½ tbsp ketchup and ½ tbsp soya sauce to the pan

22 PRESUNTO (Ham); Same Recipe **for SALTED TONGUE**

Blanche (Moniz) Viegas

1 kg pork shoulder (remove bone)
Jab the pork with fork well and then add the following masala.

Grind in magic bullet

1 head of garlic
1 ½ inch ginger
10 whole cloves
1 1/2 stick pieces cinnamon
2 tbsp sea salt

½ tsp saltpeter (heat with lighter till it flames up?)
Juice of 2 limes
2 tbsp of vinegar
2 small chunks of black juggery
½ tsp turmeric

Apply to the meat and keep under weight for 2 to 3 days.
Then remove excess masala. Wash the cooking pot, then put 1/3 cup water, 1/3 cup of feni (white rum), 3 red Kashmiri chilis. Cook covered on medium fire.

23 PORK TORRADO (Pork Roast) #1

Ethel (Pereira) Moniz

This recipe was a common way of preparing tender pork meat (pigling). Thus a tender pork meat cut and a fatty meat cut is desirable.

½ kilo pork meat
1 tsp black pepper
Pinch of saffron

½ tsp salt
Juice of 1 lime
1-2 cups water

Add all the above ingredients, bring to a boil and then cover and let cook on low to medium heat until water dries up. Remove and let cool. Cut into bits and put back into gravy. Then fry in oil. Serve with onions cut into long strips, put in a little vinegar, a little sugar and a green chilly cut into small bits.

23A PORK TORRADO (Pork Roast) #2
Blanche (Moniz) Viegas

Slice pork (not too much fat) thinly.
Apply lemon juice and a little vinegar, little recheado masala and following ground masala- green chillies, ginger, garlic, cloves, cinnamon, turmeric, onion, little sugar and little pepper.
Keep at least for 24 hrs- massage the meat occasionally.
Cook in it's juice (do not add any water) till all liquid is dried up.
Fry when desired.

24 FISH CALDINHO (Fish in Broth)
Serena (Moniz) Diniz

Ingredients

½ kg fish (pomfret or pompano)
2 cups grated coconut
or 1½ can coconut milk
4 garlic cloves
2 tsp coriander seeds
1 tsp cumin seeds
1½ tsp turmeric powder

4 black peppercorns
2 tbsp oil
1 tomato, finely chopped (Optional)
1 onion, finely chopped
2 green chillies, slit
1 tsp vinegar
1 tsp salt

Directions

Clean fish, wash and cut into pieces of desired size.
Apply salt and vinegar and keep aside.
Extract thick and thin milk of grated coconut. If using coconut milk can, divide into half and dilute 1 part as thin milk.
Grind cumin, coriander, peppercorns, turmeric and thick coconut milk and set aside.
In a vessel, heat oil and fry onions until soft. Add tomato and fry until soft. Add thin coconut milk and bring to a boil.
Add the fish pieces, slit green chillies, cover and cook for 4-5 mins (until fish is cooked).

Add thick coconut milk mixture and combine (do not over stir). Simmer for 2-3 mins on low fire. Don't allow to boil as the curry can curdle due to vinegar. Serve with hot basmati rice.

25 GOAN WEDDING STEW #1
Maria Lurdes Moniz Original from Fulu (Barreto House)

The Goan stew, or the Goan Wedding Stew, so called, as it was a staple or one of the principal dishes served at most wedding receptions of yesteryear. I loved it then and I still do.

Ingredients

1 lb of pork meat	pepper
1 lb of any meat (chicken or beef)	5 cloves
1/2 lb of pork sausages	Cinnamon stick
2 large onions -diced fine	2 chicken flavoured bouillon cubes
1 tomato - diced	2 tablespoons of oil
garlic and ginger - chopped fine	diced potatoes
a dash of sugar	diced carrots
salt to taste	macaroni
1/2 tsp of turmeric	

Procedure

Clean the meats (pork and chicken or beef) and cut into small cubes.
Add 1/2 tsp of turmeric, pepper and a dash of vinegar.
Saute onion until soft and until lightly brown.
Add chopped tomato, garlic and ginger.
Add the pork meat and let it season with the above mixture.
Add the sausages and then the chicken or beef.
Add the bouillon cubes.
Add diced carrots, let the carrots cook 1/3 cook.
Add diced potatoes and let all the flavor blend in.
When the both the carrots and potatoes are cooked
Add macaroni. Watch that the macaroni does not overcook.
Add pepper and Salt to taste.

25A GOAN WEDDING STEW #2
Blanche Moniz Viegas

Equal quantities of pork belly (pork), beef, chicken – apply salt
Saute onions – good amount
1 green chilli, chopped very fine
Once golden brown add (sausage optional)
Ginger garlic paste
(6) cloves
¼ tsp cinnamon
½ tsp pepper

Continue sautéing for short time, add beef and pork and after a little while
add chicken – cook closed
Carrots (in cubes) and potatoes, let cook for a short while.
Last add green peas and add cooked elbow macaroni.

26 BEEF CROQUETTES
Michelle (Moniz) Rebelo

Ingredients

500 gms mince meat (beef)	1 tsp ginger garlic paste
1 large onion chopped	Salt
1 medium tomato	Vinegar
1/2 tsp turmeric	Coriander leaves
1/ 2 tsp chilli powder	1/4 tsp cumin powder
1/4 tsp garam masala	1/4 coriander powder

Cook it together and make a semi-paste of it
Add One egg and green chillies (to your taste and heat tolerance)
to the cooked beef mixture and mix well.
Make crockets shaped approximately 2 to 2 ½ inches long and ½ -3/4 inch
thick (5 x 1 cm) and coat with semolina and deep fry.

27 BEBINCA (Goan rich layered pudding)
Heriberto Moniz

Bebinca is a Goan speciality dessert, popularly known as the Queen of Goan Sweets; it has a rich golden brown colour and an enticing flavor; a multi-layered sweetness that melts in the mouth.

In a village life setting, they baked the bibinca in an oven in the form of two big double earthen containers, where coconut husks were used for fire in the bottom container and inside the top container. The Bibinca container was placed inside the bottom container.

The process is time consuming, even by today's standards where we have electric or gas fired ovens, mainly because the bibinca is made with at least 7 layers, each layer baked individually. This lengthy baking process combined with the fact that the recipe demands a dozen egg yolks, made bibinca more of a rare or special commodity, in the good old days.

Now-a-days Bibinca is lot more commercially available; there are individual mom and pop suppliers in villages and cities in Goa and even cities worldwide, where there is significant presence of Goan origin folks.

The recipe given here is Heriberto's. He has been making this bibinca recipe at Christmas time, now for a number of years.

This is a whole day production for Heriberto at Christmas time, not only for home consumption, but also to share with friends, who have come to expect to receive a good piece of Bibinca from Heriberto and Maria Lurdes at this time of the year.

What I like about Heriberto's recipe, is that it gives ingredients in the form available in ready to use form for city folks or Goan diaspora.

Ingredients

1 can of coconut cream (A)	12 egg yolks
1 can of coconut milk (B)	1 tsp of salt
2 cups of sugar	1 1/2 tsp nutmeg
2 cups of all purpose flour	Ghee or clarified butter as needed

Method

Add to (A) 12 egg yolks and mix thoroughly

Add to (B) 2 cups of sugar and dissolve it completely

Join mixtures (A) and (B). To this add 2 cups of flour, salt and nutmeg; mix it to a smooth batter leaving no lumps.

Suggestion: Run through a fine sieve.

Optional: you may add 1/4 cup sugar caramel to give the bebinca a darker hue

BAKING: The pan should be of adequate size to accommodate the above batter and make at least 8-10 layers.

Heat the oven to 350 degrees with the pan in it. once the oven is ready remove the pan, pour some ghee or use a brush to grease the pan bottom and the side copiously.

Using a 3/4 cup or full cup measure (the layer should be about 1/4 inch thick when baked) use the same measure for consistency of layers. Bake it for about 20 minutes and then another 10 mins on BROIL LOW.

After each layer, run a smooth edge around the layer(s), shake it vigorously clockwise and anti-clockwise direction to make sure the layer is not stuck at the bottom.

Then brush more ghee to the top and sides of the pan. Pour in the second layer and bake it as per the first layer. Follow the same procedure for the rest of the layers, making sure that once all layers are baked the BEBINCA will be easily inverted when warm.

Tip: Once half the layers are done, you could place the bibinca container on aluminum foil with shiny side facing down. This may help to prevent the bottom getting over baked.

28 BOLINHAS (Little Balls) Goan coconut macaroons
Serena Moniz Diniz

Makes 20-22 small ones (5 cm) or 16 medium size ones.
This sweet has a Goan DNA, with grated coconut being the predominant ingredient. It happens to be one my top three Goan sweets-favourites.

Ingredients

2 c (250 g) semolina
2½ cup fresh or frozen grated coconut
3 egg yolks
1 whole egg (or one white of egg well beaten)

1¼ cup fine sugar
¼ cup water
2 tbsp ghee or butter
½ tsp vanilla essence
¼ tsp cardamom powder
¼ tsp salt

Directions

Lightly roast semolina (med heat 5-10 mins) with little (1/2tbsp) ghee. Allow to cool.
In a separate bowl, whisk egg yolks. Stir in vanilla. Set aside.
Make sugar syrup with sugar and water. Once dissolved (slightly thickened), add coconut. Cook for 2-3 minutes.
Add cardamom and mix well. When cool, add semolina, egg yolks and whole egg and mix well.
Set aside for 5-6 hours or overnight in the fridge.
When ready, make round balls (dough at room temp.) by applying ghee or flour to palms. Then flatten the balls and create a line design on top with fork tines or a knife or tooth pick. A convenient way is to flour a wooden cutting board, place the dough as a ball and divide it into 16 parts.
Bake at 350 degrees for 30-35 mins till lightly brown. Bottom will be slightly browner than the rest.

28A BOLINHAS #2 Makes 18 pieces
Fatima's Bolinhas (Modified by Emano Moniz)

Ingredients

1c Sugar (adjust to desired sweetness level)	1 TBSP Butter
	2 Pinches Salt
1/4c Water	2 Egg Yolks
1c Semolina	¼ tsp. Baking Powder
2c Grated Coconut	½-1 tsp. Cardamom Powder

Method

Use wooden spoon when mixing the ingredients.
In a deep frying pan melt sugar and water and bring to boil
Add semolina and mix and cook for 2-3 mins
Add grated coconut and mix well and cook for 2-3 mins.
Add butter, mix well, and take it off fire and let it cool fully.
Once fully cooked add remainder of ingredients and mix well by hand.
Leave mixture to rest 4-5 hours or overnight (in the fridge or outside)
Heat oven to 400F (200C).
With floured hands make small balls (about 1 ½ TBSP quantity) and place them on parchment paper lined metal pan (30cmx30cm – 12"x12"). Bolinhas are ready when lightly to medium brown and bottom is little darker brown. It should take approximately 20 mins.

29 BHATICA

Noemia Araujo and Curtorim Loutulim Raia (CLR) Association

Bhatica or Bhat is similar to bolinhas, except that it is made in cake form. When growing up in Curtorim, I don't believe Bhatica was something our folks made or even heard of. It was always bolinhas.

Ingredients

1 1/2 cups sugar

2 cups coconut

2 cups fine Semolina (450gms)

5 eggs (yolks and whites separated)

400 gms margarine or butter

1 tsp baking powder

1 tsp cardomon powder

Method

(Some folks say if you buy Rawa or Sooji from the Indian stores, instead of Semolina, it comes out better)

1. Roast semolina on a low fire (appr 5 mins) and keep aside.
2. Beat margarine or butter and sugar until light and fluffy, add egg yolks and beat well.

Add ground coconut along with semolina, baking powder and cardamom powder. Finally, add (fold in) stiff beaten egg-whites. Mix well (do not beat). Divide the mixture in TWO greased moulds and bake in a pre-heated oven 350F, for approx. 40 mins until ready.

It is ready when top is golden brown and tester comes out clean.

30 KULKULS (Benildes Coutinho Moniz)

A great sweet to prepare with the family. Kulkuls is a sweet popular with Goans, in particular at Christmas time. They are now made all over India. They are fun to make as a family affair and keep very well if stored in a airtight container.

¼ kg flour (2 cups)
¼ kg rawa /semolina (2 cups)
2- 3 Tbsp rice flour
3-4 Tbsp melted ghee or butter
(1/4 c)

¼ cup fine sugar (not icing sugar)-
increase sugar to your taste
1 cup Coconut cream/dairy milk
or water (more as needed)
1 egg
Pinch of Salt

Method

Mix well egg, sugar, ghee/butter, portion of milk in a bowl.
In a separate bowl mix flour, rawa, salt and sugar.
Make a well in the center and add the egg, milk mixture to make a dough.
Cover with a damp cloth and keep for at least 15 mins.
When you touch the dough with your dry hand, your hand will be shiny.
Form small marble-sized balls out of dough.
Grease the back of a fork with some oil and flatten and press a ball of dough onto it. In place of fork, you can use kulkul paddles available on sale in India.

Starting at one end, roll the dough off the fork and into a tight curl.
The end result will be a tube-like curl with the design from the fork on it!
Continue the process with remaining small dough balls.
Heat the oil (300F) in a deep, heavy-bottomed pan on a medium flame
When hot, fry the kulkuls in it, making sure to turn often, till they are a light golden brown in color. Drain and cool on paper towels.
NOTES: We have baked the kulkuls in the oven 400F for approximately 12 minutes, or until golden brown.
You can increase the level of sweetness by increasing the amount of sugar added in the dough.

Alternatively, you can prepare a simple 50/50 sugar/water mixture and cook till the sugar melts fully; it is important to thicken the syrup mixture a little. In a bowl put the a few cooled kulkuls at a time and pour a little of the water/sugar syrup and coat well. Repeat the process with more kulkuls. Remove and allow to sit on a plate till the syrup coated kulkuls dry. When the kulkuls are stored in a air-tight container, kulkuls will last for a considerable amount of time.

31 PATOLEOS

Serena (Moniz) Diniz

Ingredients

1 cup raw rice	2 cups grated coconut
1 cup jaggery (half Goan palm dark	½ tsp cardamom powder
+ half cane light)	12-13 turmeric leaves

Note: Leaves can be grown in pots from turmeric roots, or buy them from West Indian or Indian stores. Leaves can be frozen for future use.

Directions

Soak rice for 3-4 hours and grind to a fine paste, adding salt to taste.

Do not add too much water; paste should be thick.

Mix coconut, jaggery, cardamom powder for filling.

Alternative method: Boil 1/4 cup water, add jaggery and melt. When dissolved, strain the jaggery liquid and add coconut and cardamom powder.

Wipe turmeric leaves with moist cloth. Take spoonful of rice batter and place at the top of the leaf. Dip fingers in water to help spread paste thinly across leaf.

Place coconut filling in the centre along the rib of leaf, close leaf and press gently to secure sides.

Place patoleos in a steamer for 10-12 mins. Rest for 10 mins, unwrap centre from leaves and enjoy.

32 **XMAS Cake** or Goan Wedding Cake
I call it MARLIZ Café Cake (Margao)

Recipe from an Anonymous Lady with modification by Emano Moniz
This is a classic Goan "wedding cake" which was served at Goan wedding receptions. At the end of the wedding reception each guest received a piece of this cake as a parting mouth sweetener. My parents would bring these pieces of cake home which were so much appreciated by us kids.

During our College/University days, during the summer vacations, it was common for us classmates and friends to congregate in Margao from time to time, always at a location at Margao central park. Nearby on the other side of the street was a reputable Café place called Marliz, which among other snacks, served this type of cake. Therefore, I have been calling it Cake a la Marliz.

After close to 30 years of being out of Goa, I had the pleasure of enjoying again the taste of this particular cake and took me back to Marliz cake. It was made by an elderly Goan lady, a friend of a friend, but who was not willing to part with her recipe for the longest time. Funnily she finally gave her recipe to our friend, less than a year before she died.

It goes without saying that, once the recipe came into our hands, it got circulated far and wide and it is now being baked and enjoyed across the continents.

GOAN WEDDING CAKE

Recipe makes 2 regular size, 10in cakes
(Prep. Time 1 ½ hr, Baking time 1 ½+hr)

Ingredients

12 eggs at room temp. (separate yolks from whites)
200 to 250g EACH of the following dry fruits marinated in Brandy (or rum)
(I marinate this in 10oz Bottle full)

2c or 450g butter	Ginger in Syrup
2c or 450g sugar	Peeled Dates (optional)
4 ¼ c flour (450g +1/4c)	1 tbsp Vanilla
Black Raisins	1 tbsp Baking Powder
White Raisins	1 tbsp EACH of: Clove, Nutmeg,
Orange Skin	Pumpkin Spice
Lemon Skin	1 1/2 tbsp Cinnamon

½ kg Petha (optional) (crystalized pumpkin) chopped finely for added moisture available at Indian sweet shops

Caramel Preparation

150g (6 oz) sugar + 1oz water. In a pan, at medium heat <u>Caramelize</u> the sugar (make it dark to give the cake the dark colour you want, do not burn) and cool till hard. (b) Add ½c water and at low heat (setting 3) melt caramel, stirring constantly. When it comes to boil, take it off heat, cool fully, keep stirring frequently.

Cake Preparation

Butter 2 biscuit tins and line them with wax paper. Butter the wax paper also. Mix in a bowl the dry ingredients (flour, baking powder, spices). Fold in the brandied dry fruit (drained of liquid) and petha, to coat the fruit with flour mixture (thus fruit will not settle to the bottom).
Using a separate (deep) container and electric mixer, mix butter and sugar together well, till creamy.
Add the yolks in two parts, and continue mixing.

Add lightly beaten whites in installments and fold with a wooden spoon; do not over mix.

Add caramel liquid and vanilla

With electric mixer, mix just enough to have consistent batter, i.e. no butter blobs.

Fold the flour mixture gradually into the wet mixture with a spoon. Mix gently, until all dry and wet mixes are nicely blended.

Pour batter into prepared tins (max to 2/3 full, as the cake rises well). Cover the tin with aluminum foil.

BAKE. For 15 mins at 400F (200C) and then at 300F (150C) until cake is baked (approximately 1 ½ hr, use your tester). Remove the Aluminum foil for the last 10 to 15 mins.

Once the cake is out of the oven, sprinkle it immediately with 2 tbsp of brandy. Let it cool before closing the lid of the container

(Tip: To prevent the bottom of cake from getting overdone, place baking sheet (aluminum foil) below the cake container, when baking.)

If you use tins of different sizes, remember the smaller tin cakes get done faster.

33 CARAMEL CUSTARD (in Goa commonly called Caramel Pudding)
Eufemiano Moniz and Blanche Moniz Viegas and Maria Lurdes Moniz

This traditional dessert, frequently made in our households in Curtorim and our families elsewhere, has been my most favourite dessert going back to my childhood, and I can never get enough of it. When I arrived in Canada in 1971, I lived in the University residence for a year. When I moved out and I had to cook for myself, the first Goan dish I had my mind set upon, was the Caramel custard. And I managed to make it, with advice through mail from Goa. From my childhood memory, I have been aware that the most important element of this dessert is preparation of caramel (dark but not burnt) and properly coating the bottom and the sides of the cooking utensil or the baking mold.

Caramel

1/2 cup sugar 4 tablespoons water
In the baking dish or mould, heat sugar with water till sugar is dark amber in color. Swirl the melted sugar to coat the bottom and sides of the dish. Set aside to cool completely.

Custard Ingredients

4 Eggs	¼ tsp nutmeg
2 cups (500ml) Milk	1 Tbsp Custard powder (optional)
½ cup (125 ml) Sugar	½ tsp vanilla (optional)

Blend the ingredients well in a mixing bowl and then the mixture to the fully cooled caramel dish. Note: You can cut back the eggs to two.

Baking Method Preheat oven to 300 F or 150 C. Cover the dish with aluminum foil and bake in a water bath or bain-marie until the custard has set all around with a slight jiggle in the centre. It should take approximately 30 minutes, but the time required depends on size of the dish and oven efficiency. Alternatively, the custard can be steamed.

Steaming Method: Instapot (Pressure cooker) Method. Place a trivet at the bottom (or 3-4 crumpled balls of aluminum foil), add 1 cup of water and then carefully place the caramel and custard dish, with its top covered in foil. Close the lid and turn the valve to sealed.

Hit the manual button to high and set to 7 minutes. After 7 minutes, press cancel and release the steam. Total cooking time approximately 25 mins.

Cover and chill overnight in the refrigerator. When serving, run a knife all around the edge of the custard. Invert onto a serving dish with raised edge to hold the liquid caramel.

In the instapot, I have baked two stacked custard dishes at a time.

34 CARAMEL BREAD PUDDING
Michelle (Moniz) Rebelo

10 slices of bread (white)	1 tsp vanilla essence
2 eggs	1/4 tsp cardamom powder
1/2 cup or 100 gm sugar (adjust to your taste)	1 1/2 cup or 360-375 ml milk
	2 tbsp butter

Directions

With 4 tbsp sugar make caramel and coat the baking pan. Let it cool.
Warm up the milk and add the sugar and butter, until sugar is dissolved.
Add bread, cut in pieces, to milk mixture and let it soak for 5-10 mins.
Mix separately the eggs, vanilla and cardamom powder and add to the bread and milk mixture.
Pour this mixture gently into the caramel lined pan.
Bake in preheated 350 F oven for approximately 45 minutes or till done.
Turn upside down on a serving plate, and enjoy.

35 BOLACHA (Goan Coconut Cookies)

Normally tea time was when we would get a sweet snack. Fruit, (mango, jackfruit, bananas, custard apple, papaya) was always the first choice when in season or available. Then there were a few concoctions with main ingredients being rice, coconut or juggery.

When our folks felt like making some sweet other than the above, the most common and easy to make was Bolacha (Portuguese for cookie). Our bolacha is made with ingredients, readily available in the house. Absent is butter, because of lack of electricity and fridges at the time.

Ingredients

1 coconut grated (3 c)	Pinch cardamom powder
450g (2c) (1/2 lb) sugar	1 tbsp ghee
3 egg Yolks	½ tsp baking soda
450g (2c) (1/2 lb) flour	

Method

Grind together coconut and sugar fine (consistency between paste and coarse) without water. Add egg yolks n ghee and mix
Sift flour n baking soda.
Mix everything n keep it covered for 1/2 day.
Then take small portion of batter roll it flat like roti (appr ¼ cm thickness).
Cut into rectangular or diamond shape or any other cookie cutter shapes and transfer them to a lightly dusted or parchment paper covered baking pan.
Bake at 350 F for approximately 12 minutes, or until lightly golden brown.

36 DOCE (Doce de grão)(Gram Sweet)

Blanche Viegas Moniz and Goan Cookbook by Joyce Fernandes

Doce is a popular sweet prepared in Goa for various occasions. It is a part of the kuswar, a range of sweets typically prepared during Christmas. Most often the sweet was served in square or diamond shapes.

It is another favourite sweet or dessert of mine with a little bit of history behind it for me. There was a custom in our villages, wherein on January 1, of each year, the mother would send "janeiro", or a basketful of sweets and fruit to the married daughter's house, which we, as young kids, looked forward to. In a way, my mother was not only the oldest child, but also the only married daughter of my grandma. I remember there was always a 'bolo' of doce in this basket, made by ti Albertina.

Somehow ti Helena, came to know that doce was a favourite of mine. Thus, after I moved to Canada, at every trip back to India, ti Helena would have a "bolo" of doce ready for me.

Ingredients

2 coconuts (grated)
250 g gram dal (boiled)
500 g sugar
2-3 Tbsp ghee
6 crushed cardamons

Method

Grate and grind coconuts fine. Grind the gram dal fine.

In a cooking pot, make a thick syrup of sugar and little water; add the ground ingredients. Add ghee and cardamons.

Cook on medium heat, stirring constantly, till the mixture leaves the sides of the pan.

Remove the mixture to a slightly greased plate and either mound it as "bolo". Alternatively you can flatten the mixture to about ½ inch (12 mm) thickness, and then cut it into square or diamond shapes.

37 GODXEM OR Goan Vonn and Kondguel

Blanche Moniz Viegas and Danielle Moniz Mascarenhas
https://thedaniverse.wordpress.com/2020/10/04/goan-vonno-recipe-goa-sweet-dessert-goa-vonn-vegan-veg/

Godxem and Konnguel are similar in preparation and ingredients, the difference being that gram/channa dhal in Godxem is substituted with sweet potato in konnguel. The latter is commonly prepared in the months of March-April, to coincide with the sweet potato season and also the lent season. It is my understanding that Vonn is the name given by the folks in North Goa to what the south Goa folks call Godxem.

Ingredients

Split Chickpeas (Chana Dal)- 125gms
Coconut Milk- 400ml can (or the milk from two fresh coconuts)
Water- 800ml
Rice Flour- 3 tbsp

4 Cardamom crushed OR 1 tsp fennel / saunf seed
Goa Jaggery / Palm Jaggery- 225gms
Salt- a pinch

Method

Boil the chickpeas with salt until soft
Pour the coconut milk into a bowl and rinse the tin with water
Add 200ml coconut milk (1/2 of coconut milk can), 800ml water into a big vessel

Heat on medium flame, bring to boiling point
Add Jaggery piece by piece (crushed), stirring continuously
Let the jaggery melt. You should get light brown mixture
Mix the rice flour in cold water to make a smooth paste and add to above mixture
Add salt to taste and continue stirring until it thickens
Add the remainder of coconut milk. Bring to boiling point and take off the heat.
If making konnguell, slice sweet potatoes to 6 mm (1/4 inch) thickness.
Keep stiring the milk/water/jiggery mixture till potatoes are done.

CHAPTER 14

Outward Migration from India of Family Members

The idea for this chapter came to me one day as an afterthought when I was working out in the gymnasium. My original book idea has been to tell stories about the ancestors of our families, including our parents' generation. That generation is nearly gone and the generations that followed are in the 60s to 80s age bracket, a few of them pushing into 90.

To fully do justice in this book to the achievements of the next generation, i.e. all our cousins, would amount to substantially greater effort and demand greater treatment and space than what I have covered thus far. And truly I felt I need to complete this project first.

Our family, and here we are talking first and second cousins, is truly a worldwide family, and is now spread out from India to Australia and New Zealand, to Europe (Portugal, U.K., France) to North America (USA and Canada) and South America (Brazil). How many families are so blessed?

I came up with an alternative approach to get my cousins involved and achieve a twin set of goals. One is to pull together their experiences as first-generation immigrants in their new adopted countries. The second, in my mind, is my goal to close the circle of immigration: our ancestors came to Goa from as far as Central Asia and the current generation in a way closing the circle, or starting a new cycle of immigration by doing the journey outwards from India to so many parts of the world. Watch out World!

The contributors to the effort of including my cousins are: Eufemiano Moniz in Mississauga, Canada (my apologies if I have taken a bit more space than others), Oscar Souza (Lisbon, Portugal), Ethel's cousin, Egidio Moniz (Sao Paulo, Brazil), his brother Antonio Moniz (San Francisco, USA), the latter two my uncle Riario's sons, my brother Heriberto Moniz (Edmonton, Canada), Valerie Viegas (Florida, USA), wife of my sister Blanche's nephew Prazeres Viegas and Karen Lobo (Toronto, Canada) daughter of Ethel's cousin Joe Menezes. My sincere thanks go to the above authors.

First let me present some context to the modern day immigration.

During the Portuguese reign, Goa was mostly rural and consisted of villages, surrounding four main cities of Margao servicing the south, Panaji, the capital city and relatively centrally located, Mapuca, servicing the north and Vasco da Gama, located at Goa's main harbour of Mormugao.

The village folk's most of consumer staple needs were met at the village level. For consumer staples not available at the village level (clothing, pharmacies, etc) and administrative and commercial services, such as visit to a hospital, or the municipal services, and for other discretionary services, one would have to travel to the city.

Post-elementary school education and job opportunities within Goa's Portuguese territory were limited. Thus, many Goans migrated principally to Mumbai and to a lesser extent to other major cities of India (Delhi, Calcutta, Chennai, Bangaloru and Belgaum) for post-secondary studies and or in search of job opportunities during the British colonial rule.

Then in the late nineteenth and twentieth century, opportunities arose in the other places of the British colonial empire, including Pakistan, Middle East and East Africa (Kenya, Tanzania and Uganda). To a much lesser extent there were also job opportunities in the Portuguese colonies, in particular Mozambique, in East Africa.

Many Goans, including men from our villages, took up to seafaring, in particular on transatlantic ships (P&O later named Cunard Line comes to mind) and made a good living out it.

To my knowledge more people from North Goa (Bardez in particular) embarked on the outward migration. Folks in the south, blessed with more expansive fertile land, were able to live off the land, and were less prone to leave the comforts of their village life.

Because of the Portuguese influence- their religion and food habits and ease with learning of English or Portuguese languages- Christian Goans found it easy to adapt themselves anywhere they travelled in the world. For example, in East Africa, during the British rule, Goans excelled as school teachers, as office workers and in professions such as tailors and musicians. When these countries attained their independence from the British and the Portuguese rule, most of the Goan population (descendants) left these countries; few moved back to Goa but most migrated to UK, Portugal, Canada and Australia.

Goa was the "home" for the Goan diaspora, whether within the Indian subcontinent or the Middle East or the Eastern Africa, and they would travel back to Goa annually or at greater but regular intervals, to visit their families and ancestral homes.

After the British and Portuguese colonies attained their independence (from 1947 on), emigration pattern for the Goans changed. Now the destinations of choice, for the first wave were England and Portugal. Soon Australia, Canada and the USA were beckoning. All these countries were offering citizenship to the new arrivals, after permanent residence of three to five years. This fact and the greater distance from the "old home" of Goa, have diluted the pull to visit Goa frequently. Our elders were also passing out one by one. The pride of Goan heritage has never been lost.

Since I have information about current immigration patterns in Canada let me attempt to give a perspective of the effects of immigration on the ethnic make-up of the Canadian population in the years to come.

Canada is geographically the second largest country in the world, and like all the developed countries, has a low birth rate and hence it depends on immigration to make up for the necessary self-sustaining population growth. For years, till early 1970s, Canada preferred to attract immigrants from European countries, in particular Britain and Ireland and French speaking countries such as France and Belgium.

From late 1960s, immigration from non-European countries kept rising incrementally, both because less Europeans wanted to migrate to Canada, and more non-European migrants, with good formal education in their own countries were ready and willing to move for better opportunities. This was a big gain for the Canadian economy and in reverse a brain-drain and economic loss to the developing countries.

Canada is relatively a young new country, whose ethnic make-up is changing dynamically. As per Statistics Canada, in 2020 "currently more than 20 percent of the Canadian population is born outside Canada. Ethnically 23 percent of the population is visible minority, which at current trend is expected to increase to 32-36 percent by 2036. Canada as a whole, based on current immigration patterns, will be almost 80 per cent non-white in less than a century (or 20 percent white, 65 percent non-white, and 15 percent mixed race by 2106.) By 2031 visible minority groups are estimated to comprise 63 percent of the population of Toronto, 59 percent of Vancouver, and 31 percent of Montréal."

Coming down to our own families, we have a generation of family members, who have migrated to different parts of the world in search of better opportunities. Two of my mother's brothers, who went to Portugal for further studies, were the pioneers in our family. The rest of the migration is my generation or younger. Currently we are spread out from Australia and New Zealand to Europe (Portugal, UK and France) to Canada, USA and Brazil. Through honest and hard work and God's blessings, all our cousins and their families are professionally and financially well settled in their respective adopted countries. They have shown that their new countries are richer for having them, and they are active members of the society and community in which they live.

My generation still maintains close ties to Goa and India and the family members back there. As we raise our own families in the new countries, one can see significant dilution of the bonds to Goa/India, my generation continues to hold. It is only natural that our children feel loyalty, patriotism and love for the country of their birth or to their adopted country. The important thing is that we pass on to our children the values, we have inherited from our parents: honesty, importance of formal education, hard work and family ties.

The process of sending their children overseas, involved major financial sacrifices on parents' part. In some situations, they did not have savings to pay for travel ticket to the new destination, and thus would take a loan for that purpose. And this was the case with me. Luckily my aunt Belmira Moniz (married to my uncle Alex) offered me an unsolicited loan for the ticket from India to Canada.

The primary objective of agreeing to or encouraging your child to migrate out, has been for financial gains for the child and in many cases to contribute towards improvement of the lot of your parents and siblings back home. What is forgotten is that this was an emotionally hard experience for our parents to let their child go to a faraway place, with no guaranteed outcome, and in most cases no family members for guidance.

Those were the days when there was no telephone connection in rural households. In such a situation, like for my folks, correspondence was via letters which took 10 to 15 days to arrive. And for those in urban areas with a telephone connection, the long-distance call charges, were

relatively high. For example, when we would call Ethel's home, who had a land line telephone at home, there was this "perceived" need to keep the call short and sweet.

My own mother's concern was whether I would marry a girl from the new country, with the result that my bonds to my Goan family would be further diluted. It also took my mother a while to appreciate that I was better off in Canada than working in the Middle East.

My mother wanted to see her son like the folks who had migrated to the Middle East: they were coming on vacation to Goa every year, they were building modern residences and owned a car. And this would add up to her perceived standing in the village. Only after her second visit to us in Canada, she agreed that I was better off in Canada than if I gone to the Middle East, which had never crossed my mind in the first place.

They say that birds of the same feather flock together. And you see this in the social circle of friends that the first-generation immigrants, keep and most relate to. In most of the major urban centres around the world, there are formal or informal associations of Goans, through which they attend social functions such as dances, picnics and sports events. Goans have this particular desire to sub-identify themselves by the village where they or their ancestors originated from.

My family has called Mississauga home for the last thirty plus years. Mississauga is a city of 800,000 plus and is part of the Greater Toronto Region (GTA). For the last 50 years Goans have had an umbrella association aptly named G.O.A. (Goan Overseas Association), which is fairly active in servicing the Goan diaspora. This group was formed principally by Goan diaspora originating from East Africa. Goans coming from Pakistan, formed their own Canorient Association. Then there have been or there are village associations, some of which are barely active as the founding members are deceased or too old to continue running the activities of the associations. The prominent of these have been Aldona, Calangute and Moira, all from North Goa.

Six families, including Ethel and I, got together twenty four years ago (1999) and formed our own CLR Association (Curtorim Loutulim Raia). The uniqueness of the CLR Association is that the participating members have migrated directly from India, with a few taking a sojourn through the Middle East countries. Currently the CLR Association is the most vibrant and active village association of Goans in the GTA. The principal current events for the CLR Association are the feasts of Sao Joao in June, a picnic in July or August and a "Social" on the last weekend of September. I guess it is called social, as the principal objective of the function is socializing of people with common roots.

The average attendance at the CLR annual Social has been 250-300 plus and is principally from folks with roots in these villages. The function commences with celebration of mass. This is followed by Goan entertainment (Mando performance by the CLR Mando Group, and usually one or two dance performances by kids or the youth of the villages). The remainder of the function is undoubtedly, enjoying good food, good company and good music and dancing.

Most first-generation immigrant parents try their best to bring their children for the community functions. Once the kids reach their youth, one can see many of them moving away from the ethnic heritage groups of their parents. Their friends and partners are the ones they meet and bond with, at school, college or other social environments.

It is just a coincidence that as I decided to include this chapter in this book, there was a write-up in the opinion pages of the Canada's national newspaper Globe and Mail, January 20, 2020, "Harry and Meghan have no idea: Immigrating to Canada is hard", referring to Prince Harry (UK) and his commoner spouse Meghan Markle, who had given up their royal duties were migrating to Canada. I have taken the last one third of the article as I thought appropriate as an introduction to this topic. By the way it did not take long for Harry and Meghan to move to the USA, where Meghan held her citizenship.

"Canada's success is reliant on immigration. According to Statistics Canada, population growth (rate) in the country has fallen by more than half since 1950s, and its people are aging faster than those in all Group of Seven countries, except Japan and Germany."

"That's why organizations such as the Century Initiative are calling for Canada's population to grow almost threefold to 100 million by 2100, arguing this will significantly increase our economic growth and international influence."

"And there's no better time for Canada to be enticing talent from around the world. Its open, welcoming reputation is a beacon for scientists and entrepreneurs fleeing the persecution (current racial unwelcome) of experts in the United States and Britain. Amid rising global instability, Canada has never been more attractive to workers and families, eager to build the country's economic and civic life."

"So why is Canada's immigration system so profoundly unfriendly? Why does it welcome immigrants with bureaucracy and expense instead of open arms? Is Canada really a liberal bastion when it imposes so many burdens on immigrants from even its closest political and cultural allies?"

"Meanwhile, the cost of this bureaucracy is astonishing. It's $240 for a medical exam, $210 for degree verification, and $328 for a language test. Then there's $85 for biometrics, the $550 application fee and the $490 charge for the right of permanent residence. These costs total $1,903. And that's without the help of a lawyer."

"I know the government has no electoral incentive to invest in IRCC (Immigration Refugees and Citizenship Canada) and nothing to gain by eliminating all the excessive fees for its prospective residents."

"But here's my challenge. Do it anyway."

"Abolish the language tests for native English and French speakers. Stop the monopolies and the mafias exploiting newcomers. Invest in websites that don't malfunction more often than they work. Streamline the application process. Cut the waiting times. Show that you don't just think migration is good for Canada – you actively support and encourage it, because you believe in the future of this country and you want it to grow."

Western countries benefit from immigration as much if not more than the immigrants moving in for better opportunities

Here is another article from CBC (Canadian Broadcasting Corporation), by Anthony King

"I have seen Canadian diversity at work, and I'm still amazed by its subtle charm. I share my work days with Canadians of every colour and creed, but our differences are absorbed by common values we're hardly aware of.

Everyone I encounter has an interesting background and many are the offspring of immigrant parents who were never exposed to such cultural and ethnic diversity — until they came to Canada."

"My respect for the rights of the LGBTQ community, my tolerance for religious diversity and cultural expression, these are values that some people around the world find hard to wrap their heads around. Ideas, beliefs and economic roles are stratified and deeply polarized in many places outside of Canada. We are not immune to the forces of division either, but we are better prepared than most."

"And while other countries are coming undone by festering bigotry; while their leaders lose credibility and self-respect, we sleepy, dull Canadians are quietly just getting along, keeping our little secret."

Eufemiano (Emano) Moniz
My Canadian Experience

My own experience in Canada, can be summarised as "all is well that ends well." The very early stage of this journey was not a smooth one. Most new immigrants go through an adjustment period, the severity of which depends on many factors: the age at arrival, whether married or not and with children or not, the formal education you come equipped with and how easy it is to get re-qualified, financial assets you bring along and most of all having family or friends to guide you and support you in the initial stage of settling down in the new country.

I have been lucky in life and I like to say so. So often when I said that, my business clients used to remind me that you "make your own luck." In a way it is true, but then I look around and I see so many people, who work hard all their lives, and are still struggling. I carry with me this feeling of being lucky, because more often than not, I win at bingo and draws at social functions, and in a small way, even with the public lotteries, where I have occasionally bought some tickets.

I had started the process of migrating to Canada, in 1969, in my third year of engineering, by applying to a few Canadian Universities, for a

Master's Degree, and I was offered admission in three of them. One of them, Carleton University in Ottawa, offered me admission in the Geotechnical field and also offered me a Teaching Assistantship (TA). By March 1970, I had graduated in B.Eng. (U. of Bombay) and had a job based in Panaji, Goa.

My uncle, Jose Menezes, who was based in Ottawa at the time, sponsored me for landed immigrant status, (now called permanent resident (PR) status, similar to the Green card in the USA) because at the time, most foreign students, after completing their studies in Canada, were readily accepted for the landed immigrant status.

I was called to the Canadian Embassy in New Delhi, where I was interviewed by one Mr. Campbell, from the Canadian Embassy. He made it his job to intimidate me, and he tried it, through locking his eyes on me and through a question 'why do you wish to go to Canada", repeated seven times. To my responses to this question, a few of his retorts were: "do you know how cold Canada is and you can freeze to death?"; "do you think your uncle will spend all his savings to support you"; 'why don't you go to Australia?"

Within a week I received a two-paragraph letter from the Canadian Embassy which said "considering your age, education and experience, it is our opinion, you will not be able to settle successfully in Canada" (underlining is mine). The next paragraph was "we wish you all the best in your future endeavours".

I am proud to say that not only have I settled successfully in Canada, I have contributed in a big way in taxes to the government coffers. As I was coasting to retirement, as per the Department of Statistics Canada, our family was in the top 2-5 percent of the Canadian population.

When I advised my uncle of the letter from the Canadian Embassy, he suggested I apply for student visa. When the Canadian Embassy, received my student visa application, it was rejected, because, in their words I "had already shown my wish to settle in Canada".

My uncle called the Immigration Department in Ottawa, and to my luck he had an interview with the Deputy Immigration Minister Mr. William Bell. When he reviewed the documents, his verdict was "I don't know why his immigration application has been rejected. Be assured that your nephew will be in Canada within one week". He said that, as I was getting late for the start of the new academic year.

I received a telegram from the Canadian Embassy to "comeback for re-interview". Off I went by train again to New Delhi. This time I had my interview with the Ambassador Mr. Shaw. As I entered his office, he had completed the paperwork and he said to me "I understand we had rejected your application. But since you insist in going to Canada, we have no objection. I am going to arrange medical test for you tomorrow, and if you pass it, I will give you the visa immediately. I understand you are running late for your University year".

I had my medical tests the next day, and I was informed that I had passed to the satisfaction of the Canadian Embassy standards. It should be noted that when I was picking up my visa, the following day, there was a Punjabi male, who was also picking up his visa and this individual's English language abilities were non-existent.

Thus, within a week, with $4 in my pocket (the maximum allowance by the Indian Government) I landed in Canada on September 21, and ti Jose was there at the airport to pick me up. I was 24 years old.

I was 3 weeks late for the start of the academic year. It was not only a matter of catching up to the missed lectures, but also adjusting to a completely new system of studies. I had also to get my act together, to bring myself current, on my duties as Teaching Assistant, which was paying my bills. Add to this the new environment and the fact that, three days after my arrival, ti Jose left for Sweden, for his post-doctoral studies at the Karolinska Institute in Stockholm. I remember that day so well, as I felt the bottom just falling out from beneath me.

Before he left for Sweden Ti Jose introduced me to three of his friends: an elderly and sweet Belgian couple Mr. and Mrs. Robinet, who could only speak French; Doug (and Helen) Kennedy and Ravindra Chaudury, the latter two his Ph.D. colleagues. I kept in touch with these families visiting them occasionally, when I was still in Ottawa.

Ti Jose was kind enough to hand me $2,000 for sundry expenses. He also advised me to let him know, if and when I needed more help from him. When I was fully employed and wanted to pay him back, his suggestion was that I use the money, in a similar fashion, to help somebody else in the family, if I so wished. I paid him back the "loan" and I have done my bit, to help other family members.

With most of students returning to their homes and families during the school break, my first Christmas and New Year season in Canada was a cold and lonely time, even though I spent the Christmas and the New Year with ti Jose's friends. I used the time to get myself on track on my academic work, as the first term results were not what I expected of myself, due to my 3-week late arrival and having to get adjusted to a completely new system of studies, compared to the one in India.

With some guidance from new friends, all Egyptian students, my second term results were good. For the following year, I was lucky to have as my Master's Degree supervisor, Prof. (Dr.) Don Shields, from Ottawa University, who took me under his wings. Carleton University and Ottawa University had a mutual cooperative program. And even though I graduated from Carleton University I ended up taking more courses from Ottawa U. than Carleton U.

Don and his wife Carol Shields were wonderful and kind persons, who, even with their own four little kids, made time to invite foreign students to their house during special occasions and make us really feel at home. Don was a smart professor and Carol later became the highly celebrated Canadian novelist, winning many literature awards, including the U.S. Pulitzer Prize for Fiction as well as the Governor General's Award in Canada for her novel **The Stone Diaries**. In 2002, she was made Companion of the Order of Canada - Canada's highest honor. Sadly, she succumbed to breast cancer, in 2003 at age of 68.

At Ottawa University, I was blessed to meet and become close friend with **Narendra Verma**, a Ph.D. candidate. Pretty soon we were constant companions and I became part of his young family: his wife Kanta and three young children. Narendra was my first bestie and we are still good friends

Narendra was also an accomplished Tabla player (Indian classical music drum) and he was a student of Ustad Alla Rakha, the Tabla player accompanying the famous North Indian Classical musician, the Sitar virtuoso **Ravi Shankar**, whose music was very popular in the second half of 20th century in the West, in particular the USA.

Often, when they had a break from performances, they would fly to Ottawa to be with the Vermas. I was lucky to meet and interact with Mr. Shankar and Mr. Rakha, a number of times. I remember he even spoke to me in Konkani, saying his sister-in-law hailed from Ratnagiri, north of Goa and Konkani speaking area.

Being new to the country and arriving late for the school year, I had a lot on my plate. I did not pay attention to applying for a summer job as most students would do. At the end of my first academic year, I was running out of money to support myself. The University Student Services Department, came to my help by finding me a job washing dishes ($1.50/hr), with school kids, in the University cafeteria, during summer months, when the University opened up its student residences as an Inn for vacationers and travelling public. I lasted on that position for a week, as I got promoted ($2 /hr and later to $2.50/hr) to being a server at the cafeteria and at many of the evening receptions and functions for outside public.

My French language proficiency came in handy and was probably the major reason for being moved from dish washer to cafeteria server. As much as my mother had us do worse things than washing dishes, it still bothered me to think what she would think of her son, the engineer, trying to survive with this kind of a job in a foreign land.

Those were the days, when to save a dime (10 cents) on a phone call at the department location, I would wait till I got back to my residence room, where I could make the call for free. Still at my first Christmas in Canada, I managed to send $25 ($110 in today's dollars for 3 percent inflation) for my siblings. I learnt this from Ti Jose who used to send our family (kids) an annual money draft as Christmas gift. My wife and I continued for many years, this Christmas gift routine for our nephews and nieces, until they were all grown up and working and the need or appreciation for that gift was no longer meaningful.

When I arrived in Canada and by the time I graduated, the Canadian economy was in recession and at the dining table with my Egyptian colleagues, there was the ongoing chat about how difficult it would be for me to find employment, upon graduation, due to my lack of "Canadian experience" and the current state of the economy. Taking a hint from this conversation, and in order to differentiate myself from other graduating colleagues, I chose to take a couple courses in the specialized field of Permafrost Engineering.

Luck would smile upon me as my professor in that field, Dr. William Slusarchuk, left the University to take up a position in Calgary, Alberta. From there he offered me a position with R.M. Hardy and Associates, an engineering consulting company. I would be seconded immediately to Northern Engineering Services (NES), a group put together by the consortium of the main Oil and gas companies. NES was entrusted to prepare all the engineering design work for the proposed mega project Arctic Gas Pipeline, to ship natural gas from the Canadian Arctic to Alberta and further south to the USA.

This project basically launched my engineering career both professionally and financially. Professionally, I owe it to Dr. Slusarchuk, for not only being my mentor, but also a kind of father figure to me. It helped that his wife Mary and their young daughter Cheryl, enjoyed dropping in regularly at our house to play with our infant daughter Celine.

Oil and gas industry was booming at the time, and manpower was in short supply. When personnel accepted field assignments, away from home, for extended periods (1 month plus), it was customary at the time, to raise their regular salary by 20 percent, and also be eligible for overtime on top of it. I gladly accepted a full summer assignment of field work along the pipeline route starting at Inuvik near the Arctic, in the North West Territories and proceeding south along the Mackenzie River (Norman Wells and Fort Simpson) all the way to the Great Slave Lake in Alberta. This was before I got married.

As a young engineer this assignment was God sent for my pocket book, and I grabbed the opportunity. As a result, I had enough savings in the bank for me to put a down payment on our first house, at a new subdivision, Silver Springs in Calgary. A few of the colleagues had also moved to this subdivision and one of them convinced me to take the plunge. Ethel and I were civilly married but she was not in Canada yet. The construction got completed and we moved in, just a few days before our first child Celine was born.

During my work assignment in the north, the land of 24-hour day light during summers, our main bases were Fort Simpson, Fort Good Hope and Fort Norman. From there all travel was by helicopter, and we would be out on the field daily for 16 hours. By the time the helicopter moved the personnel and the equipment from site to site, and accounting for equipment set-up time, the actual daily productive time for my work as an engineer, ranged from 4 to 6 hours.

As much as I could fill up many pages on my experiences in this one full summer of work, there is one sad scene that still to this date tugs at the strings of my heart. At Fort Simpson, on more than one occasion, we used to see an Indigenous couple, with two little kids in tow, early morning (our breakfast time was 6 am) waiting for the bar to open. One could see they had not yet recovered, from their previous night's state of stupor.

We used to hire local Indigenous labourers to clear the brush for our work sites, and helicopter landing pad. Once the weekly payday arrived and they got paid, we got used to expect, the hired hands not to show up the next morning for work. When we would go to their homes looking for them, they were in no state to work that day, due to their state of drunkenness.

In the end, the Arctic Gas Pipeline project did not go through because the Oil companies proposing the project and the Canadian Government, could not get agreement from all the Indian Reservations, whose territories the pipeline would cross. I accepted a transfer to Hardy Associates office in Edmonton in 1977. The gas pipeline has still not been built.

Lot of the specialized research work has been done towards the building of the pipeline from the North and I hope that it will be put to good use some day in the future. If the Arctic waters become navigable, due to worldwide warmer temperatures, it is quite probable that the natural gas reserves already discovered in the Canadian Arctic, could be shipped as LNG through the Arctic water channels.

The year 1975 was a very eventful year for me and my bride, Ethelwyn Xavier Pereira, who was introduced to me by her cousin Fatima Barreto Pimenta Pereira. Fatima's sister Maria de Lurdes, was my brother Heriberto's girlfriend at that time and then became his wife. We got civilly married in Goa, with an engagement celebration in April in Mumbai. We had our church wedding in Calgary on September 5, 1975. Our first child Celine was born two months and three weeks premature at the Calgary Foothills Hospital. She stayed in the ICU for two and half months. All we had to pay was a $5 entrance fee. The nursing care Celine received was phenomenal. After this experience, I have never begrudged paying my share of taxes in Canada.

Before we move out of Calgary, let me share some immigrant stories. The first one is about my experiences at getting the driver's license. I failed the road driving test at my first three tries as I did not have a car of my own and I was too cheap to spend on necessary amount of driving lessons. When Ethel came over, and after she did her written test, I put her behind the wheel immediately and she would drive everywhere we would go together. The upshot of the driving experience is that she passed her driver's test at her first attempt.

Then Heriberto came along and after a few days of practice on my car I drove him for the driver's test. He had some experience driving in Goa. But he failed at his first attempt too. For his second driver's test, Ethel drove him to the test site, and spreading a blanket, she sat down on a patch of grass, with little Celine, near where the car was parked, waiting for the examiner. At the end of the test the examiner tells Heriberto, "I am not fully happy with your driving. I see your wife has driven you here and you have a small child. I am going to pass you, but be careful with your driving and take care of your family."

In Calgary, we had our first vegetable garden. The Government of Canada Agriculture Department would produce booklets giving advice on how to grow different vegetables. In not a big patch we had grown tomatoes, beans, carrots, cabbage and beetroot. The crop was abundant and more than we could eat. We could not even share some of the vegetables with our close friends as they had their own. But we froze some of it. The satisfaction of the first garden and plentiful produce was unbelievable, and I remember, when got home from work I would sometimes bypass the front door, to visit the garden first.

In Edmonton (1977-1980) we lived approximately a block or two south of the now gigantic West Edmonton Mall, which did not exist when we were there, but construction had just started when we packed up for our next stop, Vancouver in 1980.

At the Edmonton office of Hardy Associates, the principal projects I worked on were: field testing with a nuclear probe and monitoring work during winter months (the outside temperatures were usually at -35C, during the field work) at the Great Canadian Oil Sands or GCOS (now Suncor), which had been in operation for a number of years; design of starter dam for the tailings dams for the new Syncrude Tar Sands project, which was under construction at the time.

We had our second child Larissa, born on March 31, 1979 at the Misericordia Hospital, during our Edmonton days. Interestingly, our two elder children are born on the same day, three years apart.

From Edmonton, I followed my boss Dr. Vinod Garga, who had moved to Klohn Leonoff and Associates in Vancouver. It was really Richmond

Hill, an island south of Vancouver city, and the location of the Vancouver International Airport. It was early 1980.

This was already a third house and city move in our short married life. There were a few more to come, between this move and the last move, which was a return from Chicago to Toronto. We have owned 6 houses and have had three short term rentals in all.

Each move was professionally and financially beneficial, but I realize it now, it was hard on Ethel. You see, her quiet nature, just like her father's, meant she had to leave behind the few close friendships she made during the short time we were at each place. She did not complain then. However, when we look back, it is plain that these moves were less than pleasant for Ethel.

"No man succeeds without a strong woman behind him. Wife or mother, if it is both, he is twice blessed", a saying attributed to Harold MacMillan (UK Prime Minister, 1957-63) is so true in Ethel's case. She was relatively young, and had not been exposed to house work, when we got married in Calgary in 1975. I am sure it was hard for Ethel to come to Calgary, where neither she nor I had any family to support us in our early days of wedded life. The words of My Little Corner of the World by Anita Bryant, best reflect my invitation to her to join me up in Canada, leaving her parents behind in Mumbai

"Come along with me,
To my little corner of the world,
And dream a little dream,
In my little corner of the world.
I always knew,
I'd find someone like you,
So welcome to,
My little corner of the world."

Ethel deserves full credit for handling with aplomb, the roles of house work, cooking, looking after the children's school and extra-curricular activities. On occasions, she even used to mow the lawn, and together we painted the walls and fences, at some of our houses. Other than the investments, which I looked after, Ethel has been the domestic financial controller, putting to good use her sharp eye for a good deal. She has practiced admirably the balance between being frugal and spend-thrift, which I believe has rubbed off on our children.

To support my career, Ethel has had to make a lot of sacrifices due to my career transfers across Canada and the US and my extended periods of my absence on field assignments when we were based in Alberta and British Columbia. In my job as a financial planner, many of my client appointments were in the evenings, to enable me to meet both husband and wife, and I would return home close to 10 pm. Through it all, I enjoyed the peace of mind, knowing I had her support at home, and that the family was in good hands.

A big bonus for me has been that Ethel and I have not had any in-law problems. In fact, it often looked like my side of the family (The Monizes) liked her more than me. I can accept that. I had my mother-in-law in my corner. If my dad had not died prematurely, Ethel would have received even higher level of appreciation from him.

Just a few days before we moved to Vancouver, the Pereiras (mummy, daddy and Maria Aurora) arrived in Edmonton. Maria Aurora was the one who was migrating to Canada, but it was more expedient to sponsor the parents along with Maria Aurora. By this time, I had already started working in Vancouver and had bought our new home, a recently completed new house which was ready for the family's arrival.

My new company's engineering expertise was designing Tailings Dams to store byproducts of mining operations after separating the ore from the soil material and I was involved in a few of them, including one in the interior of British Columbia (B.C.) for Teck Corporation and Barahona Tailings Dam of the biggest copper mine in the world, the El Teniente Copper Mine in south of Chile. Unfortunately, I did not get to travel to Chile on this project.

There are two memorable projects for me. One was laying out a 6 km section of the railway route to transport thermal coal from B.C. interior.

The 6 km section was located in the Canadian Rockies at the Canadian Continental Divide between Table Mountain and Wolverine Mountain. The continental divide is so named because waters from the east side drain to the east into the Atlantic Ocean and from the west side the waters drain to the Pacific Ocean.

The location was a valley with heavy bush and shrub growth. I was given a map with the route outline, a compass and a distance measuring meter. The helicopter would drop off my support technician and me in the morning, and would come back to pick us up late afternoon, our location being transmitted to the helicopter pilot by shooting smoke flares in the air. We laid out the line by walking on the deep snow ground in snowshoes (old style/vintage bearpaw snowshoes) and it took us just over a week to lay out the 6 km route. I marvel myself on this feat: a boy from India comes to Canada and lays down a railway line route in snow shoes. I bet that ninety percent of Canadian born individuals have not even trudged on deep snow wearing snowshoes.

The other assignment was as the Senior Resident Engineer at a project involving construction of a tailings dam at Fermont mine, in Northern Quebec, then owned by US Steel Company. Fermont (meaning iron mountain) is a small mining town, which could only be reached by air, the nearest airport being Labrador, also a mining town, and connected to Fermont by a straight 30 km road. The mining personnel and their families live in the township, which is self-sufficient with stores and schools and the sort. The ore was transported by train to the nearest port of Sept-Illes.

I moved to Fermont at the end of May 1982, with Ethel and two kids, aged 6 and 3 at the time. We were lucky to rent for a short term, our house in Richmond, B.C., to a couple who were awaiting completion of their own house and they kept our house spic and span. At Fermont, our residence was near the mine site, in typical construction camp trailer complex, along with other staff involved in this tailings project. When we arrived, the snow was still up to window level. The cold and snow returned in early October.

When we returned to Vancouver in November, I was a casualty of the Canada-wide recession, which had reduced staffing at my office by half, in the period of those 6-7 months I was away in Fermont. With good savings from the latest work assignment, and immediate eligibility (special rule because of the tough recession) for payments from the unemployment insurance, the temporary financial hardship was quite bearable.

When I was posted at Fermont, I came to the conclusion that the project manager's position is what I wanted to be in, rather than performing the pure technical role of an engineer. I figured that I needed education and training in accounting and management and I had decided that an MBA degree would give me the tools.

The loss of employment was an opportunity to get started on this path. After doing the GMAT (entrance exam for MBA) I secured admission for 2-year full time MBA course (U. of Alberta, Edmonton). I also found an engineering job in Edmonton, where I worked till the week before the start of MBA classes.

Heriberto and Maria Lurdes kindly agreed for me to stay with them from mid-summer 1983, to the end of the year. We sold our house in Vancouver and the rest of the family moved for 6 months to Mumbai, to stay with Ethel's parents. I went down for Christmas and the whole family came back together to Edmonton, where we lived in the University's married student quarters till my graduation in April 1985.

Upon graduation (MBA) an opportunity arose for a 2-year engineering assignment, with a big Canadian firm SNC Lavalin, at a dam construction project in Nicaragua, Central America. The rationalization for accepting this posting was twofold: the earnings would be tax free (as non-resident) which would help replenish our depleted savings in the bank and the potential for me to get some project manager's experience. My family was also expected to join me down there.

Nicaragua was going through an internal conflict between the Sandinistas which, with support from Cuba and Russia, had taken over the political power from the corrupt government of dictator Anastasio Samosa, who was supported by the USA for years. Because of my education in Portuguese, I picked up the Spanish language very quickly. I fell in love with the country and the common people who were relatively poor but big hearted. With my salary being paid in US$ and on top of it having a daily living allowance, the life for us ex-patriates, was a life of luxury in Nicaragua, when the common people were struggling.

Unfortunately, even before I arrived in Nicaragua, the project execution had fallen behind, and a decision was taken by the company, at the insistence of financing institution, IDB or the Inter- American Development Bank, to change the whole project team. In the interim, Ethel and the girls had moved to Yvonne's place in New York, on their potential route to Nicaragua, which did not happen.

Next stop was Toronto, with Trow Associates, a reputable and preeminent engineering company, providing geotechnical, environmental and other building testing and quality control services. Trow was expanding at a fast rate due to a major building boom in progress and its own high level of expertise which was very much in demand (e.g. concrete quality control during accelerated construction of the CN Tower in Toronto, which at 553 m was at that time the tallest free-standing structure in the world). I quickly learnt that the high level engineering expertise costs the client more but it brings even greater savings for the customer, both in time and material, in addition to the higher level of client confidence.

I was hired (1985) as Assistant to the President. My previous experience in similar engineering consulting firms, my recent MBA education and relative strength in computer technology, were a great fit with the needs of the fast-expanding company. Besides assisting the President, I was taking on various other responsibilities: Business development, Project management and Human Resources. Within two years I was promoted to Vice-President Business Development and appointed to the 6 member Senior Management Committee.

In 1990 I was entrusted in setting up a Boston area office for Trow, with the acquisition of a small existing firm in Newton, Massachusetts. Then followed a similar opportunity in Chicago in 1991, where we wanted to replicate what we had done in Boston. I was offered the opportunity to move to Chicago and terms were attractive, including the potential of becoming the Vice-President of Trow's US operations.

At the time of this move the economies in Canada and the USA, were in recession. I had developed excellent contacts, and made good inroads into the Chicago market, but there was a need for more investments from the corporate office in Toronto. As they could not see the end of the recession, there was not the appetite to invest more capital from Toronto, and the company decided to wind down their short-lived venture in Chicago. I was disappointed, and because I had not yet acquired the professional engineer's designation (P.E.) in the USA, I chose the more certain route back to Canada.

In the face of deepening recession, soon after my return to base, the whole management team took a 20 percent pay cut, which I found unpalatable, and I believed that I could do better being self-employed. At my request the company agreed to give me severance of 7 months' pay for the 7 years of service. Out of a number of options, I chose to join the Financial Industry, as a personal Financial Planner with the support of a premier financial planning company, Investors Group (IG).

As a Financial Planner my role was to help individuals or couples build personal wealth through advice and products in the fields of savings, investments (mutual funds), insurance, taxation and estate planning. I was a self-employed individual, and had to bring in my own clients. But I had to direct all my business through a single company IG, akin to a franchise, and thus I was an IG Representative or IG Financial Consultant. IG provided training, administration and back-office support, along with products manufactured in house or provided by other companies for the sole use of IG representatives.

The first two years were tough, as I had to study and pass a multitude of courses to gain professional designations for financial planning (CFP) and Insurance License (Level 1 and Level2). At the same time, I had to find clients to service and build up my business. The first full year's earnings were close 20 percent of my previous job.

In the second year I promised myself that I "would piss or get off the pot", something I had learned from one of my previous bosses. For that I adopted a "winning attitude" and projected that to my clients and warm prospects, by a simple response of "excellent" when my client or prospect would ask me "how are you". That response of "excellent" had, over time, a two-way effect of boosting my confidence and projecting the same unto my client. This response of "excellent" has stayed with me to this date, and it occasionally catches people by surprise.

From the second year onwards my financial planning professional career took off, and in hind sight the 25 years as a Financial Planner, have been the best of my working life, in terms of personal satisfaction, with the job stress level being insignificant compared to my previous corporate environment. The client satisfaction was measurable, not only through seeing my client's financial affairs put in order, but also making them financially independent and to boot, my clients achieved an excellent compound annual rate of return, during my stewardship (approximately 8 percent compound growth rate over 20 plus years).

My love for financial investment field and the financial expertise gained during my 25-year financial career have now become a hobby during my retirement years. I am also always ready and happy to share my knowledge with others, in particular young adults.

I will take a little liberty to share with the next generation, my passion for financial education for the young. Achieving financial independence is not a rocket science. The following, if practiced, will take you a long way towards that goal.

Save and save early. This part of savings is not for the short or medium-term use, but rather for your retirement years. The secret here is to take advantage of the "compounding effect" of your savings, which, I believe Einstein called the eighth wonder of the world. To start with save 10 percent of your take home income and then move to 10 percent of your gross income. Expect a return on your investments of long-term inflation plus three percent or better.

Live within your means. This involves avoiding spending on credit that you cannot pay off in full at end of the month. If you have to take a mortgage on your house, keep it within comfortable level.

Buying your own house is not a financial decision; it is lifestyle decision.

Buy Life Insurance, to manage life's risks and to cover major debts and provide for your dependents. After you start working, the earlier you purchase the cheap Term Life insurance (preferably the 20-year term), better it will be. After that, when you can afford, you should also consider buying a Whole life Insurance policy.

Find yourself a knowledgeable and trusted financial advisor. He or she should be more than a securities broker, but a person who can hold your hand, and can provide you holistic advice for your financial affairs, including investments, taxation, insurance and estate planning (wills). Very few people have the time and character to self-manage their long-term finances.

A combination of engineering training, business education and the financial planning training through IG and through my own successes and failures, allowed me to enjoy this career and achieve optimum outcomes for my clients.

All good things come to an end, some day. I decided to retire in July 2018, at age 71, even though I could have continued as long as I wanted. It was sad to move on, and it was also tough on my clients, for whom I was not only their sole financial consultant for such a long period of time, but also, we had developed that special bond of trust and friendship. I had prepared my clients for the transition over a period of one to two years, including joint meetings with their new Consultant.

In retrospect, my vagabond and adventure seeking nature, willingness to take risk, and my perennial optimistic attitude, have resulted in a successful and happy outcome for the family. I could have not achieved all that without the support of my wife at home.

Canada has been good to me, and I have returned the favour. I have had the privilege of working and travelling through most of this large mass of land, Canada. If I had an opportunity again to choose a country to emigrate to, and knowing what I know now about Canada, its rich land, and caring society, I would have no hesitation in choosing Canada, "The True North, strong and free". And to Anita Bryant's song lyrics:

"And if you care to stay,
In my little corner of the world,
Then we can hide away,
In my little corner of the world."

It has been 5 plus years that I have retired, and I am enjoying it. God has been good to our family!

As I am writing this chapter there is an active movement in Canada about addressing "systemic racism" against the black population and the Indigenous people, in particular as reflected on police behaviour against these two groups and laws that unduly criminalize these two groups. It is not just Canada's problem. It is even worse in the USA, where differential treatment of the black population (descendants of slaves) is systemic and indirectly enshrined into laws that criminalize this group unduly. The current upheaval and street protests follow police brutality towards George Floyd, a black person.

I thought I should share my own and my family's experience. Having experienced and known Portuguese and English colonialisms in Goa and India, I grew up being aware what the colour of your skin means when it comes to job opportunity and upward mobility. But I also have known that racism or classism is a result of ignorance of the other person and is often practiced without being aware of it. Coming from India, where the caste and class systems are widely practiced, it is easy to relate to racism based on the colour of person's skin.

I am happy to say that over half a century that I have lived in Canada and raised a family here, we have not openly experienced racism. I attribute this good experience with lack of racism experience by the first-generation immigrant family to a combination of factors: easy adaptability into the Canadian society due to our religion and the western or Portuguese influence in Goa; high level of formal education; good command of the English and French (and Portuguese) languages; communicating with people you meet, about yourself and your family background.

Contribution from Oscar Sousa (Portugal)

Story of a life with several paths
(Original in Portuguese, translated by Eufemiano Moniz)

"At the age of 19, I joined the Salesians in Goa and was sent to Lisbon in July 1960 to study for priesthood. There I started my experience as an emigrant which would have a long route. I studied in Manique, near Lisbon, Portugal, followed by an internship in Arouca, near Porto, Portugal. I completed my theology studies in Sanlúcar la Mayor, near Seville, Spain.

I was ordained priest in 1967 in Goa and started my pastoral activity in Funchal, Madeira, where I shared the responsibilities of overseeing a boarding school, owned by the Salesians. I taught mathematics at the same school and extended my participation to other schools, to other Catholic-oriented groups in the diocese, JIC, to the movement for adults for a better world. There were 3 years of great involvement with the problems experienced by people in an attempt to find answers in the light of the evangelical message, adapted to the context.

I found myself surrounded by very active youth and together we promoted meetings for young people, old Salesian students, walks, days of reflection, camps, summer camps especially for the youngest, organized by the older ones. I encouraged the need for all of them to resume their studies, which was achieved on a large scale. I still maintain bonds of great trust and friendship with many of them.

In 1971 I left Funchal at the request of my Congregation. I later learned that I had an invitation to go to Timor to take charge of the College of Dili, but there was a change of plans, when I set out to study the problems and find local solutions for them, instead of taking all the guidelines from Lisbon. I had realized in those early years of pastoral activity that it was necessary to find new answers to new problems.

In Lisbon, I spent a few months without having specific duties. It was in these circumstances that I enrolled at the Higher Institute of Applied Psychology to take the Psychology Course. As I had no regular duties, I was invited to support a rural community on the outskirts of Lisbon. I accepted and took a team of young university students with me. We soon realized that the community needed community animation (involvement).

In 1973, the village 15 km from Lisbon, had no running water, and schooling practically ended with the 4th class. The village lived on agriculture and its mission was only to supply the city with vegetables. We started by organizing catechesis, involving the little ones in other activities, preparing a feast with the involvement of the community. We were in the old political regime. All intervention on behalf of the communities was suspect.

Our group was made up of university students and we would have our gatherings on Sunday afternoon. In the first holidays, in August, the group programmed and held a camp in the village where we reinforced the knowledge and the bonds of friendship with the elements of the group and simultaneously opened channels to better know the community: we would try to understand the works of the people with whom we already lived, we would help with the work, we would listen to their problems, we would organize activities for the children, and at the end of the camp, we even put up a children's drama with the little ones acting in it.. Trust between the group and the community increased and the group believed that more could be done.

We asked the Congregation for authorization to dedicate more effort to the community, a request that was accepted. For the academic year that began in September (1973-1974), a group of 3 Salesians was allowed to leave the Salesian Community to go live separately and take care of the needs of the Community, especially to promote literacy for adults from the 1ˢᵗ cycle and start the 2nd cycle for the little ones who had just finished the 4th class. We chose to live in Odivelas, just outside Lisbon and close to the village we sponsored. We were teachers and university students during the day and at the end of the afternoon we were scheduled to go to the village to teach. We had an audience for both initiatives.

Everything was running smoothly when the Revolution in Portugal took place on April 25, 1974 and the old regime fell. The Church did not see a new dawning there.

The experience of living in Odivelas lasted only one year. Meanwhile, the direction of the Salesian Congregation in Portugal had changed. We were invited to join the Salesian Community of Lisbon in order not to waste energy on other work proposals.

We were in charge of guiding the Parish of Our Lady of Mary Help of Christians. We carried on with three tasks: parish work, teachers in the College and university students. We were also able to fulfill our commitments to the former Community group and help students in their 4th and 6th years of schooling. The experience was so positive that other young people decided to continue their studies in a normal and after-work regime until they started to enter the University.

The direction given to the parish did not please the Provincial and we were discharged the following year with no function assigned in the year that we remained connected to the Congregation building. We all chose to continue to be teachers and university students.

In 1976 I requested my departure from the Congregation. I completed my Psychology course in 1977 and was invited to be part of the Board of a large Diocesan Day School, as a Psychologist and as Deputy Director of Escola Jardim Infantil and Escola de 1º Ciclo. I remained in the position for 3 years until the change of direction. I married in 1980 to Cynthia

Diniz Rodrigues and have lived in Almada. We had our first and only son in 1983, Gonçalo Rodrigues de Sousa.

Upon leaving Externato, I accepted invitation to serve as Executive Director of a Training and Recruitment Company in Lisbon, which had a team of 9 psychologists. I left the place 3 years later to pursue the Master in Educational Psychology, guiding my future for Education. While finishing my master's degree I went to teach Music Education in public education.

Once I completed my master's degree in Educational Psychology, I was invited by two Higher Institutes to give classes, in Tomar as Professor of Psychology, and in Santarém as Advisor for Music Education teachers, both in the post of Associate Professor. When I was in Santarém, at the suggestion of the Director, I started my studies for PhD at the Complutense University of Madrid, which I completed in 1996.

In 1998 I was invited to teach at the Lusophone University of Humanities and Technologies, Lisbon, first at the Faculty of Psychology and then at the Institute of Education. My desire to contribute to higher education was fulfilled, participating in the integral development of people. I feel fully fulfilled over these 22 years that I am at the University, teaching courses related to Psychology in the Bachelor, Master and Doctorate degrees. I have been Director (Dean) of Graduate Studies for many years and, since 2013, I am Director of the Master's Degree in Educational Sciences. I hold seminars in the PhD course and I have supervised several PhD theses and at least a hundred Master's dissertations.

Looking back, I can say that in my travels I always felt wholesome. I felt that people respected my abilities and skills in the successive invitations that I received to perform in different positions.

I was fortunate to be born in Goa into a large, affectionate, dynamic and stimulating family, and to receive a culture that was itself a breeding ground for cultures, with a mixture of East and West in terms of education, music, literature, gastronomy and all with a good level of quality.

My initial training was rich in all kinds of experiences, whether in terms of family, groups, music, sports and schools where I went. When I left Goa, I had the tools with me to find paths of happiness. So, it all seemed easy. I would like to conclude this write-up with a word of thanks to everyone I met along my journey, to my family and to the friends who offered me not only the warmth of their friendship but opened doors to other realities that might not be within my reach."

Egidio Moniz's Submission (Brazil)

I am a Moniz from Curtorim, Goa, and after graduating in agronomy from Poona, migrated to the world's food cellar- Brazil.

My dear cousin and friend Eufemiano who lives in Toronto is writing a book on our families and Goa. This article is my small contribution to his book.

We Goans have a fascinating history.

On the 25th of November 1510, the Portuguese Admiral Dom Afonso de Albuquerque defeated the Sultan of Bijapur and Portugal took over Goa. The destiny of the Goan people changed forever on that day. After 451 years, on the 19th of December 1961, India conquered Goa back.

A lot has happened between those two very important dates for all Goans.

My ancestors were Hindus, Saraswati Brahmins and our surname was Pai.

The Catholic Church, a very powerful entity at that time, believed there was no Divine salvation outside the church and they wanted to save us by converting us to Christianity.

The Catholic church, the moral arm of the Portuguese Government, was represented strongly by the Jesuits. St Francis Xavier, the pioneer missionary for conversions in Goa, is Goa's patron saint and very revered by Goans. The Jesuits, the world's greatest educators played a very important role in our lives.

There is a curious incident involving St Francis Xavier which I would like to share with you. About 30 years ago, I was visiting Registro, a town in the interior of the State of São Paulo, Brazil and it was the 3rd of December. The town was closed and I was told it was a holiday as it was the feast of their patron saint! I was amazed because like any Goan, I knew that the 3rd of December in the Catholic calendar is the feast of St Francis Xavier. When I asked the Hotel manager if there was a large Portuguese community in that town, he replied that it was the Japanese immigrants and not the Portuguese who brought St Francis Xavier to that town. Francis Xavier had also converted the ancestors of those Japanese immigrants as he had converted my ancestors and here, we were 400 years later, worshiping the same God and practicing the same beliefs in a different continent. Francis Xavier established Christianity in India, Malay Archipelago and Japan and had a tremendous impact on successive generations. I am amazed by the power of a single individual!

In 1575 my Family was converted from Hinduism to Catholicism, which was the end of "Pai "and all that it represented for thousands of years and the beginning of the Portuguese surname "Moniz", the new identity and its metamorphosis to a new mold. This meant a very big change: new Gods, a new philosophical and cultural approach to life. The Portuguese being Latins taught us to appreciate "Religion, Wine, Women and Song" and westernized us, bringing about an approach to life totally different from Hinduism.

We are Gaunkars and to date Zonkars from Raia, but the Family at some point migrated to nearby Curtorim. We have been here for over 200 years. Curtorim is a very beautiful village, situated in a valley surrounded by hills, a beautiful lake and a big river passing by and has a peaceful, fun loving and "sussegado" community.

Our ancestral heritage home in Curtorim is 100 years old, imposing, well-built and well taken care of. It was built by my paternal grandfather in 1924. It stood us well socially as it was a pillar of unspoken status in society. We all felt proud to belong to this house and all it represented.

Although Goans are adventurous by nature and went abroad to work in the British and Portuguese colonies in Africa and elsewhere, they always returned home to Goa to retire. My siblings and cousins were the first generation in the family to migrate to distant lands permanently, never to come back. We made our new adopted countries our home and became an asset to the nations in return for all the opportunities, generosity and hospitality with which we were received. Our rich culture and cuisine soon became a part of these new countries.

There has been an exodus of Christian Goans in the last 60 years. In my own immediate family, four of seven siblings migrated to California in the USA. It started with my priest brother Fr Joe Moniz, who in the nineteen sixties went to get his Masters degree in California and ended up working till his retirement last year for the Los Angeles diocese. He paved the way for my two brothers and sister, Avito and Jeanette who live in LA and Antonio who lives in Walnut Creek, San Francisco. All three, are very successful American citizens. In 1975 I migrated to Brazil. My sister Carol and brother Joaquim stayed back in India and of the second-generation Clint Misquitta, my sister Carol Moniz Misquitta's son is the only representative of the family in India.

My wife Valeria Lourdes Lobo was born and brought up in Uganda till University, as her father worked for the British government. She joined me in Brazil after our marriage in Goa in 1977. We have two sons, Nilesh, the eldest, who is a Maxillo Facial surgeon and Otolaryngologist is married to Giovanna Toffoli, a professor and researcher in Pharmacology at the Medical University in Campinas, São Paulo and they have a lovely 6-year-old daughter Manuela.

Our younger son Ravendra, a Urologist is married to Camila Venchiarutti who is an Oncologist and they have two lovely daughters Helena, 7, named after my mother and Luiza 5.

I arrived in Brazil in July 1975 at a prosperous time for Brazil. Brazil is a fascinating country with very hospitable, fun loving, hardworking and passionate people. It is three times the size of India with one sixth its population - a land of immigrants. A tropical agricultural country which is destined to feed the planet. They enchant the world with their football, music and carnival.

The country gets its "Soul" mainly from 3 different cultures: The Portuguese, the first colonizers who had the fantastic capacity to maintain this continental size country together, even though it was flanked on the entire western and Northern borders by the Spanish;

the Africans, who were formerly brought as slaves, today are definitely a vibrant and integral part of this society; the two world wars in Europe brought the Europeans, especially the Italians.

These three fantastic fun loving and gregarious cultures blended to bring about an exquisite touch to the Brazilian culture. Also, very much present are the Japanese, Arabs, Koreans, Chinese, Germans, Greeks and a small Indian community.

My first good job was with ICI an English agrochemical multinational. They were introducing a fantastic agricultural innovation called "Zero Tillage" in Brazil. Zero Tillage means you do not till the land, but the weeds are killed with a herbicide and the crop seeds planted directly into a slot cut into the soil by a special planter. Since prehistoric times man had always tilled the land to plant and produce. This was a tremendous innovation. I had the privilege to work with the first team that implemented the system. Today more than 95% of Brazil's Soybeans and Corn are planted using the Zero Tillage system. It was an honor to have participated in introducing this innovative system in Brazil.

Although I had a good job, I had a strong desire to buy my own farm to be economically independent. In 1982, seven years after I arrived in Brazil, I bought a small 10-hectare forest area in Araguari, in the State of Minas Gerais, which is 950 meters above sea level and ideal for planting Arabica Coffee. I obtained Government approval to remove the forest and planted my first 10 hectares of coffee. To obey Brazilian law, I also bought another 2 hectares of forest to be permanently kept as a forest reserve area of the farm.

Fifteen years later (1997) I sold my first farm and started from zero again on a 32-hectare farm. This time the land had already been farmed with Soybeans and corn. I planted coffee, my passion.

My love for the coffee crop dates back to my infancy, my ancestral home in Curtorim. My grandmother had about 6 Robusta Coffee trees in our garden for our own consumption. The coffee plant when it flowers has very pretty white flowers with a lovely scent that lasts for around 15 days. Those flowers and the scent remained fixed in my memory. Life is amazing! Thirty years later, I was a coffee farmer in South America because of these childhood memories!

Ten years ago I retired after 36 years with the Anglo Swiss multinational and I run my farm from Sao Paulo where I reside. It is 800 kms from Araguari. I fly to my farm once a month. I have my farm manager who lives on the farm and does the daily farm chores which are recommended by an agronomist who visits the farm every fortnight. I keep in touch daily with my manager. My farm is 100 % irrigated with the modern Israeli-system, tractor run, with sprayers, harvesters etc. using precision agriculture techniques to obtain high production.

Cooxupe, the world's biggest coffee cooperative has a branch in Araguari and is an important partner, supplying fertilizers, agro-chemicals and commercializing our coffee production, 80 % of which is for export.

We also have our own brand of gourmet coffee known as "Café Goa" that we mainly sell to "Madeleine Bakery", a top gourmet cafeteria in Sao Paulo.

Our efforts and conquests are dedicated to wonderful Brazil from this Moniz family, once upon a time from Curtorim. Goa.

C'est la vie!

Contribution from Antonio Moniz (San Francisco USA)

My Immigrant Experience:

May 2020 This is Tony.

Thanks for the opportunity to include us in your book.

Life for me has always been about movement and motion. As a child growing up in India, I saw people, cars, trains, buses, birds, animals-everything was in motion. It was as if you had to be in motion to be alive, to survive.

I was 19 years old when I moved away from home to branch out on my own. I remember hesitantly informing my mother that I got a job in Goa and would be leaving and was surprised at how well she took this news. She said "you have our address in Mumbai if you need to come back home for whatever reason. Write us a letter once in a while."

My parents always encouraged us to be independent and also gave us the tools to do so. I definitely believed I could make it on my own, even though I was only on a stipend. After 3 years in Goa, I started to get antsy and upon reading an advertisement in the Times of India for a job Saudi Arabia, I felt I had to move.

I was so enticed by the job posting: "Wanted immediately Chefs for the Municipality of Riyadh-Saudi Arabia. Excellent benefits including free food, housing and 21 days leave every year." What a challenge, how exciting, I could not resist. I thought I could market myself with the 3 years of experience I had acquired with the Taj Intercontinental in Mumbai and Goa. I applied for the job and after several interviews, was recruited, much to my delight, as an Assistant Chef.

Meeting people from all walks of life, different cultures, religion and ethnicities, language, created enthusiasm and a challenge for me. I did not have a passport when I got the job, but Dad was well connected and arranged to get one for me through a friend of his in Goa. At the age of 22,

I moved from Goa to Riyadh-Saudi Arabia. I left India with 100 rupees in my pocket and got swindled out of the entire amount before I even reached my destination ….at the layover at Abu Dhabi Airport buying a coke.

It was 1977 and I arrived in Riyadh with zero dollars but I was young and enjoyed the adventure. Most Saudi laws are very rigid bordering on the fanatical. However, I believed that my upbringing with parents that were strict disciplinarians and fervent Roman Catholics would help me adjust. Riyadh was especially strict and even though the company provided plenty of entertainment (after work hours), I became bored and homesick and just wanted something different. I managed to work in Riyadh for 4 years but I had to move again.

In 1980, while still in Riyadh, I asked my brother, Joe, to sponsor me to the US, thinking it would be a quick and easy process; however, it took 5 years. At that same time, I was offered an opportunity to work for a sister company in Jeddah-Saudi Arabia. As I did not know how long my visa for the US would take, I grabbed the job and was happy I did.

I lived a stone's throw from the Red Sea and loved that I could just lay in the water and not drown (the salinity kept me afloat). I was happier here and the work load was a lot less. My responsibilities included catering 2400 meals a day, (compared to Riyadh where we fed 12,000 meals a day). After 4 years in Jeddah, I finally got my visa to emigrate to the US in 1985.

I had to move again and I did. My brothers, Joe and Avito, gave me the warmest welcome to Los Angeles, thus beginning a smooth transition to California. I lived with my brother Avito and his lovely wife, Grace and family for over 3 years. They (Joe included) helped me adapt to my new home in the US, look for work, find a car (a 1974 Pontiac: the price was right and I loved it), experience living with a family and I will be eternally grateful for that.

My first job was with a Greek Restaurant chain (Spires) as a Manager and as I was just getting settled into this wonderful place called the City of Angels when I met my beautiful bride. We dated for about a year before

I proposed, thus setting me up for yet another move. This time the move was to find my heart in San Francisco.

Although it was hard leaving my brothers in LA, I was excited to start this new chapter with my wife. I married Melanie Mary Lobo on May 13, 1989 and together we have two awesome sons: Nathan Anthony and Jeremy William. Nathan teaches Math for Middle School and Jeremy is a Financial Planner.

Albert Einstein said that "nothing happens until something moves"….. and I'm glad I moved.

Author's Note. 2024: Nathan and Grace and Jeremy and Mackenzie are happy parents to Elia (October 2023) and Violet (January 2024) respectively. Tony and Melanie are super-happy grandparents

Contribution from Heriberto Moniz (Edmonton, Canada)

I am the second of seven children born of Caetano Moniz and Maria Florinda (Marcelina) Moniz. Loyola is the oldest, Eufemiano, Violeta, Blanche, Flaviano and Serena, the others.

Growing up in the village of Curtorim was simple, easy and charming at the same time. We walked bare feet, played football bare feet. Only to church on Sundays and good occasions we wore shoes or sandals.

My dad was a civil contractor, a proprietor (farmer), sarpanch of the village among other things. My mother, a homemaker and manager of inhouse activities. We had enough to eat, but never a choice. Whatever was cooked that day, was eaten.

The first five children, were raised, having to do different chores around the house, like sweeping the rooms, watering the garden plot or help in cooking, which has served us well in our adult life. The last two in spite of having a easier life, have also done well in life.

Schooling was in Portuguese medium till 1961, when Goa was invaded by the Indian army and became part of India.

After finishing my grade XI at St. Rita's High School, I enrolled in Chowgule College in sciences. From here, after Inter Science (two years), got admission to V.J.T.I. (Victoria Jubilee Technical Institute) in Mumbai where I finished the Mechanical Engineering degree. I did not secure high marks though, and as a result was difficult to secure a good job in well established companies.

My first job was in Goa, at Narcinva Damodar Naik, as a trainee supervisor, with a salary of Rs.450/month, which was then equivalent of Can.$75/month.

Soon I joined the merchant marine industry and after six months of training at Bombay Port Trust, I sailed with Shipping Corporation of India. My first port of call was Singapore, then onwards to Taiwan, Malaysia, Japan and onwards to the west coast of U.S and Canada.

It was a good life, in that I got to see different parts of the world and make good salary, compared to what was available in India at that time.

Around this time, I had a girlfriend, Maria Lourdes, who is my wife now. It was a long-distance relationship, which both of us did not like, to say the least. And my future mother-in-law did not approve at all.

My brother Eufemiano by then was quite established in Canada, having completed the Master in Civil Engineering from Carleton University and successfully employed. He encouraged me to migrate to Canada, suggesting it was a good country and all that jazz. He initiated the process through immigration sponsorship, and guided me with some contacts and procedures.

I landed in Montreal, in June of 1976, where I was met by my maternal uncle tio Jose. It was very painful to leave home, my parents, friends, and travel to a distant country, Canada, not knowing what the future held and when I would return home. It was a time of such emotions and such uncertainties. I remember crying bitterly when leaving home for Canada. I had the comfort of knowing that I had Eufemiano and my uncle tio. Jose (with whom I stayed the first few months in Montreal) for guidance and financial help if needed.

In less than a month of my arrival in Montreal, I had cleared some exams needed to be recertified as Marine Engineer, and was sailing the Great Lakes and the East coast of Canada.

I consider myself lucky all my life and the luck followed me to Canada too.

Within one year, my fiancee, came to Canada as a landed Immigrant. We got married in Boston by Fr. Caetano Costa, my first cousin who was posted in one of the parishes in New York. Boston was where Sales, Maria Lourdes older brother lived. Other family members lived in New York or close by.

After two years of sailing, it was time to change jobs. My wife was expecting our first child, Nadine, and as luck would have it, I was accompanying my uncle priest, Fr. Rosario, returning from his posting in Venezuela and wanting to visit Eufemiano, then in Edmonton. I used this opportunity to sound out any prospects for a job. To my great surprise and joy, I quickly secured employment with Imperial Oil, as a Steam Engineer. I could not have asked for anything more.

One of the highlights of my life in Canada is a two-year job assignment by Imperial Oil in Norman Wells (land of the midnight sun). Norman Wells, is a town in North Western Territories., located 81 miles south of the arctic circle. Located on the banks of Mackenzie River, it is only accessible by air. During winter, the river freezes and it is then used as an ice road to access other communities. In the summer the river is used to bring in goods by barges from Hay River to the south.

The Norman Wells community consisted of about 350 people during winter and about 450 people during summer. The majority of people worked for Esso Resources (Imperial Oil), who had conventional oil producing wells and a small 3000 barrels/day refinery. This refinery was originally built to supply the American troops in Alaska (WW II), through a small pipeline, which has since been abandoned. People not working for Imperial Oil, were personnel from a two men R.C.M.P. detachment, a nursing station, a bank, a grocery store, liquor store and a few indigenous people.

Because it is located that far north, Norman Wells experiences almost 24 hour sunshine during summer and 24 hour darkness during winter. The land is very fertile, and due to the copious amount of sunlight, vegetables grow in abundance with ease and minimal care, during the summer.

This posting for me came at such opportune time, and I thank my lucky stars. With a generous northern allowance and fully furnished free housing, we lived a good life. Being a small community, everyone knew everyone else. To this day we still maintain a few friendships fostered up north. It gave us a chance to save a lot of money and give ourselves a leg up, in those early years.

After 18 years with Imperial Oil, and a few more years as Power Engineering Instructor at Northern Alberta Institute of Technology, I am enjoying the good life in retirement.

I wish to thank Eufemiano, tio. Jose and also say thanks to Canada, for the country that you are. My children are lucky to be born in such a great country.

Contribution from Valerie Viegas (Florida, USA)

My experience as an immigrant to the United States

It is said that the path of your life pivots on the basis of decisions that you make. Little did I know that a couple of decisions that I made, small and insignificant as they then appeared to me, would change the trajectory of my life in such an incredible manner. Good or bad, this is the story of my life.

I started law school in Goa in the year 1991, determined to stay in Goa and practice as an attorney and eventually be a judge. That was a clear path in my mind. At the young age of 21, I was confident I knew all the answers to questions that life held in store. So sure was I, that I did not want to leave Goa, that I chose Portuguese Civil Code as my specialty (also known as Goa Family Law) as my focus in my third year of law school. I graduated with top honors and a gold medal in my specialty and started my apprenticeship practice under a female attorney, Mrs. Anarkali Agni.

It was at this time, in April 1995, that I got a phone call from a young man who wanted to meet me. I was very wary of meeting any young men, that too, ones I had never heard of before, but since he came through my best friend I agreed to meet him. I met him in my office on April 10, 1995 and my life has never been the same. That chance meeting was with Prazeres who is now my husband of 27 years and the love of my life.

When I met Prazeres, I had no idea that he would take me away from my precious Goa, from my path that I had worked so hard for or from my family and all that was familiar. I had no idea that he had all these plans to come to the US to study and I doubt even he knew at that time that we would be here for the rest of our lives. But again, those were the small, insignificant decisions that we made along the way that have brought us to where we are today.

We got married in April 1997 and a mere two weeks later I was on the longest ever flight of my life from sunny Goa to cold Detroit, Michigan. I moved from a 4-bedroom, 4 bath house where I lived with my family and two maids to a small one-bedroom apartment with my husband where I was the maid! Having been raised in a home where I did limited house work and cooking since we always had help, I was woefully unprepared to run my own home.

The first trip to the grocery store is still etched in my memory so clearly. There I saw several different kinds of onions, and several different kinds of potatoes. I had no idea what the difference was, how they tasted, nothing. The food was packaged differently, tasted different and all the spices I needed to cook. Goan food could only be found in the Indian store which was over an hour and half away by car.

Remember, I could not yet drive in the US at that time, having driven in Goa on the "wrong" side of the road, and needing to take a driver's test to get my license here. The expressways and the 18-wheelers on them made my hands clammy with sweat. But slowly and surely, with Prazeres' help as much as he could, as a busy second year medical resident, I learnt the nuances of living in America.

I started working in the legal department of the hospital (for free initially, since I did not have work papers yet) and I really believe that is what helped me assimilate into the American culture quickly. I had some great friends there, a couple of whom are still friends of mine all these years later. My boss was a wonderful female attorney who kept encouraging me to try new things, American things.

Coming from Goa, I was very comfortable with western clothes, so that was not an issue but the way in which one dressed, the fact that I had to wear everyday a blazer and pantyhose to work, that was new. We also went out to lunch often at the office, and that is where I tried a bagel for the first time. I could not understand their fascination for sandwiches for lunch.

In our apartment complex, there were several other residents like Prazeres who had wives that had given up their careers like me. Those women are still some of my closest friends. A lot of them were Indian and taught me to make great Indian food with American ingredients that were commonly available. My Hindi got so much better as we watched Hindi movies together or just conversed in Hindi. I guess that was our homesickness coming out. This was another small decision that shaped my life later on.

Several years later, we moved from Michigan to Washington State. By then we had a young baby girl who kept me on my toes. Parenting her with no guidance was a challenge but she and I grew up together. I finally got my work permit again in Washington and I used all the experience I had cooking Indian food to teach Indian cooking at the local community college in their food and wine division.

I, who never cooked in my first 25 years of growing up except for rare occasions, was now teaching others far older than I how to cook! It has never ceased to amaze me, even when they featured me in the local newspaper. I had reinvented myself once again and this brought me so much joy. I finally had a "career" of my own again, however small and insignificant it seemed to anyone.

And a few years later we moved again – to Florida – since Prazeres found a different job. By now the thought of going back to Goa had long gone away. We had two children who were going through the American school system and how they would adjust to life in Goa was one of the major concerns. Prazeres also confessed he could never imagine practicing medicine in Goa or living there again, so assimilated was he to life in the US. With both kids in school in Florida, I started to look at trying to figure out what to do with my life. They still needed me around once they were home, but when they were in school, I had some free time.

I had received my BA in English Literature before I went to law school and so I got my educational requirements recertified and started teaching as a substitute teacher in the schools where my children studied. It worked great! I worked as many or as few days as I needed, my schedule was flexible and I was always home when the children were home to help with after school activities, homework or whatever else needed to be done. Prazeres' practice picked up and he worked in the next town over. So, he was gone for the whole day.

And in yet another insignificant meeting, I happened to mention to a colleague who sat with me on the School Advisory Council, that I would love to go back to law. And he called me up one day and offered me a position to work as his paralegal. I have been there for six years now and have learnt so much and grown up even more. Who knew you could still grow at almost 50!

I think of all these moments in my life that pivoted me to the next phase of my life and I can never imagine what I thought my life was going to be like and what it is now. I have a sign in my office that says "Life is a journey, travel it well" and for me that has never been more true. I do not regret any of the choices that have brought me to where I am today. This was what my life was always meant to be.

Contribution from Karen (Menezes) Lobo

Across the Ocean: a Canadian Odyssey

When my husband Rohan and I decided to immigrate in 1995, we had just got married and exchanged comfortable lives in south Mumbai for the faraway suburb of Thane, the only affordable place. My husband was in financial services, with a south Mumbai office. It looked like a 2-plus hour commute was here to stay, since the outward bound corporate migration of offices had yet to take place.

It wasn't just the local train, which in itself was horrendous, as anyone who has experienced rush hour in Mumbai will attest to. It was the additional half hour commute from Thane station to our apartment which was the clincher. That and the pollution; droves of auto rickshaws pumping fumes into the air at Thane station, forcing many commuters to hold cloths to their faces. One monsoon on the local trains decided it for us.

We had been noodling immigration before we got married to be sure. I had cousins in Australia, and my husband's brother was already in America, so Canada made the list. Those countries and New Zealand were the only three first world countries that actively allowed immigration at the time. We settled on Canada.

Delayed by a year by the birth of our daughter Julia, the three of us finally set off in the summer of 1997. My husband left in August, on the day India celebrated its 50th anniversary of independence; at the airport he recalled feeling really odd with all the bunting and celebrations around him, just as he was pulling up stakes and leaving for good. I followed with Julia (10 months old) 5 weeks later. We were not to return for nine years.

We spent the first 2 years in London, where my husband requalified with an MBA from Canada's best business school, Western University. It was a struggle with 2 kids (Julia and Peter) both under the age of 2, but it was also fun. We were young and optimistic and full of life and energy.

We made some really good friends with whom we have kept in touch over the years. And they took us everywhere: sugar-bushing, apple picking, strawberry picking. They introduced us to the concept of garage sales, from where we bought so many great things, at such throw away prices. We learnt that the best price for anything is free…

Rohan finally found a good job and we moved to Toronto, the Big Smoke. Toronto had a different feel to it, more of a big city and we took full advantage of it. We took the kids to the museums and the science centres and the parks. We found so many things for free here: the library, the skating rinks, the community centres. Remember I said that the best price is free?

Well, we still use the library to the hilt. I have re-learned an old skill that my mother taught me when I was a child thanks to all the books at the library: knitting. And I did not have to pay a single penny for any of the books. We borrowed movies and documentaries on history and geography and taught the kids. The kids made good friends at school. Peter still keeps in touch with his old elementary school buddies.

We bought our home in 2001 in North York. That first year we invited all the neighbourhood kids for both our kids' birthday parties, and our kids were in and out of the neighbours' houses all summer long. It was like we were back in 1950s Canada, we didn't see our kids except at meal times, and if we didn't see them at lunch we were confident that whichever home they were at, that mother would be feeding them, just as we sometimes had six children at our home for lunch. This was before the days of monster homes, electronic games, and locked doors in North York.

Meanwhile I went back to night school myself in 2002 and acquired a law clerk diploma, and by 2003, when our youngest was in kindergarten, had started working full time. Then I got into the teaching industry and taught elementary school for a few years, before deciding to give it all up and go back to corporate life, but in the automotive finance industry.

We went back to India for the first time after nine years, in 2006, for my sister's wedding. It was the kids' first trip back and they were wide eyed. As they alighted at Bombay airport, they asked my husband in ringing tomes, "Daddy, what is that SMELL?", as I tried to shush them up. The trip was a great learning experience for them, and us. India had progressed beyond what we could have imagined, but the pollution and the corruption were still there.

We took the kids on great road trips all across the US and Canada. We have criss-crossed the United States east of the Mississippi by car and have had great experiences. We have taken the kids white water rafting, bungee jumping and visited museums and battle grounds all over the U.S. We have taught the kids about the Civil War and the American Revolution, warships, aircraft and breweries – experiences that we never had in India, but that were available for the asking here. We even have a DVD of me almost drowning whilst white water rafting in West Virginia, and my husband saving my shoe instead of me from the water, whilst other men fished me out of the water.

Today our kids are grown and graduated from university with their own circle of friends. They are what are affectionately known as coconuts: brown on the outside and white on the inside, with views that are a nice blend of Indian and Canadian values. They move seamlessly from one culture to another when we go to parties hosted by Indians, and those by Canadians, know how to comport themselves depending on the setting, can interpret Canadian nuances and non-verbals with ease. Their take on the world is truly international.

We will always have a soft spot for India, having been born there and grown up there. And we will always relate better culturally to India. But we have learnt over the years to incorporate into our lives the best of Canada as well as the best of India and have tried to give our children the best of both worlds. So much so, that recently Julia asked us, "What will happen when you are gone and there is nobody to explain the Indian nuances to us?" And we answered, "That is why we are teaching you as much as we can right now".

If you were to ask me today, if we made the right decision to come to Canada, I would say, 'Yes, definitely yes!" We gave up much, but have gained much, much more. Immigration broadens the mind and the heart and we are the better for it.

GENEALOGY MENEZES GODD FAMILY

1 Antonio Francisco de Menezes (1758?-)
m Ana Maria de Menezes
  2 Aleixo Manoel de Menezes (1793?-)
  m Theodesia de Menezes
    3 Antonio Francisco de Menezes
    m Ana Florinda de Menezes
      4 **Manoel Xavier do Rosario de Menezes** (1831-)
      m Maria Severina Conceicao de Cruz
        5 **Maria Quiteria** (1865?-1927) m Romualdo Francisco da Costa
            Rosarinho m Maria Mascarenhas
            had seven children (two priests, three doctors), 4 gr children
            Maria Carmelina m Salvador da Costa
            had two children
            Domingos m Maria Batista
            had seven children (9 grandchildren)
            Jose Rafael m Teresa (Arsentina) Pereira
            had nine children (two priests,) 12 grandchildren
            Maria Elizenia m Salvador da Costa
            had six children (26 grandchildren)
            Maria Piedade m Aniceto Diniz
            had three children (nine grandchildren)
            Carmelina m Martinho Soares
            had seven children (16 grandchildren)

        5 **Francisco Xavier** (1866? -1929) m Maria Anunciacao Severina
                Sardinha
            Maria Conceicao m Rozario Joaquim Francisco Medeira
            had two children (one nun)
            Maria Anunciacao m Pedro Salvador Rodrigues

had three children (8? grandchildren)
Maria Estafania (Madrinha) m Rozario Salema
had four children (8? Grandchildren)
Maria Quiteria m Manoel Afonso Coutinho
had one child and 4 grandchildren
Rosa Maria m Luis Caetano Sardinha
had nine children, all boys (16 grandchildren)
Maria Felicidade m Salvador da Costa
had one child (4 grandchildren)
Maria Esperanca (not married)

5 **Idalina** (Id man) m Joao Francisco (Janflu) Menezes
    Gabriel (children Liliana, (Motte) Joao, Carminho, Teofilo)
        (gr children 10+)
    Funchu irmao (Francisco?) (Only son Jorge, whose daughter
        Linda married Milagres Menezes)
    Jeronimo m Lurdina (?) Pereira from Benaulim
        (Pereira, Sebastiao Vicente; Menezes - Daniel,
        Marianinha, Aramita) (Aurita Pereira married (1)
        Sebastiao Vicente (Ida, Eva and Ina) and (2) Daniel
        (Palmira, Stanislau, Maria, Sabby, Jennifer, Savia,
        Edith) (Anita /Aurita is Dr. Roque Menezes niece from
        Chandor)
    Joaquim Santana (1898-1939 not married)
        gifted music composer of mando, and khell
    Lurdes (Ludman had a daughter Quiteria)
5 **Maria Felicidade** (1873-1934) m Sebastiao Aleixo da Piedade
        Veiga (Maina)
    Joaquim Veiga (Lourenco Rosario, Joao, Maria Rita
        Gracias, Maria Felicidade Rodrigues, Filomena)
        (24 grandchildren)
    Constancio Veiga (Jose, Sebastiao, Maria Borges) (17
        grandchildren)

5. **Fr. Milagres Menezes**   (1875-1948)
5 **Fr. Carminho Menezes**   (1878-1919)

5. **Inacio Caetano Cornelio de Menezes (1878-1970) - Caetaninho m Maria Teresa Fernandes** (19 grandchildren)

Maria Florinda (Marcelina) (1921-2014) m Caetano Acacio Moniz had seven children (4 boys, 3 girls) (19 grandchildren)

See Info on Moniz/Menkar Family Tree

Fr. **Rosario** Menezes (1923-)

Carmo Menezes (1925-2013) m Carolina Viegas
 Maria D'O / Francisco Carvalho (1 child)
 Milagres /Linda Menezes (2 Children)
 Celita/Antonio de Menezes (2 children)
 Nilza / Erson Viegas (1 child)
 Savio (Ninush)

Albertina (1927-2006)

Dr. **Francisco Xavier** (1929-2006) m Maria Angela Massa
 Francisco (Xico) / Magdalena/ Isabel (4 children)
 Maria Teresa/ Americo (1 child)

Constancio (1932-2019) m Ida d'Silva
 Edgar/ Sharon Fernandes (2 children)
 Noel /Menaka Costa Frias (2 children)
 Selwyn/Sheena Vaz (2 children)
 Neville/Karen Rodrigues (2 children)

Lourencinho (1936-)

Dr. **Jose** Menezes (1939-) m Guilhermina Gouveia (1946-)
 Natasja 1972/Michael Michel (3 children)
 Ravi 1975/ Linh Nguyen (1 child)
 Leila 1979/Eric Wand (1 child)

ADDENDUM

5A **Maria Teresa Fernandes** (Xamae) Her sister Leopoldina (ummarried) her Parents Caetano Xavier Fernandes and Quiteria Angelica Figueiredo

> Quiteria's Parents
>
> Joaquim Vicente and Beatriz Carlota

Quiteria's Brother: Dr. Francisco Figueiredo

Dr. Francisco Figueiredo's children

> Luis, Bernardino, Joaquim, Carlotina, Carl
>
> Beatriz married in Cortalim

Quiteria's sister Ana Severina (??) married Pedro Marcos Coelho

Their children: Angelina, Gracianinha and son Michael Coelho

Angelina married Antonio Reginaldo Pimenta
Their children: Enio, Cristov, Marie, Elsa, Josico

4 Maria Severina Conceicao da Cruz (Borda)

her Parents
Joaquim Joao de Cruz and Ana Teresa de Cruz
Her sister Maria Angelica married Felipe Neri Pereira (Raia)
Their son
Regalado Pereira married Maria Quiteria Pimenta
Their Children - All Pimenta Pereira: Maria Palmira do Rosario, Maria Angelica, Pe. Caetano, Maria Olivia, Babush, Zezito, Marta Wiseman Pinto, Maria Alda Viegas

Genealogy of MONIZ Family

1 **Caetano Francisco Moniz** (1850-1887) **m Otilia Vas** (1857-1921)

Note: Caetano had a brother Pe. Alcinho (not much is known about him)

Children: Inacio de Loiola, Eufemiano, Joaozinho and Amelina Moniz Luis

2 **Inacio de Loiola** m 1909 Ana Maria Riarinha Pereira (from Raia)

3 **Riario** Moniz (mother died after child birth and Loiola remarried in 4 years)

2 **Inacio de Loiola** (1878-1937) m 1913 **Cecilia** Monteiro (1894?-1964)

3 **Riario Moniz** (1910-1979) m. Maria **Helena** Quadros (1919-2016)

4 **Jose (Fr. Joe)** Luis Moniz, (1941)
4 **Carolina** Luis Moniz (1942) m. 1966 **Lynus** Misquitta (1936)
    5 Lygia Misquitta (1966)
    m. 1994 Adrian Dias (1966)
        6 Jadyn (1999)
        6 Apryl (2007)
    5. Lizette Lorraine Misquitta (1969)
    m. 2001 Dilip Nogueira (1960)
        6 Naomi (2004)
        6 Reuben (2006)
    5. Chrisann Misquitta (1974)
    m. 1998 Joseph Barnetto (1968)
        6 Mirelle (2012)
    5. Clint Misquitta (1981)
        m. 2015 Meghann Mascarenhas (1982)
        6 Emily (2017)

4 **Joaquim** Luis Moniz (1944) m. **Maria** Lopes Pereira
    5 Nigel Moniz m Pryanca
    5. Craig Moniz m Jeanne
    5. Megan Moniz (1988) m Wassem Chaudry
4 **Egidio** Luis Moniz (1948) *m 1977 Valeria **Lourdes** Lobo (1944)*
    5 Nilesh Joriel Moniz (1977) m 2007 Giovana Tofoli
        6 Manuela (2013)
    5. Ravendra Moniz (1980)
        m 2010 Camila Venchiarutti (1984)
        6 Helena (2012)
        6 Luiza (2014)

4 **Avito** Luis Moniz (1950-2023) m. 1979 **Grace** Welch (1956)
    5 Michelle Moniz 1982 m 2011 Andy King 1982
        6 Lily 2012
        6 Samuel 2016
        6 Caroline 2019
    5. Ryan Moniz 1984 m 2015 Liana Ching 1988
        6 Oliver 2018
        6 Milo 2021
    5. Marissa Moniz 1988 m 2021 Monica Leon
    5. Lauren Moniz 1991 m 2022 Taylor Bowlin

4 **Antonio** Luis Moniz (1955) m. 1989 **Melanie** Mary Lobo (1961)
    5 Nathan Moniz (1993) m 2022 Grace Ling Wu 1991
    5. Jeremy Moniz (1996) m 2023 Mackenzie Baysinger 1997

4 **Jeanette** Luis Moniz (1966) m. 1993 **Ronald** Dalgado (1964)
    5 Chelsea Dalgado (1998)
    5. Riley Dalgado (2006)

3 **Caetano Moniz** (1914-1978)
m. 1942 Maria Florinda (**Marcelina**) Menezes (1921-2015).

4 Inacio de **Loiola** Moniz (1943 -)
m 1971 Especiosa **Benildes** Coutinho (1947)
    5 Michelle (1973) m. 1999 Moreno Rebelo (1967)

        6 Shane (2001)
        6 Seraiah (2008)
    5. Rochelle (1973) m. 1999 Kevin Pacheco (1973)
        6 Natalie (2003)
        6 Nathan (2008)
    5. Danielle (1985) m. 2014 Alinio Mascarenhas 1983

4 **Heriberto** Aleixo Moniz (1945)
m. 1977 **Maria de Lurdes** Barreto (1952)
    5 Nadine (1977)
    5. Ralph (1977) m 2023 Anne Sophie Belisle
        6 Rafael Alexio (2023)
    5. Simone (1984)

4 **Eufemiano** Moniz (1947)
m 1975 **Ethelwyn** *Pereira (1953)*
    5 Celine (1976) m 2006 Russell De Souza (1974
        6 Phoebe (2009-2009)
        6 Evan (2009-2009)
        6 Ethan (2010)
    5 Larissa (1979)
    5. Francis (1990) m 2021 Kim Rodrigues

4 **Violeta** Moniz (1950) m. 1974 **Albino** Fernandes (1944)
    5 Ashly (1976) m 2013 Nadia D'Souza 1978
    5. Nadia (1978-2022) m 1997 Calvin Gomes (1972)
        6 Alyssa 2002
        6 Sasha 2003
        6 Natasha 2006
        6 Cassandra 2008
        6 Samantha 2011
        6 David 2015
    5. Pierre (1981) m 2014 Jolene Lobo (1986)
        6 Megan (2017)
        6 Dylan (2019)

4 **Blanche** Moniz (1953) m.1976 **Placido** Viegas (1942-2011)
    5 Olancio (1977-2013) m 2010 Michelle Araujo 1984
        6 Erwin (2011)
        6 Jayden (2012)
    5. Muriel (1982) m 2005 Brian Mascarenhas
        6 Brielle (2012)
        6 Breanne (2016)
4 **Flaviano** Moniz (1957-2015)
m. 1987 **Amelia** Mesquita (1962)
    5 Agnetha (1988)
    5. Caeteana (1993)
4 **Serena** Moniz (1953)
m. 1983 Belrosario (Belo) Diniz (1957)
    5 Synuae (1986) m 2021 Vincent Fernandes (1982)
        6 Vienna (2022)
    5. Byanca (1990) m 2019 Wendall Mascarenhas (1989)
        Lennox (2020)
        Zander (2023)
    5 Dayne (1993)

3 **Atilia Moniz** (1919-2007) m Roque da Costa
        Alzira (1937)
        Fr. Caetano (1941-2019
        Sr. Laura (1939-)
        Carlos (1943-2019) m Alzira Rodrigues
        Mario (1949-1988) m Maria Rita
        Belivia (1951-) m Arlindo Miranda
3 **Aurelia Moniz** (1921-2007) m Remedios Soares
        Aida (1947) m Anastasio Cabral
        Alexandrina (Alcina) (1949) m Hillary Furtado
        Augusto m Maria P Rodrigues Cana
        Antonieta (Neta) m Sebastiao da Costa
        Miguel M Blanche
        Maria de Neves m Joseph Noronha
        Olavo m Marta

3 **Alcinho (Alex) Moniz** (1921-2008) m Belmira Mesquita
    4 Lira (1954) *m Cornel d'Melo*
    Sherna m Ajay
    Danaye m Regan
    4 Ralph (1957) *m Rohita*
    4 Cecilia (Cecy) (1960) *m Stephen D'Silva*
    4 Kevin (1970)
3 **Antonio Joao Moniz** (1930-2007) m Filomena Da Costa
    Sailesh (1962-2020)
    Dean (1966-)
    Seville (1968-)

ADDENDUM

2A **Cecilia** Monteiro (1894?-1964) m 1913 Loiola Moniz (1878-1937)
Parents: Sebastiao Manoel Nascimento and Quiteria Liberata Petomila
Sister: **Crescencia** (1886-1956) m Antonio Jose Soares (??- 1945) (Ghor Zanvoi)
    Children: Monteiro Soares
    Marta,
    Nascimento m Lucilia Quadros
        Antonio (Tonito)   Hugo   Saozinha
        Cynthia   Vitinho   Jill   Precioso
    Liberata (1919-) m Guilherme Menezes (1916-1999)
        Virgilia m Carmo de Quadros (1937-2015)
        Antush (1944 -) m Annie Lourenco
        Jose (Zezito) (1946-2006) m Celina Pacheco
        Terezinha m William Meneses (1944-2015)
        Savio m Grisela
        Maria An
        a (1957-) m Aurio Pereira
        Sunita
    Aspulqueta (Queta)

PEREIRA FAMILY GENEALOGY

(original by Fr. Luis Menezes; updated with data from Berardo Pinto Pereira and Emano Moniz)

Descendants of Joao Baptista Aniceto Pereira

1 Joao Baptista **Aniceto** Pereira (1883-1878)
m. Maria Cristina Josefina (1848-1925)
  2. Estela Estefania **Etelvina** Pereira (1865-1948)
  2. **Msgr. Aniceto** de Menino Jesus Pereira (1871-1961) **De-facto Patriarch of Family**
2 Pascoal Do Rosario **Epifanio** Pereira (1868- 1949)
m. **Maria Aurora** Quiteria Valeriano-Baretto (1877-1956)
  3 Ana Joaquina **Ofelia** De Jesus Maria Josefa Piedade De Imaculada Conceicao (1904-1980)
  m Roque Piedade **Menezes**, Dr (1902-1974)
    4 **Arthur** Menezes (1927-1999) m. Olivia D'Sousa 1928
      5 Francesca Pia Menezes 1959
      5. Monica Menezes 1960
      5 Vasco Menezes 1964 m. Kathryn Jones
        6 Phoebe Jeanne Menezes
        6. Jevan Arthur Menezes
        6. Naomi Star Menezes
    4 **Caesar** Piedade Menezes (1931-2010) m. 1961 Anita Pimenta (1929-2020)
      5 Sunita Maria Menezes (1962) m. 1990 Michael Anthony Grevi Desouza 1960
        6. Larissa Desouza 1991 m Keith de Gama
      5. Francis Joseph Piedade Menezes (1964) m. 1998 Ida Saldanha (1964)
        6. Aaron Menezes (1999-)

5. Louis Anthony Piedade Menezes (1966)

5 Ivan John Menezes (1972) m. 2001 Supriya Peres Da Silva 1964

    6 Ari Joseph Menezes (2003)

    6. Mia Anya Menezes (2007)

4 Aires Jesus Piedade Menezes (1933-)

m. 1961 Theresa Antoinette Inez Cordeiro (1940-)

    5 Flavia Judith Menezes (1961) m. 1989 Clive Vincent Pereira (1960)

        6 Sean Louis Pereira (1990) m 2021 Bridget Vale

        6. Franz Pereira (1993)

        6. Joshua William Pereira (1999)

    5. Celia Maria Menezes (1963) m. 2003 Rohit Walter Rao (1971)

        6. Nadine Marise Walter Rao (2007)

    5. Leah Jacinta Menezes (1965)

    5. Savio Antonio Pio Menezes (1969)

    m. 1999 Priya Maria Colaco (1976)

        6. Ayesha Johanna Pia Menezes (2008)

    5. Julian Joseph Pio Menezes (1980-)

4. **Fr Louis SJ** Menezes (1934-2019)

4 Joseph (**Joe**) Piedade Menezes (1937)

m. 1966 Antoinette Mathias (1944)

    5 Karen Menezes (1967) m. 1995 Rohan Lobo (~1966-)

        6 Julia Amanda Lobo (1996)

        6. Peter William Lobo (1998)

    5. Kenneth Savio Pio Menezes (1969) m. 2000 Gillian D'Sousa (1968)

        6. Malaika Menezes

    5. Elizabeth Pia Menezes (1971) m. 2006 Brian Colaco

        6. Nikhil Colaco (2012-)

    5. David Pio Menezes (1973-) m. Marilia Correia

4. **Fr Albert** Menezes, SJ (1939-)

4 **Roque** (Roquito) Piedade Menezes, Sr. (1943-2000) m. Monique Demortier (~1944-)

5. Joanna Menezes (1975-) m. Paul Henri-Renard
    6 Luca Henri-Renard
    6. Lola Henri-Renard (2011-)
5. Anthony Menezes (1979-) m. ~2005 Ruth
    6. Oliver Menezes (2008-)
5 Roque Menezes, Jr. (1979-) m. 2007 Claire Smilie
    6 Zach Menezes (2008-)
    6. Lucy Eve Menezes (2010-)

3. **Vasco** Menezes (1949-1949)

3 **Julieta** do Sagrado Coração de Maria Pereira (1906-1963)
m. 1931 Sebastian Cotta (1901-1972)
  4 Maria Stela Cotta (1932) m. 1967 Gopal Ramesh Menon (1941-1997)
    5 Nirmala Maria Ramesh Menon (1968-) m. Prasad Naik
      6 Abhishek Naik
      6. Raj Naik
    5. Savita Julieta Menon (1970) m. Christo Mascarenhas
      6. Kenneth Christo Mascarenhas
    5. Satya Menon (1972) m. Robin Nagvi
      6. Nathan Savio Nagvi
  4. Fr Mariano Cotta (1934)
  4 Maurelio Antonio de Piedade Cotta (1936-2022) m. Fatima Cabral
    5 Julieta Maria Cotta m. Arvind Odrick Clemente
      6 Jean Louie Clemente
      6. Anabelle Clemente
      6 Olivier Clemente
    5. Sebastian Jacinto Cotta m Clotilda Fernandes
      6. Andre Xavier

  4 Manuel (Maneka) Caetano de Piedade Cotta (1941-2004)
m. 1975 Maria Goretti Menezes (1952)
    5 Sasha Julieta Cotta (1976) m. Sergio D'Silva (1976)
      6 Joaquim 2004
      6. Caroline 2008

5. Helga Mitzie Cotta 1977 m. 2012 Ryan D'Costa
6 Aaron2014
4 Miguel (Mikito) Cotta (1944) m. 1975 Lizette Fatima de Xavier Miranda (1951)
5 Chantale Cotta (1977) m. Sidney Viegas
6 Simplicio
5. Franz Schubert Cotta (1978-) m Sharmila Menezes
6 Franz Haiden
6 Manuel Jose
4. Fr Antonio Aristides de Piedade Cotta (1949-2022)
4 Maria da Graça (Gracinha) das Neves Cotta (1952) 5 m. 1985 John Sequeira
5 Reuben Sequeira (1987)
5. Raoul Sequeira (1989)

3 Joao Baptista **Aniceto** Pereira (1909-1988)
m. 1971 Maria Alice Antonieta Pereira (1909-1988)
4 Orlando Pereira 1941 m. 1979 Nicolette D'sousa 1948
5 Cherise Maria Domenique Pereira (1979)
5. Carlos Savio Epifanio Pereira (1984)
4 Churchill Pereira (1942-2001) m. Ruth Cunha (?-?)
5 Samantha Alice Pereira (1979) m. Rishi Sachdev (1977)
6. Siana Sachdev
5. Amanda Pereira (1981) m. Joshua Alury
4 Jeanette Pereira (1944) m. Peter Fortes (1942)
5 Sr. Michelle Fortes (1975-)
5 Judith Ann Fortes (1977) m. Oscar Edwin Sequeira
6 Marushka Ruth Sequeira, 1975
6. Son Sequeira
4. Indira Pereira m. Joseph Bernard Pimento (?-2010)
4 Oscar Pereira (1948- 2020?) m. 1979 Arlene D'Sousa (1951-2022)
5 Aniceto Pereira (1980)
5. Joseph Pereira (1982)
5. Sally-Ann Alicia Pereira (1983)

3 **Clarissa** Pereira (1912-1998)

m. Jose Joaquim Lazaro Tome do Nascimento Sousa (1893-1969)

   4 Maria Estela **Celina** Sousa (1934-2020)

   m. 1954 Antonio (Antush) Soares (1918-2003)

      5 Carlos Alberto Antonio Soares 1955 m.1990 Lalita Doreen Noronha 1964

         6 Desiree Dorathae Celina Soares 1991

         6. Elaine Marie Soares 1992

         6. Simone Clarissa Soares 1998

         6. Giselle Lauren Soares 2000

      5 Maria Conceicao (Baei) Soares 1956

      m. 1983 Alirio Placido Agnelo Sidharth D'Costa 1947

         6 Carla Maria Guilhermina Shabana D'Costa 1984

         6. Luis Filipe Manuel D'Costa 1987

      5 Maria Luiza Terezinha (Bebe) Soares 1957

      m. 1981Sebastian Joseph Quadros 1955

         6 Reuben Joe Quadros 1984

         6. Samantha Jean Quadros 1987

      5 Maria Yvonne Indira (Bibioca) Soares 1959

      m. 1983 Everard Carvalho 1959

         6 Falon Ema Carvalho 1985

         6. Kelvin Anthony Carvalho 1990

      5 Frederico Ravindra Antonio (Delish) Soares 1961

      m. 1990 Fatima Leopoldina Facho 1959

         6 Farcia Celine Soares 1991

         6. Fiona Rose Soares 1993

         6. Christine Marie Soares 1994

         6. Neves Antonio Soares 1999

         6. Kevin Andre Soares 2001

      5 Maria Fernanda Sarojini (Balu) Soares 1962 m. Dick Van Der Linden 1949

         6 Shaun Van Der Linden 1989

         6. Ryan Van Der Linden 1991 m. Cyril Lopez

      5. Maria Inez Sushila (Boneca) Soares 1963 m. 1995 Dennis Menezes 1959

         6. Nathan John Menezes 1996

5 Maria Jose Shakuntala Soares 1965 m 1990 Bonny Rito
    D'Silva 1961
        6 Savannah Nathalie D'Silva 1992
        6. Bradley D'Silva 1996
5 Jose (Zezito) Candido Victor dos Neves Soares 1967
m 1995 Cheryl Anne Fernandes 1970
        6 Rheya Celine Soares 1996
        6. Arianna Eryka Soares 1998
5. Maria Irene Shalini Soares 1969

4. Carlos (**Carlito**) Januario Sousa (1936-2021)
m. 1965 Estefania Asteria Diniz (1940-2010)
    5. Paula Alexandra Diniz Sousa 1968

4 Maria **Clelia** Natividade Sousa (1938)
m. 1969 Aires Jose Caetano Mascarenhas (1934-2020)
    5 Maria Sandra Mascarenhas 1970 m. Saba Vincent Da Silva
        6 Jaime Carl Da Silva
        6 Jean Marie da Silva
    5 Bosco Mascarenhas m. 2007 Karen Pimenta-Pereira
        6 Ethan 2009
        6 Eryn 2011
        6 Eva 2013
    5. Oswald Gavin Mascarenhas (1975) m. Amousha Menezes
        6. Kiara Lisa
        6 Kian
4. **Oscar** Conceicao Sousa 1941 m. 1980 Cynthia Diniz 1956
    5. Gonzalo De Sousa 1983
4 **Maria Angela** Sousa (1942) m. Louis Vaz (1936-2022)
    5 Lara Vaz, 1970
    5. Louise Vaz, 1979
    5. Lenny Vaz. 1984
4 **Mario** Piedade Sousa (1946) m. 1975 Lynette Ribeiro Soares
    1947
    5 Kay De Sousa 1976
    5. Nadine De Sousa 1979

4. Maria Fatima (**Fatu**) Terezinha De Sousa (1950-)

    5 Ricardo de Sousa Dias 1982

4 **Olavo** Santana dos Reis Sousa 1952 m.1981 Carmen Mascarenhas 1950

    5 Kathleen Di-Ann Sousa (1982)

    5. Jose Joaquim Sousa (1984)

4 Maria **Bernadette** Imaculada Sousa (1954) m. 1981 MervinLopez 1956

    5 Clive Elton 1983

        6 Liam Alexander

        6 Jacob Anthony

        6 Keira Elizabeth

    5. Joann Melina 1989

4 **Edgar** Savio do Carmo Sousa (1956) m. 1983 Celia Barneto (1954)

    5 Darinka Sousa (1985) m Tristan Gupta

        Troy Sousa Gupta

    5 Brensley Sousa (1988)

3 Francisco Xavier (FX / Chico) Pereira (1914-1999)

m. Phoebe Menezes (1917-1998)

    4 **Marjorie** Pereira (1948)

    4 **Yvonne** Pereira (1949) m 1978 Ralph d' Souza (1942)

        5 Simone D'Souza (1979) m 2011 Michael Brody 1979

            6 Keira Brody 2012

            6 Luke Brody 2015

            6 Ryan Brody 2017

        5 Marise D'Souza (1980) m 2011 Casey Butterley 1981

            6 Dillon Butterly (2013)

            6 Maxwell Butterly (2016)

            6 Aurora Butterly (2020)

        5 Andre D'Souza (1985) m 2017 Rita Celebrezze 1987

            6 Roxanne D'Souza 2021

            6 Sybil D'Souza 2021

    4 **Ethelwyn** Pereira (1953) m 1975 Eufemiano Moniz (1947)

        5 Celine Moniz (1976) m 2006 Russell D'Souza 1974

6 Ethan de Souza (2010)
5. Larissa Moniz (1979)
5. Francis Moniz (1990) m 2021 Kimberley Rodrigues
ancis Pereira (1954--1957)
ia Aurora Pereira (1959) m.1988 Geoffery Pinto (1953)
Kyle Pinto (1989) m 2023 Alexandra (Aly) Goc
yan Pinto (1990) m 2020 Anna Spengen
6 Raya Pinto (2022)
opher Pinto (1994-2012)
os Reis Pereira (1917-1998) m. Antonio Vicente Pinto

Pereira (1943-2007) m. 1978 Lexley Maureen Da

Pereira (1980-) m Shevana Rupnarine
en Pinto Pereira (1981-) m 2013 Paul Barret

ise Barret 2014
ex) Barret 2019
(1986) m 2013 Cherisse

their

danha,

Ligorio

ia),
lim),
ceto Pereira)

Pereira (1834-

miano Alvares

D'Souza, Yvonne

-2014)

cisco Xavier Pereira
-1935) m **Filomena**

hoebe (1917-1998)

-1989)

anio Pereira) was the 6th of
le Quadros and Martinho

en of Manuel Antonio

Manuel Antonio de

2. *Maria Aurora* Valeriano Barreto's brother **Caetano** V. Barreto m Maria
Eulalia Pinto

        Children: Joao, Ludovina, Cosme, Rafael and Sales

        Rafael (1902-1978) m Cremina Menezes

        Children: Sales (m Yvonne Menezes), Fatima (m Zezito Pimen[...]
                Pereira), Filomena (m Jose Vicente Silva)

        Maria de Lurdes (m Heriberto Moniz), Suzette (m Nev[...]
                Mascarenhas)

Ludovina m Roque Wiseman Pinto

        Children: Felizardo, Maria and Fausta Lobo

        Felizardo Wiseman Pinto *m Marta Pimenta Pereira,*
                children

        Roque/Lalita Correia Afonso, Maria Joao/Trevor Sa[...]
                Maria Jose/Savio Rodrigues

2. *Maria Aurora* Valeriano Barreto's sister Luzia m Joao Caetan[...]
Pereira

        Children: Lilia Andrade (Borda), Otilia Faleiro, (Ra[...]
        Quiteria Barbosa (Chandor), Luceta Torrado (Lout[...]
        Narcisco Pereira (Raia), Maria Alice Pereira (m Ani[...]

1A Emiliana Ludovina de Quadros had a sister Ana Leticia[...]
Ana Leticia (*1844-1926*) *m Antonio Xavier Braz Gomes [...]*
1884) in Divar

    Her grand-daughter Margarida (1918-2006) m Euf[...]
        (Loutulim)

      Their son Manuel (1938-2020) married Wilma [...]
        Pereira's sister in law.

3A **Phoebe Blenure Pereira** (nee Meneses, Raia) *m Fra[...]*
Her parents: **Floriano** Antonio Vicente Meneses (186[...]
        Fernandes (1880-1966)

Phoebe's siblings:
Nina (1910-1998), Anthony Grevi (1912-1992), [...]
Grevi m *Thelma Alvares (1918-95),*
Their children: Geeta (1952-2017) and Nisha (195[...]

Filomena's parents: Augusto Fernandes and Carolina Fernandes
(Curtorim)

Filomena's sister: Maria Herminia Joaquina *m Joseph Santana Miranda
(Loutulim)*

    Their Children: Cajetan Joseph Vincent (CJV) and Miquelina

        Cajetan (1911-1998) *m Ernestina Guido; their children*

            Vernon (1945) *m* Sheila Albuquerque

            and Carmen (1952) m F.J. Da Cunha

        Miquelina *m Louis Xavier Lourenco*

                Their Children: Florencio, Lewis and Atilia

Floriano's parents: Joao Nepuceno Menezes and Efigenia Severina (Raia)

Floriano's brothers:

Jose Joaquim (UK); his son Trelawn Menezes

Luis Caetano (Caetaninho) (1864-1937):

    Children: Luis (Portugal), Humiliana Colaco (Portugal)

        Berta, Fr. Raul

    Mario/Celisa:

    Children: Gilbert/Julieta Barreto, Cedric/Marina Saldanha, Nalini
/ John Almeida, Veena / Frederick de Souza, Indira / Anwar
Vahanvaty,

    Zelma m Jose Joaquim Silva

    *Children: Wilfredo, Jose Vicente, Alice, Ceusita, Arlette, Ninette,
Maria dos Anjos.*

        __Jose Vicente__ (1946-) m 1975 __Filomena__ V. Barreto (1947-1999)

    Their children: Paulo (1976) Nicole (1980) Mark (1983)

        *Filomena Barreto: daughter of Cosme Barreto, this one first
cousin to F.X. Pereira*

Descendants of Piedade Xavier Menezes

(Prepared by Fr. Luis Menezes)

1 Piedade Xavier Menezes
m. Maria Conceicao Medeira
  2 **Roque Piedade Menezes**, Dr (1902-1974)
  m. 1926 Ana Joaquina **Ofelia** De Jesus Maria Josefa Piedade De Imaculada Conceicao Pereira (1904-1980)
    3 **Arthur** Menezes (1927-1999) m. Olivia D'Sousa
      4 Francesca Pia Menezes
      4. Monica Menezes
      4 Vasco Menezes
      m. Kathryn Jones
        5 Phoebe Jeanne Menezes
        5. Jevan Arthur Menezes
        5. Naomi Star Menezes
    3 **Caesar** Piedade Menezes (1931-2010)
    m. 1961 Anita Pimenta (1929-2020)
      Sunita Maria Menezes (1962-)
      m. 1990 Michael Anthony Grevi Desouza (1960-)
        5. Larissa Desouza (1991-) m 2018 Keith de Gama
      4. Francis Joseph Piedade Menezes (1964-)
      m. 1998 Ida Saldanha (1964-)
        5. Aaron Menezes (1999-)
      4. Louis Anthony Piedade Menezes (1966-)
      4 Ivan John Menezes (1972-)
      m. 2001 Supriya Peres Da Silva (1964-)
        5 Ari Joseph Menezes (2003-)
        5. Mia Anya Menezes (2007-)
    3 **Aires** Jesus Piedade Menezes (1933-)
    m. 1961 Theresa Antoinette Inez Cordeiro (1940-)
      4 Flavia Judith Menezes (1961-)
      m. 1989 Clive Vincent Pereira (1960-)
        5 Sean Louis Pereira (1990-) m 2021 Bridget Vale
        5. Franz Pereira (1993-)
        5. Joshua William Pereira (1999-)

4. Celia Maria Menezes (1963-)
m. 2003 Rohit Walter Rao (1971-)
   5. Nadine Marise Walter Rao (2007-)
4. Leah Jacinta Menezes (1965-)
4. Savio Antonio Pio Menezes (1969-)
m. 1999 Priya Maria Colaco (1976-)
   5. Ayesha Johanna Pia Menezes (2008-)
4. Julian Joseph Pio Menezes (1980-)

3. **Fr Louis Sj** Menezes (1934-)
3 **Joseph** (Joe) Piedade Menezes (1937-)
m. 1966 Antoinette Mathias (1944-)
  4 Karen Menezes (1967-)
  m. 1995 Rohan Lobo (~1966-)
     5 Julia Amanda Lobo (1996-)
     5. Peter William Lobo (1998-)
  4. Kenneth Savio Pio Menezes (1969-)
  m. 2000 Gillian D'Sousa (1968-)
     5. Malaika Menezes
  4. Elizabeth Pia Menezes (1971-)
  m. 2006 Brian Colaco
     5. Nikhil Colaco (2012-)
  4. David Pio Menezes (1973-) m. Marilia Correia
3. **Fr Albert** Menezes, Sj (1939-)
3 **Roque** Piedade Menezes, Sr. (1943-2000) m. Monique Demortier (~1944-)
  4. Joanna Menezes (1975-) m. Paul Henri-Renard
     5 Luca Henri-Renard
     5. Lola Henri-Renard (2011-)
  4. Anthony Menezes (1979-)
  m. ~2005 Ruth
     5. Oliver Menezes (2008-)
  Roque Menezes, Jr. (1979-)
  m. 2007 Claire Smilie
     5 Zach Menezes (2008-)
     5. Lucy Eve Menezes (2010-)

3. **Vasco** Menezes (1949-1949)

2 **Rosarinho** Menezes
m. Elizenia Rodgrigues
   3 Piedade Menezes (?-2009) m. Rosinha Araujo
     4 Joaquim Menezes
     m. Edith Menezes
         5 Joshua Menezes
         5. Elisha Menezes
         m. Edith Menezes
         5. Joshua Menezes
         5. Elisha Menezes
     4 Tessie Menezes
     m Emerico Costa
         5 Alzira Costa
         5. Caetano Costa

     4 Yvette Menezes
     m. Antonio da Costa
         5 Keith da Costa
         5. Reuben da Costa
     4. Hazel Menezes
     m. Ignatius Barnetto
         5. Aaron Barnetto (?-?)
     4. Trevor Menezes
   3 **Flaviano** Menezes
   m. Filomena Clemente
     4 Cynthia Menezes
     m. John Paul Fernandes
     Dione Fernandes
         5. Desiree Fernandes
     4. Rosy Menezes
     m. Savio Clemente
   3 **Conceicao** Menezes (?-2009) m. Hilda Rodgrigues
     4 Maria Goretti Menezes (1952-)
     m. Manuel Caetano de Piedade Cotta (1941-2004)

5 Sasha Julieta Cotta (1976-) m. 2003 Sergio D'Silva (1976-)
        6 Joaquim Joel 2004
        6. Caroline 2008
    5. Helga Mitzie Cotta
    m. 2012 Ryan Da Costa
        6 Aaron 2014
4 Roy Menezes
m. Jacinta D'Souza
    5 Kimberley Menezes
    5. Daniel David Menezes
4 Alan Menezes
m. Linda Dreisbach
    5 Cameron Menezes
    5. Colette Menezes
4. Conrad Roque Menezes
3 **Caetano** Menezes m. Annie D'sa
4 Lynette Menezes
m. Louis Clemente
    5 Lynessa Clemente
    5 Gerald Clemente
4 Ameeta Menezes
m Frederick Lobo
    5 Janus Lobo
4 Alwyn Menezes
m Elaine D'Souza

2. **Espiciosa** Menezes
m. Agostinho Quadros
  3. Camilo Quadros (?-?)
  3. Ernestina Quadros
  3 Domingos **Manuel** José Quadros
  m. Margarida Cordeiro
    4 Amelia Quadros (?-?) m. Ravindrata Karmali
        5 Amalindo Karmali
        5. Ranjan Karmali
        5. Rajnandan Karmali

4. Ernestina Quadros m. Tome Menezes
m Rui Santa Rita Vaz (previous marriage)
    5. Kirl Santa Rita Vaz
4 Agostinho Quadros m. Eulalia Fernandes
    5 Andrea Quadros
    5. Angus Quadros
4. Fr Agnelo Quadros
4 Bernadette Quadros m. Augustine D'Souza
    5 Cedric D'Souza
    5. Derrick D'Souza
    5. Erica D'Souza
4 Rachel Quadros m. George D'Souza
    5 Gaye D'Souza
    5. Giselle D'Souza m. Brian Marchon
    5. Darcy D'Souza

4 Valerio Quadros m. Melita Correia
    5 Amyas Quadros
    5. Emmanuela Quadros
4 Blasco Quadros m. Lydia Rangel
    5 Faye Quadros
    5. Andre Quadros
    5. Shane Quadros
4. Sandra Quadros m Christopher Xavier

3 **Carolina** Quadros m Damiao Menezes
4 Alvaro Menezes m. Angela Castelo
    5. Ravi Menezes
4 Guilhermina Menezes m. Custodio Pimenta
    5 Noel Pimenta
    5. Selwyn Pimenta
    5 Elvino Pimenta m. Christine Gomes
        6 Dylan Pimenta
        6. Karen Pimenta
    5. Daryl Pimenta
    5. Evelyn Pimenta

4. Olinda Menezes m. Milton Baracho

4 Olivia Maria Aurora Menezes (1936-2021) m. Leandro Mascarenhas (?-?)

    5 Sarita Mascarenhas

    5. Manuel Mascarenhas

4. Grancinda Menezes

3 Helena Quadros (1919-2016)

m. **Riario Moniz (1914-1979)** (see family tree under Genealogy of MONIZ Family)

3 **Francisco Xavier** Quadros

m Maria Soares

    4 Judith Quadros m. Mario Godinho

        5 Fernando Godinho

        5. Soraya Godinho

    4 Zezito Quadros m. Maria Rita Brito

        5 Carolina Quadros

        5. Elton Quadros

    4. Francis Quadros m. Alison Dias

    4. Sarla Quadros m. Mario Furtado

        5. Chelsea Furtado

    4. Kevin Quadros

3 **Raquel Quadros**

m. Manuel Xavier

    4 Caetano Xavier (1944-2001) m. Julia (Lila) Gomes Pereira

        5 Rachel Xavier m. Cesar Vaz

            6 Raoul Vaz

            6. Natalie Vaz

            6. Ana Karina Vaz

        5. Manuel Roy Xavier

        5. Lara Xavier m. Zubin Pereira

        5. Isabel Xavier m. Alan Costa

        5. Sonia Xavier

        5. Rui Xavier

4 Maria Xavier m. Jose Carvalho

    5 Priya Carvalho m. Leonardo Viegas

        6 Rohit Viegas

        6. Rashmi Viegas

        6. Rohan Viegas

    5. Ravi Carvalho

    5. Siddhartha Carvalho m. Yvette Carvalho

    5. Nisha Carvalho m. Dr Ryan Costa

        6. Leah Costa

4 Manuela Xavier m. Newton Andrade

    5 Celina Andrade m Franzil Miranda

    5. Karl Andrade

    5. Fernanda Andrade

3 Jorge Quadros m. Imelda Gomes

  4 Tania Quadros m Gavin Semelhago

  4. Claret Quadros m. Allwyn Soares

2 Ermelinda Menezes m. Roque Pereira (Chandor)

  3 Aurita Pereira (?-2001) m. **Sebastiao Vicente** Pereira (?-1946?)

    4 Ida Ana Pereira (1942-2018) m. Manuel (Manekas) da Costa

        5. Vincente da Costa m. Nina Colaco

    4 Eva Pereira m. Alan Rangel

        5 Ann Rangel

        5. Gerson Rangel

    4 Ena Pereira m. Fabian D'Cunha

        5 Sonia D'Cunha m. Mario Leitao

            6 Child 1 Leitao

            6. Child 2 Leitao

        5. Lisa D'Cunha

        5. Ryan D'Cunha m. D'Cunha

            6. Child 1 D'Cunha

3 Aurita (??-2001) **m. Daniel Menezes** (?-?)

  4 Sebastian Menezes m. Jeannine Mathias

    5 Llana Menezes

    5. Liesel Menezes

4 Stanislaus Menezes m. Joyce Mascarenhas
    5 Joanne Menezes
    5. Sharon Menezes
4 Jennifer Menezes m. Charles Sollis
    5 Daniel Sollis
    5. Dionne Sollis
4 Marie Lourdes Menezes m. Lloyd D'Souza
    5 Reyna D'Souza m. Rhys Fernandes
    5. Rebecca D'Souza
    5. Rachel D'Souza
    5. Rhea D'Souza
4 Palmira Menezes m. Colin de Lesseps Fonseca
    5 Waylon de Lesseps Fonseca
    5. Christoff de Lesseps Fonseca

4 Edith Menezes m. Joaquim Menezes
    5 Joshua Menezes
    5. Elisha Menezes

4 Savia Menezes m. John Fernandes
    5 Stacy Fernandes
    5. Jillian Fernandes
    5. Chiara (Adopted) Fernandes
3. Remedes Pereira (?-?)
3. Aramita Pereira (?-?) m. Lawrence D'Costa
    4. Amelia D'Costa
3 Rosario Pereira (?-?) m. Greta Rosario
    4 Cecil Pereira m. Cheryl Pinto
        5. Chelsea Pereira
    4 Clyde Pereira m. Nhu Sheena Coelho
        5 Shanelle Pereira
        5. Rhys Pereira
    4 Caren Pereira m. Kingsley D'Souza
        5 Naomi D'Souza
        5. Olenka D'Souza
    4 Clint Pereira m. Joan Kinny

5 Nathan Pereira
5. Brandon Pereira
5. Vernon Pereira

3 Santana Pereira m. Reynah Sequeira
    4 Maria Pereira
    4. Franca Pereira m. Errol Viegas
        5. Mikaela Viegas
    4. Nicole Pereira m. Joseph D'Cunha
3 Lourdes Pereira (?-?) m. Ethelvina D'Sa
    4 Ermelinda Pereira m. Peter Vaz
        5 Girl Vaz
    4. Carmo Pereira
    4. Savio Pereira
2 Maria Claudina Menezes m. Militão Fernandes
    3 Artemisia Fernandes (1922-2009)
    3 Edwin Baptista Fernandes (1943-2011) m. Branca Antunes
        4 Ana Claudia Fernandes
        4 Joao Pedro Fernandes m. Ana Inês Silva
            5 Vasco Fernandes
    3 Caetano Fernandes m. Crescencia Costa
        4 Wilson Fernandes m. Maria Valladares
            5 Sonalia Fernandes
            5. Sovina Fernandes
        4 Milton Fernandes m. Olivia Fernandes
            5 Liesha Fernandes
            5. Nileen Fernandes
        4 Clelia Fernandes m. Leslie Barbosa
            5 Snezzy Barbosa
            5. Melvin Barbosa
        4 Sarita Fernandes m. John Cabral
            5 Josico Cabral
            5. Sanford Cabral
            5. Zenon Cabral
        4. Edwin Fernandes (?-1995)
    3. Fr Joao Pedro Fernandes

3 Olga Fernandes m. Eusebio Inacio Pinto
    4 Savio Pinto m. Venita Pinto
        5 Ullian Pinto
        5. Senia Pinto
3. Edwin Fernandes (?-1941)
3 Leonora Fernandes m. Simplicio Noronha
    4 Sebastião Noronha m Euphemia Noronha
        5 Maria Lourdes Noronha
        5. Maria Lumen Noronha
        5. Savio Noronha
    4. José Neves Noronha
    4. Maria Noronha m Fransisco (?-?)
    4. António Noronha m. Lourdes Noronha
    4. Agnes Noronha m. Dominic
    4. Camu Noronha m. Joseph (?-?)
    4. Paul Noronha m. Olivia Noronha
2 Miguel Menezes m. Joyce
    3 Lea Menezes m. Nolasco Rodrigues
2 Isabel Menezes m. Jose Coelho
    3 Lucia Coelho (?-2015) m. Angelo Pereira
        4 Leo Pereira m. Marina Misquitta
            5 Andrea Pereira
            5. Sarah Pereira
            5. Natasha Pereira
        4 Melwyn Pereira m. Pratima Rosario
            5 Aaron Pereira
            5. Jason Pereira
    3. Laura Coelho
    3. Sr Ubaldina Coelho
    3 Rosario Coelho m. Umbelina Figueiredo
        4 Jose (Jesito) Coelho m. Brenda Barreto
        4. Darryl Coelho m. Daphne Dias
        4. Bosco Coelho
        4. Carl Coelho
        4. Conrad Coelho
    3. Palmira Coelho (1940-1955)

3 Peter Coelho m. Imelda Vaz
    4 Isabelle Coelho m. Pedro (Pedrito) Correia Afonso
        5 Natalie Ann Correia Afonso
        5. Aidan Correia Afonso
    4 Michelle Coelho m. Alden do Rosario
        5 Anna do Rosario
        5. Rui do Rosario
        5. Lara do Rosario
    4 Rochelle Coelho m. Clayton Mascarenhas
        5 Rafael Mascarenhas
3 Antonio Coelho m. Terezita Coelho
    4 Annabelle Coelho
    4. Laura Coelho
3 Raul Coelho m. Estefania Cruz
    4 Roshan Coelho m??
    4. Savio Coelho m Supriya Coelho
    4. Neville Coelho

3 Anselmo Coelho m. Sandra Monteiro
    4 Kim Coelho m. Vanita Coelho
        5 Diya Coelho
    4. Ken Coelho
    4. Kay Coelho
2. **Flaviano** Menezes